NOV 0 6 2014

THE MARQUIS

THE MARQUIS
Lafayette Reconsidered

Laura Auricchio

Alfred A. Knopf
New York
2014

A portion of this work first appeared in The Yale Review (October 2014).

Library of Congress Cataloging-in-Publication Data

Auricchio, Laura.
The marquis : Lafayette reconsidered / Laura Auricchio. —First Edition.
pages cm
Includes bibliographical references.
ISBN 978-0-307-26755-9 (hardcover : alk. paper)   ISBN 978-0-385-35324-3 (eBook)
1. Lafayette, Marie Joseph Paul Yves Roch Gilbert Du Motier, marquis de, 1757–1834.
2. Generals—France—Biography. 3. Statesmen—France—Biography. 4. Generals—United States—Biography. 5. France. Armée—Biography. 6. United States—History—Revolution, 1775–1783—Participation, French. 7. United States—History—Revolution, 1775–1783—Biography. I. Title.
DC146.L2A87 2014
944.04092—dc23 [B]
2013046386

Front-of-jacket image: Marquis de Lafayette, 18th c. etching. Musée Franco-Américain du Château de Blérancourt, France © RMN–Grand Palais/Art Resource, NY

Back-of-jacket image: Marquis de Lafayette, c. 1781–85, by Francesco Giuseppe Casanova © Collection of the New-York Historical Society, USA / Bridgeman Images

Jacket design by Stephanie Ross
Manufactured in the United States of America

First Edition

For everyone who made it possible

CONTENTS

Map of France highlighting Paris, Versailles, Chavaniac, and La Grange.

ILLUSTRATIONS

INTRODUCTION

O
n a rainy April afternoon in 2009, I found myself scrambling to keep up with a French curator who was striding purposefully across a cobblestoned courtyard at the Château de Versailles. Coming to a sudden stop at an unmarked door, he rifled through a ring of oversized keys, turned the latch, and switched on a light to reveal a small, sparsely furnished room coated with a fine film of dust. This was clearly not one of the château's most popular locations, but it contained the treasure I had come to see: a white marble bust of Gilbert du Motier, Marquis de Lafayette (1757–1834). Carved in 1790 by the renowned sculptor Jean-Antoine Houdon, the bust portrays Lafayette as an officer and a gentleman: his uniform signals his cherished role as commander of the French National Guard, his powdered coiffure is expertly arranged, and his firm jaw and oblique gaze suggest absorption in matters of grave importance.

As I admired this noble countenance of stone, a wry smile crept across the curator's face. Suddenly, the silence was broken. "Why," asked the curator, "should we have a bust of Lafayette?"

The question surprised me. After all, I said, Lafayette is the French hero of the American Revolution—the Hero of Two Worlds, the Apostle of Liberty. I had learned about him in school and knew that he was worthy of admiration. Lafayette was just nineteen years old and one of the richest men in France when he relinquished the comforts of his station to serve the cause of freedom half a world away. "The Marquis," as Americans called him, led our troops into battle, froze with them at

Jean-Antoine Houdon. *Lafayette in the Uniform of the National Guard.* 1790. Marble. Châteaux de Versailles et de Trianon.

Valley Forge, and clothed and fed them at his own expense. News of Lafayette's daring adventures thrilled all of France, and that excitement encouraged the French king, Louis XVI—an absolute monarch—to support a revolution. Knowing that Lafayette helped us win independence, generations of Americans have expressed our nation's gratitude by naming countless towns, counties, streets, parks, and schools in his honor. Lafayette is so esteemed in the United States that his statue stands across from the White House, in Washington, D.C.'s Lafayette Square. A bust is just one more token of well-deserved appreciation.

After listening politely, the curator shook his head and pointed to a plaque installed a few feet away. It was a memorial commemorating the deaths of thousands of French soldiers and sailors who, sent across the Atlantic by their king, had lost their lives fighting for American freedom. He repeated the question, a bit louder this time: "Why should we have a bust of Lafayette?" These men were killed in the American Revolution, he said, but they have no statues. Louis XVI bankrupted France for the cause of American liberty and received his thanks from the guillotine. Besides, it was not Lafayette but the Comte de Rochambeau who led the French forces in America. How and why did we come to revere—of all the sons of France who came to America's aid—the Marquis de Lafayette?

I began to see his point. During the winter of 1776, Lafayette's interest in the American cause was not unique. In fact, it could hardly be called unusual. The fashionable salons of Paris were abuzz that season with talk of *"les insurgents,"* as the envoys sent by Congress were fondly known, and a card game called *"Le Boston"* was sweeping through high society. The best French homes feted George Washington in absentia, and Benjamin Franklin delighted all of Paris, where he cut a conspicuous figure in a marten-fur cap—an accessory that toyed with French perceptions of rustic Americans.

If pleasure-loving Parisians enjoyed the novelty of these New World republicans, many military men saw the Americans' cause as an opportunity for revenge. The army had been nursing its wounds since 1763, when the French and Indian War (known in France as the Seven Years' War) had ended with France ceding its Canadian colonies to Great Britain. By helping to wrest thirteen valuable colonies from British control, a humiliated French officers' corps hoped to redeem itself. So pervasive was enthusiasm for the American fight that the economist and author André Morellet—an astute social observer who often accompanied Franklin on his rounds—quipped in 1777 that "there is more support for American independence in Paris than in the entire province of New York."

Yet there was something uncommon about Lafayette's commitment to America. His devotion was deeper than his countrymen's, his drive more intense. While other Frenchmen sailed for the New World seeking riches or retribution, Lafayette sought nothing short of a new life. Earnest, enthusiastic—as optimistic as Voltaire's naïf Candide—Lafayette was out of place in the glittering Parisian world of wit and cynicism that the urbane Franklin so effortlessly mastered.

Lafayette had married into one of the best-connected families of the French court, but he hailed from the Auvergne region of south-central France, and the uncontrived manners of that rural area marked him as a stranger in the refined circles of his in-laws. At Versailles, even Lafayette's rugged appearance counted against him. The young marquis was large for his time: five feet, nine inches tall and endowed with a broad frame that one contemporary described as "decidedly inclined to *embonpoint.*" In other words, he tended to be stout. As Lafayette grew older, his bold features would be called distinguished, but as a youth he was not widely perceived as handsome. He had a long, oval face with a prominent aquiline nose, gray-blue eyes that peered out from a pale complexion, and a shock of unfashionably red hair atop a high, sloping forehead. Friends and admirers saw Lafayette's open and frank expression as a window to his soul, but this transparent credulity placed him at a disadvantage in the dissimulating games of intrigue that passed for sociability at Versailles.

Lafayette felt more comfortable in the saddle than perched on a gilded stool, and he remained uneasy in a society that cultivated an ideal of disaffected nonchalance; feigned detachment was foreign to his character. Reared on tales of his ancestors' military exploits, Lafayette yearned to prove himself worthy of such a legacy. Enthusiasm may have been unfashionable, but Lafayette made no attempt to hide his zeal. The "love of glory," Lafayette recalled in his memoirs, inspired him to excel at school, where he vied for academic prizes bestowed in public ceremonies. The urge to escape "a life without glory," he explained to his wife in 1777, compelled him to sail for America. "Glory," he assured George Washington in 1778, was his only ambition. To be clear, the glory Lafayette sought was quite divorced from notions of splendor. In 1762, a French dictionary defined "glory" as a "reputation" garnered through "virtue, merit, great qualities, good actions and beautiful works"; synonyms included "honor, esteem, praise." Once earned, glory was its own reward. Many men of Lafayette's generation hoped for glory, but Lafayette was single-mindedly devoted to its pursuit.

In America, Lafayette found glory and more. Here, for the first time since leaving the Auvergne, he was surrounded by people who saw his sincerity as a virtue, not a flaw. The public welcomed him immediately—Lafayette was the only marquis in the American army, and his title all but guaranteed his renown. The same nation that rejected Old World traditions of hereditary privilege rejoiced to find a highborn nobleman on its side, as if his interest in the American cause proved its universal appeal. And if Lafayette's rank opened doors, his personality won hearts. As news of Lafayette's unaffected charm made its way through the colonies, even the most hardened anti-French feelings began to dissolve. Then as now, Americans prided themselves on plain dealing, and those who met Lafayette were pleasantly surprised to discover that this exceptional Frenchman shared their sensibility.

Surely Lafayette deserves to be remembered. Why, then, had the French curator seemed perplexed by the bust?

Part of the answer is that Lafayette succeeded so completely in cultivating an American identity that, even in France, he remains a distinctly American hero. In 1781, after the British surrendered to allied forces at Yorktown, most of the French officers in America returned to France and to the pursuits they had left behind. But Lafayette, who had left his homeland as an outcast, had no career to reprise. Serving as America's foremost French advocate became his primary occupation, and the spirit of the new nation assumed a position at the very core of his being. Lafayette, who called Washington his adoptive father, turned his Left Bank town house into a home away from home for visiting Americans. The Adamses, the Jeffersons, and the ubiquitous Franklin were frequent guests at Monday suppers, where English was the language of choice and where Lafayette's children—including his son, named George Washington, and a daughter known as Virginie—sang songs in English. Mementos of the United States abounded: a gold-engraved copy of the Declaration of Independence hung on a wall of honor, plants from the New World decorated the terrace, and books on American history filled the shelves. For a time, a young man of Iroquois descent lived with Lafayette's family as "a favourite Servant." As the explorer John Ledyard wrote of Lafayette in 1787, "he has planted a tree in America, and sits under its shade at Versailles."

But the curator may not have been objecting to Lafayette's Americanization; more likely he was hinting at a darker chapter of Lafayette's story. Although Lafayette was an indefatigable champion of righteous causes, he did not always meet with success. During the French Revolution, he failed spectacularly. In America, we remember his triumphs; in France, few outside of his native Auvergne see him as a hero. So little does France love Lafayette that the monumental *Critical Dictionary of the French Revolution,* published by a leading team of French historians in 1988, states flatly that "the man has drawn few eulogies."

At the outset of the French Revolution, in 1789, Lafayette's moment of glory seemed to be at hand. On July 15, the morning after the storming of the Bastille prison, popular acclaim placed Lafayette at the helm of the newly established National Guard. The following month, Lafayette became the first person to submit a proposal for a "Declaration of the Rights of Man"—a set of principles that would serve as the foundation of a new constitution—to France's newly formed legislature. On

La Nation Française assistée de Mᵉ De la Fayette terrasse le Despotisme et les
Abus du Regne Feodal qui terrassoient le Peuple

The French Nation Helped by Mr de la Fayette Stops
the Despotism and Abuses of the Feudal King Who
Oppresses His People. 1791.

July 14, 1790, Paris commemorated the first anniversary of the Bastille's fall with a grand public festival featuring Lafayette as its undisputed star. Newspapers and broadsides compared Lafayette to Washington, and prints depicted him as a vanquisher of despotism, wielding a sword of justice.

Yet Lafayette's French triumphs were troubled from the start. As commander of the National Guard, Lafayette was charged with the impossible task of keeping the peace in a city racked by violence. Time and again Lafayette looked on helplessly as brutal justice was meted out in the streets, and he grew to loathe the politicians who, in his view, incited the crowds to further their own interests. Although he had assisted at the birth of the United States, Lafayette rejected the notion that France could sustain an American-style republic. He believed that France's monarchical traditions were too ancient and revered to be cast aside, and he deemed the French people too uneducated and uninterested, perhaps even temperamentally unsuited, to shoulder the burden of self-governance. Lafayette never embraced radical politics, and he made enemies of those who did. As he saw it, a constitutional monarchy was the only form of government that could guarantee liberty in France, and he defended this view to the end. In the revolution's early days, many forward-thinking men and women shared the same hope. But as the nation grew increasingly polarized, most of his allies abandoned the dream, while Lafayette stood fast on a middle ground that was rapidly eroding.

Lafayette was proud to call himself a moderate in an era of extremes. Explaining his philosophy later in life, he insisted that "true moderation consists, not as many people seem to think, in always seeking the middle between any two points . . . but in trying to recognize the point of truth and holding to it." Rarely has a man held to moderate principles with such tenacity. By 1791, partisans on both the left and the right (these political terms emerged precisely during this period) came to see him as a traitor to their respective causes. Supporters of the monarchy denounced him as a rabble-rouser. Centrist rivals falsely accused him of carrying on an affair with the despised queen Marie Antoinette— and commissioned a memorable series of pornographic pamphlets and prints to drive the point home. Republicans lambasted him for perceived attacks on freedom of the press. As circumstances grew ever

Lafayette and Marie Antoinette. c. 1790.

more desperate, Lafayette made increasingly grievous mistakes. One by one, the crown, the people, and, finally, the army turned against him. Had he not fled the country in 1792, Lafayette would surely have been executed. Still he clung to his principles. By the end, they were very nearly all he had left.

Lafayette was only thirty-four years old when he went into exile, and although he lived to be seventy-six and remained active in French politics until his final days, he never stopped thinking, writing, and talking about the historic events of his young adulthood. Those events defined his life, and for that reason, they form the core of this book. Writing in 1815 to the author Benjamin Constant—a friend and political ally—Lafayette took a moment to reflect on a remarkable lifetime that had been filled with bold dreams, tremendous achievements, and tragic failures. "I have been reproached all my life," he wrote, "for giving in too much to my hopeful disposition; I will respond that it is the only way to do something out of the ordinary. One would, indeed, never try anything extraordinary if one despaired of success."

Why should we have a bust of Lafayette? Not because he was infallible or superhuman or endowed with gifts that the rest of us lack. We should have a bust of Lafayette precisely because he was all too human. He lived in treacherous times and made imperfect choices. He failed at more ventures than most of us will ever attempt and succeeded at efforts that stymied countless men, but he never abandoned the belief that he could change the world, and he never despaired of success. Of all his accomplishments, these might be the most extraordinary.

THE MARQUIS

PART ONE

FROM PROVINCE TO PARIS

Facing page: Lafayette's birthplace. Château de Chavaniac in the Auvergne region of France, as depicted by Clara Greenleaf Perry, c. 1920. Lithograph. Collection of the Boston Athenaeum.

CHAPTER 1

FAMILY PRIDE

Lafayette was born on September 6, 1757, at the Château de Chavaniac—an eighteen-room fortress of a home located some three hundred miles south of Paris. Built of dark, rough-hewn stones and capped with terra-cotta roof tiles, Chavaniac projects like a rocky outcropping from the volcanic hills and jagged gorges that cut through the landscape of the Auvergne. Although the château had

been ravaged by fire in 1701 and reconstructed in the decades before Lafayette's birth, the rebuilding made no concessions to the classical elegance that had begun altering the face of Paris in the 1500s. Instead, Chavaniac retained the squat, utilitarian character of the house erected on the site in the Middle Ages. In architecture, as in most things, change came slowly to this part of France.

Today, the Auvergne beckons travelers seeking unspoiled nature and hearty fare. Visitors lodge in centuries-old stone shelters, hike craggy terrain, and dine on pungent cheeses, rich sausages, and green lentils deemed among the best in the world. But in Lafayette's time, few outsiders appreciated the region's untamed charm. Passing through the area in 1789, the English agronomist Arthur Young (who found little to admire in France as a whole) reserved special disdain for the town of Clermont-Ferrand, the capital of the Auvergne. As Young described it,

> Clermont . . . forms one of the worst built, dirtiest, and most stinking places I have met with. There are many streets that can, for blackness, dirt and ill scents, only be represented by narrow channels cut in a night dunghill. The contention of nauseous savours, with which the air is impregnated, when brisk mountain gales do not ventilate these excrementitious lanes, made me envy the nerves of the good people, who, for what I know, may be happy in them.

Dearly though Lafayette may have loved the Auvergne, it was not a fashionable place to call home.

By the standards of the high nobility, Lafayette's ancestry was equally disserviceable. Although the senior branch of the family could trace its roots to the turn of the millennium and had produced dignitaries including Madame de La Fayette, the acclaimed author of the classic early novel *La Princesse de Clèves* (1678), Lafayette himself descended from the junior branch—a less distinguished lot. As Lafayette put it, his direct ancestors had "left the province only to make war and played no role at all at court." Making matters worse, several generations of his forefathers had been on the losing end of primogeniture—the custom of passing all of a man's resources to his eldest son. The capital that had trickled down through Lafayette's father's family was relatively slight, and a large portion of it had been amassed through a tradition of marrying well. Although Lafayette exaggerated his misfortune by writing in his memoirs that he had been "born poor," he had certainly been born far less rich than he would eventually become. If not for a series of almost freakishly premature deaths, he might have inherited nothing at all.

Jacques-Roch du Motier—the older brother of Lafayette's father, Roch-Gilbert—was the first of his generation to die, expiring at the age of eighteen in 1734 when he was shot in the back at close range by an Austrian prisoner in Italy during the War of the Polish Succession. Perhaps the nearly preternatural credulity that marked Lafayette's character was a trait common to the family as a whole: Jacques-Roch had placed the Austrian behind him on a saddle without confiscating the captive's pistol. Just a few years later, Jacques-Roch's father, Édouard, met his end through hapless misadventure after a brief career at the Château de Versailles. According to the diaries of the Duc de Luynes, a consummate courtier and an invaluable recorder of palace life under King Louis XV, Édouard was a newly titled marquis working his way up the ranks in the King's Bodyguard—and, evidently, making a poor impression; Luynes describes him as "a man of high birth, or so they say." On October 8, 1736, Édouard was granted the honor of riding on horseback beside the monarch's carriage during the return from the hunt, a ritualized ceremony that occurred several times a week and usually went off without a hitch. But after bagging their quarry at the hunting grounds of Les Alluets-le-Roi, some ten miles northwest of Versailles, the royal party was nearing the ironwork gate near the Trianon pavilion, on the edge of the palace gardens, when Édouard's mount took a spill that brought down horse and rider. As Luynes put it, Édouard "broke his head" and was carried, unconscious, to the château, where, upon awakening, he lingered in agony to await the inevitable; about a year after the fall, Louis XV still felt obliged to ask a surgeon if the poor man's suffering could be eased, but it was to no avail.

Édouard's death, in 1740, left his infant son and two daughters in the hands of his wife, Marie-Catherine de Chavaniac-Lafayette, a formidable woman who, many years later, would be Lafayette's grandmother, godmother, and primary caretaker. Abandoning her husband's château at Vissac, the widowed Marquise de Lafayette moved the household some ten miles northeast to the newer and larger Château de Chavaniac, inherited through her father. There, as Lafayette remembered it, his grandmother grew into something of a local legend; she was held in such high regard that people took onerous journeys from the farthest reaches of the province to seek her advice.

Roch-Gilbert became the first of his line to marry into the prestigious nobility of the court—the men and women who lived in the
circles of the royal family. Thanks to the intervention of Jean Bretagne
Charles de La Trémoïlle, whose grandmother belonged to the influential senior branch of the Lafayette family, Roch-Gilbert wed Marie-
Julie de La Rivière on May 22, 1754. Like the Motiers, the Rivières had
been ennobled for centuries, but Julie's family was more distinguished,
better connected, and far wealthier than her husband's. Julie's paternal
grandfather, the Comte de La Rivière, had performed brilliantly in his
military career and in 1756 would be awarded the Grand Cross—the
highest class of membership in the chivalric Order of Saint Louis—
in recognition of his service. Julie's mother, who died a year before
the marriage, had served as a lady-in-waiting to Madame Adélaïde,
the powerful maiden daughter of King Louis XV, while her father, the
Marquis de La Rivière, devoted himself to his lucrative Breton estates
and amassed a fortune in the process. Whenever they were in Paris, the
Rivière men resided in grand apartments at the Luxembourg Palace
granted by the king. At the time of the betrothal, Julie too was living in
Paris, in the convent where she had been educated.

Despite her family's wealth, Julie brought only modest resources to
the union. She had an older brother whose interests took precedence
over hers, and her father—renowned for his parsimonious habits—was
willing to part with no more than a small dowry that would generate about 1,000 livres a year. It was not a lot by the standards of high
society, but the Marquis de La Rivière was willing to send his daughter
to live in the Auvergne, an idea to which Julie herself obligingly raised
no objection. This was no small sacrifice. By permitting Julie to trade
Paris for Chavaniac, the Rivières effectively abandoned hope that she
might advance their dynastic ambition at court, and their benevolent
attitude toward the newly married couple didn't end there. Thanks to
Rivière influence, Roch-Gilbert received a commission as colonel in
the elite grenadiers. It was a higher rank than any Motier had previously attained but, alas, Roch-Gilbert did not enjoy it for long. On
August 1, 1759, he was fighting in the conflict known today as the Seven
Years' War when he was killed by an English cannonball at Minden, in
northern Germany. With that fatal injury, Roch-Gilbert's two-year-old
son—Gilbert, our Lafayette—became a full-fledged marquis.

For the second time in two decades, Lafayette's grandmother found
herself at the head of a household, responsible for the well-being of a

boy who had lost his father. Concerned about her grandson's precarious finances, she wrote to Louis XV in October, requesting a pension for the child. As she explained to the king, Roch-Gilbert's four campaigns had drained the family resources. Most of the income from their estates and investments had gone to feeding, clothing, and arming the men under Roch-Gilbert's command—obligations that traditionally fell to commanding officers. Making matters worse, Roch-Gilbert had failed to draft a will. As a result of this oversight, most of Julie's dowry would revert to the Rivière family. Without the benefit of royal generosity, she suggested, no funds would be available to educate the young Marquis de Lafayette.

A modest pension was awarded, but Lafayette did not have to rely on such largesse for long: in 1761, the early death of Lafayette's uncle—his mother's brother—promised a lifetime of financial security as Lafayette, suddenly and unexpectedly, became the heir to the substantial Rivière fortune. At that point, it was his mother's turn to act. The widowed Julie de La Rivière returned to Paris to live with her family, and on February 28, 1762, she was presented at court, where she began building a network of connections that would pave her son's path to Versailles.

Over the next five years, Lafayette saw his mother for only a scant few months at a time, when she returned to the Auvergne for visits. To modern sensibilities, such separation might seem heart-wrenching, but members of the French nobility routinely handed infants over to wet nurses and placed older children under the control of governesses and tutors. Raised by a devoted grandmother, Lafayette was luckier than most. "Although my mother loved me a great deal," he later wrote, "the thought of taking me away from my grandmother La Fayette never crossed her mind." A honeyed sense of nostalgia infuses his descriptions of his childhood, which he spent in the close-knit company of his grandmother, her two grown daughters (one was widowed, the other never married), and a female cousin just a year older than he. His grandmother made considerable efforts to further his social and financial interests and did everything in her power to fill the boy with family pride. Lafayette remembered thrilling to tales of his father's, grandfather's, and uncles' heroic battlefield exploits; if he ever learned that the stories were embellished for his benefit, he never let on.

These grand stories were, no doubt, in the back of his mind when, at the age of eight, Lafayette began to hope that he might attain glory for himself in the very near future. The fearsome and mysterious Beast

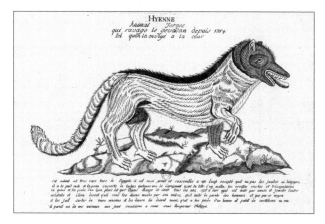

The Beast of the Gévaudan as pictured in a 1765 broadside.

of the Gévaudan was roaming the hills of south-central France, devouring livestock and murdering women and children in the vicinity of Lafayette's home—or so people said. Between 1764 and 1767, scores of human deaths were attributed to this chimerical predator, whose rampages quickly became the stuff of tall tales and folklore. Living at the epicenter of the putative carnage, Lafayette might well have been frightened—he was still a child, after all—but instead he saw the creature as an opportunity for him to leave a mark on the world. Drafting his memoirs a dozen years later, he recalled that "my heart Beat" for the beast, "and the hope of Encountering it Enlivened my walks."

What, exactly, was this beast? Lafayette called it a hyena; others said it was a wolf; one particularly inventive account described a monstrous hybrid the size of a bull with talons "the length of a finger" and a mouth "measuring at least a foot" wide. Some insisted the creature had been sent by the devil. Though two centuries have passed, conflicting theories still abound. The "real" Beast of the Gévaudan has been variously described as an exceptionally large lynx, a cross between a wolf and a dog, or a villain of the human variety. Maybe its exploits were the inventions of a greedy landlord intent on extracting protection from his tenants. Or perhaps, as some have maliciously suggested, the fable was an ingenious cover story concocted by a bloodthirsty Protestant exacting a gruesome revenge for decades of Catholic oppression. In all likelihood, more than one creature was responsible for the carnage; an overabundant population of wolves seems a plausible culprit. Then again, the beast may have been nothing more than a figment of mass hysteria. One thing, however, is clear: Lafayette never encountered the fabled creature.

Whatever else it may have been, the Beast of the Gévaudan was the talk of France. Chilling stories of its lethal exploits spread from the villages of the Massif Central to the salons of Paris and the court of Versailles. Government officials were implored to capture it, while earnest journalists, high-handed moralists, and hack writers alike exploited its potential to sell newspapers, pamphlets, and broadsides. No less a figure than King Louis XV took a keen interest in the uproar, sending hunters and bloodhounds to the countryside with instructions to capture and kill the beast. Members of the local nobility assembled their own hunting parties, and over the course of three years, several wolves and other creatures were slain, dissected, and documented, with their measurements widely reported and their images disseminated through engravings. The culprit may well have been slaughtered, or it may have died a natural death, although popular legends contend that the beast continues to wander the fields and mountains, possessed of a supernatural spirit.

When Lafayette first wrote down his recollections of the beast, during a hiatus from General Washington's army, the tale was still a cause célèbre ripped from the headlines. So familiar was the terrifying creature that a reference needed no explanation. In his winningly self-deprecating manner, Lafayette played down the horror that had gripped the land, describing the beast as having "caused some damage, and even more commotion." Only in later drafts of the much-revised memoirs did he go on to elaborate the crimes laid at the creature's feet. But in 1780, the mere mention of his yearning for the beast stood as sufficient proof of Lafayette's central claim: "I recall nothing in my life that preceded my enthusiasm for glorious tales or my plans to travel the world in search of renown."

Although Lafayette dreamed of world travel, he was wary when the time came for him to accompany his mother on a two-week journey to Paris, in December 1767. The ten-year-old Lafayette had never imagined that his life might be different from that of his father or grandfather, and he "separated with the utmost chagrin from a grandmother, two aunts, and a cousin whom I adored." Shortly after the carriage bearing mother and child started its northward journey, Lafayette sensed that everything was about to change. At home, local adults had treated him

Lafayette's first home in Paris, the Luxembourg Palace.

with the respect required by the rank of marquis, and village children had been too daunted by his station to approach him. On the road to Paris, he noticed something unusual: the men he passed did not tip their hats in deference to his position. For most of us, the process of growing up entails discovering the limits of our own, individual significance. But few people can pinpoint with precision the exact moment of that humbling realization. For Lafayette, it was seared into his memory.

When Lafayette descended from the carriage in the courtyard of the Luxembourg Palace, in Paris, he stood before a building that had no equal in the Auvergne. One of the greatest architectural achievements of seventeenth-century France, the palace was located in the university quarter, on the Left Bank of the Seine. In a 1765 essay on Paris, Louis, Chevalier de Jaucourt ranked the Luxembourg on par with the Tuileries and the still-unfinished Louvre as one of the city's "three superb palaces, distinguished above all the others." Designed in 1615 for Marie de' Medici, wife of King Henri IV, it had been loosely inspired by the Medicis' Pitti Palace, in Florence; it catered to Marie's Italianate taste and incorporated the classicizing tendencies of its primary architect, Salomon de Brosse. Extensive gardens added to the grandeur of the place, with a broad parterre branching into wide allées bordered with carefully trimmed rows of yew and boxwood. The garden's intricate symmetries suggested the power of culture to bend nature to its will. Once Lafayette settled into the apartments where his grandfather and great-grandfather lived at the discretion of the king, he too would have to be shaped in conformity with the refined ways of the capital.

Paris in the mid-1700s was a thriving metropolis of 700,000 people and the second most populous city in Europe, surpassed only by London. Both capitals had seen their populations double since the first wave of mass urbanization began sweeping across the continent and the British Isles at the turn of the century. An incomparable center of cultural excellence, Paris boasted three theatrical companies, five public libraries, six Royal Academies, scores of churches, monasteries, and convents, and one world-renowned university, with thirty-six subordinate colleges. For the rich and well-connected, the city was an opulent playground where renowned artists, writers, and thinkers mingled with political leaders, ecclesiastical dignitaries, and financial titans in chic cafés and stylish salons. Shop windows displayed merchandise from the four corners of the globe, and luxury goods fabricated in the city—fashions, tapestries, mirrors, and more—were coveted throughout Europe and beyond. In short, the taste of the Western world was formed in Paris. For a provincial youth who had spent his first decade at the top of the only society he knew, this was a brave new world indeed.

The ways of Paris were equally foreign to the Abbé Fayon, Lafayette's longtime tutor, who accompanied his young charge to Paris. In the Auvergne, Fayon had supplied Lafayette with an education entirely in keeping with tradition among the Nobility of the Sword—families like Lafayette's whose inherited privileges derived from generations of military service. Boys of Lafayette's station were schooled in the history of their lineages, and their intellects were stretched just enough to equip them with a smattering of Greek and Latin. Destined to become army officers and feudal landholders, noble boys from the provinces seldom needed much in the way of book learning. But Lafayette was no longer such a boy, and although Fayon remained in Lafayette's employ for the rest of his life, the good abbé's lessons were no longer sufficient.

In Paris, a new era was dawning in education and in most areas of life as rational principles of Enlightenment philosophy ushered in sweeping reassessments of society's most fundamental assumptions and cherished institutions. By the time Lafayette began daydreaming about the Beast of the Gévaudan, seventeen volumes of the magisterial *Encylopédie,* edited by two of the era's most influential philosophers—the author and art critic Denis Diderot and the mathematician and physicist Jean Le Rond d'Alembert—had already been published. This vast and formidable undertaking was intended to be nothing less than a compendium of all human knowledge. The *Encyclopédie* represented the pinnacle of Enlightenment-era erudition, offering lengthy entries on ideas and practices from reason and faith to wigmaking and apiculture.

When it came to education, the *Encyclopédie* authors and other reformist philosophers insisted that instilling virtue should be the primary goal of a noble's course of study. As Charles Rollin, former rector of the University of Paris, put it in his influential *Treatise on Education* (1726), "virtue alone puts men in a position to fill public offices. . . . It is virtue that gives [a man] the taste for true and solid glory, which inspires in him love of the *patrie* and the desire to serve it well, which teaches him always to prefer the public good to private good." For Rollin, such a solid moral footing could be attained only by studying the classics of Greek and Roman antiquity. Noble boys, he argued, should emulate the selfless actions of ancient heroes rather than fanciful tales passed down through family lore.

On a practical level, studying philosophy, rhetoric, and the other classical disciplines was becoming a necessity for scions of the sword nobility, who, for the first time in anyone's memory, had to consider careers outside the army. France's humiliation in the Seven Years' War had generated loud calls for changes in the way the army selected and promoted its personnel. As critics pointed out, a sterling genealogy was no guarantee of strong leadership, yet lineage and wealth had been the only prerequisites for advancement to influential positions. Reformers insisted that merit alone should determine who rose through the ranks. As high posts gradually opened up to qualified commoners, young noblemen from military families could no longer count on living military lives.

All of this left Lafayette in a bind: when it came to seeking an occupation, his options were quite limited. Noblemen were prohibited by longstanding tradition from engaging in commercial professions; to become a tradesman or a financier would be to suffer *dérogeance*—the loss of the rights and privileges that accompanied noble status. Nor could Lafayette have entered the clergy. That he lacked any religious calling was not the problem. French ecclesiastical rosters were filled with second sons who, expecting no inheritance, were unable to marry, yet lived fully carnal lives despite their vows; faith and devotion were afterthoughts in such circumstances. But as his family's sole heir, Lafayette had to marry, procreate, and continue the line. Of course, a provincial nobleman could always stay close to home and tend to his lands and dependencies, but to widen his family's circle of influence Lafayette would need to find a place at court or in public service, perhaps undertaking a diplomatic career. Whatever route he followed, he would almost certainly require a more rigorous formal education than his father had received.

In 1768, Lafayette's family enrolled him in the Collège du Plessis, one of the competitive secondary schools under the jurisdiction of the University of Paris. Located on the Rue Saint-Jacques, the Collège du Plessis was just a short walk away from the lodgings of Lafayette's family. The school dated back to 1322, but its building was much newer, having been reconstructed in the seventeenth century, thanks to a bequest from Louis XIII's powerful chief minister, Armand Jean du Plessis—the famed Cardinal Richelieu—a descendant of the founder.

As a member of the sword nobility, Lafayette was unusual among the school's student body. Most of his classmates hailed from the less prestigious Nobility of the Robe, whose families owed their rank to judicial or governmental service. There were even a handful of outstanding scholarship students from bourgeois backgrounds, like Antoine-Joseph Gorsas, the son of a shoemaker from Limoges. Having lived in near isolation until now, Lafayette discovered that he enjoyed the camaraderie and respect he found among his fellow students. They liked him, and Lafayette felt like a rising star among devoted friends who gave him his first taste of leadership. Although he traveled in a circle of older boys, he recalled that the other students acted like "disciples" who "would have defended me fiercely if there was ever a need." The boys' dedication did not, however, necessarily extend to the causes Lafayette championed, as he learned on the day he "wanted to mount a revolt to prevent the unjust punishment of one of my comrades." To Lafayette's surprise, he found that "I was not as well-supported as I might have hoped." This was to become a lifelong theme, as Lafayette's unbounded zeal frequently generated both admiration and bewilderment.

Lafayette later recalled in his memoirs that he learned to enjoy the playful pomp that his newfound wealth allowed. His boys' nights out must have been a sight to behold. It was his habit to dine in the city with classmates, whom he described as "children sporting épées . . . which went quite well with their embroidered suits, their bourses [taf-

feta sacs that collected long hair at the back of the neck], and their curls
garnished with powder and pomade."

This is not to say that Lafayette gave up his dreams of military distinction. He remembered "burning with the desire to have a uniform,"
and when he was thirteen years old, he finally received one, thanks to
his great-grandfather the Comte de La Rivière, who secured him a place
in a unit that had welcomed many earlier members of the family: the
Black Musketeers, soldiers of the king's guard. Lafayette was delighted
with this turn of events at the time, but in retrospect he recognized that
the appointment was ceremonial. The troops of the Maison du Roi
had disgraced themselves in the War of Austrian Succession, during
the 1740s, when they'd bolted from combat, and thereafter they were
relied upon to be little more than mannequins in smart uniforms. Still,
Lafayette took an adolescent pride in his membership and was pleased
to discover that participating in a picturesque review before the king
counted as an excused absence from class—a bonus that any schoolboy
would have appreciated. Writing about this in his memoirs, he adopted
the self-deprecating tone that so endeared him to the American public,
noting that he had been thrilled "to ride to Versailles in full uniform to
hear the king tell me . . . that he had nothing to order, and to report
back to the commander of the musketeers the same news that was
repeated to him three hundred and sixty-five days a year."

Nonetheless, four years at the Collège du Plessis helped Lafayette
grow into the serious man who would leave his mark on history. The
yearning for achievement that had inspired him to pursue the Beast of
the Gévaudan motivated him to prove his mettle in the academic arena,
and he succeeded admirably—albeit not admirably enough to satisfy
his desires. Lafayette recalled with pride that he won the prize for Latin
rhetoric given out by his *collège,* but he remained disappointed that he
had not triumphed in the university-wide stage of competition. Implying a miscarriage of justice, his memoirs lament that boys who had
taken the same Latin class several times over were permitted to compete
in the contest, while he had completed the course only once. Lafayette
believed that he would have carried the day despite the handicap if only
he had been a better copyist, as his paper had been graded harshly by a
judge who took off one point for each missing word of an inadvertently
omitted sentence.

Although the study of Latin did not immediately yield the laurels
that Lafayette craved, it may well have been the single most important

undertaking of his young life. Latin gave the excitable lad a potent means of focusing his youthful enthusiasms—through the language, history, and philosophy of the ancient Roman republic and the classical world. Through his coursework, he imbibed the moral and ethical principles put forth in such texts as Cicero's "On Moral Duties," Virgil's pastorals and *Georgics,* and the odes and satires of Horace—all standard reading in the colleges of Paris. History, represented in the curriculum by the Grecian progenitor of the discipline, Herodotus, and biography, where Plutarch loomed large, both became lifelong passions. Books by these authors, their contemporaries, and their followers lined the shelves of his libraries, and the lessons they taught shaped the outlines of his life.

Lafayette was hardly alone in his fascination with republican Rome, whose citizens shunned despotism to govern themselves according to principles of virtue and honor. Louis-Sébastien Mercier, an incisive chronicler of eighteenth-century Paris, wrote in 1781 that "Rome was the first name that reached my ears . . . the names of Brutus, of Cato and Scipio followed me in my sleep." So fully did the *Decades* of the Roman historian Livy fill his mind that Mercier reported it took him "a good deal of time to return to being a citizen of my own country" after he put down his schoolbooks. Mercier did not miss the irony that France's absolute monarchy employed teachers to "explain solemnly all the eloquent declarations advanced against the power of kings" by the ancient Romans. "One comes away from the study of the Latin language with a taste for republics," he observed. But he warned that young men emerging from the *collèges* "must lose and forget" such political lessons quickly "for their safety, for their advancement and for their happiness." As Mercier suggested, any student who found "himself at Versailles" dreaming, "despite himself, of Tarquin, of Brutus, of all the proud enemies of royalty" was in a highly awkward situation.

On April 3, 1770, Lafayette was still immersed in tales of Roman virtue when his mother died in the family's rooms at the Luxembourg Palace. A few weeks later his grandfather, too, was lost—perhaps, as Lafayette wrote, due to grief. At twelve years old, Lafayette was an orphan—an extraordinarily wealthy orphan. Lafayette's inheritance from his grandfather dwarfed the income from the lands in the Auvergne. From those southern properties, Lafayette received approximately 18,000 livres annually, while his grandfather's estates in Brittany and Touraine yielded more than 60,000 livres per year. And upon the death of his great-grandfather in 1781, another 17,000 livres would be expected every twelve months. Altogether, with investments in the East India Company and rent from properties in Paris, Lafayette's annual revenues routinely topped 100,000 livres. In some years, he brought in nearly 130,000 livres—all of it returns on investments. By way of comparison, a skilled laborer with steady employment seldom earned more than 1,000 livres per year at this time. Incomes as large as Lafayette's were rarely found outside of the highest levels of nobility, and they were almost never seen in the hands of a young boy from the provinces.

Lafayette was too young, too naïve, and too lost in mourning to manage such sums. Even in the best of times, money interested him very little; for much of his life he relied on friends, family members, and advisers to help him watch over his wealth. In the early years, relatives in Paris managed Lafayette's day-to-day finances while his grandmother kept tabs on developments from Chavaniac, and the entire clan began to look for a suitable bride to marry the suddenly rich young heir. Arranging a marriage among noble families naturally involved an intricate social and financial calculus. That the bride and groom might be personally compatible was always to be desired, but the preferences of two individuals carried less weight than the benefits a proposed alliance might bring the families. Given Lafayette's stunning fortune, his guardians were not obliged to find a bride who would bring a large dowry, but they were eager to find a match that would give the young man a ready-made network of influence. To avoid a lifetime of obscurity at Chavaniac, Lafayette needed an advantageous marriage that would provide entrée to court.

Lafayette could not have hoped for a wife better suited to this purpose than the young woman selected for him, Adrienne de Noailles, who was descended from one of France's most distinguished and influential families. Her father, the Duc d'Ayen, was renowned as both a chemist and a courtier; other close kin ranked among Louis XV's most trusted advisers. Adrienne's great-uncle the Duc de Mouchy had been inducted into several prestigious chivalric orders—the Order of the Golden Fleece, the Order of the Holy Spirit, the Order of Saint Louis—and in 1775 he would be named *maréchal de France,* the nation's highest military honor. Élisabeth Vigée-LeBrun, the most sought-after portraitist in Paris and a favorite of Marie Antoinette's, dined frequently at the home of the *maréchal,* where she shared the table with a select roster of guests who, she wrote in her *Souvenirs,* were chosen from among "the literary celebrities and the most distinguished figures of the city and the court." The *maréchal*'s wife, the Comtesse de Noailles, had been appointed *dame d'honneur* to Marie Antoinette upon the dauphine's arrival in France and charged with the daunting task of introducing the notoriously informal Austrian princess to the intricate social protocol required of the wife of the French heir apparent. So renowned was the comtesse for her stern demeanor and unyielding insistence on propriety that Marie Antoinette bestowed upon her the affectionately mocking nickname "Madame l'Étiquette." Aside from princes and princesses of royal blood, few families wielded as much power as the Noailleses.

Why would such a family marry their daughter to an unknown youth from a distant outpost? The Duc d'Ayen had his reasons. As the father of five girls, d'Ayen faced the unenviable task of assembling five dowries hefty enough for five sons-in-law to accept. Lafayette, with his solid finances but comparatively undistinguished social status, was the rare marital prospect who would care little about Adrienne's fortune.

Adrienne's mother, Henriette Anne Louise d'Aguesseau, the Duchesse d'Ayen, was less sanguine. She had just arranged an ideal union for her eldest daughter, who was set to marry the well-bred Vicomte de Noailles, a cousin of the Duc d'Ayen's. Perhaps she shared the prejudice articulated by the Comte de Ségur, a friend of Lafayette's, who nonetheless thought ill of noblemen from the provinces in general. In his memoirs, Ségur blithely pronounced that "one almost always recognized a man of the court by his politeness, and it was among the young country gentlemen that one most frequently encountered arrogance and a tendency to be easily offended." In the duchesse's view, Adrienne, who was just twelve years old, still had plenty of time. Lafayette's would surely not be the last offer, and the duchesse sincerely hoped that it would not be the best. So vehemently did duc and duchesse disagree that they could not bear to live under the same roof for several months. He stayed at the family home in Versailles while she remained in Paris until a compromise was struck: the marriage contract would be signed but kept secret—above all, from Adrienne—and the wedding would be put off for two years. If Lafayette were to embarrass himself in the interval, his prospective in-laws could break off the engagement and be spared the taint. Long before news of the planned union became public, the young man moved into a wing of the Noailles town house in Versailles in the capacity of a privileged lodger. He paid a rent of 8,000 livres a year, supplied his own servants, paid for his own food and fuel, and—most important from the perspective of the duchesse—remained under the constant surveillance of his future in-laws. Transforming the provincial marquis into a suitable husband was not a matter to be taken lightly.

Lafayette was therefore uprooted once more and would have to adjust to a new home, a new family, and a new school, not to mention a new set of expectations from his prospective in-laws. The transition was rocky. He abandoned the Collège du Plessis and its classical curriculum for the Académie de Versailles, which offered instruction in the finer points of comportment to children of the court nobility. There, Lafayette was expected to learn to ride like a gentleman officer, to dance with grace, and to wield an épée with aplomb. These skills could make or break a man at court, where impeccable manners were demanded at all times and a single miscue could mark a man for life. As the historian David A. Bell points out, a courtier's emphasis on bodily performances was not purely arbitrary, since "the same qualities that made him a graceful and well-mannered noble . . . would also, he believed, make him an able warrior." As a result, esoteric rules of behavior governed every moment at Versailles, and most of Lafayette's new classmates had already absorbed this unwritten code of conduct as if by osmosis. Since early childhood, they had watched their elders perform rarefied rituals. By the time these boys reached adolescence, even outlandishly contrived postures and poses seemed like the most natural movements on earth. But all of this was foreign to Lafayette, who in truth was never able to master the finer points of a courtly existence.

The Académie also taught Lafayette harsh new lessons in social rank. For the first time in his life, he was immersed in a society of young men whose lineages surpassed his own in every respect. Their families were more ancient, better educated, and more successful in every way than any Lafayette had ever known. They wielded enormous power, enjoyed unchallenged esteem, and possessed truly breathtaking wealth. His most notable classmate was the Comte d'Artois, a brother of the future King Louis XVI. Lafayette had been transported into the most elevated of all possible realms, one where the battlefield deaths of his progenitors, the provincial fame of his grandmother, and his appointment to the Black Musketeers counted for much less than the dreamy boy from the Auvergne had once believed.

CHAPTER 2

THE OUTSIDER

On the morning of Saturday, March 26, 1774, the sixteen-year-old Lafayette played a central role in the recurring drama known as the presentation at court. Although the leading players changed with each performance, the essence of the event had remained essentially the same since the age of Louis XIV—the Sun King—who'd transformed the Château de Versailles from a hunting lodge into a dazzling theater of royal power during the seventeenth century.

As the clock approached ten, the jaded denizens of Versailles assembled in the palace's richly decorated corridors to watch the spectacle unfold. Soon a nobleman would appear in their midst, offering himself up for dissection by their sharp eyes and sharper tongues. Even garments made of the softest silks would do nothing to soothe his anxieties: the ceremonial sword hanging by his side might cause him to stumble; worse still, his powdered wig might be styled in last year's fashion. Surreptitious glances would size him up as he passed through towering gates of gilded iron, climbed the vibrantly colored marble steps of the Queen's Staircase, and walked through the collection of martial regalia that filled the King's Guard Room on the way to the king's bedchamber, at the center of the palace. The antechamber to the king's bedroom, the Salon de l'Oeil de Boeuf, named for its bull's-eye window, was the newcomer's hall of judgment, its gilt paneling punctuated by mirrors facing mirrors that multiplied his every gesture. His self-consciousness might increase as murmurs reached his ears; courtiers might wonder aloud about this stranger, but none would speak to him. At long last a door would open and, as His Majesty entered the room, a *maréchal* would whisper the name of the newcomer. The king might gaze upon the debutant—or he might not—without ever breaking his stride as he continued on his way.

Lafayette was presented as a member of the "nobility of old extraction"—an honor reserved for those whose aristocratic lineages dated back at least to the year 1500. But even with an ancient family tree, most sons of the provincial nobility could not expect to bask in the presence of the king for more than a single day. Lafayette's own father had made just one appearance at Versailles before returning to the countryside. In general, men who lived in the rural regions of France did not possess the financial resources to acquire elevated military appointments, the social connections to serve in the royal household, or the education needed for diplomatic or ministerial posts. Lafayette, however, was not typical. His fortune was substantial, and he was set to marry into one of the court's most respected families in less than a month. For him, this would be the first of many visits to the Salon de l'Oeil de Boeuf.

Lafayette's place at Versailles had seemed to be assured when he'd married the fourteen-year-old Adrienne de Noailles on April 11, 1774. The wedding Mass was celebrated by the Abbé Murat, the same cousin who had baptized Lafayette sixteen years earlier. As the family gathered to witness the holy union in the lavish chapel of the Hôtel de Noailles in Paris, a grand complex just a few blocks from the Tuileries Palace, there could be no doubt that Lafayette had come a long way from the simple village church where he'd received his first sacrament. And yet, although the building was surely one of the city's architectural treasures, for Lafayette it was a gilded cage.

The animated boy who'd attracted a following at the Collège du Plessis became taciturn and awkward at the Hôtel de Noailles. The Comte d'Espinchal, a fellow Auvergnat who served as captain of the Regiment of the Queen's Dragoons and never forgave Lafayette for his part in the French Revolution, described him as "pale, cold and lifeless." Even the Comte de Ségur, one of Lafayette's closest friends, remembered him having "a cold and serious bearing, which sometimes created a false impression of timidity and embarrassment." Lafayette became notorious for refusing to participate in discussions that did not, in his opinion, merit consideration; naturally forthright, he was uncomfortable in conversations that privileged style over substance. Worse than unfashionable, his silence generated widespread disfavor—an effect, Lafayette acknowledged, exacerbated "by the gaucheness of my manners which, without being out of place on any important occasion, never yielded to the graces of the court or to the charms of supper in the capital." With a touch of remorse, Lafayette confessed in his memoirs that "disguised pride" lay at the root of his reticence. His withdrawn manner was a protective feint, intended to stave off any embarrassment that he might unwittingly bring upon himself while he got his bearings in a world that was as unfamiliar as it was unforgiving.

Ségur, Lafayette's friend, was one of the few people who understood that the young marquis's cold exterior "concealed the most active spirit, the firmest character, and the most burning soul." Ségur had firsthand knowledge of Lafayette's hidden fervor, recounting in his memoirs that, in the mid-1770s, Lafayette "had become attached to a lady as amiable as she was beautiful." Mistakenly believing Ségur to be his rival, Lafayette flew into "a fit of jealousy" and "spent almost an entire night" attempting to goad him into a duel. Ségur recalled the difficulty he experienced in reasoning with Lafayette, who was determined "to persuade me to fight with him, sword in hand, over the heart of a beauty on whom I did not have the least claim." Ségur was amused when, just a few days later, the Maréchal de Noailles asked what could be done to breathe some life into his taciturn in-law—"to rouse him from his indolence, and to add a little fire in his character."

Ségur knew well that Lafayette's difficulties arose not from innate timidity but from being trapped in an atmosphere to which he was temperamentally unsuited. Now, as a member of the Noailles clan, Lafayette was expected to socialize with the fast-living young men and women who occupied the upper tier of the court nobility. High-stakes gambling on cards and horses, constant, heavy drinking, and all manner of carousing were the favorite pastimes of this privileged set, which included not only the Vicomte de Noailles (the favored son-in-law) but also the Comte d'Artois, the Duc de Chartres (a cousin of the French royal family), and at times even Marie Antoinette herself. Throwing propriety to the wind, they amused themselves by racing sleek, lightweight cabriolets through the streets of Paris and slumming at workmen's dance halls on the outskirts of the city. Seasoned courtiers looked askance at such goings-on and reprimanded Lafayette and his companions on at least one occasion for mounting an amateur theatrical performance that mocked the pretensions of the arriviste robe nobility. The farce, which parodied the bureaucratic procedures and legalistic posturing of lesser-born nobles, was not only unkind but—more ominously—it was also politically tone-deaf.

An awkward adolescent eager to be liked, Lafayette did his best to keep up. He was generous to a fault and happy to put his copious resources—money, horses, hospitality—at the disposal of his companions, even those with ample fortunes of their own. But the memoirs of his contemporaries make it clear that he was not cut out for a life of distraction and dissolution. Some of the most pointed examples of Lafayette's social discomfort come from the writings of the Comte de La Marck, a Belgian nobleman in the French army and a confidant of Marie Antoinette's. La Marck, who traveled in the circles of the Noailles family in the 1770s, described Lafayette as perpetually striving to affect a *"bon air"* and often failing spectacularly. The Belgian oozed disdain as he recalled that Lafayette "danced without grace [and] sat badly on his horse." At his most cutting, La Marck describes an episode when, thanks to the Noailleses, Lafayette secured a coveted invitation to a quadrille hosted by Marie Antoinette and "proved himself to be so maladroit" at the sprightly dance "that the Queen could not stop herself from laughing." On another night out, Lafayette reportedly drank so much that he had to be helped to his waiting carriage and, once deposited inside, was disappointed to realize that the Vicomte de Noailles, whom he always wanted to impress, was not among the company that evening. All the way home, Lafayette pleaded with his companions, "Don't forget to tell Noailles how well I drank!"

As long as Lafayette remained in the realm of the Noailleses, the prospects before him were bleak. Although he possessed neither the desire nor the personality to succeed at court, his in-laws continued to hope against hope that they might guide him in that direction. The most disastrous moment came in 1775, when the Maréchal de Noailles sought to place Lafayette in the service of the Comte de Provence, the elder of Louis XVI's two brothers. A natural-born courtier who had performed regularly in the operas staged by Madame de Pompadour, the official mistress of Louis XV, the *maréchal* seems not to have understood how completely the notion of courtly behavior ran against the grain of Lafayette's character.

The *maréchal's* plan horrified Lafayette. Determined as he was "to travel the world in search of renown," he saw no path to glory emerging from the entourage of the king's brother, and he followed the first escape route that presented itself. As Lafayette later told the story to his physician and confidant Jules Cloquet, the opportunity arose at one of the masked balls that traditionally enlivened Paris in the weeks before Lent. There, Lafayette reported, he went out of his way to insult his prospective employer. As Lafayette and Provence were conversing, the young royal began to boast of his superior memory. Unable to abide bluster, even when it issued from the mouth of a prince, Lafayette interjected with his opinion that "memory is a fool's intellect." In deference to the *maréchal,* Provence was willing to give Lafayette the benefit of the doubt. Provence had, after all, been disguised in costume; perhaps Lafayette had genuinely failed to recognize him. The following day, Provence asked Lafayette if he knew whom he had insulted. Yes, Lafayette replied, it was the man then standing before him. After that conversation, there was no more talk of placing Lafayette at Versailles. Lafayette was pleased to have spared himself the inglorious life of a courtier but he had mortified his in-laws in the process.

For all their differences, Lafayette and the Noailleses saw eye to eye on at least one matter: they believed that a man of the sword nobility must possess an honorable military rank. To Lafayette and his in-laws, the brass buttons of an officer's uniform were far more than ornaments; they were signs of personal and family pride. On April 7, 1773, thanks to the intervention of the Duc d'Ayen, Lafayette was named lieutenant in the mounted regiment of the French army known as the Noailles Dragoons. Like most military commissions of the period, this one had been bought and paid for, yet money alone could never have procured such a place for a provincial, even if the provincial in question was a marquis. D'Ayen had to pull every string he could at the Ministry of War to clear the young man's way. Before Lafayette had spent a day in training, Ayen secured him the promise of a promotion. In the summer of 1774, when the regiment set off for its annual exercises in the northeastern French town of Metz, near the German border, the untested Lafayette was on his way to the army career he had always dreamed of. Or so he thought. When Lafayette returned to Metz in the summer of 1775, now wearing the insignia of captain and commanding a full company, he could not have known that his life was about to change forever.

Long before most Frenchmen heard about the conflict brewing in England's American colonies, one man had been following the rebellion with great interest—the Comte de Broglie, a former ambassador to the court of Poland, who was serving as the governor of Metz. During the reign of Louis XV, Broglie had played a central role in the king's "Secret Ministry," maintaining a covert correspondence with the monarch and implementing private policies that the French court deemed too controversial or embarrassing to acknowledge in public. Reestablishing France's supremacy over England in the wake of the Seven Years' War had been a priority for Broglie since at least 1765, when, at the behest of the king, he'd crafted a plan to invade England. In 1775, the Americans' efforts to throw off the English yoke cheered Broglie's heart. The American cause struck Broglie not only as an opportunity for France but also as a chance for personal advancement; a master manipulator with a taste for subterfuge, Broglie wrongly believed that George Washington was eminently replaceable, and envisioned himself at the helm of the rebel forces. It was no coincidence that Lafayette—a rich, free-spending young man in search of a worthy cause—attracted Broglie's attention.

Lafayette, who knew nothing of these background intrigues, perceived only the best in Broglie. Broglie was not generally well-liked—contemporaries described him as a small, headstrong man whose "sparkling eyes" signaled a "restless spirit" and whose overweening ambition kept him on constant alert for new prey—but Lafayette saw only a senior officer and accomplished courtier who took an interest in him and, refreshingly, did not attempt to transform him into someone he could never become. Broglie brought Lafayette into his circle, treated him as an equal, and introduced him to influential friends and innovative ideas. A grand master in the international society of Freemasons, Broglie might well have sparked Lafayette's interest in that fraternal organization, launching an affiliation that Lafayette retained throughout his life. Freemasonry may be best known today for its esoteric mystical system rooted in Newtonian science; emphasizing the rationality of the universe, the society refers to God as the Great Architect and adapts symbols from the building trades—calipers, T squares, levels—to represent and convey its tenets. But in Lafayette's time, the order helped advance reformist political views by propounding universal principles of virtue, espousing meritocracy as its organizing structure, and promoting a social vision that the historian Margaret C. Jacob has described as "stability under a strong, but constitutional monarchy."

Thanks in part to its universally legible symbols, Freemasonry became a worldwide phenomenon. Having arrived in France as an English import in the early 1700s, the society grew increasingly popular throughout the nation as the eighteenth century progressed; Jacob counted 62 lodges (as Masonic meetinghouses are called) in France in 1759, and 314 by 1770. Members of the bourgeoisie and the nobility mingled in the lodges, which also sprouted in the Holy Roman Empire, the Dutch Republic, and elsewhere on the European continent. Crucially for Lafayette, who appears to have joined the Parisian lodge of Saint-Jean de la Candeur in December 1775, Freemasonry also crossed the Atlantic. George Washington, who had been inducted into the Masonic lodge in Fredericksburg, Virginia, in 1752, was one of the many Founding Fathers who embraced Freemasonry, and when Lafayette arrived in America, Freemasonry would serve as a bond that united him to his comrades-in-arms.

Broglie's role in facilitating Lafayette's initiation into the order remains undocumented, but it is certain that Broglie introduced Lafayette to one of Freemasonry's highest-ranking members, Prince William Henry, Duke of Gloucester and Edinburgh, who was also England's most controversial spokesman for the American cause. Gloucester, as he was generally known, was King George III's younger brother and the black sheep of the royal family—a profligate spender whose secret marriage to Maria Walpole, the widowed niece of the writer and politician Horace Walpole, scandalized king and court when it became known. Equally vexing to George III was Gloucester's support of the liberal minority in the House of Lords, where the independent-minded prince joined a chorus of peers who objected to the king's American policies and sympathized with the colonists' grievances.

During the summer of 1775, Gloucester and his wife traveled through France en route to Italy, where the warmer climate was deemed beneficial to Gloucester's delicate health. Along the way, the French king allowed the English prince to tour fortifications throughout the nation and to inspect the royal troops. Such a visit brought Gloucester to Metz, where, one day in August, he sat down to dine at the table of the Comte de Broglie and found Lafayette among the invited guests. That dinner ignited Lafayette's passion for the American cause. In 1828 Lafayette told his American biographer, Jared Sparks, that he had "listened with ardent curiosity" throughout the meal and "pressed the duke with questions." The responses he received inspired him so fully that, before he left the table, "he had conceived of the idea of going to America."

The looming fight against the British could almost have been tailor-made to appeal to Lafayette, whose initial enthusiasm for the American cause quickly transformed into an urgent mission. For Lafayette, aiding the colonists represented an opportunity to right the wrongs of the Seven Years' War by avenging both his father's death and his nation's losses. Moreover, the prospect of assisting a rebellion excited the always active imagination of the adolescent Lafayette, who craved self-determination and who, according to his memoirs, once responded to a schoolmaster's prompt by describing an ideal horse as one that threw off its rider. Although his determination to serve under the banner of liberty was nothing if not earnest, Lafayette also had a more immediate reason to join the fight: America might well have been the only land where Lafayette could continue to wear the uniform of an officer.

When King Louis XVI of France named the Comte de Saint-Germain his minister of war, on October 25, 1775, it was only a matter of time before wide-ranging changes would sound the death knell for Lafayette's military career. Saint-Germain's goals were commendable; committed to making the army both a more equitable institution and a more effective fighting force, he introduced reforms designed to ensure that merit, rather than ties to Versailles, would determine who rose through the ranks. For Saint-Germain, the matter was personal. Born in the Franche-Comté region of eastern France, he had firsthand experience with the injustices suffered by hardworking officers from rural areas: having won commendations for his conduct on the battlefields of the Seven Years' War, he'd seen his bids for promotion scuttled by the machinations of better-connected rivals. In his memoirs, Saint-Germain lamented the army's "pernicious distinction between the nobility of the Court and that of the provinces . . . between the rich and the poor, such that one has everything, without meriting anything, and the other gets nothing, no matter what they merit." As minister of war, Saint-Germain devised a wholesale reorganization of the army intended to spare others the indignities he had suffered. Only a portion of his proposed changes were adopted before he tendered his resignation in the face of stiff opposition, but those changes were enough to place many young noblemen in the army reserves until such time as their services were required. With the nation now at peace, that time might be long in coming. On June 11, 1776, Saint-Germain's plans forced Lafayette out of active duty; in the euphemistic parlance of the day, Lafayette had been "reformed."

Having given no serious thought to the possibility of a career outside of the military, and having definitively closed the door to an appointment at court, Lafayette had no clear path forward. Throwing his lack of direction into high relief, Adrienne was blossoming in her role as wife and mother, having given birth to a daughter, Henriette, in December 1775. When Lafayette had learned of Adrienne's pregnancy, he had been overjoyed at the prospect of becoming "the father of a wonderfully loving family." But, according to the reigning mores of the day, fatherhood—unlike motherhood—could not be a vocation. To live an honorable life, Lafayette had to devote himself to some project that would benefit the public good, and to attain the renown that he dreamed of, his service would have to be widely recognized. Thanks to clandestine negotiations held six months earlier, on the other side of the Atlantic Ocean, just such an endeavor would soon be at hand.

CHAPTER 3

LES INSURGENTS

On a dark December night in 1775, the sixty-nine-year-old Benjamin Franklin and two other members of the Committee of Congress for Secret Correspondence set out for a meeting at Carpenters' Hall—the elegant Georgian building that had hosted the Continental Congress in 1774. Although the men shared a destination, they traced separate paths through the streets of Philadelphia to avoid being followed. Reaching Carpenters' Hall, Franklin climbed the stairs to the second-floor headquarters of the Library Company of Philadelphia where, surrounded by books that he had helped amass, he sat down with his colleagues to begin a series of talks with an emissary from the French court. The topic? Joining forces against Great Britain, France's traditional enemy, in a war that was already under way.

Julien-Alexandre Achard de Bonvouloir, the French secret agent who visited Carpenters' Hall that night, had been sent by Louis XVI to assess the likelihood of American success and the wisdom of forging a covert Franco-American alliance against King George III. Following explicit orders given by France's foreign minister, Charles Gravier, Comte de Vergennes, Bonvouloir was to leave no evidence of collusion that might fall into the hands of British spies. And although overt French support would have been invaluable for the Americans, they too kept the discussions quiet—Franklin's committee sent no official notification to Congress—in order to avoid public embarrassment in case of failure, which probably seemed like a distinct possibility to many rational observers. A French-American alliance was not a natural fit; not only were the two peoples divided by distinctions of language, manners, and mores but they harbored deep-seated mutual suspicions grounded in religious and political differences. In the recent past, long-standing animosities between the nominally Catholic French and the predominantly Protestant Americans had been compounded by fierce fighting in the French and Indian War, which had left lingering resentments on both sides. Yet the men who met at Carpenters' Hall during Christmas week in 1775 were somehow able to bridge the divide well enough to agree on a tentative plan that was designed to be disavowed if the need ever arose.

On July 6, 1776, Connecticut lawyer-turned-businessman Silas Deane arrived in Paris to pick up where the Philadelphia discussions left off. Deane had instructions to keep his presence and purpose under wraps; if anyone asked, he was to identify himself as an American merchant "engaged in the business of providing goods for the Indian trade." Meanwhile, a handful of trustworthy allies would work behind the scenes to arrange an audience with Vergennes. Once the introduction was made, Deane was to ask Vergennes to supply the Continental Army with four military engineers, "clothing and arms for twenty-five thousand men with a suitable quantity of ammunition, and one hundred field pieces," all to be acquired on credit. Deane had little to offer in return, but he was to suggest that, if France would help free the colonies, "it is likely [that a] great part of our commerce will naturally fall to the share of France." That part of the plan worked smoothly: by July 20, Deane and Vergennes had agreed that the crown would send clothing, guns, and ammunition—all the while denying any involvement in American affairs. Deane's cover story, however, was short-lived.

Barely had Deane settled into his Left Bank lodgings in the Hôtel du Grand Villars than the Parisian elite began flocking to his rooms. By December, when Arthur Lee and Benjamin Franklin arrived as the first official American emissaries to France, *"les insurgents,"* as the patriots were called, were all the rage. In the fashionable salons of Paris and the halls of Versailles, a new card game dubbed *Le Boston* supplanted the English whist as a favorite pastime. By the following spring, a ditty celebrating Washington, his mission, and the American continent was raising smiles. Stressing the first syllable of "continent" in every verse, singers found themselves mischievously uttering a word barred from polite company. Even Marie Antoinette embraced the fad for the New World, pressing Deane for Narragansett horses that might add an American touch to her stables.

Schooled in the Roman classics, the men of Lafayette's generation heard echoes of antiquity in the foreigners' voices. As Ségur put it, the visitors appeared to his circle of friends like "some wise contemporaries of Plato, or republicans from the time of Cato and Fabius." Ségur observed that "nothing was more surprising than the contrast between the luxury of our capital, the elegance of our fashions, the magnificence of Versailles," and the manner of the Americans, who arrived with their "almost rustic dress, simple but proud bearing, free and direct language, hair without preparation or powder, in short, with this antique air that seemed to have carried itself suddenly inside our walls." So taken was France with these men and their cause that "opinions from every quarter pressed the royal government to declare itself on the side of republican liberty." Perceptive as always, Ségur noted the irony of a world where the court "applauded the republican maxims" of *Brutus*—Voltaire's theatrical sensation—and where "the monarchs were inclined to embrace the cause of a people in revolt against their king; in short, independence was spoken of in the camps, democracy among the nobles, philosophy at the balls, morality in the boudoirs."

Military men were particularly smitten with America, especially those who, like Lafayette, had been "reformed." On December 2, 1776, an astonished Deane wrote to John Jay, "I have a levee of officers and others every morning. . . . I have had occasionally dukes, generals and marqueses and even bishops, and comtes and chevaliers without number." These high-ranking noblemen, Deane explained, "being out of employ here, or having friends they wish to advance in the cause of liberty," were eager to learn what assistance the American army might need. Spurring these officers on were the Comte de Broglie and his ally the "Baron" Johann de Kalb—a Bavarian peasant who, thanks to his wife's fortune, was able to enjoy an extravagant lifestyle suited to his self-invented title. Both hoped to play important roles in the American war, and they were actively recruiting anyone who might wish to join their transatlantic ventures. In their elegantly appointed town houses, Broglie and de Kalb hosted soirées in honor of the ever-popular Deane, who, they imagined, might provide their tickets to America.

At first, Deane was pleased with the offers of assistance. In August, he reported to the Secret Committee that "several young gentlemen of fortune, whose families are nearly connected with the Court, are preparing to embark for America." By November, the offers had multiplied, and Deane's excitement had cooled. "I am well nigh harrassed to death with applications of officers to go out to America," he complained. And before the year was out, he would write with growing alarm, "Had I ten ships here I could fill them all with passengers for America." Although nothing in his instructions suggested that he should recruit French officers, Deane was soon appointing major generals at a rapid clip. Perhaps he believed that a bit of European expertise would help the struggling Continental Army, and he may well have been so daunted by the intricate webs of influence that defined the French aristocracy that he feared displeasing even people whose titles were spurious, like de Kalb.

This was the opportunity Lafayette had been waiting for, but he continued to bide his time before joining the fray. Although he often described himself as a man of action, Lafayette was more deliberative than he let on, and he habitually watched and waited before determining the best way to proceed; once he chose his course, however, it was almost impossible to steer him away. In an early version of his memoirs, drafted in 1779, before his legend as a firebrand had fully developed, Lafayette wrote that "we were afraid to visit" Deane, the rebel, whose "voice was muffled by the cries of Lord Stormont," England's ambassador to the court of Louis XVI. By way of warning his French hosts not to back the wrong horse in the American conflict, Stormont was blustering about the halls of Versailles predicting the colonists' imminent defeat at every turn. If Deane's reports are accurate, Lafayette must have been one of the few men in Paris to let the Englishman's barrage of words delay his approach.

As summer turned to autumn, Lafayette could wait no longer. Compelled by "the desire to right the wrongs of the last war, to fight the English and to fly to the aid of the Americans," Lafayette, Ségur, and Noailles made a pact in October, pledging to join General Washington's army together. Noailles advocated seeking permission from the Duc d'Ayen, but Lafayette thought it safer to keep the news secret. As he recalled, "circumstances . . . had taught me to expect nothing but obstacles . . . from my family; therefore I counted on myself." Rather than turn to his father-in-law, Lafayette asked the Comte de Broglie— the man who had first whetted his interest in the American cause—for an introduction to Silas Deane. Broglie directed Lafayette to de Kalb, who spoke English and was already negotiating with Deane for transportation to America. Like Broglie, de Kalb saw in Lafayette a path to the New World, and was therefore happy to oblige.

Noailles joined Lafayette for his first meeting with de Kalb but, still convinced of the need for official approval, took it upon himself to write to the Comte de Maurepas, adviser to the king. By then, it was clear that the king had no objections to French officers sailing to the aid of America—scores of Frenchmen had departed in recent months, all but waving their papers from Deane as they left—but the crown was not ready to drop the façade of neutrality by granting permission in writing. Receiving no reply from Maurepas, Noailles asked d'Ayen to intercede. According to some accounts, d'Ayen considered the request and may well have been tempted to join his cousin-turned-son-in-law on an American venture. But, upon hearing that Lafayette was involved in the scheme, d'Ayen soured on it. He told Noailles to inform de Kalb that the plan was off.

Noailles dutifully withdrew from the conversation, but Lafayette refused to turn back and, in fact, redoubled his efforts, meeting regularly with Deane and de Kalb throughout the month of November, continually impressing upon them how much he could help their cause. Lafayette, who was barely nineteen years old, recalled speaking "more of my zeal than of my experience" in presenting himself to Deane. Desperate for a chance to prove his mettle, Lafayette insisted that he could offer more than just passion—he could also generate publicity, a valuable skill in eighteenth-century Paris, where public opinion was beginning to wield political clout. As the men talked, the young marquis "dwelt upon the minor sensation my departure would raise." Sweetening the pot, he made it clear that he expected no remuneration for his services. Instead, he asked for something that he cherished more than money: a high military rank and the respect that came with it.

Deane had his own reasons for awarding the incongruously elevated rank of major general to a man who had never seen battlefield action. Avoiding matters of skill or experience altogether, the letter of agreement signed by Deane and Lafayette on December 7, 1776, observed that Lafayette's "high Birth, his Alliances, the great Dignities which his Family holds at this Court, his considerable Estates in this Realm, his personal merit, his Reputation, his disinterestedness, and above all his Zeal for the Liberty of our Provinces" rendered him worthy of the appointment. Noting that Lafayette believed he could not "obtain leave of his Family to pass the seas and serve in a foreign Country till he can go as a General Officer," Deane explained, "I have thought that I could not better serve my Country . . . than by granting to him in the name of the very honorable Congress the Rank of Major General."

Evidently he didn't consider that seasoned American officers might see the matter of Lafayette's rank in a rather different light.

Only one detail remained unsettled: Lafayette and de Kalb needed a way across the ocean. Here, at last, was a problem that Lafayette's wealth could solve. He proudly announced to Deane that "hitherto . . . you saw only my zeal"; now Lafayette would prove himself useful by "purchasing a ship that will transport your officers." With the help of Broglie's secretary and friends, Lafayette spent 112,000 livres, approximately one year's income, on a vessel known as *La Victoire*—"Victory." A slow and ungainly merchant ship weighing in at 220 tons, the *Victoire* was hardly the ideal craft. Even after being outfitted with six cannons, it could scarcely have mounted a defense in the event of attack. But eager to distinguish himself in the New World, Lafayette was delighted to call the ship his own.

Who was aware of these preparations? With deniability serving as the overriding principle in those early days of the French-American alliance, it's difficult to say. The story that Lafayette related in his 1779 memoir protected both his family and the French government by marveling at "the secrecy" of his conversations with de Kalb and Deane and insisting that "family, friends, ministers, French spies, English spies, all were blind to them." But in 1777, de Kalb told a different story. Finding himself shouldering the blame for Lafayette's unapproved departure, de Kalb insisted that no secrecy whatsoever had surrounded their meetings. "We saw each other every day," de Kalb wrote to the French Department of War. "He came to my house openly and without the least mystery . . . and I did the same visiting him at the hôtel de Noailles." De Kalb was "always admitted without any difficulty," even when Madame de Lafayette was with her husband. De Kalb had no idea, he claimed, that d'Ayen and the rest of the family were not aware of Lafayette's imminent departure. In fact, Lafayette had always told him that d'Ayen "desired it and consented." Lafayette must surely have been spotted going in and out of Deane's lodgings, which were placed under surveillance by the Paris chief of police the moment of the American's arrival. And even if all this traffic had somehow gone unnoticed, someone had to have signed off on the formal leaves of absence from the French army that had been acquired by thirteen of the fourteen men under de Kalb's command. Those who later claimed to have been unaware of the planning may simply have been looking the other way or, perhaps, hoping that no one would be able to prove their complicity.

A great clamor nonetheless arose in mid-March when two letters from Lafayette—one to Adrienne and one to d'Ayen—reached the Hôtel de Noailles. Informing the family that Lafayette was en route to Bordeaux and about to set sail, the letters made conspicuous mention of the fact that their recipients were ignorant of his plans. In his letter to Adrienne, Lafayette acknowledged that he was leaving at a difficult moment (Adrienne was expecting their second child), but he asked her not to be unhappy with him. As he explained, he was already "too cruelly punished" by sorrow. "Had I believed that I would feel my sacrifices in such a frightful manner," he wrote, "I would not now be the most unhappy of men." He simply "had never understood how much I loved you." Lafayette crafted a more high-minded letter to his father-in-law. "I have found a unique opportunity to distinguish myself, and to learn my craft," he wrote to d'Ayen. "I am a general officer in the army of the United States of America. My zeal for their cause and my frankness won their confidence. . . . I have done all I could for them, and their interest will always be more dear to me than my own."

Lafayette was sincere, but d'Ayen was outraged, his pique exacerbated by a specific circumstance. Just a few weeks earlier, Lafayette had traveled to London, where he had visited d'Ayen's brother, who was then serving as France's ambassador to England, and the ambassador had gone so far as to present Lafayette to King George III. In light of Lafayette's decision to take up arms with the Americans, that ill-timed introduction could now be perceived as a provocation on the part of the ambassador, if not the French crown. At the very least, it threatened to jeopardize the standing of the Noailleses at court.

D'Ayen could not stand idly by. Hoping to stop Lafayette from leaving the country, he wrote to Louis XVI, who, in turn, issued orders forbidding Lafayette's departure. The message reached Bordeaux too late—the *Victoire* had already sailed—but d'Ayen would have another chance. Rather than steering due west for America, Lafayette headed for the Bay of Biscay, at the foothills of the Pyrenees in northern Spain. Evidently, Lafayette believed that d'Ayen would bless the American adventure at the eleventh hour, if only to save face, and he was happy to delay the transatlantic crossing for a few days while awaiting the good news. But the message that reached Lafayette was not what he had hoped for. Containing harsh words of remonstrance from both d'Ayen and Louis XVI, it instructed the wayward marquis to retrace his steps and hasten to Marseilles. There, the message said, Lafayette was to meet his in-laws, who would accompany him on an educational tour of Italy.

Lafayette was undeterred. Surely, he thought, d'Ayen would eventually grant permission; the case only had to be presented in the right light. Leaving ship and comrades at the harbor in Spain, Lafayette rode three days by coach back to Bordeaux, took a public carriage that was heading for Marseilles, and then returned to the *Victoire* on horseback. Conflicting rumors proliferated in Paris and London—and eventually in America, as well. For every report that Lafayette had given up on his "folly," as Stormont called it, there was another asserting that the *Victoire* was already in the middle of the ocean. Some whispered that the court had secretly permitted the departure, while others contended that Louis XVI had ordered Lafayette clapped in irons and was readying a cell in the Bastille. Adding to the confusion, Lafayette dispatched a peculiar and contradictory series of letters that can only have been designed for self-protection. Two were sent in quick succession to the king's minister: the first requested permission to sail, and the second, noting that no reply had been received, declared silence tantamount to approval and announced that Lafayette was on his way. This line of defense might not have held up in a court of law, but it was received well by the tribunal of public opinion.

On April 17, Lafayette arrived for the second and last time at Puerto de Pasajes, on the Bay of Biscay, and on April 20 his ship set sail for the New World. As Lafayette had promised Deane, his departure caused a bit of a "stir," with his comings and goings from various ports only agitating matters further. In the midst of the hullabaloo, Stormont had reported on April 2 that Lafayette's "Relations seem to be much displeased with his Conduct" and that "his friends and the Public at Large" deemed Lafayette's actions "imprudent and Irregular." Yet even the British ambassador had to admit that the general consensus was favorable. Those who heard of Lafayette's great escape held that "it shews a spirit of Enterprize, and strong Enthusiasm for a good cause." Few people thought Lafayette had it in him, but the boldness of his actions in the New World would surprise his detractors and his defenders alike.

PART TWO

American Patriot

CHAPTER 4

FIRST IMPRESSIONS

Captain Charles Biddle had no desire to meet a boatload of Frenchmen. A merchant mariner from Philadelphia who happened to be in Georgetown, South Carolina, on June 13, 1777, when the *Victoire* touched ground on nearby North Island, Biddle wrote in his autobiography that he "had heard so much of the French officers who came over to enter into the American service" that he had "conceived a very unfavorable opinion of them." They were all mercenaries, as far as he could tell, and probably not even real military men at that. Biddle scoffed that the latest group most likely consisted of "only barbers or tailors" seeking an easy fortune. Yet Biddle could not deny his French fluency, and he grudgingly granted an associate's request that he serve as an interpreter for the newcomers. He soon discovered that none of the forty-five Frenchmen who had descended on North Island would have been able to trim his beard or fit him for a suit of clothes.

The crossing had not been easy for Lafayette. In a plaintive letter to Adrienne written aboard ship on May 30, he confessed that he did not take naturally to the sea. Lafayette had been "quite ill during the first part of my voyage," he wrote, adding with his usual dry humor that at least he could take comfort in the fact that his shipmates shared his suffering. The seasickness eventually subsided, but six weeks had already passed since the *Victoire* had left port, and Lafayette despaired that he would not reach land for another "eight or ten" days; in fact, he would be on board for another two weeks. Lafayette found the North Atlantic to be "the most tedious of regions." "The sea is so sad," he lamented, "and I believe we sadden each other, she and I." Yet tedium was no match for Lafayette's enthusiasm. Once he recovered from the nausea—which, he boasted, he did more quickly than his companions—he immersed himself so fully in English books that, although he had not studied the language before sailing, he arrived with passable skills and would be fluent in less than a year.

Many of Lafayette's shipmates shared his excitement, but others were more jaded—none more so than the Vicomte de Mauroy. Mauroy, a native of Burgundy, had served as an infantry captain for fifteen years before being promoted to lieutenant colonel in the grenadiers but had since been decommissioned, thanks to Saint-Germain's army reforms. Like Lafayette, Mauroy held a letter of appointment granting him the rank of major general, but unlike Lafayette, Mauroy had had money, not laurels, in his sights when he'd signed on with Silas Deane on November 20, 1776. Whereas Lafayette plainly stated that he would serve as a volunteer, Mauroy demanded "the same pay prerogatives and honours as the American officers of the same rank" and was promised "additional pay as a foreigner which he leaves to the discretion of the States" as well as a further "sum of twelve thousand livres . . . one half thereof as a bounty and the other half as an advance of his pay."

The very model of a mercenary officer, Mauroy was as cynical as he was avaricious. He actively tried to poison Lafayette's idealistic views during the long ocean crossing, later explaining that "I wanted by my objections to prepare him for the disappointments he might experience." Determined to shake Lafayette's belief that Americans "are unified by the love of virtue, of liberty . . . that they are simple, good, hospitable people who prefer beneficence to all our vain pleasures," Mauroy argued that Americans were no different from their European brethren. Having come from Europe, they brought "the views and prejudices of their respective homelands" to the "unspoiled gound" they now inhabited. In fact, Mauroy believed that Americans might be even less admirable than the men and women they'd left behind because, to his mind, "fanaticism, the insatiable desire for wealth, and misery" were the three motivations that kept a "nearly uninterrupted stream of immigrants" flowing to the New World. Where Lafayette perceived only goodness, Mauroy saw greedy men who "sword in hand . . . cut down, under a sky that is new to them, forests as ancient as the world, water a still virgin land with the blood of its primitive inhabitants, and fertilize with thousands of scattered cadavers the fields they conquered through crime." Still, Lafayette was unfazed. He landed on North

Island as optimistic as the boy who'd once hoped to slay the Beast of the Gévaudan.

The *Victoire* dropped anchor under inauspicious circumstances. To begin with, the ship had strayed far off its intended course. The Frenchmen had been heading for Charleston when adverse winds combined with the crew's scant knowledge of the region to leave them more than fifty miles northeast of their destination at ten o'clock at night. The landing party sent ashore at North Island encountered four dark-skinned men who were out fishing by moonlight, and soon the weary travelers were trudging behind the fishermen to an unknown house where they hoped to receive hospitality from strangers. Their guides, it turned out, were slaves who belonged to one Major Huger; Lafayette had been welcomed to the land of liberty by men who were not free.

None of this seems to have affected Lafayette's sunny attitude. Seeing the world through rose-colored glasses, Lafayette was consistently charmed by the places and people of South Carolina. When he met Charles Biddle, he apparently had no idea that the unwilling translator harbored any ill will toward the French. In fact, during his first few weeks in America, Lafayette seems to have remained blissfully ignorant of the hostility routinely directed toward French officers in general. Writing from North Island on his second day in America, Lafayette crafted a glowing letter to Adrienne in which he confirmed his highest hopes. "The manners of this world," he observed, "are simple, polite, and worthy in every respect of the country where the good name of liberty resounds." A few days later he elaborated on the theme in a letter from Charleston, praising "the simplicity of manners, the desire to oblige, the love of country and of liberty," and the "sweet equality" that "reigns over all." He lauded not only the town—"one of the most attractive, best built, and most pleasantly populated cities that I have ever seen"—but also, and perhaps unwisely in a letter to his wife, its "very pretty" female inhabitants. Sweeping aphorisms about equality and possibility pepper these early letters, which, making no mention of the institution of slavery, take a selective view of already limited experiences. "What enchants me," Lafayette rhapsodized, "is that all citizens are brothers; in America, there are no poor, and none that one could even call peasants." He later remembered being struck by the sight of "new products and methods of cultivation" during his first trip to the New World. Even the landscape captured his imagination: where Mauroy saw destruction wrought by European colonists, Lafayette described "vast forests, immense rivers" where "nature adorns everything . . . with an air of youth and majesty."

Lafayette was only nineteen years old and innocent enough to trust his first impressions; he also had a tendency to express himself in rapturous tones no matter the occasion. Although he had come to fight the British, just a few months earlier he had been lavishing praise on the city and people of London. Writing to Adrienne from the English capital on February 28, he had reported feeling completely at home— something that he had never quite felt in Paris. "For once, my love, I am just like these gentlemen," he wrote, explaining that "we dance all night and, perhaps because my dancing is more on a par with everyone else's, I like the ball here." He also liked Englishwomen. As he put it to Adrienne, "to us, all the women are pretty, and good company." Strikingly, he referred to England—the nation with which he was about to go to war—as "my new country." Then again, as he admitted, "it is true that I am inclined to see everything in the best light."

In America, a unique set of circumstances boosted Lafayette's natural optimism. Lafayette was the only marquis around—and although his rank counted for little in the drawing rooms of Paris and Versailles, it never failed to dazzle his American hosts. Many of Lafayette's shipmates bore titles of nobility, but none so exalted as his. And while some could boast of accomplishments that dwarfed Lafayette's, none of them enjoyed the benefits that were lavished upon the young marquis.

Lafayette's less privileged companions had a very different experience of their arrival in the New World. The passengers from the *Victoire* set off for Charleston in two groups: one, including Mauroy, sailed with the ship to its destination, while the rest, including Lafayette and de Kalb, made the journey overland. De Kalb described the three-day march from North Island to Charleston as an exhausting ordeal made with great difficulty in unbearable heat. His letters report on the fevers and illnesses suffered by his companions, as well as the purges and rest cures they underwent. Perhaps a bit of boasting was involved—"I believe I'll bury all our young men," the fifty-six-year-old de Kalb wrote to his wife—but his story tallies with the recollections of his aide-de-camp, the Chevalier Dubuysson. In a lengthy memoir sent back to France that autumn, Dubuysson elaborated on the journey to Charleston. Offering details overlooked by Lafayette and de Kalb, Dubuysson recalled that a shortage of horses had left the group to set out on foot. Armed to the hilt for fear of marauders, and too weighed down to carry any fresh clothing, they plodded slowly through the oppressive humidity. It did not take long for the men to realize that their heavy riding boots were adding to their misery, and with no other shoes at their disposal, they chose to walk barefoot through stretches of "burning sand" and dense woods. Three days later, Lafayette and his companions arrived in Charleston looking a great deal like "beggars and bandits," as Dubuysson put it, and they "were received accordingly."

Dubuysson encountered anti-French sentiment everywhere. He offered no excuses for the swarms of ill-mannered French soldiers of fortune he witnessed in Charleston, many of whom, he believed, were bad seeds who had been "ruined by debt" or "chased out of their corps." But he was nonetheless critical of Americans who routinely heaped invective upon the foreign soldiers who had come to the colonies' aid. With an unseemly harshness, he complained that "all the French here are paid very little for the sacrifices they make on behalf of a populace that offers them no gratitude, and that merits just as little."

Lafayette was immune to such problems. Dubuysson found the honors abundantly bestowed upon his companion bewildering and altogether out of proportion to the middling rank of a marquis. But in America, the sudden appearance of a group of titled Frenchmen in South Carolina was so noteworthy that it made the papers as far north as Boston. The *Independent Chronicle and the Universal Advertiser* carried a dispatch from Charleston reporting that "a number of Volunteers and French Officers, who have three Years Leave to serve in America, are just arrived here." The author seemed not to be entirely clear who the important personages were: "among them," the article announced, "are the Marquis de Moncaim, and the Marquis de Fayette, the last said to be Son-in Law to the Duke d'Aguen." The identities are garbled, but the errors didn't make much difference in this context. The foreign names were all the same to an American audience seeing them for the first time, and the salient idea was conveyed quite clearly: highborn, influential French officers were joining the American army. To the reading public, the men's arrival must have seemed a sign of hope.

On June 26, 1777, the group set off for Philadelphia, where they expected the Continental Congress to confirm their appointments, assign them commands, and send them off to fight in General Washington's army. The 650-mile trip north began comfortably enough for the dozen or so officers and their servants, or at least for the lucky ones who started out in open carriages—the most luxurious means of transportation they could find, albeit a step down from the sleek cabriolets, ornamented with lacquer and gilt, that Lafayette and his friends had once raced through the narrow streets of Paris. As Dubuysson describes it, the European convoy must have made for an unlikely spectacle: homespun wagons, piled high with baggage and pulled by teams of wheezing horses, lurched violently as they crept along behind an incongruously majestic guide—one of Lafayette's servants dressed for the occasion in the colorful costume of a hussar, which customarily featured horizontal gold braids running across the jacket, vertical gold braids coursing down the legs of the trousers, and a tall black hat surmounted by a prominent plume completing the opulent look.

The parade was nearly as brief as it was conspicuous. Four days of jostling over rocky paths proved too much for the rickety vehicles; somewhere in North Carolina the axles gave way and the coaches ground to a halt. Leaving behind a trail of baggage, the men continued on horseback through Maryland, Delaware, and Pennsylvania. Writing from Petersburg, Virginia, on July 17, Lafayette related the scene to Adrienne with a measure of self-deprecating humor: "I started out brilliantly by carriage," he reported, but now "we are all on horseback, after having broken the carriage, in my usual laudable fashion, and I hope to write to you in a few days that we have arrived on foot."

And so they would. Over the course of the next ten days, the horses proceeded to collapse of exhaustion, one by one, in the steamy heat of the mid-Atlantic summer. On the morning of Sunday, July 27, the Frenchmen reached Philadelphia, a bedraggled crew plagued by fever and dysentery. No military campaign in all of Europe, Dubuysson complained, could have been "harder than this voyage," which offered no pleasures to mitigate the pain. But the men had been buoyed by the infectious "zeal of Lafayette" and now, with the thirty-two-day journey ended, a grateful Congress would soon welcome the travelers—or so the Frenchmen imagined.

The reception they received was in fact rather cold. John Hancock of Massachusetts was serving as president of the Second Continental Congress, and with Congress out of session for the day, his home was a natural destination for the French visitors. Pausing just long enough to wash up, the exhausted but still eager officers made their way to Hancock's pleasantly situated house at the intersection of Arch and Fourth Streets. But Hancock was not interested in speaking with these disheveled foreigners who appeared unbidden on his doorstep. He suggested they call on Robert Morris, a wealthy Philadelphia merchant who represented Pennsylvania in Congress and was a member of the Committee of Congress for Secret Correspondence—the same body that had appointed Silas Deane to drum up French support for the revolution. As far as Hancock was concerned, if Deane had sent these men to America, Morris should be the one to deal with them. So off they went to find Morris, who at least had the courtesy to arrange an appointment for the following day before putting them back on the streets of Philadelphia.

The next morning, Lafayette and twelve other French officers gathered in front of the Chestnut Street entrance to Independence Hall, ready for what they hoped would be a history-making conversation with Morris. After waiting quite some time, they saw Morris walking toward them in the company of yet another American representative, James Lovell of Massachusetts, who was hastily introduced as a gentleman who "speaks French very well and has been charged with dealing with all of your countrymen." Having been passed around like so many hot potatoes the day before, Lafayette and his compatriots were disheartened when Morris departed just as brusquely as he had arrived. But as far as Lovell's language skills were concerned, the visitors were indeed impressed. Dubuysson recalled that Lovell "received us in the street, which is where he left us after calling us, in very good French, adventurers."

If nothing else, the abbreviated conversation with Lovell explained the hostility they had experienced since reaching Philadelphia. Lovell "ended his harangue," as Dubuysson put it, by complaining about Silas Deane. It seems that Deane had been asked to send back four French engineers but had instead inflicted upon Congress a certain Monsieur du Coudray, who had made a very poor impression, along with "some so-called engineers . . . and some useless artillerymen." Fortunately, Lovell continued, Benjamin Franklin had saved the day by locating four real engineers in Paris. Since those engineers had recently arrived, no further Frenchmen would be required. Lafayette and his companions, Lovell concluded, should feel free to head home.

Major General Philippe Charles Tronson du Coudray had all but ensured his countrymen's icy reception when he'd arrived in the colonies bearing exorbitant demands, an imperious manner, and exaggerated claims to political influence. Lovell's denunciation notwithstanding, du

Coudray did possess some valuable qualities. He was an experienced army engineer selected by France's minister of war to oversee the transfer of French guns to ships bound for America, but he had arrived in June bearing a letter from Silas Deane placing him in charge of all of America's artillery and engineers and promising tremendous funds to match this high authority. Unfortunately, the position Deane so freely assigned to du Coudray was already occupied. The occupant— Brigadier General Henry Knox, for whom Fort Knox is named—was only one of the many American generals who threatened to resign if Deane's agreement with du Coudray was to be honored.

Du Coudray's intimations of close ties to the French court had left Congress in a quandary. On June 19, John Adams was among those who had equivocated. Acknowledging that du Coudray's "terms are very high," Adams nonetheless concluded that "he has done us such essential service in France, and his interest is so great and so near the throne that it would be impolitic, not to avail ourselves of him." Undaunted by the disputes raging around him, du Coudray persisted in inspecting the region's fortifications, which he critiqued in contemptuous reports. And although his bleak assessments of Philadelphia's defenses would unfortunately prove to be accurate, his high-handed denunciations of the Delaware River forts, designed and built by American hands, endeared him to no one. Writing of Fort Billingsport, du Coudray deemed its plan "very bad" and executed "without judgment." Fort Mifflin he termed "badly situated," its battery "improperly directed," its embrasures "badly constructed"—in short, "it can answer no valuable purpose." And the best he could say of Fort Bull was that its faults "do not render it as useless as the two former Forts."

By the time Lafayette's group arrived, the far more satisfactory Louis Lebègue Duportail, handpicked by Franklin, had appeared to save the day. He, too, was exasperated by the sad state of American military affairs, but being more discreet than du Coudray, he shared his caustic, condescending thoughts primarily with the French foreign minister, the Comte de Vergennes. "There is a hundred times more enthusiasm for this revolution in a single café in Paris than in all the united colonies," Duportail ludicrously lamented to Vergennes in a November letter. Nonetheless, he believed the revolution a fight worth having. Duportail was well aware that "shepherding the colonies to victory would cost France several millions," but he deemed it an investment that would "be amply repaid by the destruction of the maritime power of England, which, having no more colonies, will soon have no marine." Shortly after reaching America's shores, Duportail was placed at the head of the army corps of engineers. With that, the American army had received all that it imagined it needed from France.

Convinced that their cause was hopeless, Lafayette and his companions were surprised the following morning when the man who had dismissed them so unceremoniously in front of Independence Hall appeared at Lafayette's door. Mistakes had been made, explained the contrite Lovell, who was now accompanied by another French-speaking congressman, William Duer of New York. Congress wanted to make amends—but only to Lafayette, and only on America's terms. If Lafayette would renegotiate some details, he would be granted "the rank and commission of major general in the army of the United States" that Deane had promised. First, in the interest of fairness to American officers who had been fighting for months before Lafayette's arrival, Congress would rescind the misleading seniority Deane had awarded him: Deane had stipulated that Lafayette's tenure begin on the date of their agreement, December 7, 1776, but Congress changed his official start date to July 31. Second, no salary would be attached to this commission—a condition already written into Lafayette's appointment. Lafayette eagerly agreed, and on July 31, he was in possession of a major general's sash and a letter from Congress confirming his rank.

Why the change of heart? Presumably, members of Congress had taken the time to read the papers Lafayette had furnished to them. Although Deane's credibility had been tarnished by the du Coudray fiasco, he'd lavished such high praise on Lafayette that Congress took notice. As the resolution passed by Congress on July 31 put it, Lafayette's "zeal, illustrious family and connexions," combined with the financial resources that enabled him to cross the ocean "at his own expence" and "to offer his service to the United States without pension or particular allowance," were sufficient to warrant a commission as major general. Writing in a private letter, Congressman Henry Laurens further explained that Lafayette was expected to "have a Short Campaign & then probably return to France & Secure to us the powerful Interest of his high & extensive connections." Lafayette's companions promised no such influence. Although the experienced de Kalb and his aide-de-camp Dubuysson did, eventually, join Lafayette in the Continental Army, most of the men who had sailed on the *Victoire* headed back to France before the year was out.

Lafayette was elated, and his delight increased when he learned that he would soon meet his new commander. As chance would have it, General Washington happened to be leading some 11,000 troops from their camp in New Jersey to Chester, Pennsylvania, just outside of Philadelphia and, on the night of July 31, he was scheduled to attend a dinner in his honor at the City Tavern on Second Street—the unofficial clubhouse of the Continental Congress.

Lafayette remembered being awed when he first caught sight of "that great man." Washington was standing across a crowded room at the City Tavern "surrounded by officers and citizens," yet despite the throng, "the majesty of his figure and of his size made it impossible" to mistake his identity. In some ways, the forty-five-year-old Washington represented all that Lafayette hoped to become—a figure universally respected for his dignity, honor, and restraint. There were even physical similarities. Like the young Frenchman, Washington was considerably larger than the average man of the era; standing six feet tall, he towered over even Lafayette. Yet, whereas Lafayette's bulk made him something of an awkward presence in the refined salons of Paris and Versailles—a bull in a china shop, gingerly stepping around the delicate furnishings that represented the height of fashionable interior design in 1770s France—Washington bore his height regally, his great size seeming like a mark of great character. Even before the two men were formally introduced, Washington had achieved the status of an idol to the fatherless Lafayette, who, brimming with hope, yearned for glory in a strange land.

Initially, this admiration was not altogether mutual. The circumspect Washington hid his doubts from Lafayette, but he was not well-disposed toward the French in general. Having fought against their troops in the French and Indian War, Washington spoke out against French meddling during the du Coudray imbroglio. Writing from Morristown, New Jersey, on July 27, he complained mightily about the unwelcome influx of French officers, who "embarrass me beyond measure." Not only did the army have all the officers it needed, he insisted, but the difficulties in dealing with the Frenchmen were "increased by the immoderate expectations, which, almost every one of them, I have seen, entertains, and which make it impossible to satisfy them." Suggesting an abiding distrust of the Gallic character, Washington continued, "I have found by experience that however modest, they may seem at first to be, by proposing to serve as volunteers, they very soon extend their views, and become importunate for offices they have no right to look for." And had Washington surmised that one or more of Lafayette's companions might have designs on his own position, he would not have been mistaken.

It was just four days after writing these remarks that Washington first encountered Lafayette—yet another French volunteer claiming that he had come "to learn and not to teach." The inexperienced youth waited not even a month before making it clear that he expected to be placed in command of a division, much to Washington's exasperation. Writing to Congressman Benjamin Harrison on August 19, Washington explained that a difference of opinion had arisen concerning the nature of Lafayette's appointment. Washington believed that Lafayette's rank was purely honorary, but the Frenchman clearly had other ideas. "What the designs of Congress respecting this Gentn. were," Washington wrote, "and what line of Conduct I am to pursue . . . I know no more than the Child unborn." Harrison confirmed that Congress "never meant" for Lafayette to have a command, but it was Washington who had to devise increasingly inventive ways to put off the persistent young marquis.

To Washington's credit, Lafayette seems not to have noticed the discomfort he was causing his newfound hero. In his memoirs Lafayette remembered only that Washington welcomed him with open arms at City Tavern, invited him to join in the following day's inspection of the Delaware River forts, and asked him to share lodgings and meals for the duration of his stay in America. From that day on, Lafayette considered Washington's home—wherever it might be—as his own. Leaving behind his companions in Philadelphia, he moved to Washington's Bucks County encampment, reviewed American troops alongside the general, and began traveling with the army. In Lafayette's nostalgic words, it was "with this ease and simplicity that two friends were united."

Throughout August and early September, Washington and his army were readying for a long-anticipated attack on Philadelphia by British forces under General William Howe. Lafayette was spending as much time as possible at Washington's side; fully expecting to be awarded a division at any moment, he was making arrangements for two aides-de-camp. Lafayette's earnest enthusiasm was already beginning to grow on Washington when a batch of mail arrived from France furthering the young man's cause. One letter, signed not only by Silas Deane but also by the more trusted Benjamin Franklin, urged Congress and the army

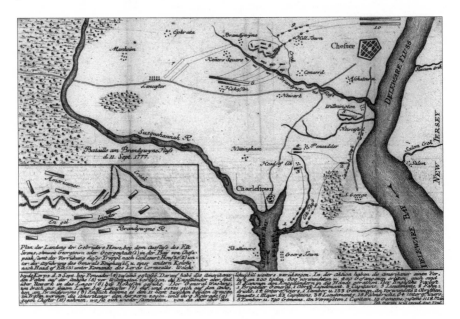

Map of the Battle of Brandywine, September 11, 1777.

to exhibit "a friendly Affection" toward Lafayette. This was not simply a matter of personal opinion, explained the Americans in Paris. Rather, a warm welcome would be a wise political gesture, "pleasing not only to [Lafayette's] powerful relations and to the court but to the whole of the French nation." Imagining that Lafayette was merely interested in achieving some small honor that he could boast about at home, the envoys asked Washington "not to permit [Lafayette's] being hazarded much, but on some important occasion."

Just such an occasion happened to be at hand. Howe and his men had spent much of the summer sailing from New York, which was now firmly under British control. Having arrived at Head of Elk, Maryland, in late July, Howe's 17,000 British and Hessian troops spent the month of August making their way overland in a northeasterly direction, heading toward the seat of the Continental Congress at Philadelphia. Facing imminent battle with an experienced enemy, Washington could not place a division in the hands of Lafayette—a foreigner whose entire military experience consisted of two summers of training at Metz—but he did allow the eager youth to participate in the fight.

When they awoke on September 11, 1777, the 10,500 American troops positioned along the banks of the Brandywine River could barely see the tops of the surrounding hills through the thick blanket of fog.

Early that morning, Washington received word that Howe's soldiers had started their eastward march, and he surmised that they would attempt to cross the Brandywine at Chadds Ford—the most traversable route to Philadelphia. American troops were mustered along the river accordingly, with the strongest presence at the presumed target of attack. Lafayette was assigned to a division led by Major General John Sullivan of New Hampshire, who was positioned a mile or so north of Chadds Ford—a posting that may have been intended to keep the eager marquis out of harm's way. By late morning, the battle had begun, and by midafternoon, an even exchange of cannon fire and musket shot was crossing Chadds Ford in the scorching heat of the bright, late-summer day.

What the Americans didn't know was that they were engaged with just half of the British troops. While the Hessian general Wilhelm von Knyphausen was sustaining the attack at Chadds Ford, General Howe had spent the better part of the day leading a second column farther north. And, having crossed the river several miles above the Americans' uppermost positions, Howe was now driving south, descending on Sullivan's surprised troops. Lines of British and American muskets faced off across an open plain, with both sides suffering heavy casualties. Lafayette was in the thick of the action, trying to make himself as useful as possible. As he later described it, he was "rallying the troops" when a musket ball tore through his left calf. Eager to continue the fight but weak from the loss of blood, he was helped to his horse by an aide-de-camp and exited the field.

The day ended with the British encamped along the Brandywine and the Americans in retreat. Two hundred and fifty Americans and eighty-nine British soldiers were killed, with many more wounded. Four hundred Americans were taken prisoner. Besting the Americans in intermittent skirmishes over the course of the following days and weeks, the British continued their march east. On September 18, the Continental Congress held its final session in Philadelphia before relocating to York, Pennyslvania. And on September 26, the British took the City of Brotherly Love.

The Battle of Brandywine was a catastrophe for the American army but a crucial turning point for Lafayette, whose dramatic wound ended up doing him more good than harm. The shot that wounded him was almost providential. Passing through the fleshy part of his lower leg, it caused damage serious enough to merit the attention of Washington's personal surgeon but minor enough to leave Lafayette in good spirits and with relatively little fear of grave consequences. After the battle, Lafayette was transported by boat to Philadelphia, where he found himself "surrounded by citizens intrigued by his youth and his situation." And while the British were on their way to victory in Philadelphia, Lafayette was on the path to American fame. Washington, perhaps mindful of the letter from Franklin and Deane, inaugurated Lafayette's celebrity with a widely published dispatch written on the night of September 11, 1777. In his account of the loss at Brandywine, which had left so many dead and wounded, Washington mentioned just two officers by name: "the Marquis La Fayette was wounded in the leg, and General Woodford in the hand." Throughout the month of September, as Washington's letter made its way into newspapers around the colonies, the American public was introduced to Lafayette as the French aristocrat who had risked life and limb on behalf of their freedom.

Transferred from one safe haven to the next while Congress scrambled to evacuate Philadelphia, Lafayette enjoyed little rest during the first week after the battle. But on September 21, he finally arrived at Bethlehem, Pennsylvania, where he was to spend four weeks of convalescence in the care of the Moravian fellowship—a missionary Protestant denomination that was exempt from military service and assisted the American army off the field of battle by storing baggage and munitions, housing prisoners of war, supplying blankets and clothing, and tending hundreds of sick and wounded soldiers. (According to a diary maintained by the community, some seven hundred men were lodged in just one of the Moravians' makeshift hospitals on December 28, 1777.) At least sixteen members of Congress also took refuge in Bethlehem that September, including the Massachusetts representatives John Hancock, John Adams, and Samuel Adams, and Henry Laurens, a congressman from South Carolina who would begin serving as president of the Continental Congress on November 1. All were treated with kindness and respect, but Lafayette received particularly attentive care from his nurses, the wife and daughter of George Frederick Boeckel, the overseer of the congregation's farm, who transferred him out of his tavern lodgings and welcomed him into their own home. In the months and years that followed, the connections Lafayette forged in Bethlehem would prove invaluable.

Lafayette described his forced "inaction" as more painful than his wound, but he approached the Moravians, whose ancestors had fled persecution in central Europe, with the same earnest curiosity that he brought to all of his interactions with Americans. When Lafayette took leave of Bethlehem on October 18, the congregation's diarist remembered him as "a very intelligent and pleasant young man" who spent much of his time reading—in English—a history of the Moravian mission in Greenland, with which he declared himself to be "highly pleased." For his part, Lafayette came away impressed by "the gentle religion" of his hosts—he referred to them as this "innocent family"—whose "community of goods, education and interests . . . contrasted with the scenes of carnage and civil war" that were devastating the surrounding land.

While confined to bed, Lafayette could do nothing but read and write. And write he did, drafting scores of letters to recipients on both sides of the Atlantic. Aflame with ideas for new ways to harm, or at least harass, the English, Lafayette proposed his ventures to anyone he could think of. Writing to the Marquis de Bouillé, a cousin then serving as governor of the French colony of Martinique, Lafayette suggested an assault on the islands of the British West Indies. To the Comte de Maurepas, Louis XVI's aging but powerful minister of the marine, he proposed an attack on British interests in India. Both ideas were rebuffed, but Lafayette's bold determination was starting to impress even Maurepas. As Lafayette later recalled, Maurepas took to jesting that the eager young soldier would probably succeed in selling "all the furniture of Versailles to support the American cause; because, once he gets something in his head, it's impossible to resist him."

Although these military schemes found no takers, the letter-writing campaign succeeded in at least one respect: Lafayette began to establish himself as the default intermediary between France and America. Writing to Laurens and Washington in America, and to Adrienne, the king's ministers, and others in France, he made a point of praising each land to citizens of the other. Letters to Adrienne lauded Washington—an "intimate friend" and "excellent man" abounding with "talents and virtues"—while attempting to inoculate French society against any ill will that might be spread by his disgruntled companions from the *Victoire* who were then returning to France. These and other dissatisfied Europeans, Lafayette cautioned, "will naturally give an unjust account of America, because the disconcerted, anxious to revenge their fancied injuries, cannot be impartial." At the same time, Lafayette took it upon himself to represent France to America by sending missives to Congress extolling the merits of newly arrived French officers. Lafayette did not know all of the men he recommended, but as he explained to Henry Laurens, "being honour'd with the name of French, I consider it my duty, to recommend you every honest countryman of mine." Meanwhile, he continued to press his own cause: he desperately wanted to be granted a command.

By the time Lafayette rejoined Washington's troops, on October 19, his displays of ardor and goodwill had made an impression, and Washington was prepared to reward him. On December 1, while Lafayette was marching toward Valley Forge, Pennsylvania, Congress passed a resolution naming him commander of a division. Six months after arriving on foreign shores, Lafayette was on his way to achieving the military dream that had been thwarted in his native land.

CHAPTER 5

DISENCHANTMENT

*W*hat a date, my dearest love, and from what a region I am now writing, in the month of January!" Lafayette wrote to Adrienne from frigid Valley Forge on January 6, 1778. Pondering the vagaries of fate, he marveled to find himself in such harsh conditions, confined "in a camp . . . in the middle of the woods . . . 1500 leagues from you . . . in the middle of the winter." Yet there he was, a major general responsible for three brigades—some three thousand men—who were destined to spend the coldest months of the year "in little huts that are about as pleasant as dungeon cells."

Lafayette described to Adrienne the "dreariness" of his lodgings, but he knew all too well that the army had much larger concerns. Lacking sufficient food and clothing to hold out against the bitter chill, Washington's 12,000 soldiers were succumbing to illness at an alarming rate. Despite a steady stream of letters from Washington, Lafayette, and others to Henry Laurens, now presiding over Congress, no provisions appeared to be forthcoming. Lafayette had received word that clothing shipped from France had arrived in America but, maddeningly, it had been detained in Yorktown and was not making its way north. In a brave attempt to jest in a new language, Lafayette asked Laurens to "consider, if you please," that the parcels of clothing "are innocent strangers, travelling [through] this state, and very desirous of meeting the Virginian regiments they belong to." Continuing the conceit, he added, "if they are detained only for exerting the most respectable rights of hospitality receive here my thanks. . . . But if it is possible, I do not want they should be entertained longer."

Lafayette's English was far from perfect, but it was improving. And as it did, so did Lafayette's grasp of the difficulties that Washington and the American army faced. Little by little, Lafayette began to understand that politics were roiling the colonies he so admired. In a letter of December 30, 1777, he told Washington that the scales had fallen from his eyes. "When I was in Europe," Lafayette acknowledged, "I thought that Here almost every man was a lover of liberty and would Rather die free than live slave. You Can Conceive my astonishment when I saw that Toryism was as openly professed as Whigism." More gravely, Lafayette was coming to understand that neither the war effort nor Washington's place at its helm was immune to partisan attack. In what Lafayette perceived to be a dangerous move, Congress had just established the five-member Board of War. Now that Washington had to report to a civilian body, he would be at the mercy of political wrangling. "There are open dissensions in Congress," Lafayette wrote to Washington, who surely did not need to be told that America's representatives had dissolved into "parties who Hate one another as much as the Common Enemy."

Not only was Lafayette concerned that internal bickering would hurt America's prospects for freedom, but he was also dismayed at the effect it was having on Washington's reputation. Expressing himself frankly, Lafayette raged to Washington against the "stupid men who without knowing a single word about war undertake to judge you, to make Ridiculous Comparisons." The comparisons Lafayette found so insulting were being made by a handful of congressmen and officers who considered Washington less capable than General Horatio Gates, who had earned praise for his engagement with British forces in the vicinity of Saratoga, New York, which had ended in victory on October 17, 1777, about a month after Washington's defeat at Brandywine. But Gates had faced forces considerably smaller than his own, while Washington had been outnumbered by troops fighting under no less a figure than the commander in chief of the British Army in America. Gates was a key player in the so-called Conway Cabal—a loose conspiracy, named after General Thomas Conway, that aimed to topple Washington. Both Lafayette and Washington believed that the English-born Gates was maneuvering himself into the position of heir apparent. What Lafayette didn't know was that Gates and his allies perceived Lafayette himself to be the weakest link in Washington's chain of command. Young, credulous, and eager to please, he was an easy mark for men with years of experience in military politics and intrigue. It didn't take long for these men to lure Lafayette with custom-made bait, embroiling him in machinations that would vex, if not offend, his esteemed commander.

The first hint of trouble came in a letter from Lafayette to Washington dated January 20, 1778. Lafayette reported hearing from Conway's aide-de-camp that Conway would soon lead an invasion of France's former Canadian colonies, but as Lafayette saw it, the selection of Conway over himself was not merely a personal slight but also a mistake that would jeopardize the success of the mission and besmirch the honor of France. He insisted to Washington that "they will laugh in France when they'l hear that [Conway] is choosen upon such a commission out of the same army where I am." The principal problem was that although Conway had served in the French military, he was "an irishman . . . when the project should be to show to the frenchmen of that country a man of their nation, who by his rank in France could inspire with them some confidence." Not wishing to seem too forward, Lafayette added a disclaimer, noting that "I mention that only as a remark (of their folly, Sir)." As he avowed, he had no "idea of leaving your army neither my Virginian division." He merely wanted Washington to know about the plan lest it prove to be part of "some much worse scheme against yourself or your army."

A scheme is, indeed, what it turned out to be. On January 24, Horatio Gates wrote a letter on behalf of the Board of War notifying Lafayette of an unexpected appointment: having observed "your Ardent Desire to signalize yourself in the Service of these States," Congress has decided "to appoint you to the Command of an Expedition meditated against Montreal." Lafayette was to "lose no Time in repairing to the Northward." Albany was to be his destination. Conway, who apparently was to be his second-in-command, would meet him there with further instructions. Presumably, by spending some time with the impressionable young man, Conway hoped to coax Lafayette over to his way of thinking and persuade him to abandon his allegiance to Washington. The wealthy Frenchman with the ear of Louis XVI's court could surely be a valuable ally.

Nearly everything about Gates's letter to Lafayette posed a direct challenge to Washington's authority. Not only had the Board of War neglected to consult the commander in chief for advice on the Canadian expedition, but they had not so much as notified him before ordering Lafayette—an officer under Washington's command—to leave Valley Forge. Even the method of the letter's delivery was a slap in the face to

Washington. It turned up in a batch of Washington's mail. Although he knew nothing of its contents, Washington would be the one to deliver it to Lafayette. On January 27, Washington sent a reply to the Board of War that couched his displeasure in the cool and measured tones that characterized his masterful leadership in both war and peacetime. "As I neither know the extent of the Objects in view, nor the means to be employed to effect them, it is not in my power to pass any judgment upon the subject," he wrote. But a sharp warning followed: "I can only sincerely wish, that success may attend it," not only in the interest of the public good but also "on account of the personal Honor of the Marquis de la Fayette, for whom I have a very particular esteem and regard."

For his part, Lafayette was delighted but wary. Writing to Laurens in terms overflowing with gratitude, he expressed deep appreciation for the faith Congress placed in him and promised that "every thing nature could have granted to me, all my exertions, and the last drop of my blood, schall be employed in showing my acknowledgment for such a favor and how I wish to deserve it." But out of "love and friendship" for Washington—and perhaps coached by Washington himself—Lafayette refused to accept Conway as his second-in-command. "How can I support the society of a man who has spoken of my friend in the most insolent and abusive terms, who has done, and does every day all his power to ruin him . . . ?" He would not accept the commission if it meant taking Conway. If Conway was not removed, Lafayette threatened, he would return to France and, he added in a letter of January 31, he would take all of the other French officers with him. Clearly, Lafayette was not quite so easily manipulated as Gates and Conway might have hoped.

On February 2, a resolution of Congress removed Conway from the project and assented to most of Lafayette's other requests. On February 3, Lafayette put pen to paper to share his news with Adrienne. Exuding enthusiasm, he explained that he had been ordered to "see if some harm can be done to the English" fleet and forts north of the border. But he added that "the idea of liberating all of New France and delivering it from a heavy yoke is too brilliant to stop there." Lafayette seemed to believe that his dreams were coming true—he had "a large number of French officers" under his command, and he found it "very glorious being their head."

At the same time, Lafayette admitted to feelings of self-doubt. Most of Lafayette's letters to Adrienne had been filled with platitudes about America and praise for its people. On the rare occasions when he described his disappointments, he generally wrapped them in self-deprecating humor, lessening any sense of fear or regret. But in this letter, Lafayette let down his guard. "I am undertaking a terrifying task," he confessed. "At twenty, one is not prepared to be at the head of an army, responsible for all the numberless details that devolve upon a general, and having under my direct orders a great expanse of country." Beneath the veil of self-assurance that he had donned in America, Lafayette remained a largely untested youth straining to make his mark and frightened that he might fail.

When Lafayette arrived in Albany on February 17, he found a disastrous state of affairs. Instead of the 2,500 troops he had been promised, only 1,200 were on hand. Albany was even colder than Valley Forge, and its soldiers were clothed just as poorly as those in Pennsylvania. Food, arms, ammunition—everything was lacking. Lafayette saw no option but to spend his own funds to acquire necessities. He wrote to Washington that he didn't know whether "blunders of madness or treachery" were responsible for this sorry situation—although, in all fairness, more prosaic problems, including logistical snags and overextended resources, were mostly to blame. Whatever the root of these problems, a winter incursion into Canada was clearly impossible under the circumstances, and so, with a heavy heart, Lafayette soon resolved to abandon the plan.

In an anguished letter to Henry Laurens on February 19, Lafayette confessed that, after crossing an ocean in search of honor, he now felt personally humiliated. How could he possibly descend "from a precipice where I embarked myself out of my love for your country, my desire of distinguishing myself in doing good to America?" he asked in his earnest but still choppy English. "My situation," he wrote, "is such that I am reduced to wish to have never put the foot in America." Having already shared news of his impending expedition with the French court, he now realized that "men will have [a] right to laugh at me, and I'll be almost ashamed to appear before some." His letter to Washington was more personal. "Why am I so far from you," he lamented, "and what business had that board of war to hurry me through the ice and snow without knowing what I should do, neither what they were doing themselves?" Perhaps, Lafayette mused, he should seek a new campaign to cover the smirch of a failure.

Washington replied with the reassuring words of an older and more experienced friend who understood a young man's pain and doubts. "However sensibly your ardour for Glory may make you feel this disappointment," he wrote, "you may be assured that your Character stands as fair as it ever did, and that no new Enterprise is necessary to wipe off this imaginary stain." In offering this advice, Washington was abiding by one of the 110 items listed in "The Rules of Civility and Decent Behaviour in Company and Conversation," which he had copied into his schoolbook as a youth: "When a man does all he can though it Succeeds not well blame not him that did it." Lafayette had indeed done all he could. And when he began the long trek back to Valley Forge on March 31, 1778, he was marching back to Washington's side. Never again would he be lured away by empty promises.

Like most people, Lafayette learned by trial and error. But he did not have the luxury of erring in private, even at this early point in his career. Few of the men involved with the military struggle for America's independence were granted so much autonomous responsibility with so little life experience. Hailing from a sheltered background with little more than idealism to guide him, Lafayette was a stranger in a strange land. Although he adapted with remarkable speed, his inevitable missteps came with the whole world watching. A less determined man might have been discouraged, but Lafayette was nothing if not determined.

CHAPTER 6

ALLIANCES

On May 1, 1778, George Washington wrote "with infinite pleasure" to congratulate Congress on a set of long-awaited "good
tidings." He was referring to news that the Franco-American
Treaty of Alliance and Treaty of Amity and Commerce had both been
signed on February 6 in Paris. Now that the charade of neutrality was
over, French ships would soon be sailing to America's aid. As Washington reported, "I have mentioned the matter to such Officers as I have
seen, and I believe no event was ever received with a more heart felt
joy."

Lafayette's response was particularly demonstrative. According to the
early chronicler David Ramsay, whose *History of the American Revolution* was published in 1789, Lafayette broke with both military protocol and American convention when, swept up "in a transport of joy,
mingled with an effusion of tears, he embraced General Washington,
exclaiming 'The king my master has acknowledged your independence.'" With the enthusiasm of a twenty-year-old whose dream has
come true, Lafayette sent his own letter to Congress, declaring, "I am
myself fit to receive as well as to offer congratulations in this happy circumstance," and predicting that "immortality" would reward America's
leaders. As he explained to Adrienne in June, he had always believed
"that in serving the cause of humanity and that of America, I was fighting for the interests of France." Now that the three causes were formally
united, his belief had been vindicated.

Congress's ratification of the treaties meant a day of celebration for
the troops at Valley Forge. Cannon and musket fire filled the air on
May 6, as did "huzzas" for the French king, the "friendly European

powers," and "the American States." Under the watchful eye of Baron Friedrich Wilhelm von Steuben—the Prussian-born adviser whose relentless drilling had transformed the Continental Army into a disciplined fighting force of the highest caliber—ten thousand men took to the parade ground for a display of military exercises carried out with unprecedented precision. Lafayette donned the colors of the Bourbon monarchy for the occasion, wrapping a white kerchief around his neck before leading the French troops through the assembly. When the official events ended, less formal festivities began. Washington was willing to relax the usual rules of behavior for the evening, declaring that the men "must have more than the common quantity of liquor and perhaps there will be some little drunkenness among them."

It was clear that the French-American treaties heralded a new role for Lafayette, but it was less clear what that role would be. For a time, rumor circulated that Lafayette had been appointed France's minister to the United States. So seemingly credible was this report that, on May 23, the executive council of Pennsylvania asked Washington to clarify when, precisely, Lafayette could be expected to pass through the state. They hoped to receive advance notice "in order that due honour might be done to so respectable a personage" as the new ambassador. Henry Laurens, for one, was relieved when the rumor proved to be false. Much as Laurens liked and admired Lafayette, he found the young Frenchman's boyish enthusiasm and utter refusal to participate in what we might today call Realpolitik distinctly enervating.

Conrad Alexandre Gérard, the man actually named to the post, was considerably more pragmatic. A career diplomat who had played a crucial role in negotiating the treaties of alliance with Deane, Franklin, and Lee, he was uniquely well versed in the intricacies of these important documents. At his first meeting with Laurens, in July 1778, Gérard assured the American that he had "refused to listen" to the droves of Frenchmen wanting places in the Continental Army who had called on him since he arrived. They all hoped that he might recommend them, but Gérard was adamant that "Congress would never be troubled with Petitions under his auspices." Laurens praised this "sensible declaration" in a letter to Washington, adding, "I most earnestly wish our noble friend the Marquis could be persuaded to adopt the [same] determinations."

Having no interest in Gérard's position, Lafayette had no need for the diplomat's circumspection. His hope was that the Franco-American alliance would provide the opportunity he had craved all his life—a chance to serve in the French army. Writing on May 14 to Lazare-Jean Théveneau de Francy, a French agent in America, Lafayette proclaimed that "if my compatriots make war in any corner of the world, I will fly to their colors." In fact, he insisted that he would not wait for orders from the king but would "leave on the spot" with the first French ship headed for the Caribbean. If no action could be found against British forces in the islands, he would return to Europe and fight there. Regardless of the arena, Lafayette felt confident that he would be in the French fight, and equally confident that France would emerge triumphant. As he explained to Théveneau de Francy, France's finances were strong and its army "invincible." Moreover, he added, "we are *Frenchmen,* a matter of no small weight in the balance of advantages."

With the French on the way, Washington began preparing Lafayette for a turn in the spotlight. On May 18, he sent Lafayette on his most important mission to date. The British seemed to be readying for an evacuation of Philadelphia, but Washington wanted to be sure that the redcoats' apparent departure was not a ruse intended to disguise an attack on his men. He assigned Lafayette to find out.

From Washington's standpoint, the mission gave Lafayette a chance to hone his craft as a budding general without sending him too far afield. But it was nonetheless a genuinely sensitive task that required careful coordination across languages, cultures, and chains of command, as Lafayette would lead not only the soldiers he had come to know during his time at Valley Forge but also hundreds of Pennsylvania militiamen and forty-seven Oneida warriors who had recently arrived from Fort Stanwix, near Albany, where Lafayette had recruited them in March. With more than two thousand men involved, success would require clear and effective communications on all sides, and failure could have lasting repercussions.

Everyone understood that this was a delicate coalition, and sound advice was freely distributed on all sides. Before leaving Fort Stanwix on April 24, the Oneida men had received instruction from a sachem known, according to the New Haven–based *Connecticut Journal,* as "Ojistalale, alias Grasshopper." Samuel Kirkland, a Presbyterian missionary who lived among the Oneidas, translated the sachem's speech for the Anglophone press. "Young warriors often need advice," began Grasshopper. "You are undertaking a long march, you will be exposed to fatigue and many temptations, and many will be your observers."

The men were told to "beware of strong liquors" and to abjure both "private revenge" and the "abuse and plunder" of innocent families. "Nephews," the sachem implored, "keep in mind you are bound to the grand army of America, and will be introduced to General Washington, the chief warrior; to a great officer of our Father the French King, the Marquis de la Fayette, at whose particular application you go." Finally, the warriors were to "be all of one mind, have one object in view," and "yield implicit obedience to Major de Tousard," one of Lafayette's aides-de-camp, "who will conduct you in the march and fight with you."

Lafayette was likewise prepared by his mentor. Notably, the instructions Washington issued on May 18 featured little of the clipped language or matter-of-fact tone typical of his orders. Instead, he took the time to spell out his reasoning and elucidate his goals. "The detachment under your command," Washington explained to Lafayette, should endeavor to provide "security to this camp," to disrupt British communications with Philadelphia, to "obstruct the incursions of the enemies parties, and obtain intelligence of their motions and designs." "This last," Washington emphasized, "is a matter of very interesting moment, and ought to claim your particular attention." To achieve this goal, Lafayette was "to procure trusty and intelligent spies, who will advise you faithfully of whatever may be passing in the city," and to "communicate to me every piece of material information you obtain."

Well aware that Lafayette's zeal sometimes outpaced his wisdom, Washington hoped to temper the young man's enthusiasm with a measure of circumspection. Acknowledging that it would be "very desirable" to attack the last British troops as they withdrew from Philadelphia, Washington warned that "this will be a matter of no small difficulty and will require the greatest caution and prudence in the execution." Washington reminded Lafayette "that your detachment is a very valuable one, and that any accident happening to it would be a severe blow to this army" and admonished him to "use every possible precaution for its security and to guard against surprise. No attempt should be made nor any thing risked without the greatest prospect of success, and with every reasonable advantage on your side." Like any good teacher, Washington described the parameters of the assignment but ultimately expected Lafayette to make his own decisions. He refrained from directing Lafayette to any "precise position," choosing instead to "leave it to your discretion to take such posts occasionally as shall appear to you best adapted to the purposes of your detachment." To this, Washington added simply that "in general . . . a stationary post is unadvisable, as it gives the enemy an opportunity of knowing your situation and concerting [plans] successfully against you."

Unfortunately, Lafayette failed to heed this last point as fully as Washington might have hoped. Lafayette marched to within eleven miles of Philadelphia, where he set up camp on an elevation in an area known as Barren Hill and remained there for two nights. As Lafayette described it, his position was "of good height," affording a clear view of its surroundings, and securely situated, having "at right rocks and the [Schuylkill] River, at left excellent stone houses and a stand of woods, its front supported by five pieces of well-placed cannon, and some roads at the rear" protected by six hundred militiamen. The detachment stayed in place long enough for General Howe to learn their location. Howe was having a busy week, filled with farewell parties, but he was willing to delay his departure for a few days if it would mean leaving with Lafayette in tow. He immediately began planning an attack on Barren Hill.

On the morning of May 20, Lafayette was recruiting a young woman to serve as a spy when he was told that a British column was approaching from the left. Next, he heard that troops were advancing from the rear. The Pennsylvania militiamen, he learned, had abandoned their posts. Someone cried that Lafayette's detachment was surrounded— and it was. With 5,000 British soldiers advancing toward him from three directions, and seeing no way through enemy lines, Lafayette maintained his composure. Thanks to a cool head and some clever feints, he managed to elude the enemy while directing an orderly retreat along a low road that led through the woods, across the Schuylkill, and back to camp. That Lafayette's detachment escaped with only nine dead was all but miraculous.

News of Lafayette's retreat at Barren Hill spread throughout America and around the world as it made its way from personal letters and official documents to newspapers and magazines. Interpretations of the story varied according to each author's politics, some presenting Lafayette as a hero and others painting him as the hapless beneficiary of a lucky break. Washington, who understood how deeply Lafayette cherished his honor, was careful to cast the event as "a timely and handsome retreat" in a letter to Congress that was published in the *Pennsylvania Packet* on June 3. Another writer, whose letter appeared on the same

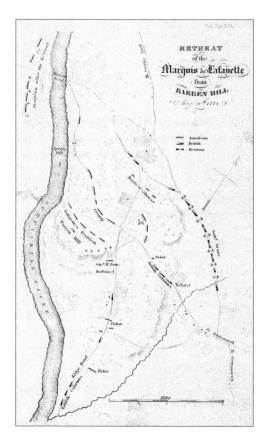

Lafayette's Retreat at Barren Hill.

page, attributed Lafayette's success either to cowardice or to confusion on the part of the British. "The commander of the enemy's party," the author opined, "must have been deceived by the regularity and good order of the retreat, and apprehensive of being drawn into an ambuscade, otherwise nothing but want of courage can excuse him from letting the Marquis get off with so trifling a loss." The London papers, which habitually derided the "French mercenaries" serving America's cause, carried a letter from a British soldier who blamed Lafayette's escape on nothing more than good timing. The "rebels," wrote the man, who claimed to have been at the scene, had received intelligence of the British march and escaped across the Schuylkill "with the utmost precipitation." "Had we been half an hour sooner," he averred, "we should have given a good account of them, for the army was never in higher spirits."

The most colorful accounts of the day are those that describe the actions—some real, others likely fabricated—of the forty-seven Oneidas who served as Lafayette's advance scouts. The *Pennsylvania Packet* reported that the Oneidas' harassment of the British facilitated Lafayette's retreat: after firing at the British light cavalry, the story relates, the Indians "set up the war whoop, and scampered about according to their custom." The British were said to have been so "terrified at the unusual sound" that they "scampered off too as fast as their horses would carry them," dropping their cloaks behind them. This account paints the Native Americans as scavengers who collected the discarded clothing "and soon converted them into leggings." Another version of the story appears in the diary of Joseph Plumb Martin, a soldier in the 8th Connecticut Regiment. Overestimating the number of Oneidas present, Martin remembered that "a company of about a hundred Indians, from some northern tribe"—men he described as "stout looking fellows and remarkably neat for that race of mortals"—had joined the detachment at Barren Hill. Martin came away unimpressed by the Oneida scouts, who, "with all their alertness," had failed to notice that the British were coming until it was very nearly too late, and then proceeded to spend the afternoon "whooping and hallooing like wild beasts."

There are no accurate records of the numbers of Native Americans who died at Barren Hill, but evidence suggests that the Oneida warriors were among the last to leave the site, and a plaque installed many decades later in a nearby cemetery commemorates "six Indian scouts

Major General Charles Lee with one of the dogs whose company he preferred to humans'.

who died in battle May 1778." Before the summer was out, the Native Americans were headed back to upstate New York, but Lafayette's association with the Oneidas was just beginning.

Of all the alliances Lafayette forged in 1778, the most valuable was surely his friendship with Washington. The bond between the men was cemented in late June, when the chaotic Battle of Monmouth pitted them not only against the British Army but also against the volatile temper of their comrade-in-arms Major General Charles Lee—a scrawny man with an outsized ego whose service as second-in-command of the Continental Army was about to come to a spectacularly bad end.

Lee and Washington had a long and contentious history. The men were the same age (both were born in February 1732—Washington in Virginia, Lee in Cheshire, England), and both had served in the wars against France. But Lee, who had fought in Europe and was still a British soldier when he took up the American cause, deemed himself the wiser and more accomplished officer. Lee's disdain for Washington was not personal; he regarded nearly everyone in the same imperious manner. An eccentric character, Lee took pride in his misanthropy and openly admitted preferring the company of dogs and horses to that of humans; in a letter to a friend, Lee promised that he would turn philanthropic "when my honest quadruped friends are equaled by the bipeds in fidelity, gratitude, or good sense." Exhibiting a fine disregard for military protocol, he treated orders like unwelcome suggestions— which is to say, he generally ignored them.

In the early days of the Revolutionary War, relations between Lee and Washington had been cordial. But they took a turn for the worse in November and December 1776, when Lee repeatedly disregarded Washington's directive to hasten his troops from their camp near White Plains, some fifteen miles north of British-held New York, in order to reinforce Washington and his men in New Jersey. Rather than simply cross the Hudson as instructed, Lee wrote letter after letter—to Washington, to other officers, to state officials—justifying his inaction on the grounds that he had insufficient troops to make the journey safely. As the days wore on, elaborate complaints began to creep into his letters. Writing to the president of the Massachusetts Council on November 22, Lee railed against the "indecision" he observed in the nation's military and political leadership and insisted that a draft be raised—a suggestion that ran counter to the wishes of Congress. "There are times," Lee argued, "when we must commit treason against the law of the State for the salvation of the State." Still in New York on November 30, he further argued that a conscripted army would make for a superior fighting force, since volunteers tend to come from "the most idle, vicious, and dissolute part of every society." Such men might easily "become the tools of some General, more artful than the rest," he warned, and be compelled to turn their arms "against their country's bosom." Meanwhile, Washington—who, we might presume, was the "artful" general to whom Lee alluded—was growing impatient. Writing from Newark on November 27, Washington had expressed astonishment that Lee had not yet budged, given that "my former letters were so full and explicit, as to the necessity of your marching as early as possible." Lee and his men finally crossed the river in early December, but they would not be on the move long. On the morning of December 13, Lee was captured by British dragoons while staying at a suspiciously unguarded farmhouse in northern New Jersey. He remained in custody until May 1778.

Released as part of a prisoner exchange, Lee reached Valley Forge the day after Lafayette returned from Barren Hill. He was just in time to join in the councils of war that Washington convened in June to debate whether—and, if so, how—to engage the British troops that were evacuating Philadelphia and marching north toward New York. Opinions were divided. Lee joined with Benedict Arnold and others in insisting that the Continental Army would be no match for the British in an open engagement, while Lafayette was among those who encouraged bold action. Washington chose a middle course: the Americans would harass the withdrawing troops as they headed north but would be prepared for a general engagement should success seem likely. On June 18, Washington drew up orders that placed Lee in command of the first division, assigned "to move the morning after Intelligence is received of the Enemy's Evacuation of the City." But Lee declined the offer, and Washington selected Lafayette to lead the advance force.

On June 25, Washington placed Lafayette in command of 4,400 troops with orders to use "the most effectual means for gaining the enemys left flanck and rear, and giving them every degree of annoyance." On June 26, at least seven letters flew back and forth between Lafayette and Washington between five in the morning and ten-thirty at night. In them, Lafayette stressed his desire to move as quickly as possible while Washington stressed the need for circumspection. "I must repeat again my wish that you do not push on with too much rapidity,"

Washington wrote from Cranbury, New Jersey, at nine forty-five in the morning. "You may be, in case of Action, at too great a distance to receive succor and exposed from thence to great Hazard," he explained.

Before the night was over, Washington had replaced Lafayette with Lee. Lee had not changed his mind about the feasibility of the mission but felt that he had been too hasty in declining the opportunity to lead it. As Lee had explained to Washington on June 25, it "is undoubtedly the most honorable command next to the Commander in Chief" and "my ceding it would of course have an odd appearance." Lee made a similar appeal to Lafayette, who yielded to the senior officer's request. If Lee's objective in declining had been to scuttle the mission and make himself seem indispensable, Washington's appointment of Lafayette had elegantly demonstrated that neither was the case.

After accepting a command that he did not want, the disgruntled Lee proceeded to complain mightily about it. Writing from a post in the woods near Englishtown, New Jersey, some forty-five miles south of Manhattan, at seven in the morning on June 27, Lee grumbled that he had been unable to ascertain whether or not the British were still encamped at Monmouth; by way of explanation, he added that "the People here are inconceivably stupid." The British had not moved, and they were still there on the morning of June 28, when the Americans engaged the rear of the British Army near Monmouth Court House. Lee was in command when the first shots were fired, but his leadership quickly dissolved when he ordered a retreat in the face of a charge by enemy cavalry. As Lafayette recalled the events, the Americans were soon "exchanging roles with the British." No longer on the offensive, Lee had allowed himself to be pushed back by Cornwallis. Alarmed, Lafayette dashed off a note to Washington, who arrived "at a gallop" only to find "the troops in confusion and still retreating" while Lee complained that the entire mission had been "against my advice." An outraged Washington castigated Lee, sent him to the rear, and seized control. "Cannon fire was exchanged all day," wrote Lafayette, and although both sides suffered hundreds of casualties in one-hundred-degree heat and stifling humidity, the Americans "continued to gain ground until nightfall." At the end of the day, the British withdrew and the Americans claimed the battlefield.

As measured by the number of fallen soldiers, the battle was very nearly a hard-fought draw, but the Americans saw the outcome as a victory. It was the first time Washington's army had advanced against the

British, and the first time the ragged men of Valley Forge had looked and acted like the disciplined fighting force they had become. The day also yielded the revolution's first female hero: it was at Monmouth Court House that Molly Pitcher, who had been supplying water to the troops throughout the day, reportedly took her husband's place at the cannon when he was carried off the field.

For Lee, the Battle of Monmouth was disastrous. With his pride deeply wounded by Washington's actions, Lee flew into a fit of rage and began a letter-writing campaign that might charitably be described as unwise. Writing to the Virginia congressman Richard Henry Lee (no relation) on June 29, Lee railed against Washington's decision to engage the enemy at Monmouth, writing "what the devil brought us into this level country (the very element of the enemy) or what interest we can have (in our present circumstances) to hazard an action, somebody else must tell you, for I cannot." His June 30 letter to Washington went further. Lee insisted "that nothing but the misinformation of some very stupid, or misrepresentation of some very wicked person, could have occasioned your making use of such very singular expressions as you did, on my coming up to the ground where you had taken post." The retreat, Lee claimed, had been necessary. In fact, he added, "I can assert that to these maneuvers the success of the day was entirely owing." Accusing Washington of having committed "an act of cruel injustice," he asked whether the commander in chief believed him to be guilty "of disobedience of orders, of want of conduct, or want of courage." Whatever the charge, Lee demanded an opportunity to refute it before a court-martial. Lee was arrested that day, and his court-martial began before the week was out. He was found guilty on three separate charges, and never served under America's colors again.

Lafayette emerged from the Battle of Monmouth a closer comrade to Washington. In his memoirs, Lafayette wrote that they "passed the night on the same cloak" and discussed Lee's perfidious behavior. Lafayette's star was rising, and it was about to soar far higher.

Lafayette saw his next step clearly. Having found battlefield distinction in America, he hoped that he might be welcomed back into the French fold. When Lafayette learned that the French fleet had been spotted off the coast of Maryland, it seemed that his opportunity had arrived. At last, he thought, he might don his country's uniform.

The twelve French ships of the line and four frigates that appeared in American waters on July 5, 1778, had sailed from Toulon three months earlier under the command of Admiral Charles Hector d'Estaing— a man who was much accomplished but little loved. In three decades of military service, the forty-eight-year-old d'Estaing had been stationed around the globe, risen to the ranks of both general and admiral, and received nearly every decoration available to him. Yet he had also acquired a reputation for being a meddler whose poor judgment hobbled his leadership. In 1778, d'Estaing's habit of inserting himself into matters better left to others prompted the gossipy publication known as *L'espion anglois* to predict that he would sow "ill will and insubordination" among the men who sailed for America. "I fear for this campaign," opined the author. Bearing out this forecast, an anonymous pamphlet written by a disgruntled officer four years later decried the admiral's "haughty and presumptuous" character and blamed d'Estaing's distasteful personality and routine abuses of power for generating widespread enmity that ultimately damaged the mission.

Arrogant though d'Estaing may have been, he appeared to hold Lafayette's future in his hands, and Lafayette greeted him accordingly. In a long and effusive letter of welcome, Lafayette established common cause with the admiral, emphasizing their shared Auvergnat ancestry and promising to collect and pass along intelligence concerning British maneuvers. At length, Lafayette broached the matter that was dearest to his heart: his desire to fight in the French service. "However pleasantly situated I am in America," he wrote, "I have always thought . . . that I would prefer to be a soldier under the French flag than a general officer anywhere else." Echoing the sentiments he had already expressed to Théveneau de Francy, Lafayette assured d'Estaing that, if France should decide to wage war against British interests in any part of the world— the East Indies, the Antilles, Europe—he would "leave at once" to join the cause. Writing again ten days later, Lafayette clarified that he had "no other ambition" than "to seem worthy to you of being a French soldier and of serving in this capacity under your orders."

In the weeks after the fleet's arrival, Lafayette threw himself into a whirl of activity that earned him d'Estaing's gratitude and admiration. In an autumn report to the French Ministry of the Marine, d'Estaing praised the young marquis, noting that "no one was better situated to serve as a link" between France and America. And although d'Estaing sometimes bristled at what he termed Lafayette's "extreme impatience," he understood that Lafayette's "zeal," coupled with "his valor, and his wisdom" helped to counteract the "incalculable slowness" that he encountered in his dealings with the Americans. Indeed, no one could have been more enthusiastic than Lafayette about the task at hand. Between July 14 and July 30, Lafayette sent at least six separate letters to d'Estaing. He provided introductions to Washington's aides-de-camp Alexander Hamilton and John Laurens (Henry's son) and supplied context for missives from Washington. He reported on British activities in New York, sent encrypted messages concerning American plans, and engaged skilled pilots in an effort to salvage d'Estaing's doomed attempts to navigate the shoals off New Jersey and enter New York Harbor. On July 30, en route to Rhode Island after giving up plans to attack New York, d'Estaing expressed his thanks to Lafayette, who, he predicted, would inevitably succeed in winning "the opinion and the aid" that would be "the first necessity" of a new campaign planned against the British at Newport. "You know how to get everything going," d'Estaing wrote to Lafayette, who was then marching northward, leading two American brigades overland from White Plains to Rhode Island. There, they would serve under Major General John Sullivan, who was to lead American ground troops in a joint land and sea offensive against the British and Hessian forces occupying Newport and its surrounding islands. "You will have acquired an even greater share of glory before I have the honor of embracing you," d'Estaing forecast.

Washington, too, had high hopes for Lafayette. Lafayette's good nature had already helped dissipate the army's resentment of French officers. Now Washington relied on Lafayette to smooth whatever wrinkles might mar the new alliance. Writing to Sullivan on July 27, Washington stressed the importance of maintaining "Harmony and the best understanding" between the two forces. This was no simple task. In fact, Washington himself remained wary of working with non-Americans. In a letter to the New York congressman Gouverneur Morris (who, having witnessed the privations of Valley Forge, became an ardent champion of the army), Washington exclaimed, "I do most devoutly wish that we had not a single Foreigner among us, except the Marquis de la Fayette, who acts upon very different principles than those which govern the rest."

Perhaps it was inevitable that relations between the new allies would be strained from the start. Shortly after the armies assembled at Newport, their leaders began wrangling over whose troops would land first on the British-occupied islands. Sullivan expected that American troops would be the first to disembark, with d'Estaing's French forces following them. But d'Estaing insisted that the French deserved the honor of landing before the Americans. Indeed, d'Estaing argued that for the French to land after the Americans would be not merely "militarily inadmissible" but, in fact, "impossible." Lafayette made valiant efforts to bring the two sides closer together, but with national pride at stake, there was little to be done. To d'Estaing, he emphasized that this was, after all, America's war, and that it might be "vexing for certain people to watch the beautiful monologues of a play performed by foreign actors." To Washington, Lafayette urged that the French be allowed to act quickly and decisively, lest d'Estaing's men feel unappreciated. Having boarded the French ships, Lafayette wrote, he "saw among the Fleet an ardor, and a desire of doing some thing which would soon turn into impatience if we don't give them a speedy occasion of fighting."

It did not go well. A joint attack, with both armies landing simultaneously, was planned for August 10, but Sullivan seized an opportunity to advance one day earlier. Having received word that the British were evacuating, he sent his men forward on August 9 without notifying d'Estaing. As John Laurens related the story to his father, "This measure gave much umbrage to the French officers. They conceived their troops injured by our landing first, and talked like women disputing precedence in a country dance, instead of men engaged in pursuing the common interest of two great nations." Feeling angry and betrayed, d'Estaing struck out on his own. Without consulting the Americans, he dispatched most of his fleet from Newport Harbor in pursuit of British ships, leaving Sullivan to discover that his naval protection had been reduced to a mere three ships.

Horrified, Sullivan charged Lafayette with the unenviable task of coaxing d'Estaing back to Newport. But the French had come under fire as they sailed out of Narragansett Bay and were wary of facing the same battery on their return. In a pleading letter, Lafayette promised d'Estaing that his ships would be safe and added, with underlines for emphasis, *"that the Americans do not find your situation dangerous."* Still d'Estaing refused to place his fleet in the hands of an ally he deemed untrustworthy. He remained at sea until the elements accomplished what Lafayette could not: on August 12, strong winds scattered the

French vessels and inflicted heavy damage that forced d'Estaing to turn back for Newport. Relieved as they were by the return of the fleet, the Americans were all the more livid when d'Estaing declared his intention to remain only long enough to assess the condition of his tattered ships. On August 22, the French sailed for Boston in search of needed repairs, leaving Sullivan to accuse them of desertion, cowardice, or worse. Furious at the French, he committed these and other unflattering opinions to paper and dispatched a small craft to overtake d'Estaing and deliver the missive.

For a brief moment, Lafayette snapped. He did not condone d'Estaing's departure, but neither would he abide insults to French honor. With tempers flaring on all sides, Lafayette was so irate that he dared not share his emotions with his mentor, Washington; he later confessed that he feared he might "risk our friendship by expressing the sentiments of an afflicted heart." Still, he kept striving to make peace. "Would you believe," he asked d'Estaing in a letter of August 24, "that, forgetting the general obligations owed to France and the services specifically rendered by the fleet, the greater part of these people here allow faded prejudices to revive and speak as though they had been abandoned, almost betrayed." Nonetheless, Lafayette pointed out that their mutual disgust with Sullivan's cohort "need not mean falling out with General Washington and Congress," whom he termed "the two great driving forces of all our work." The next day, he shared his horror with Washington, asking him to "Reccommend to the several chief persons of Boston to do any thing they can to put the French fleet in situation of Sailing soon."

Ultimately, it fell to Washington to calm the anger on both sides. In judiciously phrased letters to Lafayette, Washington tended to the young man's wounded honor by extolling the virtues of Lafayette, d'Estaing, and all their countrymen. In other letters written at the same time, Washington issued pleas for transatlantic understanding to Sullivan, Major General William Heath, and other American leaders, explaining his wish to "palliate and soften matters." Wisely, Washington asked his countrymen to remember that the French were "people old in war, very strict in military etiquette, and apt to take fire where others scarcely seem warmed." There was little to be done about national temperament, but military success required a degree of mutual understanding. Differences would have to be put aside.

On August 26, Lafayette rode through the night to Boston, making the sixty-mile journey in just seven hours—a remarkably rapid pace. There, he conferred with all parties and helped broker a détente. The success of the alliance depended on Lafayette, and Lafayette's future depended on that alliance.

CHAPTER 7

HOMECOMINGS

*I*n the fall of 1778, Lafayette was growing restless. Having suffered through a summer of delays and disappointments, he spent the month of September encamped near Bristol, Rhode Island, awaiting an attack that never came, prodding Washington and d'Estaing into actions they would not pursue, and lobbying for permission to return to Washington's headquarters. On September 1, Lafayette pleaded with Washington, "I long my dear general, to be again with you." Writing again on September 21, Lafayette added "our Separation has been long enough, and I am here as inactive as anywhere else."

With no new orders forthcoming, Lafayette cast about for other ways to contribute to the cause. On September 8 he wrote to Silas Talbot, an American army officer with extensive naval experience, to propose a nocturnal attack on an English frigate moored off the coast of Rhode Island. By the following week Lafayette had developed a new plan: he would challenge Lord Carlisle, the head of the British peace commission, to a duel. As Lafayette explained in a letter to d'Estaing, the commissioners had impugned the French character, alleging that France viewed the American colonies as little more than "the instrument of her ambition." Not only did Lafayette burn to right the wrong but, he informed d'Estaing, "I have nothing very interesting to do here, and even while killing Lord Carlisle, I can make some more important arrangements at White Plains." (Lafayette did extend the challenge, but Carlisle declined.) Finally, Lafayette's last hopes for imminent activity were dashed by a letter of September 25 in which Washington made it clear that a second attempt to invade Canada was not in the offing.

Adopting a firm but gracious tone, Washington wrote to his ever-eager comrade,

> If you have entertained thoughts my dear Marquis of paying a visit to your Court—To your Lady—and to your friends this Winter, but waver on acct. of an expedition into Canada, friendship induces me to tell you, that I do not conceive that the prospect of such an operation is so favourable at this time as to cause you to change your views.

Shortly after the message was written, Lafayette began planning a trip to France.

As Washington knew, a series of personal misfortunes had been weighing on Lafayette in recent months, but a steadfast commitment to the American Revolution had prevented him from returning home. Henriette, Lafayette's first daughter, had died on October 3, 1777, at the age of twenty-two months. But news traveled slowly and unreliably, especially in times of war, and Lafayette did not learn of the death until late spring. When he did, he was crushed. "How dreadful my isolation is," he wrote to Adrienne on June 16. "My heart is afflicted by my own sadness and by yours, which I was not able to share. The immense time that it took for me to learn of that event makes it that much worse." Lafayette was also facing financial troubles. Since arriving in America, he had been drawing on credit to pay for expenses that were rapidly multiplying. Making matters worse, the *Victoire* had foundered off the eastern seaboard in the summer of 1777, scuttling Lafayette's plans to recoup his investment in the ship by sending it back to France loaded with cargo.

The most pressing reason for Lafayette's return to France might well have been the one highlighted in his October 13 letter to the president of Congress requesting leave of absence from the Continental Army. "Now . . . that France is involv'd in a war," Lafayette wrote, "I am urg'd by my duty as well as by patriotic love, to present myself before the king, and know in what manner he judges proper to employ my services." Perhaps Lafayette had come to understand that he would not be permitted to fight under the French flag until he begged the king's forgiveness for sailing to America against explicit royal orders. At first, Lafayette seems not to have comprehended the difficulties of his situation, or the awkward position in which he placed d'Estaing, Bouillé, and the other French officers whom he petitioned for an appointment in the summer of 1778. But his interlocutors were more keenly attuned to questions of decorum and dared not welcome a fugitive—even a fugitive in name only—into the fold.

As Lafayette planned his return voyage, France's representatives in America began preparing carefully crafted letters to the king and his ministers in support of the wayward youth. The French ambassador, Conrad Alexandre Gérard, reported to the Comte de Vergennes on the "wisdom and dexterity" with which Lafayette had comported himself in America but deemed it prudent to distance himself from any laudatory views. In his letter of October 20, Gérard professed, "You know, Monseigneur, how far I am from adulation, but I would be unfair if I did not convey to you the testimonials that are on the lips of everyone here without any exception." Gérard noted that Lafayette had "offered very salutary advice informed by friendship and experience" and that his "prudent, courageous, and likable" conduct had made him "the idol of Congress, of the army, and of the American people." Moreover, he added, Lafayette's "military talents are held in high esteem." D'Estaing, too, wrote on Lafayette's behalf while couching his commendations in apologetic terms. In a November report to the Ministry of the Marine, d'Estaing singled out the tremendous enthusiasm exhibited by Lafayette, which, he wrote, had obliged him to receive the young man with "personal satisfaction mingled with political unease." Americans, in contrast, were unstinting in their praise of Lafayette. Knowing that the war could not be won without French support, and fully aware that Lafayette was America's strongest advocate in France, Congress did all it could to shore up Lafayette's standing in his native land. When Congress approved Lafayette's leave of absence on October 21, it also resolved to furnish him with a letter extolling his virtues to Louis XVI. The official dispatch recommended "this young Nobleman to your Majesty's notice," lauding Lafayette as "one whom we know to be Wise in Council, gallant in the Fields, and Patient under the hardships of War." Citing not only Lafayette's "Zeal, Courage and attachment" but also his "Devotion to his Sovereign," Congress attested that Lafayette had earned "the confidence of these United States . . . and the Affection of their Citizens."

William Carmichael, who had served as Silas Deane's secretary in Paris, added a personal appeal to Benjamin Franklin, asking him to manage the delicate politics of Lafayette's return. Lafayette's diplomatic skills had impressed Carmichael, who reported to Franklin that "no one but [Lafayette] has known how to reconcile the clashing parties of this Continent to his own views." He did not want to lose Lafayette's valuable voice but, having witnessed the uproar that surrounded Lafayette's departure from France, he believed that Franklin—the most beloved American in Paris—would be the best man to usher Lafayette back into the good graces of the king. Consider, Carmichael wrote to Franklin, "what a satisfaction it will be" to the Noailleses "that the Ministry should be acquainted by you rather than any one Else of the opinion entertained of [Lafayette] here." "May it not be proper," Carmichael suggested, "to put the resolves letters &c. &c. into the hands of the ministry instantly on the receipt of them & before the Marquis makes his appearance at Versailles?"

Before he left, Lafayette was promised one more token of Congress's gratitude: a ceremonial sword to be cast in silver by Lafayette's Parisian cutler through the intercession of Benjamin Franklin. The sword, its hilt decorated with vignettes commemorating four of Lafayette's battlefield accomplishments, became one of his most prized possessions. In Paris, John Adams remarked that Lafayette wore it proudly whenever he went out in company—it was tangible proof that Lafayette had found the glory he sought in America.

When Lafayette had left France in 1777, the smarter sets of Paris and Versailles had deemed him a social liability, but on February 12, 1779, he returned home a hero. His carefully scripted reentry into Paris was an unmitigated success. As he described it, "Upon my arrival, I had the honor of being consulted by all the ministers and, what was even better, embraced by all the ladies." Satisfying protocol, Lafayette immediately paid a visit to Versailles, where he was "interrogated, complimented, and exiled" to the luxurious confines of the Hôtel de Noailles for a few days of supremely comfortable house arrest—a nominal punishment for having disobeyed royal orders. But even this penalty was not paid in full: on his second day in Paris, Lafayette personally delivered a package of letters to John Adams. All doors were open to him, and even Marie Antoinette, who had so heartily disapproved of his dancing, now intervened with the king on his behalf. Thanks to the queen, Lafayette was granted the rather costly honor of paying 80,000 livres to purchase the command of the regiment of the King's Dragoons—a position that a man out of royal favor could not have acquired for any amount of money.

Like so many others before and since, Lafayette had reinvented himself in America. As the Comte de Ségur told it, Lafayette's faraway exploits had captured the imagination of his homeland. Ever since Paris learned of "the first battles in which Lafayette and his comrades in arms burnished the name of France, the approbation was universal; even people who had most opposed his foolhardy enterprise applauded him; the court nearly burst with pride, and all the young people envied him." In fact, Ségur believed that Lafayette's éclat had propelled France into open support for the Americans. "Thus," Ségur wrote, "public opinion, declaring itself more and more for war, made it inevitable, and dragged along a government too weak to resist such an impulse."

Another man might have been content to rest on his laurels, but Lafayette put his popularity to use in the service of the American cause. Throughout the spring of 1779, he corresponded and met with the highest-placed representatives on both sides of the French-American alliance, and thereby sealed his reputation as America's foremost advocate in France. Speaking with Vergennes, Maurepas, and others at court, Lafayette proposed loan agreements, lobbied for increased naval and ground support, and floated ideas for military offensives against British territories. Of these, the most daring was a bold plan to strike the coastline of England, pillaging the commercial towns of Liverpool and Bristol to raise funds for the Americans. The assault was envisioned as a joint land-and-sea venture led by Lafayette and the naval commander John Paul Jones. In honor of Benjamin Franklin, who had been deeply involved in the planning, Jones would be aboard the *Bonhomme Richard*—a reference to Franklin's *Poor Richard's Almanac*. Fully anticipating that the offensive might begin at any moment, Lafayette spent much of the summer and autumn of 1779 at the ready at the Channel port of Le Havre, but he never received the go-ahead to sail.

The attack on England was just one of many projects Lafayette and Franklin hatched together. The men made for an unlikely pair: one young, plainspoken, and painfully earnest, the other an aging wordsmith renowned for his urbanity. But both were good-natured, and although Lafayette tried not to take sides in the increasingly public feud that set Franklin against his fellow American ministers, Lafayette was drawn more to the Francophile Philadelphian than he was to John Adams, a stolid New Englander, or to the Eton-educated Virginian Arthur Lee. Franklin listened patiently to even the smallest of Lafayette's concerns; when Congress asked Franklin to procure uniforms with decorative layers of white fabric, or "facing," sewn onto the cuffs, lapels, and other parts of the coat, Lafayette objected that yellow facing would be more suitable. Lafayette, in turn, appreciated the humor when Franklin poked fun at his outsized devotion to all things American. On September 17, 1782, when Franklin learned that Lafayette intended to name his newborn daughter Virginie, "as an offering to My Western Country," Franklin jested that Lafayette did "well to begin with the most ancient State" and wished that the Lafayettes would "go thro' the Thirteen." Enjoying the conceit, Franklin added that "Miss Virginia, Miss Carolina, & Miss Georgiana will sound prettily enough for the Girls; but Massachusetts & Connecticut are too harsh even for the Boys."

All kidding aside, Franklin fully understood Lafayette's motivation for naming a daughter Virginie and a son George Washington. Franklin knew well, and Lafayette was coming to learn, that words and images could shape public opinion. In the spring of 1779, they collaborated on a telling project: an illustrated children's book to be used in schools—or so they wrote—depicting selected horrors inflicted by the British upon the Americans during the Revolutionary War. As Franklin quipped to a pro-American correspondent in England, the goal of the book's thirty-five prints was "to impress the minds of Children and Posterity with a deep sense of your bloody and insatiable Malice and Wickedness." Lafayette's tone was a bit less jocular when he wrote to Franklin, "I great deal love our project, and want to be Concern'd in it as much as possible." Although Lafayette expressed some reluctance about portraying the English as less human than other nationalities, he concluded that such a book was necessary because British atrocities "must be known By the future American posterity." Together, Franklin and Lafayette compiled a list of twenty-six possible images before abandoning the project. Those in Lafayette's handwriting include the very questionable No. 18, "Prisoners killed and roasted for a great festival where the Lenape Indians are eating American flesh; Colonel Butler, and English officers, sitting at table," and the more historically accurate No. 21, "A dusty prison ship where American officers are confined without being at liberty to take the air and so crowded that they can live but a few days—British officers come to laugh at 'em and to insult at their miseries."

Lafayette had only recently begun thinking about the power of images. In August, he had seen John Hancock give a copy of a 1776 portrait of Washington by the prominent Philadelphia artist Charles

Willson Peale to the Comte d'Estaing. Writing to Washington about the scene, Lafayette testified, "I never saw a man so glad of possessing his sweet heart's picture, as the admiral was to Receive yours." Lafayette was so struck by the event that he acquired a small copy from Peale for himself and arranged for the army engineer Pierre Charles L'Enfant (who would later become known as the city planner of Washington, D.C.), to sketch Washington from life. Lafayette's sudden interest in pictures took Washington by surprise; in a letter of September 25, Washington, who found portrait sittings rather disagreeable, explained to Lafayette that "when you requested me to set for Msr. Lanfang [*sic*] I thought it was only to obtain the outlines and a few shades of my features, to have some Prints struck from." Washington noted, "Could I have conceived that my Picture had been an object of your Wishes, or in the smallest degree worthy of your attention, I should, while Mr. Peale was in the Camp at Valley Forge, have got him to have taken the best Portrait of me he could, and presented it to you."

There was nothing out of the ordinary about Lafayette's request for a picture of Washington. In the eighteenth century, many prominent men decorated their homes with portraits of historical figures they hoped to emulate, absent friends they wished to remember, and influential contemporaries deserving of respect. Thomas Jefferson, for instance, filled Monticello with sculptures, paintings, drawings, and engravings of dignitaries. Marble busts of Voltaire, Alexander Hamilton, and others greeted guests in Jefferson's entry hall; paintings of John Locke and Isaac Newton and engravings of Louis XVI and Napoleon Bonaparte mingled with biblical scenes on the walls of the parlor; and, thanks to plaster casts of busts by Jean-Antoine Houdon, George Washington, Benjamin Franklin, John Paul Jones, and Lafayette were always among the company in the tearoom.

Lafayette would later amass his own, more focused collection of prints, paintings, and sculptures commemorating important friends and significant events, but his portraits of Washington played a unique role in 1779 and 1780. In those months, Lafayette was lobbying to be placed at the helm of a French detachment headed for America, and his close friendship with Washington was the most powerful argument at his disposal. Shortly after returning to Paris in 1779, Lafayette arranged for a French artist to paint a more didactic version of Peale's portrait of Washington. While the version that Hancock owned offers a three-quarter-length view of the standing Washington towering over a distant

Portrait of Washington.
Print commissioned by
Lafayette, linking his name
to Washington's in 1780.

landscape, the new image created for Lafayette emphasizes the demise of Great Britain and highlights the role of France as America's closest ally. As Lafayette described it, his painting shows Washington "with the French treaty and the Declaration of Independence in his hand and the edicts and proclamations of His Britannic Majesty under his feet." "Beneath," wrote Lafayette, "one reads the famous lines 'Manus haec inimica tyrannis, etc.'—'This hand is hostile only to tyrants and draws the sword only to obtain tranquil peace under liberty.'"

Lafayette took every opportunity to call attention to his intimate knowledge of Washington and of all things American. In a letter to Vergennes on July 1, 1779, Lafayette wrote, "If you are curious . . . to see a portrait resembling my friend, I beg you to send to my home for it." Lafayette added that he planned to bring the portrait with him to Benjamin Franklin's house in Passy, where it would be displayed for Franklin's Fourth of July celebration. "Things like that go over very well with our new allies," Lafayette explained to France's most senior diplomat. Soon, Lafayette commissioned yet another version—an engraving published in 1780 by Noël Le Mire after a composition by the battle painter Jean-Baptiste Le Paon. This more decorative scene places Washington at a camp in the woods and adds a decidedly exotic flavor by introducing a turbaned African servant and a Persian rug, edged with fringe, draped across the tabletop. The most significant addition to the work, though, might be its pairing of the names of Lafayette and Washington—the text beneath announces that it was "engraved after the original painting in the collection of Monsieur the Marquis de la Fayette."

As plans for a new French expedition to America got under way, Lafayette was as direct as could be about his desire to command the French detachment. In a letter to Vergennes dated February 2, 1780, he laid out his argument: in light of his friendship with Washington and so many Americans, he believed that naming him commander would be "much more advantageous to the public good and to the interests of France vis-à-vis her allies" than any other option. "If I am in command," he wrote, "you can proceed in complete confidence because the Americans know me too well for me to ignite any false rumors." So strong were his feelings on the matter that he was willing to accept a purely temporary appointment and to relinquish all claims to rank or seniority. But if he were not chosen, he warned, immediate actions would have to be taken "to prevent the ill effects that the arrival of another commander would have in America." He insisted that "the notion that I would be unable to lead this detachment is the last that would present itself over there." A cover story would have to be agreed upon; for instance, Lafayette might simply say that he "preferred an American division," implying that he had declined a French post. Whatever decision was made, Lafayette believed that he had to be kept fully apprised because "a secret that I would not know about would be regarded with great suspicion in Philadelphia."

We have no record of how Lafayette responded when he was told that the command would be given to the Comte de Rochambeau, but he must have been devastated. Rochambeau had certainly earned the position: he had been an officer since before Lafayette was born and had suffered multiple wounds in the Seven Years' War. Still, Lafayette demanded at least a face-saving role. "If [the command] is not given to me," he wrote, "I must leave immediately with the resources I request." Moreover, he would have to be the one to "instruct General Washington." The ministry was happy to grant him this much. According to Vergennes's orders of March 5, 1780, Lafayette would sail to America in advance of the French expeditionary force. Once arrived, he would "hasten to join General Washington" and "inform him confidentially that the king . . . has resolved to send to their aid six ships of the line and 6,000 regular infantry troops at the onset of spring." On March 11, Lafayette set sail from Rochefort on the *Hermione,* bearing the good news and ample provisions for the army.

Before departing, Lafayette quietly signaled his displeasure at having been passed over. As John Adams reported it, Lafayette bid adieu to his monarch "in the Uniform of an American Major General." Adams averred that when Lafayette appeared before Louis XVI in American attire, the costume "attracted the Eyes of the whole Court." And Adams had no doubt that the sword Lafayette carried that day was the one commissioned by Congress. It "is indeed a Beauty," Adams conceded, "which [Lafayette] shews with great Pleasure." Without saying a word, Lafayette let it be known that he was returning to the only nation that appreciated his merit.

Americans, in fact, did more than simply appreciate Lafayette—they celebrated him at every turn. In a letter of May 1, 1780, Abigail Adams notified her husband that "last week arrived at Boston the Marquis de la Fayette to the universal joy of all who know the Merit and Worth of that Nobleman. He was received with the ringing of Bells, fireing [*sic*] of cannon, bon fires, etc." Similar festivities erupted in every town he passed through on the 250-mile journey from Boston Harbor to Washington's headquarters at Morristown, New Jersey. "It's to the roar of cannon that I arrive or depart; the principal residents mount their horses to accompany me," Lafayette told Adrienne. "In short, my love, my reception here is greater than anything that I could describe to you."

Lafayette's return was a bright spot in a season that had been unrelentingly bleak for the American army. Privations that had plagued the war effort from the start were worsening as officers and soldiers alike faced lethal shortages of food, clothing, and blankets. With military salaries going unpaid and inflation rendering American currency next to worthless, desertion rates skyrocketed and recruitment plunged. Although Lafayette did not come with any quick fixes—even the four thousand uniforms that he had hoped to bring with him did not reach Rochefort before he sailed—his news of imminent French aid injected a note of hope into the atmosphere of despair, and the mere fact of his return had a cheering effect.

Lafayette wasted no time in proving that he merited the accolades he received. As soon as he understood the gravity of the situation, he began peppering state leaders from Massachusetts to Pennsylvania with urgent pleas for assistance. Lacing his military arguments with personal requests, Lafayette wrote to Samuel Adams in Massachusetts, George Clinton in New York, and others up and down the eastern seaboard, asking them to consider the awkward position in which he now stood. Having taken "particular delight in praising the Patriotic spirit of the United States" to his countrymen, Lafayette confessed to Adams, "I would feel most unhappy and distress'd was I to tell the people that are Coming over full of ardour and Sanguine hopes, that we have no army to Cooperate with them, No provisions to feed the few soldiers who are left." Lafayette sent similar requests to members of Congress, who, in the end, wrested control of recruitment and supply from the states' disorganized authorities.

Alarmed though Lafayette was by the depleted state of the army, nearly two years had passed since he had last seen action, and his most urgent wish was to return to the field of battle. Washington, Lafayette, and the other generals had long agreed that taking New York should be their primary objective, and shortly after he rejoined Washington's "family" (as Washington's closest circle was known) Lafayette began agitating for an immediate attack. With England's attention temporarily diverted to the war's southern front, Lafayette believed that the time to act was now. General Clinton's forces had been mercilessly bombarding Charleston, South Carolina, since mid-April, and after the devastating Siege of Charleston ended with the Americans' capitulation on May 12, the British began pouring resources into raids in North Carolina and Virginia. Lafayette understood that any action against New York would have to wait the arrival of Rochambeau's French forces, but he did not want to delay a moment longer than necessary. As he promised Vergennes in a letter of May 20, "If the French troops arrive in time, chances are good that New York is ours." But he warned that "if the English have time to regroup," the project might have to be abandoned.

So eager was Lafayette to move forward with the attack on New York that he laid out the plans in a detailed letter to Rochambeau dated July 9—one day before the French squadron had even landed at Newport, Rhode Island. But Rochambeau had more immediate concerns. He had arrived with only 5,100 men, rather than the anticipated 7,500, and he believed that many of them would require a month or so to

recover from illnesses contracted during the crossing. Arms and maté-
riel badly needed by the depleted American military were also lacking;
John Paul Jones's frigate bearing 15,000 muskets and 100,000 pounds of
gunpowder had been delayed. Meanwhile, with the English reinforcing
their position in New York and Rochambeau expecting an assault on
Newport any day, all able-bodied French troops were fully occupied in
strengthening their fortifications in Rhode Island. Perhaps, Rochambeau suggested, an assault on New York could be planned for some
time after August 15, with the details to be worked out in a face-to-face
meeting with Washington, who served as the supreme commander of
all French and American forces.

Understanding that New York would have to wait, Washington did
his best to temper Lafayette's impatience. On July 22, Washington
wrote, "I am persuaded, my D[ea]r Marquis that however ardent your
wishes to undertake the reduction of a certain place, you will not fail to
give a candid and full overview of the difficulties" to Rochambeau. "We
owe it to our allies," he added. "We owe it to ourselves." As Washington
feared, Lafayette would not be dissuaded. At a July 30 meeting with
Rochambeau and the Chevalier de Ternay, the commander of France's
naval forces in America, Lafayette listened to their concerns and dutifully reported Washington's opinion that they could not strike New
York until they had naval superiority. But he chose not to mention that
the Americans had almost no arms, and as he later informed Washington, he "added in my own name that however we must . . . act Before
the winter, and get Rid of a shamefull defensive."

On August 9, Lafayette committed these and other thoughts to paper
in a twelve-page letter, which he sent to Rochambeau and Ternay with
a copy to the Chevalier de la Luzerne, who had replaced Gérard as the
French ambassador to the United States. While purporting to offer a
factual account of the July 30 conversation, Lafayette's letter made bold
claims that neither Rochambeau nor Ternay could support. Although
the group had reached no such decision, Lafayette asserted that "it is
very clearly settled that as soon as the French attain naval superiority,
they must not lose a single day in beginning the joint effort." And the
chastising tone with which Lafayette concluded his missive did nothing
to render his opinions more palatable. "Based on an intimate understanding of our situation," he wrote, "I assure you . . . that it is important to act during this campaign." Nothing that might happen in the
future, Lafayette warned, would be sufficient to "make up for the fatal

harm of our inaction." Finally, alluding to his greater knowledge of all things American—knowledge that he'd once hoped would win him the command that Rochambeau now occupied—Lafayette added, "I believe it is very important to take advantage of the moments when you find an opportunity for cooperation . . . without which you can do nothing in America for the common cause."

Rochambeau was livid. Writing his own letter to Luzerne, Rochambeau lambasted Lafayette. "He proposes Extravagant things to us," fumed Rochambeau, "like taking Long Island and New York without a navy." And although Lafayette assures us, Rochambeau added, that he can protect our right flank, "he forgets that there is still a left flank in a landing, which the whole English navy will exterminate, if it doesn't prefer to go at the same time and do the same thing to the Chevalier de Ternay, who will be left to his own devices here" in Newport. Lafayette's letter, Rochambeau complained, included "not a word, nor an order, nor even an opinion from Mr. Washington," with whose dispatches Rochambeau was "infinitely satisfied." Unfamiliar as he was with Lafayette, Rochambeau could only assume that the letter had been written "at the instigation of some hotheads," but Luzerne disabused him of the notion that any conspiracy might be afoot. In a letter of August 24, Luzerne indicated that he was "inclined to believe that what M. de Lafayette has written to you is purely a result of his zeal and of a courage that experience will moderate." Luzerne concurred that, henceforth, Rochambeau should correspond with Washington directly; such a move, Luzerne wrote, "will prevent all the inconveniences of this premature ardor."

Lafayette was slow to see how he had erred, but Rochambeau hammered away until he got the point across, leading Lafayette to write a series of apologetic letters, each more elaborate than the last. Even at the end of the exchange Rochambeau had severe words for the presumptuous young man. "You know me well enough to believe that I do not need to be roused to action," Rochambeau wrote to Lafayette on August 27. "At my age, when one has made a decision based on military and political reasoning necessitated by circumstances, all the instigations in the world could not make me change without a direct order from my general." Lacing into Lafayette for his naïveté, Rochambeau allowed that "it is always good, my dear marquis, to believe the French invincible, but I am going to confide in you a great secret based on forty years' experience. There are none easier to defeat when they have lost confidence in their commander." And, he noted, they are inclined to "lose that confidence immediately when they have been put in danger because of private and personal ambition." In the end, however, Rochambeau eased up on Lafayette, assuring him of his "most tender friendship" and concluding his letter by observing "that the warmth of your soul and your heart rather overheated the composure and wisdom of your judgment." But that was not the end of the world. "Keep this last quality in the council," Rochambeau recommended, "and reserve all of the first for the moment of action."

For Lafayette, the fateful moment finally arrived in February 1781, when Washington placed him in command of 1,200 men, mostly composed of light infantry, with orders "to act against the corps of the enemy now in Virginia." Lafayette's primary target was to be Benedict Arnold, the traitorous American general who had crossed over to the redcoats, plotting a British takeover of West Point in September 1780. Since then, Arnold had taken a page from Cornwallis's playbook and was conducting costly raids throughout Virginia. Lafayette was meant to stop him. If Arnold were to fall into Lafayette's hands, the marquis had explicit instructions to "execute in the most summary way" the "punishment due to his treason and desertion." Lafayette set out from New Windsor, Connecticut, on February 21, and joined up with Baron von Steuben in Yorktown, Virginia, on March 14.

Although Lafayette faced a force far greater than his own and a steady stream of setbacks—pouring rain, scarce provisions, rampant desertions—the return to action restored his spirits. Lafayette estimated that he was outnumbered "four or five to one in our regular infantry and ten to one in cavalry," yet his letters were nearly as jovial as those he'd sent when he'd first arrived in Charleston. Writing on May 22 to the Vicomte de Noailles, one of several French friends who had sailed with Rochambeau and were now fighting in the north, Lafayette said expected reinforcements were slow in coming. When they arrive, he mused wryly, "we'll be in a condition to be beaten more decently; but at the moment we can only run." Finally, he asked Noailles to mention him were he to write to Paris: "Tell them that your poor brother is devilishly busy getting himself thrashed."

In reality, Lafayette was far from getting thrashed. Rising to the challenge, he kept his men on the move as he and Cornwallis played a game of cat and mouse throughout the state of Virginia. In August, as Cornwallis began maneuvering toward a secure position on the Chesapeake at the trading port of Yorktown, Lafayette learned that help was on the way. Washington and Rochambeau would soon be joining their forces and heading south together, while a French fleet under the Comte de Grasse sailed for the Chesapeake Bay. Lafayette was given a crucial task: his job was to keep Cornwallis occupied in Virginia while the allies closed in from land and sea. Cornwallis was essentially trapped. While Washington and Rochambeau were descending from the northwest, three American divisions, commanded by Lafayette, Steuben, and Benjamin Lincoln, were taking up positions to the south and west. With the Chesapeake to the east, Cornwallis had nowhere to go.

By September 28, the allied forces were in place with Washington at the helm, and in early October, Washington tightened the noose around the enemy, digging trenches closer and closer to the British defenses. More than one hundred French and American cannons opened fire on Cornwallis's fortifications on October 9, began targeting British ships the next day, and continued the bombardment for a week, inflicting heavy damage. On the night of October 14, Lafayette's detachment struck a decisive blow. Led by Colonel Alexander Hamilton, who was then serving under Lafayette's command, some 400 light infantrymen armed with axes and bayonets stormed and took one of the last remaining British redoubts. Cornwallis fought for two more days before waving the white flag on October 17. The official ceremony of surrender took place two days later, but the humiliated Cornwallis refused to attend. When the British general Charles O'Hara relinquished Cornwallis's sword to General Benjamin Lincoln of Massachusetts, the last major battle of the American Revolution officially drew to an end.

More than four years had passed since the *Victoire* had deposited Lafayette and his lost band of French officers on the shores of South Carolina. In those four years Lafayette had lived a lifetime's worth of new experiences. Yet he was still only twenty-four years old, and his remarkable life as a man living between two worlds was just getting under way.

CHAPTER 8

HONOR

*P*aris was abuzz with revelry on the day of Lafayette's return, but Lafayette was not the man of honor, who, as it happens, was a rather more diminutive figure. Marie Antoinette, who had produced only one daughter in her first eleven years of marriage, had at last given birth to a son—an heir to the throne—on October 22, 1781. When Lafayette reached Paris on January 21, 1782, the city was celebrating the three-month-old dauphin. In the morning, the queen attended services at two different churches, but the king arrived late; the streets were so densely packed with crowds that His Majesty's carriage got stuck in traffic. In the afternoon, the notables of the city toasted the future of the royal family at a grand feast at the Hôtel de Ville (city hall). At dusk, a show of fireworks lured the banqueters away from their postprandial gaming tables, if only long enough to behold the display.

Had Lafayette been any less renowned, his star would have been eclipsed. As it was, the royal fete only added to the brilliance of his return. Adrienne was not at home when Lafayette reached the Hôtel de Noailles. She had gone to the Hôtel de Ville with the rest of her family, but she'd apparently left in more exalted company. Upon the close of the festivities, Marie Antoinette bestowed a tremendous honor upon the marquise by permitting her to ride home in one of the royal carriages. The entire procession, including the carriages of the king and queen, accompanied Adrienne to the door of the Hôtel de Noailles, where they drew to a halt. The revelers gazed out from their vehicles as Adrienne descended from her coach and was reunited with her husband. She promptly collapsed into his arms.

To the author of *Correspondance secrète, politique et littéraire*—one of the clandestine serials that spread celebrity news and court gossip to the capitals of Europe in the late eighteenth century—the unprecedented scene of a monarch offering a noblewoman a ride home was not so much a mark of Lafayette's stature as a sign of Marie Antoinette's grace. As to Lafayette, the newsletter poked gentle fun at the young man who had grown accustomed to having his every arrival and departure cheered by groups of admiring Americans. The anonymous author deadpanned that, because Lafayette had reached Paris at a moment when everyone who was anyone was otherwise occupied, he must have been greeted by "a large and joyous group of fishwives" who gathered at the entrance to the stately Hôtel de Noailles bearing branches of laurel as offerings to the victorious major general. Marketwomen would certainly have been the only people in town with nothing better to do that day, but how they had gotten word of Lafayette's imminent arrival remained, the author implied, a mystery.

After spending the better part of four years as a symbol of France in America, Lafayette was about to embark on a career as an American representative in France. The congressional resolution James Madison wrote into the record on November 23, 1781, went far beyond granting Lafayette a furlough. After approving Lafayette's leave of absence and commending him for "his conduct throughout the past campaign, and particularly during the period in which he had the chief command in Virginia," Congress conferred a new set of duties upon the marquis. "The ministers plenipotentiary of the United States" in Europe were instructed to "confer with the Marquis de la Fayette, and avail themselves of his informations relative to the situation of public affairs in the United States." The minister plenipotentiary to the court of Versailles, Benjamin Franklin, was further directed to "conform to the intention of Congress by consulting with and employing the assistance of the Marquis de la Fayette in accelerating the supplies which may be afforded by his Most Christian Majesty for the use of the United States." Finally, the American "superintendant of finance, Secretary for foreign affairs and the board of war" were asked to help further these goals by keeping Lafayette apprised of developments "touching the affairs of their respective departments."

Based on the resolution's wording, it seems that Congress might have envisioned an advisory role for Lafayette. Having demonstrated at every turn that his devotion to the United States ran as deep as his love for France, Lafayette had surely earned the right to be consulted on matters concerning both nations. But Lafayette construed his position somewhat more expansively. Although he often worked closely with Franklin, he felt entirely comfortable taking matters into his own hands, and he routinely acted on America's behalf without prior approval from Congress. Over the course of the next two years, he devised his own diplomatic assignments, proffered political advice on matters both foreign and domestic (whether or not his opinion had been sought), and always made it a point to spread news of his American efforts. In short, serving as America's foremost friend in Paris and Versailles became more than a pastime for Lafayette—it was even more than a career. The nation that had welcomed him so warmly occupied a place near to his heart and was his driving passion.

One of the first tasks Lafayette set for himself was fostering trade between France and the United States. Although he had no prior experience in the field of commerce—and no one on either side appears to have asked him to address this particular problem—Lafayette did possess a keen sense of both countries' needs and was willing to do the work required to meet them. America, newly liberated from the economic yoke of Great Britain, was striving to build up both its domestic manufacturing and its capacity to exchange goods throughout the globe. Matters ranging from the navigation of inland waterways to international trade agreements ranked high on the agendas of the young nation's legislators, diplomats, farmers, sailors, and merchants. France, for its part, hoped to profit from its investments in the American war by securing advantageous trade relations with the new nation while driving an economic wedge between Great Britain and its former colonies.

Lafayette devoted much of 1782 and 1783 to studying the intricate details of transatlantic commerce. Writing to Washington in November 1783, he explained that he had been "Collecting the Opinions of Every American Merchant Within My Reach" so that he could better understand their wishes. By December, he had completed his "Observations on Commerce between France and the United States," filling twelve octavo pages with arguments designed to persuade Vergennes of the advantages to be gained by granting commercial concessions to the United States. "Since we are rivals of the British in both our manufactured goods and our sea trade," Lafayette wrote, "it is by these very means that our political rivalry will be decided someday." He was not telling Vergennes anything new, but Lafayette hoped that he might be able to help hasten the pace of a cumbersome bureaucracy, arguing that "each delay, each mistake becomes a sure gain for England."

Having lived in the comparatively pared-down manner of the New World, Lafayette understood that the finest French goods would appeal to only a select few Americans. The French would have to create "a taste for our manufactures." He was right to predict that "our broadcloth, our silks of every kind, our linens and fashionable clothing, etc. will find a considerable American market that with care can be further enlarged." Although, at first, he believed that "the less refined [*recherchées*] manufactures will be closer to American taste," he suggested that "we could cut the costs of our more refined manufactures by simplifying our methods." Thinking, perhaps, of English factories like Etruria, where Josiah Wedgwood had introduced a division of labor to boost efficiency, Lafayette suggested that "some industries would not lose by adopting the British principle that employs one person for each task, and for each task only the necessary amount of energy."

More daunting was the project of increasing American imports into France, where the protectionist practices of mercantilism imposed hefty taxes on foreign-made goods. Yet Lafayette, who was never easily dissuaded, accepted the challenge. He took part in extensive negotiations that resulted in the creation of four "free ports," where items arriving on American ships would be exempt from all duties and prohibitions, and throughout the 1780s he hammered away at efforts to open up the French market for American goods ranging from timber to whale oil. Some commodities, notably tobacco, posed particular difficulties: the farmers general, as the king's tax collectors were known, enjoyed a near monopoly over the sale of tobacco, and they were not pleased at the prospect of a sudden spike in supply; nor did they welcome the idea of American merchants competing for clients. Still, through sheer persistence, Lafayette and his American colleagues managed to wrest some concessions even on this thorny issue.

Having begun to see commerce from an American perspective, Lafayette developed a keen ability to observe and articulate some of the fundamental differences that bedeviled French-American relations. Summing up a sentiment shared by many in the United States, Lafayette's "Observations" insisted that the French way of doing business "has driven American trade away." The text asserted that "the intricacies of our regulations are even more annoying than their cost," so that "time, so precious to a merchant, is as wasted over a slight obstacle as it would be over the most important matter." Even Lafayette's boundless enthusiasm could not completely bridge such ingrained cultural differences.

Lafayette had addressed his "Observations" to Vergennes and sent copies to the French and American officials who were best situated to act upon his recommendations, but he also had a larger audience in mind: the American people. For Lafayette, it was not enough that he act tirelessly on behalf of his adopted country; it was important that those actions be widely known. As he confessed to Robert R. Livingston, secretary for foreign affairs, in a letter written in February 1783, "I Have a Great Value for My American Popularity, and I Want the people at large to know My Affection to them, and My zeal for their Service." The "Best Way" to publicize his efforts, he suggested to Livingston, would be "to Have a Resolve of Congress Published" announcing its "Approbation" of his efforts on behalf of the United States. To spread the word about his "Observations on Commerce," Lafayette turned to James McHenry, a former aide-de-camp who was then serving simultaneously in the Maryland state legislature and the Continental Congress. In a letter of December 26, 1783, enclosed with a copy of the document, Lafayette asked if McHenry would please "Be so kind only as to take Care My Commercial efforts Be known in America."

In placing a high value on his reputation, Lafayette was hardly alone. Honor, which had long ranked among the most treasured possessions of the French nobility, came to be increasingly understood in the eighteenth century as inseparable from notions of both merit and esteem. Americans, too, recognized the incomparable worth of a man's public name. In a 1780 letter to the Patriot author Mercy Otis Warren, Abigail Adams had expressed concern about unfounded rumors that accused John Adams of conspiring with the British. "I sometimes contemplate the situation of my absent Friend," Abigail wrote of John, ". . . as the most critical and hazardous Embassy to his reputation, his honour, and I know not but I may add life, that could possibly have been entrusted to him." So highly did America's founders think of public reputation that, in *The Federalist Papers*, Alexander Hamilton wrote of "the love of fame" as "the ruling passion of the noblest minds." At the same time, as the *Encyclopédie*'s entry on "reputation" makes clear, being overly interested in garnering esteem was deemed a fault. The bulk of the entry is devoted to parsing the apparent contradiction in the fact that "nature strews approbation upon the marks of esteem that one is given; and yet it attaches a sort of stain to the appearance of seeking them out." Propriety demanded recognizing the fine line between earning fame and seeming to pursue it too ardently or as an end in itself.

Cognizant of the distinction, Lafayette tried his best to tread carefully, although his enthusiasm for glory sometimes got the better of him. In his December 26 letter to McHenry, Lafayette explained that he wished to have his commercial efforts be made public, in part "Because that Entrusting Temper which You know me to be possessed of, Now and then is Altered By the Selfishness of others." Lafayette evidently felt that he had been given short shrift in the version of events provided by Franklin, Jay, and Adams concerning a loan of 6 million livres that France had made to the United States. Refraining from his habitual use of the first-person plural "we" in writing of Americans, Lafayette noted "that Your plenipotentiarie's letters, rather Gave a Ground to think I Have not Been so Active as they in obtaining the last six millions." Correcting the record, he added that "I cannot help remembering that Jay and Adams Never Went to Versailles But twice, I think, when I pushed them to it." By spreading word of the "Observations on Commerce," Lafayette implied, McHenry could help right a wrong. The American ministers, however, believed that Lafayette had developed a habit of claiming undue credit. John Adams's diary entry of November 23, 1782, records a meeting with Lafayette at Franklin's home in Passy. "The Marquis's business," wrote Adams, "was to shew us a letter he had written, to the C[omte] de V[ergennes], on the subject of money. This I saw nettled F[ranklin] as it seemed an attempt to take to himself the merit of obtaining the loan if one should be procured."

Franklin, who could more than hold his own, makes no mention of feeling particularly "nettled," but Adams was losing patience with Lafayette. In the same diary entry, Adams predicted that Lafayette's "unlimited ambition will obstruct his rise. He grasps at all civil, political, and military, and would be thought the Unum necessarium in every thing." Adams saw this habit of overreaching as a tragic flaw in the character of the marquis; it disappointed him. Lafayette "has so much real merit, such family supports, and so much favour at court," Adams wrote, "that he need not recur to artifice."

Adams had not always been so wary of Lafayette. In a 1780 letter to James Warren of Massachusetts—a fellow member of the Sons of

Liberty and the husband of Mercy Otis Warren—Adams had declared Lafayette to be "the same Friend to Us here [in Paris] that he was in America. He has been very assiduous to procure Cloths and Arms for our Army, and to promote our Interest in every other Way, within his Circle." But by 1782 Adams was struggling to wrest a modicum of respect from the Comte de Vergennes, who did nothing to disguise his preference for the more cosmopolitan (and less austere) Franklin, and Lafayette's appearance on the stage of American diplomacy threatened to force Adams still further to the margins.

Adams was in Amsterdam, recovering slowly from a debilitating fever that had plagued him for months, when, on February 19, 1782, the congressional resolution granting Lafayette a role in American affairs reached him. His initial response was entirely polite: in a letter to Lafayette dated the following day, Adams proclaimed Congress's instructions to be "so agreeable to my inclinations, that I would undertake a journey to Paris, for the sake of a personal interview with my dear general, if the state of my health, and the situation of affairs, in which I am here engaged did not render it improper." But on April 16, 1783, he expressed a very different opinion. Writing to James Warren, Adams declared "the Instruction of Congress to their foreign Ministers to consult with" Lafayette to be "very ill Judged. It was lowering themselves & their Servants." Indeed, it was "an Humiliation." "As long as Congress insists on rendering America's representatives subservient to the Marquis," wrote Adams, "Your Ministers will never be respected, never have any Influence," and "every Frenchman . . . will consider your Servants as mere Instruments in their Hands." Adams was growing increasingly disillusioned with America's French allies, whom he suspected of being willing to place their own interests ahead of America's in any peace negotiations that might be forthcoming. Adams began to doubt the wisdom of placing so much faith in a man as young and as closely connected to the court as Lafayette, in whom he perceived "the Seeds of Mischief to our Country, if We do not take care." The youth, he wrote, had "gained more applause than human Nature at 25 can bear. It has enkindled in him an unbounded Ambition, which it concerns Us much to watch." While Adams acknowledged that Lafayette was "ardent to distinguish himself in every way, especially to increase his Merit towards America," he warned that "this Mongrel Character of French Patriot and American Patriot cannot exist long."

Adams was right to perceive in Lafayette a profound devotion to both

France and America—this dual allegiance was clear to both nations—but he was wrong to fear that Lafayette might be dangerous or that his hybrid character could not be sustained. Lafayette was not a schemer. Rather, he was an idealist who seems not to have contemplated the possibility that Americans, much as they loved him, would always see him as a Frenchman or that the French court, while according him a grudging respect, would always be wary of his foreign allegiances. But where others saw divided loyalties, Lafayette's clear conscience blinded him to all difficulties.

Untroubled as he was, Lafayette even imagined for a time that he might be an ideal person to represent the French government, with sufficient latitude to speak for the United States, at the ratification of any peace treaty with Great Britain. According to Benjamin Franklin's journal, Lafayette began dropping hints during a visit to Passy in May 1782. Leaving Franklin to divine the purpose of the meeting, Lafayette recounted a tale of the Duc de Nevers, who, Lafayette reported, "during the Treaty at Paris for the last Peace," in 1763, "had been sent to reside in London, that this Court might thro' him state what was from time to time transacted, in the Light they thought best, to prevent Misrepresentations and Misunderstandings." Eventually, it became clear to Franklin that this was no mere history lesson: Lafayette hoped to be granted a similar post. As Franklin recorded it, Lafayette explained that "such an Employ would be extremely agreeable to him on many Accounts; that as he was now an American Citizen, spoke both Languages, and was well acquainted with our Interests, he believ'd he might be useful in it."

Franklin very much "lik'd the idea" of Lafayette going to London as a representative of France. To have a French diplomat in England with America's interests at heart would grant the fledgling nation considerably more leverage than its own minister could exert. Franklin was so fond of the notion that he hosted a breakfast to introduce Lafayette to the British representatives Richard Oswald and Thomas Grenville, recently arrived to lay the groundwork for negotiations. With the preliminaries taken care of, on May 26, Lafayette and Franklin decided that the time was ripe to propose the arrangement to Vergennes. Unfortunately, Vergennes liked the idea quite a bit less; if France were to send an envoy to the Court of St. James's, it would be one loyal to France alone.

But Lafayette would not be shunted aside. Although he played no formal role in the peace negotiations, mid-June found him haranguing Grenville with accusations that "the expectation of peace is a joke, and that you only amuse us without any real intention of treating." Meanwhile, Lafayette continued to suggest ways that he might make himself useful in the political and diplomatic areas. In a private letter to Robert Livingston written on February 5, he proposed several options. For instance, he indicated that it "Would Highly flatter" him to be granted the "Honorary Commission" of bearing the peace treaty to England for ratification. Lafayette elaborated on this, noting that he would "Well Enough like to Present Myself there in the Capacity of an Extraordinary Envoy from the United States."

Hoping to marshal support for the idea, Lafayette wrote to Washington, saying, "I Would take it as a Most flattering Circumstance in My life to Be Sent to England With the Ratification of the American treaty." Ideally, Lafayette continued, he would like to reach London in advance of the American ambassador so that "I Would Have the pleasure of introducing Him." As a stalwart friend, Washington dutifully wrote to Livingston of Lafayette's request to serve as "the bearer of the Ratification." Sage politician that he was, however, Washington refrained from endorsing too heartily the notion that any citizen of a foreign land, no matter how earnest, be permitted to represent America abroad. "How far it is consistent with our national honor, how far motives of policy make for or ag[ain]st sending a foreigner with it; or how far such a measure might disappoint the [ex]pectations of others, I pretend not to determine," wrote Washington. He asked only that Livingston accede to Lafayette's desire "if there is no impropriety, or injustice in it."

Quite rightly, Livingston perceived multiple improprieties. He refused even to present Lafayette's request to Congress, explaining to Washington that "the honor of the nation seems to require that it should be represented by a native . . . it should not appear to act under foreign influence." More specifically, he warned that "too close a connection with France might render her foes jealous of us." Washington offered no resistance. Instead, by way of reply, he assured Livingston that although "there is no Man upon Earth I have a greater inclination to serve than the Marquis La Fayette . . . ," he had "not a wish to do it in matters that interfere with, or are repugnant to, our National policy, dignity, or interest." Washington broke the news to his friend on October 12. Writing bluntly, Washington informed Lafayette that the "event" he desired "will not I apprehend, ever take place." The question was put to rest for good when Congress affirmed, on March 16, 1784, "that it is inconsistent with the interest of the United States to appoint any person not a citizen thereof, to the office of Minister, chargé des affaires, Consul, vice-consul, or to any other civil department in a foreign country; and that a copy of this resolve be transmitted to Messrs. Adams, Franklin and Jay, ministers of the said states in Europe." When John Adams learned of the congressional declaration, he must have felt at least a twinge of vindication.

While the Treaty of Paris was being ratified in London on April 9, 1784, Lafayette was at home preparing for his first visit to the free and independent United States of America, but John Adams remained skeptical of the Frenchman. A new bone of contention had arisen: the Society of the Cincinnati, a hereditary organization established in 1783 by a group of officers who had served under Washington. The society, which still exists today, was envisioned as a vehicle for reaffirming bonds of affection and obligation among the revolution's longest-serving and most distinguished military leaders, and for ensuring that the sacrifices of the war would not be forgotten. According to their charter, the men who founded the Cincinnati intended:

> to inculcate to the latest age the duty of laying down in peace, arms assumed for public defence, by forming an Institution which recognizes that most important principle; to continue the mutual friendships which commenced under the pressure of common danger; and to effectuate the acts of beneficence, dictated by the spirit of brotherly kindness towards those officers and their families.

Having risked their lives for the independence of the United States, most of the Cincinnati had stepped to the side to allow politicians to make the next moves toward forging an enduring republic; the society would ensure that the officers' contributions to the nation's founding would not be forgotten.

The society's name honors a man whose virtue was widely known in the eighteenth century: the Roman general Lucius Quinctius Cincinnatus, who lived in the fifth century B.C. and whose story is told by Livy. Persuaded by the Senate to leave his farm long enough to lead Rome through a time of crisis, Cincinnatus served briefly as *magister populi* (literally, "master of the people"—a dictator appointed for a limited term) but refused the role of lifelong ruler and resumed his quiet

Washington bequeathed this gold-and-
enamel medal of the Society of Cincinnati
to Lafayette. Measuring 1½ x 1⅛ inches,
it sold at auction at Sotheby's New York
for $5.3 million on December 11, 2007.

existence of private industry. In 1783, when Washington laid down his
sword and returned to his own fields at Mount Vernon, it became commonplace to link his name and image to those of Cincinnatus, and by
dubbing themselves "Cincinnati," Washington's officers honored their
general and announced that they, too, were relinquishing any claims
to power by "returning to their citizenship." Members were—and still
are—entitled to purchase and wear "a bald eagle of gold . . . suspended
by a deep blue ribbon edged with white, descriptive of the union of
America and France," its center featuring an enameled emblem depicting Cincinnatus at his plow.

Lafayette was the society's most prominent and enthusiastic French
member. He had been the one to draw up a roster of French officers
who fought under Washington. And in an event that merited several
paragraphs in the *Mémoires secrets* (like the *Correspondance secrète,* a
newsletter that reported the goings-on in French society), he had welcomed fifteen of them to his home on January 16, 1784, for a ceremony
at which he distributed the society's golden eagle insignia, designed by
Pierre Charles L'Enfant and produced by the Paris jewelry firm of Duval
and Francastel. Lafayette even went into debt for the cause: L'Enfant left
Paris for America without paying a jeweler's bill that exceeded 20,000
livres—Francastel had provided the society's gold and enamel eagles on
credit—and Lafayette voluntarily shouldered the obligation.

Few disputed the comparison between Washington and Cincinnatus, and no one denied the nation's obligations to its military heroes,

but the notions that the Cincinnati would wear insignia reminiscent of the medals distributed by Europe's chivalric orders and that its membership would be inherited made the society a lightning rod for controversy. Adams condemned the group for introducing hereditary titles in a nation that forbade them, and he (mistakenly) held Lafayette partially responsible for its existence. Writing from The Hague on January 25, 1784, Adams reported to the Baltimore-based businessman Matthew Ridley, "I have been informed that this whole Scheme, was first concerted, in France and transmitted from thence, by the Marquis." Thomas Jefferson, too, disapproved mightily of the Society of the Cincinnati, making it one of the few topics on which Jefferson and Adams agreed. On April 16, 1784, Jefferson spelled out his objections in a letter to Washington that declared the society to be "against the confederation—against the letter of some of our constitutions;—against the spirit of all of them" because "the foundation on which all these are built is the natural equality of man, the denial of every preeminence but that annexed to legal office, & particularly the denial of a preeminence by birth." Abigail Adams raised a more concrete concern in a letter to Mercy Otis Warren: Abigail hinted at the dangers of a permanent military class setting itself apart "that the people may look to them, and them only as the preservers of their Country and the supporters of their freedom."

Lafayette seems to have been genuinely unsure what to make of such criticisms, which reached him both indirectly, through the rumor mill, and directly, in letters from Adams. Writing to Washington from Paris on March 9, Lafayette told his mentor that "most of the Americans Here are indecently Violent Against our Association. . . . You Easely guess I am not Remiss in opposing them—and However if it is found that the Heredity Endangers the true principles of democraty [*sic*], I am as Ready as Any Man to Renounce it." He looked to Washington for guidance, adding, "You Will be My Compass." Washington evidently saw nothing awry in the society: he accepted the role of its first president.

Lafayette's embrace of the Cincinnati only increased the distrust felt by Adams, who had begun to suspect Lafayette's motives in all things. In a testy letter written from The Hague on March 28, 1784, Adams told Lafayette that, "as to your going to America, Surely I have no Objection against it . . . but I questioned whether you would go, as the War was over, and I knew of no particular Motive you might have to go." Adams concluded, "If you go I wish you a pleasant voyage, and an happy Sight of your Friends." Lafayette was hurt. His English faltering, as it often did when he was in an emotional state, Lafayette rebuked Adams for the coolness of his tone and rejected the implication that his motives might be anything but pure:

> A friendly letter I wrote You, and the One I Receive is not so affectionate as usual. . . . As to My Going to America, I first Went for the Revolution. . . . Now I am Going for the people, and My Motives are, that I love them, and they love me—that My Arrival will please them, and that I will Be Pleased with the sight of those whom I Have Early joined in our Noble and successfull cause. . . . How could I Refrain from Visiting a Nation whose I am an Adoptive Son . . . ?

Nearly eight weeks passed—an unusually long silence—before Lafayette wrote to Adams again. "Altho' I have not Been Honoured with an answer to My last letter," Lafayette began, "I will not loose time in Acquainting you that My departure from l'Orient is fixed on the 22d instant." Lafayette held out an olive branch, offering to deliver any letters that Adams might wish to send to Massachusetts. "As I intend landing in New York," he explained, "your letters to your family will not Have a long way to go." But Adams would not be mollified. Making no excuses, he replied flatly that he had "received in Season, the Letter mentioned in yours of the second of this Months, but as there was nothing in it which required an immediate Answer, I have not acknowledged the Recipt of it, untill now." Adams added that he had no need of Lafayette's postal services. Referring to two Americans then traveling in Europe, he informed Lafayette that "I will answer the Letters of my Friends by Mr. Reed and Coll. Herman." Lafayette, who genuinely wished to make amends, sent one more letter to Adams before sailing for New York. As far as we know, it went unanswered.

CHAPTER 9

1784

*W*hen Lafayette set foot on Manhattan Island on August 4, 1784, the city's scars from the Revolutionary War were just beginning to heal. Captured in 1776, New York had remained a British stronghold throughout the conflict, serving as a base of military operations, a refuge for Loyalists, and a haven for thousands of escaped slaves promised freedom in exchange for service in the British Army. For seven long years, the city had hosted a sprawling network of overcrowded jails, including pestilential prison ships that held as many as 11,000 captured soldiers at a time. A similar number of prisoners died from disease and starvation over the course of the war. By the time General Howe evacuated Britain's troops from Manhattan, on November 25, 1783, a third of the island's buildings had been lost in two major fires. Other structures had escaped the conflagrations only to be battered by hard use as makeshift stables, hospitals, and mess halls for the occupying army. Docks had fallen into disrepair, and streets had been rendered impassable by a labyrinthine system of trenches.

An observant visitor strolling the streets of Manhattan in 1784 would have seen the city springing back to life around the ruins. The burned-out façade of Trinity Church loomed above Wall Street, and on Bowling Green, an empty pedestal that had once supported an equestrian statue of King George III stood forlorn amid the stubbly grass—but the docks and markets were once again bustling with the exchange of goods. Having reopened after the winter thaw, the port was regularly welcoming shipments of foodstuffs and manufactured wares. In February, the *Empress of China* had sailed through the ice floes dotting New York Harbor, marking America's entrance into the China trade;

on board were piles of animal pelts, thirty tons of American ginseng, which grew wild in the mid-Atlantic region, and stores of other goods that were plentiful in the New World but precious in Canton. New York's chamber of commerce had been revived. And representatives of the Bank of New York, recently founded by Alexander Hamilton, were greasing the wheels of trade by providing commercial financing at interest from temporary offices in a yellow brick house on Pearl Street.

With so much going on, Lafayette's arrival initially attracted scant notice. He had sailed on the *Courier de New York,* one of a fleet of five French packet ships that had begun making monthly crossings in September 1783. The landing of the ship, which was carrying the June mail from Europe, was widely announced, but several papers neglected to mention its most famous passenger. It did not, however, take long for the news to spread. Approaching Philadelphia on the evening of August 9, Lafayette was escorted into the city by a ceremonial detachment of the local militia and welcomed by the sound of tolling church bells. On September 7, James Madison observed that "wherever [Lafayette] passes he receives the most flattering tokens of sincere affection from all ranks." And on September 14, during Lafayette's next trip through New York, Mayor James Duane and the city's Common Council presented Lafayette with a gold box containing a certificate that declared him to be "admitted and received a *Freeman and Citizen of the City of New York.*"

For the next five months Lafayette and his aide, the eighteen-year-old Chevalier de Caraman, captain in the Noailles Dragoons, traced and retraced routes up and down the eastern seaboard, traveling by carriage, ship, barge, horseback, and, at times, on foot. The pair visited nine states from Virginia to New Hampshire; Lafayette was feted every step along the way with banquets, balls, and toasts that fixed in American minds the image of the marquis as a hero. But Lafayette, who had turned twenty-seven in Philadelphia that September, was still a young man, and he had come to America not only to celebrate his past but also to shape his future. Since Yorktown, he had begun to see himself as more than a soldier, and his first peacetime visit to the United States gave him an opportunity to try out new roles and explore emerging interests. In America, the expectations of family, court, and tradition weighed less heavily on Lafayette than they did in France. Here, he could experiment with newfound concerns; some proved to be passing fancies, but others became lifelong passions.

In the 1780s, Lafayette became a citizen of two republics: one was the United States; the other was the imagined community known as the Republic of Letters. A loosely knit international society with no geographic boundaries, the Republic of Letters was populated by educated men and women committed to the Enlightenment ideal of disseminating thought and knowledge with no restrictions based on nationality, social status, or other distinctions. Its citizens might reside anywhere and could adhere to a range of political and intellectual views, but they were bound together by the belief, articulated by the historian Dena Goodman in 1994, that "the search for knowledge was now subordinated to the higher good of society, even of humanity as a whole." To enter, one had only to support the free and open exchange of ideas. This could mean joining an academy, subscribing to a periodical, maintaining an international correspondence, or attending one of the salons—regularly scheduled gatherings of writers, artists, political figures, and other social and intellectual luminaries—that were often hosted by prominent women and were especially influential in eighteenth-century Paris. Lafayette, who was never entirely at ease with the rigid protocols of life at court, had a greater affinity for the more open-minded and outward-looking sensibility of the Republic of Letters. It offered him an alternative path to reputation and esteem.

In one of the first organized events of his 1784 visit, Lafayette proclaimed his citizenship in this ideal realm. The occasion was a meeting of the American Philosophical Society—or, as it was officially known, the "American Philosophical Society, Held at Philadelphia, for the Promoting of Useful Knowledge." Founded by Benjamin Franklin in 1743, the society spelled out its goals and by-laws in a 1769 act of incorporation that laid out the founding principle that "the cultivation of useful knowledge, and the advancement of the liberal arts and sciences in any country, have the most direct tendency towards the improvement of agriculture, the enlargement of trade, the ease and comfort of life, the ornament of society, and the increase and happiness of mankind." To promote such endeavors, the society would maintain a collection containing "all specimens of natural Productions, whether of the Animal, Vegetable, or Fossil kingdom; all models of machines and instruments"—in short, any objects whose study might explain the laws of nature or further the progress of mankind. It would publish papers chosen for "the importance or singularity of their subjects, or the advantageous manner of treating them, without pretending to answer, or to make the society answerable, for the certainty of the facts, or propriety of the reasonings." Its members, who were to meet twice a month, would be divided into six committees, investigating topics ranging from "Geography, Mathematics, Natural Philosophy and Astronomy" to "Husbandry and American Improvements."

Lafayette had been admitted on January 19, 1781, but he remained a silent member for the better part of three years. The Marquis de Chastellux, Lafayette's countryman and comrade-in-arms who was then serving as a major general in the French army under Rochambeau, was elected at the same time. In light of his established intellectual credentials, Chastellux was probably the more viable candidate. A well-known figure in Enlightenment circles, Chastellux had written a two-volume book titled *On Public Happiness* (1772) that won high praise from Voltaire and earned its author admission to the French Academy in 1775. Lafayette could boast of no such learned accomplishments. In fact, as Chastelllux recalled, Lafayette's nomination had initially been rejected; embarrassed by this ungenerous treatment of a beloved hero, the society later let it be known that the blackballing was "thought to be a mistake."

Although Lafayette had exhibited little interest in the world of letters before joining the society, he soon entered wholeheartedly into the craze for things scientific that was captivating the imagination of Paris. On July 12, 1782, he paid the 96 livres required to become a "protector" of the "Establishment for the Correspondence of the Sciences and the Arts," or the "Salon de la Correspondance," as the enterprise was often called. It had been founded in 1779 by a young man who called himself Pahin de la Blancherie, who'd conceived of it as a for-profit version of the American Philosophical Society. To facilitate the dissemination of knowledge, La Blancherie published a weekly newsletter and invited "men of letters and artists" to gather in rented rooms near the Sorbonne and discuss the diverse objects exhibited there on a rotating basis. Jean-Baptiste Le Paon, the painter who had reimagined Lafayette's portrait of Washington as an exotic battlefield scene, was among the artists who exhibited at the Salon de la Correspondance, where his works appeared alongside "books, paintings, mechanical devices, specimens of natural history, sculptural models and, finally, all types of ancient or modern works with which one would want to be acquainted, or to learn . . . the value, the existence, or the author," as La Blancherie put it in his self-published newsletter. Not incidentally, all items on view were for sale unless otherwise indicated.

The American Philosophical Society was pursuing a similar range of interests, albeit without La Blancherie's eye to financial gain. Meetings held in 1783 and 1784 witnessed discussions of topics including the aurora borealis (May 2, 1783), "a serpent in a horse's eye" (September 26, 1783), an "improved method of quilling a harpsichord" (November 21, 1783), and "the preserving of parsnips for drying" (April 16, 1784). Cutting-edge scientific instruments were also presented and analyzed, including five thermometers (February 20, 1784), a microscope "framed in a mahogany trunked cone and stand" (March 5, 1784), and an orrery— a model of the solar system—commissioned by the society, at the suggestion of Thomas Jefferson, to be produced by David Rittenhouse as a gift to Louis XVI (January 13 and March 6, 1783).

In the spirit of transatlantic conversation, Lafayette wrote to the society on December 10, 1783, about a marvelous invention that was then the talk of Paris: the hot air balloon. On September 19, the brothers Joseph-Michel and Jacques-Étienne Montgolfier had astonished the French nation when they'd launched from the grounds of Versailles a balloon, made of toile, measuring fifty-seven feet high by forty-one feet in diameter and carrying a sheep, a duck, and a rooster in its basket. According to Barthélemy Faujas de Saint-Fond, the assistant director of the Jardin du Roi and the author of the first full account of the Montgolfiers' experiments, all of "the grandest, most illustrious, and wisest" men in France gathered as witnesses, "as if for a concert, to render a solemn homage to the sciences." French newspapers fed the balloon-mania with articles celebrating the possibilities of flight, while gossip sheets touted stories of inventors claiming to have gotten there first. Soon, fashionable women took to wearing their tresses in the *coiffure à la montgolfière*—piled high on the head with a small hot air balloon embedded in the mound—and lighthearted vignettes involving the airborne marvels appeared on curtains made from printed fabrics known as toiles de Jouy. The influential furniture maker Georges Jacob even supplied Marie Antoinette with a pair of side chairs, now housed in the Metropolitan Museum of Art, that feature gilded walnut finials carved into the shape of balloons. For his part, Lafayette sent a letter "enclosing an authentic narrative of the Experiments lately made in France with air Balloons, drawn up by Mr. Sage, an able Cheymist in the Academy of Sciences, with two Copper Plates Prints of those machines." Although the learned organization had already received news of the discovery from Benjamin Franklin, Lafayette's letter was

Frontispiece to Barthélemy Faujas de Saint-Fond's description of the hot air balloon flight launched from Versailles in 1783.

presented at the group's meeting of April 2, 1784, and "duplicated by one of the secretaries."

When it came to matters scientific, Lafayette's enthusiasm sometimes trumped his good sense. The curious marquis was taken in by an attention-seeking ploy perpetrated in December 1783 when the daily *Journal de Paris* announced that it was collecting funds to be awarded to a man who claimed to have invented a pair of elastic shoes that made it possible to walk on water. As the renowned scholar of eighteenth-century "underground" literature Robert Darnton has discussed, the inventor, identified only as "D," pledged to cross the Seine on foot on New Year's Day and to pick up the proceeds when he reached the other side. Lafayette made one of the largest contributions to the pot, which was ultimately donated to charity.

A similar triumph of wishful thinking was on exhibit in Philadelphia on August 12, 1784, when Lafayette gave a presentation to the American Philosophical Society in front of twenty-two members gathered in Carpenters' Hall—in the same room where, some nine years earlier, Louis XVI's undercover agent Bonvouloir had first met with Franklin to discuss covert Franco-American cooperation in the fight against England. Lafayette's visit was of a far more public nature, but he, too, had come to share a European secret with American friends. Lafayette's topic was mesmerism—more commonly known at the time as "Animal Magnetism." The theory, developed by the German physician Franz Anton Mesmer, posited the existence of an invisible but manipulable fluid contained within and around every object in the universe.

Mesmer had taken Paris by storm when, in February 1778, he'd arrived claiming to have discovered a means of curing various ailments by using magnetic currents to rechannel the flow of the mysterious fluid within a person's body. More grandly, Mesmer held that universal harmony—a worldwide state of perfect physical and moral health in which man and nature would coexist in ideal balance—could be achieved through similar means. It did not take long for the sick and the curious to begin flocking to Mesmer's music-filled rooms at the Place Vendôme. There, supplicants encountered an apparatus involving a large tub surrounded by several ropes, iron rods, and human chains. When activated, the eccentric machine would send mixed groups of men and women into spasms that sometimes required the afflicted to be carried off to an adjacent "crisis room," where they could recover on the mattress-lined floor.

Some deemed Mesmer a common charlatan who lined his pockets by bilking the desperate and the credulous. The academies of Paris were among the skeptics, as were Thomas Jefferson, Benjamin Franklin, and scores of satirists who produced poems and caricatures that played up the orgiastic undertones of Mesmer's convulsive groups. But those who were willing to suspend disbelief saw a promise of earthly salvation in Mesmer's omnipresent fluid, and the specter of tyranny in any attempts to squelch such a well-intentioned philosophy.

Lafayette, who was always looking for new ways to ameliorate both individual and societal ills, saw mesmerism in the best possible light. Spreading liberty was one means of bettering the world; Lafayette hoped that mesmerism might be another. He joined Mesmer's Society of Harmony (which counted Benjamin Franklin's grandson among its notable members), and shortly before departing for America, he

Caricature of Mesmer's tub in Paris.

wrote to Washington that Mesmer has "made the greatest discovery upon animal magnetism. . . . He has instructed scholars, among whom your humble servant is called one of the most enthusiastic." Perhaps acknowledging the boastful overtones of that statement, Lafayette added, with self-deprecating humor, "I know as much as any conjurer ever did." Still, he took mesmerism seriously enough to promise to let Washington in on "the secret of Mesmer, which you may depend upon is a grand philosophical discovery." Lafayette went so far as to chide Benjamin Franklin for agreeing to serve on a French royal commission investigating Mesmer's claims: writing to Franklin on May 20, Lafayette observed that "Sciences and letters are frighted a way By the Hand of despotism."

Franklin was not swayed. In fact, at the very moment that Lafayette was regaling the American Philosophical Society with tales of animal magnetism, Franklin's scientific commission was drafting its devastating assessment of Mesmer's claims. By the late autumn of 1784, news of the debunking reached American shores. In the months that followed, newspapers from Massachusetts to South Carolina gradually relayed to their readers the disappointing verdict that animal magnetism was no more than a "chimera." Lafayette never renounced the discredited theory, which continued to win adherents into the twentieth century, but neither was he tainted by association with it. One American author seems to have had Lafayette in mind when he excused the credulity of "characters distinguished for their good sense and benevolence—men, who were willing to believe almost anything that had even a shadow of probability of doing good to mankind." Incapable of knowingly perpetrating such a deception, men of good faith might simply "think it impossible that any one should be so devoid of honesty as to attempt an imposition" in a matter of such grave concern.

For Lafayette, the highlight of his American sojourn came at his next destination, Mount Vernon, the Virginia estate of George Washington. Having relinquished his military commission on December 23, 1783, Washington was enjoying the tranquil existence of a "private citizen . . . under the shadow of my own vine and my own Fig tree, free from the bustle of a camp and the busy scenes of public life," as he wrote to Lafayette on February 1, 1784. "Come . . . and view me in my domestic walks," Washington proposed. "No man could receive you in them with more friendship and affection that I should do." Lafayette happily accepted the invitation.

Lafayette and the Chevalier de Caraman, his traveling companion, reached Mount Vernon on August 17, 1784, and stayed as Washington's guests for ten days. In that time, Lafayette left the grounds only once, to dine with local gentry at Lomax's Tavern, the Alexandria, Virginia, terminus of the Baltimore stagecoach route. The other days were spent in the vicinity of the house in a state of uninterrupted serenity that Lafayette had not experienced since leaving Chavaniac, and his letters to Adrienne wax lyrical about the casual atmosphere of sociable retirement that he found at "the retreat of General Washington." Each day, Lafayette observed, was given over to a pleasurable sequence of "lunching, talking, writing, dining, talking, writing, and supping." He fretted only that the young Caraman—"poor Maurice," as Lafayette called him—might "find it a bit monotonous."

At Mount Vernon, Lafayette reflected on the full meaning of the Cincinnatus analogy, observing how Washington had turned his retirement into an expression of personal values by following the prescription offered by Horace in his epodes: *"Beatus ille qui procul negotiis / ut prisca gens mortalium / paterna rura bubus exercet suis"* ("Blessed is he who, leaving business behind him, works his life out on his ancestral land among the cattle"). Taking this as a model for his own behavior, Lafayette articulated in his letter to Adrienne an ideal vision for their new house in Paris, which was still undergoing renovations. "Since I am surrounded by domestic details, I will yield to the example of the true Cincinnatus, and although I may be a less retired Cincinnatus, I will also speak of the arrangements for the house." Lafayette directed Adrienne's "attention to my *cabinet*"—roughly the equivalent of his study or office—which he wanted to fill with objects that were emblematic of his interests in scientific progress and the young United States. He wrote that "there should be placed a barometer, a Declaration of Independence, and a smoke machine" (presumably a device intended to cut down on the smoke emanating from fireplaces) acquired during this tour of America. He added that Monsieur Pilon, one of his servants, "knows what must be done with my busts and monuments." Almost as an aside, Lafayette noted that "a rug wouldn't harm anything."

Lafayette's letters paint a picture of his visit to Mount Vernon as he wished to see it and as the reunion of the former comrades-in-arms has been commemorated since. An enormous 1859 painting by the American artists Thomas Prichard Rossiter and Louis Remy Mignot rendered the scene much as Lafayette described it. The painting—destined to be reproduced in prints, on postcards, and as decorations on collectible plates for years to come—was created to support and to capitalize on the drive to restore the deteriorating Mount Vernon in the middle of the nineteenth century. It portrays the two generals standing on the neoclassical portico of the main house engaged in leisurely conversation. Behind Washington, a young girl clings to the lap of her mother, who sits at a small tea table enjoying a hot beverage and the company of a second woman. Behind Lafayette, in the shadows of a late-afternoon summer light, a young white boy and a black woman sit together on the grass, their playful gestures echoed by the pair of scampering dogs—one white, one brown—who frolic beside them. The manicured lawn stretches into the background until it yields to the gentle flow of the distant Potomac River.

A more complete picture of Mount Vernon at the time of Lafayette's visit might be less idyllic. Looking beyond the majestic house and landscaped park, we would see five working farms, spread across eight thousand acres, where more than two hundred slaves lived and toiled. Mount Vernon was a fully functional plantation, growing wheat, corn, oats, and other grains. Washington, who firmly believed that a nation's economic worth and moral value could be measured by its management of its land, surveyed his fields every day he could. He experi-

Lafayette's 1784 visit to Mount Vernon as imagined by Thomas Prichard Rossiter
and Louis Rémy Mignot in 1859.

mented constantly, trying new agricultural tools and techniques, and
became a pioneer of modern farming systems through his advocacy of
crop rotation, fertilization with manure, and other techniques that are
now commonplace. Of course, while much of the intellectual work was
his, most of the physical labor was performed by slaves.

Lafayette seems not to have mentioned slavery in any letters he sent
to France in 1784, but he did not fail to notice the inhumane institution that enabled his adopted nation to flourish. Lafayette evidently
saw himself as part of a great American experiment whose long-term
success had not yet been fully ensured, and a sense of protective loyalty
kept him from airing in Europe his criticisms of the United States. He
had stated as much in a letter chiding John Adams, not so much for
speaking ill of the Society of the Cincinnati but for letting his grievances be known abroad. Writing on March 8, 1784, Lafayette explained
to Adams that "it Has Ever Been My duty and inclination to Set up in
the Best light Every thing that is done By a Body of Americans. . . . Had
I Amendments to Propose [to the society's by-laws], it Should Be in
America, and Not in Europe." Lafayette implied that Adams should
adopt the same policy of discretion.

On the matter of slavery, Lafayette followed his own advice. More than a year before visiting Mount Vernon he had written to Washington on the subject, proposing "a plan . . . Which Might Become Greatly Beneficial to the Black Part of Mankind." Lafayette asked Washington to join him "in Purchasing a Small Estate Where We May try the Experiment to free the Negroes, and use them only as tenants." The theory that slavery could be gradually abolished through such a program had been proposed by a handful of writers, mostly in Britain, but with little effect. Lafayette wrote to Washington that "such an example as yours, might render it a general practice. And, if we succeed in America, I will cheerfully devote a part of my time to render the method fashionable in the West Indies." Lafayette concluded by declaring that "if it be a wild scheme, I had rather be mad that way, than to be thought wise on the other tack."

Keenly aware that the issue of slavery was a political and economic powder keg threatening to explode the nascent union, Washington crafted a judicious reply. Lafayette's proposal, Washington wrote, offered "striking evidence of the benevolence of your Heart." Giving Lafayette just enough encouragement to buoy his hopes, Washington added, "I shall be happy to join you in so laudable a work; but will defer going into a detail of the business, till I have the pleasure of seeing you." We do not know whether Lafayette and Washington did discuss slavery at Mount Vernon; if they did, their conversation has not come down to us.

Nonetheless, we do know that Lafayette addressed the matter at least twice during his 1784 American visit—both times in Virginia, where arguments on the subject had grown particularly heated. On November 16, Lafayette appeared before the Virginia House of Delegates in Richmond to receive its members' official thanks for his "prudent, calm, and intrepid conduct during the campaign of 1781." As the legislators put it, they wished that Lafayette might become the "model" for those seeking "glory" and praised the work he had done on behalf of "the interests of humanity." Lafayette responded graciously, thanking the men of the chamber for the honor and voicing his appreciation for their constant affection and confidence. Yet before he concluded, he issued a plea that the state of Virginia might provide the world with "proofs of its love for the rights of all of humanity, in its entirety."

At the time, Lafayette had reason to be hopeful that slavery might soon be abolished in Virginia. Now that America had won independence, a wave of abolition and emancipation had been sweeping through many of the northern states, where influential individuals and organizations were successfully arguing that the new nation must extend its promise of liberty to all people. Although slavery had been declared illegal by just two states—Vermont in 1777 and Massachusetts in 1783—systems of gradual emancipation had been introduced in Connecticut, New Hampshire, Pennsylvania, and Rhode Island and were under consideration elsewhere. Of the southern states that relied on slave labor to perpetuate their plantation economies, Virginia had exhibited the greatest inclination to permit occasional emancipation when, in May 1782, its state legislature had passed an "Act to Authorize the Manumission of Slaves." This controversial law authorized any slaveholder to free his or her own slaves as long as the emancipation papers were written in "his or her hand and sealed, attested and proved in the county court by two witnesses, or acknowledged by the party in the court of the county where he or she resides."

But Lafayette arrived at a moment of backlash: on the same day that he addressed the Virginia legislators, two counties submitted proslavery petitions, signed by a total of 257 citizens, to the Virginia General Assembly (as the House of Delegates and Senate were collectively known). These petitions were only the beginning; six more counties submitted remonstrances supporting slavery in the next twelve months, bringing the total number of signatories to 1,244. The eight counties mounted a variety of arguments and sought a range of outcomes, but they all had one goal in common: the repeal of the law permitting manumission. According to the petitions of November 16, 1784, "many Evils have Arisen from" partial emancipation, and "many of the same Free Negroes are Agents, Factors, and Carriers to the neighboring towns" of slaves who were stolen from their owners and freed under false pretenses by unwitting county courts.

Yet Lafayette remained hopeful that the law would not be repealed, and he acted accordingly. Still in Richmond on November 21, he wrote a testimonial supporting the application for freedom submitted by a slave named James Armistead, owned by William Armistead, who sought manumission on the basis of his contributions to the success of Lafayette's 1781 campaign. As Lafayette confirmed, Armistead had "done Essential Service to Me" when he'd "Industriously Collected" intelligence "from the enemy's camp." He had, Lafayette wrote, "perfectly acquitted himself with some important commissions I gave him and appears to me entitled to every reward his situation can admit of."

Although it took more than two years, Armistead was freed on January 9, 1787, at which time he adopted the surname Lafayette. Thanks, in large part, to Lafayette's efforts to publicize his commitment to manumission, his role in securing Armistead's liberation became widely known on both sides of the Atlantic. While in Paris in 1783, Lafayette had commissioned a painting and engraving depicting himself and Armistead at the Siege of Yorktown. Envisioned as pendants to Lafayette's 1780 portraits of Washington with a turbaned African servant, the 1783 pictures depict Armistead in a fanciful costume topped by a plumed chapeau—an unlikely uniform for a black man hoping to pass unnoticed in 1781 Virginia. When Lafayette returned to the United States in 1824, a widely circulated broadside that reproduced Lafayette's handwritten letter beneath a more plausible portrait of Armistead helped secure Lafayette's reputation as a friend of the abolitionist cause.

The reputation was well earned. Throughout the 1780s and 1790s, Lafayette became increasingly active in various strains of the international abolitionist movement. His archives include correspondence on the subject with the English abolitionists Thomas Clarkson and Granville Sharp, as well as with the Marquis de Condorcet, who thanked him in 1785 for reading his *Reflections on Negro Slavery,* and Benjamin Franklin, who, as president of the Pennsylvania Society for the Abolition of Slavery, sent Lafayette several copies of the society's constitution on May 27, 1788. In 1788, Lafayette joined France's Society of the Friends of the Blacks, an organization spearheaded by the writer and humanitarian Jacques-Pierre Brissot (also known as Brissot de Warville). In the same year, Lafayette became a corresponding member of the New York Manumission Society and the British Committee for the Abolition of the Slave Trade. And he continued to keep abreast of developments in abolitionism even amid the tumult of the French Revolution, acquiring, for example, a handwritten French translation of James Phillips's anti-slavery broadside *Description of a Slave Ship,* published in London in 1789.

It would, however, be a mistake to understand Lafayette's views on slavery as being any more clear-cut than those of his abolitionist contemporaries. Although Lafayette championed liberty as an inalienable right, he never proposed the sudden or universal emancipation of slaves. Instead, his goals were similar to those articulated by Franklin, who spoke for many members of anti-slavery movements in describing the "final purposes" of the Pennsylvania Society as "the suppression of

*Marie-Joseph-Yves-Gilbert du Motier, Marquis de Lafayette
at Yorktown.* Engraving after Jean-Baptiste Le Paon by Noël
Le Mire. 1782.

the slave trade and the gradual abolition of slavery itself." Like Franklin
and like Jefferson, who wrote frequently of his efforts to improve the
lives of the roughly two hundred slaves on his plantation and devised
plans to repatriate slaves to Africa, Lafayette advocated ameliorating the
conditions of enslaved men, women, and children. He first broached
the idea of improving the lot of slaves in the French colonies (the only
territories in which France permitted slavery) in his 1783 memo on
Franco-American commerce. By way of arguing that France's colonies in the Americas should be allowed to import foodstuffs from the
United States, Lafayette appealed to "the double voice of self-interest
and humanity." He observed that "as long as feeding the slaves depends
on laws prohibiting the importation of foreign produce into the colonies the slaves will be few and poorly nourished, will work little and die
sooner." It was a cold calculus to be sure, and an unusually pragmatic
position for Lafayette—a man who usually traded in absolutes.

An 1824 broadside reproducing Lafayette's 1784 testimonial in
support of the manumission of James Armistead, who spied
for Lafayette during the 1781 Virginia campaign, beneath a
portrait of Armistead.

Tying himself into a moral knot that he never managed to untangle,
Lafayette opted paradoxically to demonstrate the benefits of gradual
emancipation by becoming a slaveholder himself. Although Washington declined to join in the venture, Lafayette put his plan for an ideal
plantation into action in 1785, when he acquired two properties in
Cayenne, the capital of the South American colony of French Guiana:
Saint Régis (which he renamed L'Adrienne, in honor of his wife) and
Le Maripa. For the fields planted with clove trees and sugarcane, and
forty-eight slaves to work them, Lafayette paid 125,000 livres. A third
property, La Gabrielle, worked by twenty-two slaves, was acquired in
1786 in a profit-sharing arrangement with the French government.
According to a list compiled on March 1, 1789, seventy slaves were liv-
ing on the three plantations. They ranged in age from the one-year-old
Seraphim, who was brought to Le Maripa from a nearby plantation

along with her parents and her four-year-old brother, to the blind sixty-year-old Hosea, who would die at L'Adrienne. As Lafayette wrote to Washington on February 6, 1786, his intention was "to free my negroes in order to make that experiment which you know is my hobby horse." Washington replied with a lament that captured the contradiction of a slaveholder who had led a nation to freedom: "would to God a like spirit would diffuse itself generally into the minds of the people of this country, but I despair of seeing it." Neither man could have foreseen that, when faced with the political and financial exigencies of the French Revolution and its aftermath, Lafayette would fail to live up to his own expectations.

On August 28, 1784, Lafayette and Caraman were once again on the road. Setting out from Mount Vernon, they were heading some four hundred miles due north to Fort Stanwix (also called Fort Schuyler), near Lake Ontario in what is now Rome, New York, to witness the signing of a treaty between the government of the United States and the Six Nations of the Iroquois Confederacy. With three appointed commissioners representing the interests of Congress, Lafayette had no official role in the proceedings, but he was eager to visit the Oneidas, whose young men had fought alongside him at the Battle of Barren Hill.

As Lafayette made his way through the mid-Atlantic region, his entourage grew. Future president James Madison, who was on a brief hiatus from public service, reported in a letter to Thomas Jefferson that he "fell in with the Marquis" at Baltimore and embraced the voyage as an opportunity to "gratify my curiosity in several respects." From Baltimore, the men set off by barge to Albany. There, they awaited the arrival of the Marquis de Barbé-Marbois, France's Philadelphia-based chargé d'affaires, whose diary offers a colorful chronicle of the group's westward journey from Albany to Fort Stanwix. A fifth man, a certain Demanche, served as an aide. Although neither rank nor position designated Lafayette the leader of his group, he overshadows all others in Barbé-Marbois's account, as even the weather played second fiddle to Lafayette's persona in Barbé-Marbois's telling. While the other members of the party bundled in cloaks and rugs to ward off the autumnal chill of central New York in late September and early October, Lafayette, the diplomat related, "seemed to be impervious to heat, cold, draught, humidity, and the inclemency of the seasons." His only protection was "an overcoat of gummed taffeta," in which he must have been a sight to behold. Evidently, the coat had been shipped from France packed "in newspapers that had stuck to the gum. There had been no time to pull them off, and the curious could read on his arm or his back the *Courrier de l'Europe* or the news from various places."

Lafayette insisted that the travelers' first stop be the settlement of Niskayuna, nestled deep in the woods near Albany. There, as Barbé-Marbois explains, Lafayette "wished to examine at firsthand phenomena that seemed very similar to those associated with Mesmer." Niskayuna had been established in 1779 by the celibate yet rapidly growing Protestant sect known as the United Society of Believers in Christ's Second Appearing—known colloquially as the Shakers. Lafayette was not disappointed. As he described them to Adrienne, the Shakers were "enthusiasts who go through incredible contortions and who claim to perform miracles, in which I have found some of the methods of magnetism."

According to Barbé-Marbois's journal, Lafayette and his friends reached Niskayuna on foot on a Sunday, and the sound of "slow, melancholy, but rather melodious music" greeted the approaching visitors, who found the Shakers "in the midst of their religious devotions." When the dancing and singing drew to a close, Lafayette set about the task he had come to perform: testing the powers of animal magnetism on one of the Shakers. An old man "of extreme simplicity" was selected for the honor, and Lafayette was soon "magnetizing him with all his power," but to no avail. The community looked on warily as Lafayette continued laying hands on the man, "trying without success the effects of magnetism on all his poles," until an elderly Shaker, presaging the question put to Dorothy in Oz, asked whether this exercise was being performed "in the name of a good spirit or of an evil spirit." So convincing was Lafayette in explaining the beneficent goals of mesmerism that the Shaker in question perceived an opportunity and attempted to convert the earnest Frenchman on the spot, hoping that Lafayette might proselytize for the community while spreading the good news about mesmerism. As Barbé-Marbois reports, "We were unable to shake him off until we left Niskayuna."

The next leg of the trip was an eighty-mile drive "across a superb" but war-torn landscape. Duties were divvied up equally: Lafayette looked after the horses, Caraman arranged lodgings, Madison served as navigator, and Barbé-Marbois "was the cook for the troop." Expecting provisions to be scarce, they had stocked their carriages with everything from cornmeal to chocolate, but the men wanted for nothing.

With Lafayette in their midst, "people gave us butter in abundance," reported Barbé-Marbois. "If we asked for milk, they brought it to us in great wooden pails." Children were eager to serve as human candlestick holders or fire screens, and fought for the privilege of turning the wooden spit on which the visitors roasted their meats.

Transportation, however, left much to be desired. After a few days' journey, Barbé-Marbois found that his phaeton carriage—lightweight, sporty, and prone to overturning—was no match for the treacherous roads and had to be abandoned. The last miles to Fort Stanwix were traversed on horseback, with stacks of blankets serving as makeshift saddles. Still, the company reached the assigned meeting place several days before the government commissioners were expected. Eager "to see the Indians in their villages, and to get acquainted with their customs," Lafayette and his companions set off once again. Here, they found the roads to be "really barbarous and wild" as they made their way on horseback, guided by Oneida scouts, through a dense forest whose only paths were chiefly intended for travel by foot. As Barbé-Marbois described it, the ground was "a muddy marsh, into which we sank at each step." They "traveled in dark and rainy weather" and "lost [their] way once" before finally emerging from the wood and crossing a series of "rivers by fording them, and sometimes by swimming our horses." At last, the company "arrived, very wet and very tired, in the territory of the Oneidas." Lafayette, as usual, offered a more upbeat version of events, describing his arrival as something of a homecoming. "My companions," he wrote to Adrienne from Fort Stanwix, "were quite surprised to find me as familiar with this country" as with the Faubourg St.-Germain.

Throughout the eighteenth century, Europeans—especially the French—were fascinated by Native American peoples and cultures. Few of the philosophers or scientists who wrote on the subject had traveled to the New World or encountered its indigenous inhabitants, but a lack of firsthand knowledge did not prevent them from citing the Indians to support their own theories about human nature. The eminent French naturalist the Comte de Buffon believed that Native Americans suffered from the "degeneration" that afflicted everything—plants, animals, people—subjected to the supposedly unhealthful conditions of the New World climate. The Abbé Raynal, who traveled in the circles of the forward-thinking men of letters who wrote and edited the *Ency-clopédie* and is believed to have cowritten his controversial *History of the Two Indies* with Diderot, espoused an opposing view. Raynal's description of the native peoples encountered by the French in Canada reads like a catalog of virtues associated with the "noble savage"—a term coined by the seventeenth-century English poet John Dryden. According to the *History,* native societies were marked by good faith, mutual respect, and selfless benevolence. Unspoiled by the vanity and artifice of Europe, the Canadian Indians were said to understand that nature created all men equal and to scorn "the respect that we have for titles, dignities, and especially hereditary nobility." Raynal, like many French authors, referred to these people as *sauvages,* but the Encyclopedists inflected the word with positive connotations absent from the English term "savage"; as the Chevalier de Jaucourt wrote, "One calls *sauvages* all the Indian peoples who are not subject to the yoke of the nation and who live apart. . . . Out of the way in the forests and mountains, they preserve their liberty."

Lafayette owned the works of Buffon and Raynal, as well as other books on the customs of the Native Americans, but his attitude toward these indigenous peoples was largely free from the judgments, either for or against, that issued from the scholars' pens. Instead, Lafayette gazed with ingenuous wonder upon people who, in his view, were so deeply connected to the American land he loved yet whose manners seemed so intensely foreign to him. Perhaps he felt a kinship with a people out of place in their own home. In memoirs drafted in 1780, Lafayette vividly described his first glimpse of a Native American assembly. He recalled seeing "five hundred men, women, and children, colored with paints and feathers, their ears pierced, their noses ornamented with jewels, and their nearly naked bodies marked with varied designs." Although he opined that "drunkenness" seemed to be an obstacle that the society had yet to overcome, he noted with approval that "as the old men smoked, they discoursed very well on politics." The sincerity with which Lafayette approached his hosts must have communicated across language barriers because, as he put it, the Iroquois "adopted" him "and gave him the name Kayewla, which had formerly been borne by one of their warriors." With a justifiable measure of pride, he noted that "whenever the army needed Indians or there was any business to be conducted with those tribes," the American leadership always turned to him for advice, counsel, and assistance.

Barbé-Marbois was less kindly disposed toward the Oneidas, in whom he perceived neither wisdom nor eloquence, yet he was moved by the realization that he was bearing witness to a vanishing way of life. He urged "Europeans who are curious to know" the Indians not to "lose time, for the advance of the European population is extremely rapid in this continent. . . . In a few centuries," he foretold, "when civilization will have extended its effects over all the world, people will be tempted to regard the reports of travelers as the ingenious dreams of a philosopher who is seeking the origin of society and is tracing the history of its advances from his imagination." In a particularly poetic passage, Barbé-Marbois envisioned the inevitable transformation of the landscape in upstate New York:

> In a century, and perhaps sooner, agriculture and commerce will give life to this savage desert. This rock will furnish stones to the city which will be built on the banks of that stream. There will be a bridge here and a quay there. Instead of this marsh there will be a public fountain; elegantly dressed ladies will stroll in the very place where I walk carefully for fear of rattlesnakes: it will be a public park, adorned with statues and fountains. A few ancient trees will be exhibited as the precious remains of the forest which to-day covers the mountain. I see already the square where the college, the academy, the house for the legislature, and the other public buildings will be placed.

As Barbé-Marbois predicted, it took far less than a hundred years for the region to be transformed. On July 4, 1817, a shovel thrust into the ground at Rome, New York, marked the beginning of the great construction project that produced the Erie Canal.

The landscape might not have shown it, but the Oneida world had been changing for some time. After decades of trading, negotiating, and warring with Europeans, many of the continent's native societies had fully incorporated foreign goods and customs into their more traditional ways of life. Barbé-Marbois noticed as much when his group arrived in the Oneida village. Entering the Council Hall, where the nation's chiefs and warriors were awaiting their guests, Barbé-Marbois recognized one of the "venerable leaders" as Great Grasshopper, who was attired in his finest regalia—"a Bavarian court hunting costume," received as a gift from the Chevalier de la Luzerne, "which he wears on all important occasions." When the meeting of the Great Council at Fort Stanwix began the following day, the forty men representing the region's native nations—Oneidas, Tuscaroras, Mohawks, Senecas, Cayugas, Onondagas, and more—appeared in costumes ranging from traditional capes made of untanned bearskin to the daintiest of embroidered European waistcoats. During the Revolutionary War, only the Oneidas and the Tuscaroras sided with the rebellious colonists, and many of their men distinguished themselves from members of the other nations by wearing belts, necklaces, and other accoutrements received from the Americans. Items given to them by Lafayette were particularly prized.

When the conference opened on October 3—a piercingly cold day—Lafayette was the first to address the assembly. Although he spoke in French, he underscored his respect and affection for local cultures by lacing his talk with references to figures and concepts gleaned from Iroquois lore. He thanked "the Great Manitou who has brought me to this spot of peace, where I find you all smoking the calumet of friendship" and praised the two nations that had joined with the Americans. Reprising the speech he had delivered six years earlier, Lafayette reiterated his promise that, if they allied with the Americans, "the great Onontio [the Indian name for the administrator of New France] like the sun will clear away the clouds which hang over your heads, and the schemes of your enemies will vanish like smoke."

Although Lafayette played no official role in the proceedings, his address became the centerpiece of the conference—much to the chagrin of his European and American colleagues. Over the course of two days, each of the chiefs replied in turn, referring to Lafayette as "our father," as the Iroquois had termed the French for at least a century, thanking him for his words and, in the case of the nations that had joined the English, apologizing for failing to heed his advice. Arthur Lee, one of the congressmen, complained to Madison "of the immoderate stress laid on the influence of the M." Apparently, Lee did not hesitate to tell Lafayette what he thought, but if he hoped to encourage Lafayette's departure, it was to no avail. Madison reported to Jefferson that Lafayette "was the only conspicuous figure" throughout the entire event, and that he had "eclipsed" the three commissioners from Congress. Trying to make sense of Lafayette's star turn, Madison offered a measured view of the marquis, writing, "I take him to be as amiable a man as his vanity will admit and as sincere an American as any Frenchman can be." Madison seems to have misconstrued Lafayette's enthusiasm as narcissism, but his assessment of Lafayette's French-American character was spot-on.

For his part, Lafayette was gratified by the warm welcome he received. Writing to Adrienne, he expressed surprise that his "personal credit with the *sauvages . . .* has proved to be much greater than I had imagined." "They made me great promises," he wrote, "and I love to think that I have contributed to a treaty that will give us a small stream of commerce and will ensure the tranquility of the Americans." Still, he was glad to be leaving his "little bark hut," which he found "about as comfortable as a taffeta suit in the month of January." On October 6, Lafayette and Caraman collected their belongings, bade good-bye to Barbé-Marbois and the others at the fort, and boarded a boat rowed by five men that was heading down the Mohawk River to Albany in weather that Lafayette described as "beautiful."

Lafayette and Caraman spent the next two months traveling as far north as New Hampshire and as far south as Virginia, visiting old friends, making new ones, and enjoying the banquets, balls, and receptions that sprang up wherever they went. Lafayette's travels were fueled, in large part, by nostalgia for his days in the army and curiosity about the nation he had helped create.

Interested though he was in the past and the present, Lafayette was also concerned about the future. One of his goals in coming to America had been to ensure the survival of his American reputation, and he attended to the matter with considerable care. Lafayette was well aware that the first histories of the American Revolution were being written even as he was being feted at a string of celebrations that had no precedent in the young country. Abigail Adams's friend Mercy Otis Warren was collecting the materials that would go into her *History of the Rise, Progress and Termination of the American Revolution* (1805); David Ramsay, a legislator from South Carolina, was doing the same for his *History of the American Revolution* (1789); and William Gordon, an irascible Massachusetts parson, was already well along in writing *The History of the Rise, Progress, and Establishment, of the Independence of the United States of America, Including an Account of the Late War; and of the Thirteen Colonies, from Their Origin to That Period* (1788).

Lafayette was most concerned about Gordon, and with good reason. Parson Gordon had already made enemies of men as eminent—and as different—as John Hancock and Alexander Hamilton. John Adams described him as "an eternal Talker, and somewhat vain, and not accurate nor judicious." Hoping to protect his own reputation from Gordon's injudicious pen, Lafayette asked James McHenry, his former aide-de-camp, to "recollect the train of his military proceedings and commit them to paper" and to forward the resulting text to Washington. Washington, in turn, was asked to send McHenry's thoughts to Gordon for inclusion in Gordon's *History*. Washington and Gordon enjoyed cordial relations of the sort that might facilitate the granting of favors; along with letters on the subject of the marquis, the men exchanged tulips, redbud trees, and other flowering plants, as part of a collective effort undertaken by many of the Founding Fathers to spread the vegetation of their respective regions throughout the new nation.

Yet even the promise of a magnolia tree from Virginia was insufficient to persuade Gordon to accept the memoir handcrafted by McHenry. "In certain places," complained Gordon, "the colouring is too strong." For instance, he refused to cast as particularly meritorious Lafayette's decision to abandon his planned incursion into Canada, observing that "it did not require the bold judgment of a most experienced general to relinquish" the project "when there were not the means of prosecuting it with any reasonable prospect of success." He was still less kind in his assessment of Lafayette's retreat at Barren Hill. Revealing, perhaps, a lack of military experience, Gordon insisted that "there was no great maneuvering in his extricating himself from the critical situation into which he had been brought." To this he added the unfounded assertion that Lafayette was partly to blame for his predicament because he had dropped "the night before the hint of his meaning to remain upon the spot till the next morning, and which was forwarded to the British commander." In defense of his unflattering words concerning Lafayette's actions at Barren Hill, Gordon cited General Knox, whose assessment of the retreat was that "here we were saved by pure providence without any interposition of our own." In the end, Barren Hill was not mentioned in Gordon's four-volume history. Whether because the author mellowed as he wrote the book or because Lafayette's fame grew too great to contest, Gordon's *History of the Rise, Progress, and Establishment, of the Independence of the United States of America* ultimately portrayed Lafayette as the hero he had become.

CHAPTER 10

AN "AMERICAN" NOBLEMAN IN PARIS

By the time Lafayette reached his mid-twenties, he had come out of his shell and fully embraced the extravagant lifestyle of a typical Parisian aristocrat. He was tremendously wealthy, and yet his expenditures grew so lavish that they outpaced his sizable income—a common predicament for men and women of his class, who routinely leveraged their assets to the hilt in order to maintain an appearance of limitless riches. Despite their devil-may-care demeanors, many Parisian nobles subsisted on a system of credit that was as complicated as it was shaky.

Lafayette's financial problems developed gradually, over a period of years. In 1782, his receipts still covered his outlays quite tidily. He was obliged to pay down substantial debt incurred during his American voyages, but his lands, investments, and inheritance brought in 224,743 livres, while his total expenses amounted to only 200,889 livres, leaving him a healthy surplus of 23,854 livres. By 1785, however, Lafayette was essentially breaking even, taking in just 845 livres more than he spent. And by June 1788, his finances were in a state of disarray; his annual income had shrunk to 115,381 livres, while his expenses remained nearly constant at 190,462, leaving a staggering deficit of 75,081 livres.

In a memo of June 30, 1788, Jacques-Philippe Grattepain-Morizot, the attorney who oversaw Lafayette's accounts, expressed alarm. Grattepain-Morizot acknowledged that some unnecessary expenses on the part of the household staff could be reined in, but he impressed upon Lafayette that even "the greatest surveillance" would never yield enough savings to balance such a lopsided budget. Instead, he insisted that the discipline required to reach "that happy state of affairs, in which one spends only what one takes in and transmits to one's children the property of their late father, can come only from you." Underscoring his point, Grattepain-Morizot produced a table featuring eight columns of flowing cursive script and carefully inked numerals that categorized Lafayette's expenses—salaries and pensions, merchants, household, children, and so on. Of the totals at the bottom of each column, the largest by far represented Lafayette's discretionary spending. Amounting to 52,284 livres, Lafayette's personal costs included such miscellany as a box at the opera (450 livres), subscriptions to publications (416 livres), and tailoring (3,215 livres). Taken together, these outlays exceeded the combined total of 49,208 livres that went to household expenses (domestic servants, linens, lighting, etc.), the children (their governess, clothing, smallpox inoculations, etc.), and Adrienne's personal needs. Lafayette's leisure activities necessitated ever greater expenditures on horses and carriages, including large sums, as Grattepain-Morizot observed, for maintenance due to Lafayette's frequent voyages and fondness for carriage races. The memo concluded by directing Lafayette's attention to a proposed austerity budget Grattepain-Morizot had drawn up, adamant that it "must commence tomorrow."

Lafayette's financial turmoil began, as is so often the case, with a real estate investment. On September 6, 1782, Lafayette reached the age of majority, finally enjoying unfettered access to his copious assets, and two months later he purchased the Left Bank town house on the Rue de Bourbon (the modern-day Rue de Lille) that he would make over entirely as his own. According to the sales contract, Lafayette paid 150,000 livres for the house and land, which stretched the length of a block, plus 50,000 livres for the furnishings, carved wood paneling, and decorations already in place. He then plowed 100,000 livres into renovations, bringing the total cost basis of the property to some 300,000 livres—an amount he raised by selling several income-producing properties, thus causing his revenues to plunge even as his expenses were growing.

Then, as now, location was all in matters of residential real estate, and Lafayette opted for a fashionable milieu quite distinct from the staid grandeur preferred by his in-laws. Whereas the Hôtel de Noailles stood on the Rue Saint-Honoré near the Tuileries Palace, Lafayette's house was located on the other side of the Seine in the stylish Faubourg Saint-Germain. Compared with the home he left behind, Lafayette's

Rue de Bourbon house was rather modest. Not only was the Hôtel de Noailles several times larger than Lafayette's town house, but the grandeur of its design both reflected and facilitated the family's high social aspirations. The Duc de Noailles had created a stir when he'd erected a barrier outside his front door; previously, such structures had marked only the entrances to the homes of princes of the blood. Indoors, too, the Duc de Noailles had mimicked the royal family by creating a formal bedroom for receiving guests. There, in a canopied bed divided from the rest of the room by an ornate railing, the host could recline in luxurious comfort while visitors were obliged to stand—although guests of sufficiently high rank might sit on stools placed on the other side of the balustrade.

The Noailles complex had grown up around a core that dated to 1453, but Lafayette's home had not even been built yet when the Turgot map of Paris—an enormous and remarkably detailed map published in atlas form—was created, between 1734 and 1739. Development in this part of the city was of such recent vintage that the Turgot map depicts construction sites and vacant lots on the blocks that would become Lafayette's neighborhood. The two areas also boasted very different political characters. The Noailleses, a family of courtiers, were situated a stone's throw from the Parisian center of royal power, but Lafayette's house was next door to the final home of the disgraced finance minister Anne-Robert-Jacques Turgot, who had purchased the building in 1779 after being exiled from Versailles and resided there until his death in 1781.

As Lafayette described it in a 1784 letter, his was "a house which, if not the most beautiful, is at least infinitely gracious." Like Turgot's, Lafayette's was one of eight built on the Rue de Bourbon by a single speculator, Pierre Salles, who used variations on a limited number of plans for all of the buildings he erected and sold in the 1730s and 1740s. Since its completion in 1744, Lafayette's house, like others funded by Salles's partnership, had functioned as a high-end rental. Three tenants in succession—all members of the nobility—had let the home from two different proprietors before Lafayette became its first owner-occupant. Although Lafayette's home was torn down in the early twentieth century, the Hôtel Turgot (as it is known) still stands between the Boulevard Saint-Germain and the Assemblée Nationale. It offers a sense of what Lafayette's home looked like, as both were built in a "horseshoe" arrangement framing a common entry court and were laid out in a very similar style. (The Hôtel Turgot, which was purchased by the renowned Dutch art historian Frits Lugt in the twentieth century, is now the location of the Fondation Custodia—one of the world's foremost collections of Old Master prints and drawings, assembled mostly by Lugt himself.)

Detail of the Turgot map of Paris, 1739. The Hôtel de Noailles is at the left, and the location of Lafayette's house is at the right.

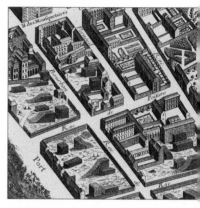

Detail of the Turgot map of Paris showing the empty lots where Lafayette's town house would be built.

The Hôtel de Noailles, located near the Tuileries and Louvre palaces on the Right Bank.

The Hôtel Turgot, built on the same plan as Lafayette's town house and still standing, on the Left Bank, adjacent to the site of Lafayette's home.

The building was large enough to accommodate Lafayette's family and household servants in a manner befitting their station, but compared with other homes in the area it was not out of the ordinary. The house's primary living quarters were distributed across two floors, with six rooms per floor, augmented by an *entresol* (partial balcony level), a *sous-sol* (basement), and an attic. Household servants had quarters in the attic, and additional servants were lodged in an outbuilding. The stables, too, were ample, but while it was certainly a luxury to maintain the fifteen horses and four carriages they could hold, nearby homes erected by the same developer accommodated as many as twenty horses and five carriages.

Conceived as just one building among many in the developer's plan, Lafayette's town house grew increasingly distinct in the 1780s as it came to embody its owner's character and ideals. From the architect who renovated the building to the furnishings that filled it, the home enhanced Lafayette's reputation as America's foremost French ally. Lafayette may well have been introduced to his architect, Adrien Mouton, through a Noailles relative, but the choice had symbolic resonance. As a student at the French Royal Academy of Architecture in the 1760s, Mouton had become a voice for religious freedom. Having won the Rome Prize, which enabled budding architects to study the great monuments of the Eternal City as guests of the French state, Mouton saw his sojourn in Italy cut short in 1767 when, at Eastertime, he refused to submit proof that his confession had been heard by a Catholic priest. Back in France, Mouton filed a lawsuit against the director of the French Academy in Rome, the painter Charles-Joseph Natoire, who responded that "it is necessary to smother in its cradle the progress of this cabal . . . which desires nothing but independence in every respect." When Mouton received a settlement of 20,000 livres, he struck a blow against religious persecution.

By the time Lafayette selected his architect, the cause of religious tolerance had grown increasingly dear to his heart. Lafayette had made many Protestant friends during his time in America and had come to abhor the intolerance that France's nominally Catholic government exhibited toward other Christian denominations. In 1785, he made his own small contribution to the cause when he returned to Paris in the company of John Edwards Caldwell, a fourteen-year-old boy from Elizabeth, New Jersey, whose father, the Reverend James Caldwell, had died during the war—"barbarously murdered by the British," as John

Quincy Adams put it. Lafayette placed Caldwell in a French boarding school, where he obtained a special dispensation releasing the Protestant student from the requirement of attending Catholic services. And in 1787, when Lafayette was selected by the French crown to authorize a set of government reforms—an event that became a precursor to revolution—Protestant rights became one of the first causes he championed.

American values were most fully on display in the rooms that Lafayette considered truly his own—the *grand cabinet* and its adjoining library. Here, Lafayette spent time alone, reading and writing, or welcomed visitors to discuss matters of state and other sober concerns. In keeping with its intimate function, the *cabinet* was relatively modest in size, but two windows leading out to a small balcony must have created an appearance of spaciousness, which would have been enhanced by three large mirrors: one mounted above the fireplace, a second directly opposite, and a third between the windows.

These spaces were filled with opulent French furniture that hinted at republican idealism. Throughout the 1780s, one of Lafayette's favorite furniture makers was the Luxembourg-born Bernard Molitor, a technically skilled and aesthetically forward-looking craftsman at the top of his profession. With his home and workshop on the Rue de Bourbon, Molitor was Lafayette's neighbor and worked for many families in Lafayette's courtly and military circles. Molitor's neoclassical style—all straight lines, with ornamentation limited to a decorative grammar borrowed from ancient Greece and Rome—was widely associated with the virtues of the ancient republics and was all the rage in the fashionable circles of Paris and Versailles.

For Lafayette's home, Molitor and other craftsmen created tables, shelves, and boxes made from the most expensive materials and constructed with the greatest care. When Lafayette's possessions were seized and sold by government order amid the tumult of the French Revolution in the 1790s, one of the items removed from the town house was a "mahogany bookcase," presumably from the library, deemed to be of such merit that it was selected for the national collection. The appraisers also noted a "mahogany *guéridon*" (a small, round table supported by a pedestal in a form inspired by antiquity) "with a white marble top," which sold for 130 livres in 1795, and a two-piece set—a "*secrétaire* surmounted by a file cabinet" and an "armoire in mahogany and decorated with gilded leather"—that together sold for 810 livres.

Lafayette clearly devoted thought to the furnishings of his *cabinet* and its surroundings, which he described in several letters as showcases for all things American. Writing from Mount Vernon in August 1784, he told Adrienne that "the true Cincinnatus" had inspired him to consider how the room should be furnished. Two months later, he reported to Adrienne from Church's Tavern, near Hartford, Connecticut, that "I have discovered here a climbing plant, always green, that will yield a marvelous effect on the two walls of our terrace. When it reaches you, I ask you to please seed it and to plant a large quantity."

Decorating the room with American mementos had been on Lafayette's mind even before he set off on his 1784 journey. On November 19, 1783, he had jotted a quick note to William Temple Franklin, the grandson and secretary of France's favorite American, expressing a desire to own a copy of the new nation's founding document. As Lafayette explained, "The object of my having a declaration of independence is to have it engraved in golden letters as the most conspicuous part of my *cabinet,* and when I wish to put myself in spirits, I will look at it, and most voluptuously read it over." He hoped that Temple would be able to "procure it for me, printed if you can, in order that a French workman may be less apt to make blunders." Lafayette admired the declaration as an inspiring document that embodied essential principles of liberty, equality, and fundamental human rights, but in his *cabinet,* paradoxically, visitors would encounter it in the deluxe form of a gold-plated curiosity. The display was a heartfelt ode to America that could have been conceived only by a Parisian nobleman.

The social hub of the Lafayette household was an airy, oval salon on the ground floor featuring three curved French doors that opened onto a garden. Light streaming through the doors' clear glass panes would have bounced among four large mirrors, each measuring more than seven and a half feet in height. During evening gatherings, when the only illumination came from candles and a fireplace, these broad expanses of silvered glass would have animated the room with flickering reflections, allowing everyone present to keep an eye on the whole assembly by casting discreet glances at the nearest mirror.

Lafayette and Adrienne spent many hours in this well-appointed salon hosting the American dignitaries who became regular visitors to the Rue de Bourbon. Accounts of afternoons and evenings spent in the company of the Lafayette family recur throughout the correspondence of the Adamses, the Jeffersons, the Jays, and others sent to Paris by the United States government in the 1780s. English was the language of choice at these gatherings, where Lafayette's two older children—Anastasie and George Washington Lafayette—were always introduced to the guests and sometimes entertained them with songs in the foreign tongue. So established did these "American dinners" become that Lafayette ordered invitations preprinted in English: "The Marquis de la Fayette has the Honor to present his Compliments to [blank] and begs the favor of his Company at Dinner on Monday next [date]." Dozens of these small cards are scattered among the copious papers Benjamin Franklin left behind at his death.

So un-French was mealtime chez Lafayette that even Abigail Adams, whose strict New England sensibilities inclined her to disdain the Parisian "life of ceremony and parade," felt at home there. Colonel William Stephens Smith, the husband of Abigail Adams Smith, similarly approved. After dining with Lafayette on April 29, 1787, he wrote to his wife that the "dinner was so perfectly to my taste that I must give you a small sketch of it." "There were only us two," he continued. "The table was laid with great neatness. By the side of each was fixed, (I'll call it) a dumb waiter. On which was placed half a dozen clean plates, knives and forks, and a small bell in the one near the Marquis, and the servants retired. The first course being over, he rung the bell and it was removed for the second. Thus we spent an hour and a half with great ease and friendship; not incommoding the servants, nor being subject to their inspection."

Just as Colonel Smith was taken by Lafayette's unprepossessing nature, the Adams women repeatedly commented on the virtues they saw in Adrienne. Abigail remarked, "I should always take pleasure in her company. She is a good and amiable Lady, exceedingly fond of her Children and attentive to their education, passionately attached to her Husband!!!" So startling was this last trait that Abigail thought it worth repeating—"A French Lady and fond of her Husband!!!" The Adamses' daughter, also named Abigail, was similarly touched by Adrienne's maternal qualities. After one dinner with the Lafayette family, she observed that "the fondness that Madame la Marquise discovers for her children, is very amiable; and the more remarkable in a country where the least trait of such a disposition is scarce known. She seems to adore them, and to live but in them." Although the Adams women counted Adrienne's company among the few features of Paris they would regret leaving behind, each hinted that there may have been something excessive in the family's Americanization. The younger Abigail mused on the all-American dinners held chez Lafayette. "It was intended as a compliment," she recognized, "but I had rather it had been thought so to introduce us to French company." As the Adamses readied for their journey to England, her incisive mother noted, "I shall lose part, and the greatest part of American intelligence by quitting France; for no person is so well informed from all the States as the Marquis de la Fayette."

In one case, unfortunately, Lafayette's enthusiasm for filling his house with American memories seems to have come at considerable cost to another person's well-being. The person in question was Peter Otsiquette, the son of a French father and an Oneida mother, who went to live with Lafayette "as a favourite Servant" at the age of nineteen, in 1786. Lafayette's first allusion to Otsiquette (whom he generally called "Otchikeita") came in a 1784 letter to Adrienne. Writing from Oneida territory, Lafayette confided, "I might well bring back a young Iroquois *sauvage:* but this negotiation is not yet complete." Lafayette and his companions saw nothing unusual in the request—since the seventeenth century, missionaries had been sending Native American boys to France to be educated—and were surprised to discover that all of Otsiquette's family had to be consulted before any arrangements could be made. Barbé-Marbois noted "the difficulty that M. le M[arqu]is de La Fayette had in procuring a *sauvage* companion. Even though the Oneidas have the greatest affection for him, they had infinite difficulty obtaining permission for him to take one of their young people to France." The matter must have been resolved by April 1785, when Lafayette wrote to the Connecticut merchant Jeremiah Wadsworth that "the whole family who are Oneidas, consented to his coming with me—and I would be much obliged to you . . . to forward the Young Indian's departure by the October packet."

Otsiquette was half French, but in France, he was defined by his Oneida heritage. Among the thousands of pieces of paper discovered by Lafayette's descendant René de Chambrun in the Château de La Grange in 1956 are a handful of small receipts listing an array of fabric and clothing purchased from the Paris boutique of Godin, l'Aîné. Godin's shop regularly provided clothing for the Lafayette children and, occasionally, for the marquis himself, but on October 9, 1786, the merchant charged Lafayette's account for two black taffeta cravats intended, according to the receipt, to be worn by *"le sauvage."* On November 4, a black silk cravat and four blue handkerchiefs with red borders were added to the tab, and identified in the same way. These purchases were for European-style clothing, but a German officer who visited Lafayette in January 1787 described the man who served as Lafayette's page as "a *sauvage* from America, dressed according to his custom." John Ledyard, a Connecticut-born explorer who was a frequent guest at Lafayette's house, and a frequent beneficiary of his largesse, observed that summer that "the Marquis, at much expense, equipped [Otsiquette] in rich Indian dresses."

An especially colorful description of Otsiquette's traditional dress comes from the memoirs of the Comte de Neuilly, who was a child in the 1780s. Neuilly remembered attending a ball honoring Lafayette at the home of Adrienne's aunt the Comtesse de Tessé, which Lafayette arrived at in the company of "a *sauvage* whom he had brought from America: a real tamed animal [*"une vraie bête apprivoisée"*] with a ring in his nose, a feathered headdress on his head, a bone placed so as to hang from the ear; legs and arms tattooed: his entire costume consisted of a belt of feathers over a flesh-colored tunic." Neuilly recalled being terrified at first by the "scalp dance" performed by the visitor, who kept time with a song by slicing the air with a tomahawk. Caraman entered into the spirit and joined in the dance, as did Neuilly, who, with a bit of encouragement from Lafayette, eventually found his nerve.

Command performances by natives of the New World had a long history in Europe, where travelers to distant lands sometimes brought back indigenous people—usually young men—to stay with them for a few weeks or a few years. In London, the 1710 visit of "Four Iroquois Kings," as they were called, occasioned endless festivities as locals followed the exotic guests through the streets and marveled at their every move. The most famous visitor in Lafayette's memory was undoubtedly the man known as Mai, who traveled to London from the South Sea Islands with the explorer Captain James Cook and lived in the home of the naturalist Joseph Banks from 1774 to 1776. For two years, Mai visited with the English elite and became the subject of paintings, prints, and newspaper articles, as well as the catalyst for debates on matters ranging from imperial policy to the relative merits of "civilization." To Lafayette's credit, he seems not to have allowed Otsiquette to become a public spectacle; we have no images of the youth, who apparently attracted little notice in Paris outside of Lafayette's family circle.

Upon his return to America, however, Otsiquette's connection to

Lafayette earned him wide acclaim. His arrival on the *Cato* in late July 1788 was reported in American papers from Maine to Pennsylvania, and those who met him that summer were impressed with the social skills and physical dexterity he had acquired in France. Sometimes, however, the precise circumstance of his journey became distorted in the telling, as at least two newspapers reported that "this young aboriginal was sent for to Paris by that benevolent nobleman the Marquis de la Fayette, for the purpose of receiving the first principles of an European education." Before going to France, readers were told, Otsiquette was "wholly in a rude and uncultivated state," but he returned with "his manners elegant and refined, and his genius quick and penetrating." One young woman who had the good fortune to dance with Otsiquette at a soirée in Providence wrote in her journal that Otsiquette had been dressed in the height of French style, wearing "a scarlet coat trimmed with gold lace," and that his skill at dancing a cotillion was "by far the best of any person I ever saw attempt it." Evidently, Otsiquette had also obliged his audience by performing a "war dance" for the assembled Rhode Islanders— creating a spectacle that they, like the young Neuilly, deemed "terrible."

The Oneidas, too, apparently held Otsiquette in high regard. In March 1792, he was among the Iroquois leaders who traveled to Philadelphia for an audience with President Adams. Tragically, he died during that visit; he was buried with military honors. Once again, Otsiquette's name spread throughout the American press. Some reported that Otsiquette had died of pleurisy, but others believed that the still young man had drunk himself to death. Francis Adrian Van der Kemp, a Dutch patriot who had immigrated to upstate New York, suggested in a letter to a friend that Otsiquette had returned from Paris "highly cultivated and master of the French language and politeness, although it was doubted if his heart was as improved as his head." Otsiquette's death prompted Van der Kemp, a deeply religious man, to ponder the ethics of European involvement with Native American peoples. Taking a bold stance for his time, Van der Kemp wrote, "It may be justly questioned if the vicinity of their white neighbors is to them not rather a curse than a blessing. How contrary is this with the genuine spirit of Christianity."

For all of his Americanization, Lafayette remained a Frenchman through and through in one realm of his life: although he and Adrienne shared a deep bond of affection—one that grew even stronger in times of trial—Lafayette was known to enjoy the favors of women other than his wife, and to do so quite openly. The subject has traditionally been a sensitive one for Lafayette's biographers, some of whom may have seen marital infidelity as an unwelcome blemish on the man's otherwise admirable character. As the late Louis Gottschalk recounted, his discovery of a love letter to a mysterious "Aglaé" ignited a "friendly controversy" among Lafayette scholars in the 1930s. Gottschalk's insistence that Aglaé was not, in fact, a pet name for the marquise met with opposition from a group of devotees, who would "entertain no doubt of Gilbert's constant fidelity to his Adrienne." But in the arranged marriages of the eighteenth-century French nobility, blissful monogamy was almost unheard of, and Lafayette was a man of his time.

Lafayette recalled his early dalliances as mere peccadilloes. So unexceptional did they seem to him that he mentioned them in the third paragraph of the memoirs he sent to the American historian Jared Sparks in 1828:

> I shall spare you also the confession of an unedifying youth, and even of the story of two romances dedicated to beauties who were then very celebrated, in which my head had a larger part than my heart. The first, scarcely begun, broke against the obstacles of jealousy with which I collided head-on. The other—in which I wanted at first to triumph less over the object herself than over a rival—I pursued, despite long interruptions, on every possible occasion. Our relationship went from esteem all the way to the contrary sentiment, and was finally terminated by a catastrophe unconnected with me. It is more pleasant for me to speak of the tender and stable affection that I never cease to feel for the woman whom I had the good fortune to marry.

Gottschalk's Aglaé, Aglaé de Barbantane, Comtesse d'Hunolstein, seems to have been the first of the two women mentioned by Lafayette. Aglaé, a young woman of about Lafayette's age, served as a lady-in-waiting to the Duchesse de Chartres in the 1770s and socialized in the circles of the Vicomte de Noailles. It was in this milieu that she and Lafayette met in 1776, before Lafayette joined the American army. At the time, she was reputed to be the mistress of the rakish Duc de

Chartres—her employer's husband—although Lafayette seems to have believed that his friend Ségur was his rival for Aglaé's affections. She is presumed to be the unnamed lady over whom Lafayette challenged Ségur to a duel.

Lafayette failed to make an impression on Aglaé before he went to America, but his heroic exploits turned her head. By the time he'd returned as one of the heroes of Yorktown, his name and Aglaé's were frequently being whispered in the same breath. They were enmeshed in a full-fledged lovers' quarrel when Lafayette wrote Gottschalk's telltale letter on March 27, 1783. "You are too cruel, my dear Aglaé," it begins. "You know the torments of my heart, you know that it is torn between love and duty, and you demand that it take a stand on this unhappy matter." Heated though it is, this rhetoric must not have been new: "It has been more than a year since you tried to break this tie," Lafayette complained. "Every day you redoubled your efforts. . . . Now you take one last approach; it's the cruelest one for me, but the only one that may succeed. The only question is whether I am an honest man."

In the end, it's not clear whether Aglaé broke the tie or whether it was broken for her. We know that she was dismissed from the Chartres household and entered a convent in the city of Nancy, in eastern France, where she remained until the French Revolution abolished religious orders. The author Stéphanie Félicité, Comtesse de Genlis, who served as tutor to the children of the Duc de Chartres and succeeded Aglaé as his mistress, had no personal fondness for her banished predecessor, yet she reported that Aglaé underwent a true conversion, embracing her Catholic faith and living an exemplary life marked by austerity and charity.

By the time Lafayette parted ways with Aglaé, his attention had drifted to the second woman referenced in his letter to Sparks—Diane-Adélaïde de Damas d'Antiguy, Comtesse de Simiane, a lady-in-waiting to the Comtesse de Provence. Gottschalk observed that Lafayette was already praising Madame de Simiane as "pretty" and "amiable" in a letter to his friend the Prince de Poix on January 13, 1783. And the celebrated painter Élisabeth Vigée-LeBrun, writing in her memoirs in the early nineteenth century, recalled Lafayette visiting her studio in 1783 "just to see the portrait that I was making of the pretty Madame de Simiane, to whom, it was said, he was paying court." With a mixture of admiration and surprise, Vigée-LeBrun, a staunch monarchist who had

Élisabeth Vigée-LeBrun, portraitist to Marie
Antoinette, was working on the *Portrait of
Diane-Adélaïde de Damas d'Antiguy, Comtesse
de Simiane,* in 1783, while Lafayette was
courting the comtesse.

been a favorite portraitist to Marie Antoinette, added that Lafayette's
"tone, his manners, had a great deal of nobility, and did not in the
least suggest revolutionary tastes." Coming from Vigée-LeBrun, this
was meant as high praise.

In telling Sparks that this second affair had terminated in "a catastrophe unconnected with me," Lafayette was not being entirely truth-
ful. On March 14, 1787, the *Mémoires secrets* reported, "Rumor has it
that Monsieur the Comte de Simiane, husband of the renowned beauty
Madame de Simiane . . . killed himself a few days ago in a fit of jealousy
over the Marquis de Lafayette." Despite the gossip, the tragedy did not
put an end to the relationship. By all accounts Madame de Simiane
remained, at the very least, one of his closest confidantes for many
decades to come.

PART THREE

FRENCH REFORMER

CHAPTER 11

A POLITICAL EDUCATION

Never did Lafayette express kinder words for Louis XVI or greater optimism about France's future than in the letter he wrote to George Washington on January 13, 1787. The cause of Lafayette's enthusiasm was a royal decree that, as he put it, promised to influence "the Happiness of 26 millions of People." To address the problem of a grossly imbalanced budget, the French king had decided to convene "an Assembly of Notables" consisting of 144 men—"ArchBishops, Bishops, Nobles, presidents of the Several parliaments, Mayors of towns," and other "principal men" selected from every corner of the realm. The dignitaries would gather in February to conduct "an Examination of the finances to Be adjusted, of the Means to alleviate the taxes of the people, and of Many abuses to Be Redressed." Lafayette blamed the crown for France's fiscal woes, pointing to "the sums squandered on Courtiers and Superfluities," yet he believed that Louis XVI was taking honorable steps to make matters right. As Lafayette wrote to Washington, "There Was no Way more patriotic, more Candid, more Noble to Effect those purposes. The King and M. de Calonne His [Finance] Minister deserve Great Credit for that. And I Hope a tribute of Gratitude and Good Will shall Reward this popular Measure."

As pleased as he was for the nation, Lafayette was also happy for himself. For the first time in his life, he had been accorded a measure of influence over France's domestic affairs. All members of the assembly had been handpicked by the government—Lafayette was one of thirty-six men chosen from the ranks of the nobility (known as the "Second Estate" in the social order of the day), with the remaining slots filled by members of the clergy ("First Estate") and the nation's wealthiest and most influential commoners ("Third Estate"). Lafayette saw his selection as more than simply an honor: it was an opportunity to introduce into France some of the liberal social and economic measures he had first encountered in the United States. He had come to consider such reforms both just and necessary if France hoped to keep pace in a rapidly changing world. Itemizing his goals, Lafayette wrote to Washington:

> My Earnest Wish, and fond Hope is that our Meeting will produce popular Assemblies in the provinces, the destruction of Many Shackles of the trade, and a change in the fate of the protestants, Events which I will promote By my friends as well as my feeble endeavours with all my Heart.

In retrospect, Lafayette's envisioned reforms were modest compared with the changes that the larger forces of history would soon bring about in France. But Lafayette, who had never imagined that the foundation of his ancient homeland would soon be shaken to the core, could hardly have known that he was about to participate in a transformation so momentous that it has been termed the "French Prerevolution."

For a time, it was not at all clear that Lafayette would be invited to the Assembly of Notables; his name appeared on an early list of participants, vanished from a second version, and then reappeared on the final roster. The crown never explained the vacillation, but the task of selecting the notables was certainly a delicate one. It was in the government's interest to choose men who would be docile enough to sign off on the king's proposed reforms while appearing sufficiently independent to withstand charges of blind subservience. Clearly, Lafayette's name had raised flags. But why? Had the royal ministers feared that Lafayette, the celebrated friend of the American republic, might add a dangerously radical voice to the proceedings? Or was Lafayette, who had been working closely with the king's advisers on American dealings, perceived to be so closely tied to the interests of the monarchy that he would be more puppet than participant? In other words: Was he too safe? Or was he not safe enough?

Both theories were floated by Lafayette's contemporaries, whose interpretations tended to break down along national lines. Thomas Jefferson, who had replaced Franklin as America's Minister Plenipotentiary to France in 1785, saw in Lafayette living proof that the Old

World could learn important lessons from the New. Jefferson believed that Lafayette's republican tendencies must have rendered the Americanized marquis persona non grata in a court "whose principles are the most absolute despotism." As Jefferson explained to his fellow Virginian Edward Carrington, Lafayette's "education in our school has drawn on him a very jealous eye." Jefferson did not blame Louis XVI. He insisted that "the king, who is a good man, is favorably disposed towards [Lafayette]." But he implied that the court's most conservative faction—which was headed by the Comte d'Artois, a former classmate of Lafayette's from the Académie de Versailles—might fear that Lafayette, an experienced general who was "supported by powerful family connections, and by the public good will," could wield undue power and use it to push for reforms, if not more.

A very different account of Lafayette's temporary exclusion from the assembly appeared in the *Mémoires secrets,* which harbored profound doubts about the entire project. In a summary guide to the notables published the day before the assembly convened, the newsletter assessed each member's potential to make a genuine contribution. Lafayette did not come off well. The guide dismissed Lafayette with harsh words that were rendered all the more damning by their telegraphic style: "Having a mild and timid character, uneducated; not much is to be expected." Worse than ineffective, Lafayette was said to be in the pocket of Charles-Alexandre de Calonne, the finance minister, who masterminded the assembly. "Coached by the Noailleses," the *Mémoires secrets* predicted, "he will be counseled to be on the side of the court and not to compromise." According to this logic, neither animosity nor fear led to Lafayette's omission from the notables. Rather, Lafayette was excluded on the solid grounds that he "was very young"—he was, in fact, younger than all but one of the notables—and "that he had not demonstrated any knowledge of administration, that he held no office that would entitle him to be called to this Assembly." The author reported that Calonne had, in the end, praised Lafayette's "commendable character" and agreed to propose his name to the king. In return for the favor, Lafayette was said to have promised "zeal and submission," not to the American principles endorsed by Jefferson but to whatever plans might be hatched by the royal ministry.

The truth was probably somewhere in between. Lafayette was all but certain to participate with zeal, but accepting the role of a pawn—for the sake of a king or anyone else—was not in his character. Iconoclastic in his views and spirited in the pursuit of his goals, Lafayette was not easily swayed on any topic, and he may simply have been considered too much of a loose cannon for the government to trust him. If the monarch expected quick affirmation of plans already devised, Lafayette could be trouble.

At ten o'clock in the morning on February 22, 1787, Lafayette and the other notables filed into a vast meeting hall erected in the courtyard of the Hôtel des Menus Plaisirs du Roi—the bureau of the "King's diversions"—in the town of Versailles. Measuring 120 feet long by 100 feet wide, the hangar dwarfed the men who gathered beneath its coffered ceilings. The space had been used as a warehouse for storing the piles of furniture and props constantly churned out for the lavish festivities that punctuated court life, but it had been transformed so thoroughly for the occasion that it was barely recognizable. Now every nook and cranny overflowed with symbols of the monarchy: niches held orbs covered with fleurs-de-lis; walls and seats were cloaked in tapestries produced in royal manufactories; and, at the far end of the room, the king's throne towered above the scene, surmounted by a richly decorated canopy of purple fabric. These silent signals reminded the notables that they were guests of the king, serving at his pleasure.

In retrospect, a less charged locale might have been a better choice for a meeting intended to address a budget crisis. The Menus Plaisirs

Meeting room of the Assembly of Notables constructed at Versailles. 1787.

had earned a reputation as the epicenter of extravagant spending. In 1781, Louis-Sébastien Mercier had criticized the bureau, writing that "any frugal-minded citizen must deplore the waste of time and good money upon ceremonies and shows." While the hall was being readied for the arrival of the notables, the *Mémoires secrets* waxed indignant that the king, unsatisfied with any of the existing spaces within the enormous expanse of Versailles, had seen fit to transform a warehouse into an assembly hall; the government, opined the newsletter, had opened an austerity meeting by "tossing several millions out the window for a vain and ephemeral ceremony." This was a monarchy famously tone-deaf to matters of public image, and the assembly would be asked to ponder the nation's fiscal woes in a setting that reeked of profligacy.

Inside the chamber, clusters of long, backless benches were arranged on two levels, with every notable assigned a seat. Lafayette sat at the periphery of the upper level, where he looked out on a sea of costumed dignitaries: clergymen wore cassocks surmounted by long tunics of white linen; noblemen dressed in suits complemented by lace cravats, velvet capes, and plumed hats; members of the legal profession appeared in black robes and square hats; and others sported garb befitting their respective stations. The king's bodyguard stood at attention, ceremonial weaponry in hand, and officers of the chancellery, representing the judicial system, silently asserted the king's power over the law by assuming kneeling poses on the dais. Shortly after eleven o'clock, all stood to witness the arrival of heralds, princes, dukes, captains of the guard, high-ranking members of the royal household, the ever important comptroller of finances, Charles-Alexandre de Calonne, and, of course, the king.

Louis XVI strode across a fleur-de-lis-patterned carpet, climbed two steps to the dais indicating his position of honor, then sat down in a duly appointed throne. "Gentlemen," he began, "I have chosen you from among the various orders of the state, and have gathered you around me to inform you of my plans." As Louis described his intentions, they seemed very much in line with those articulated by Lafayette. The king said his aim was to "improve the nation's revenues" through a series of changes that would place France in the vanguard of free trade. He would institute a more equitable system of taxation, "liberate commerce from the obstacles that have impeded circulation," and, in the end, "bring relief . . . to the most indigent of my subjects."

Taking up no more than twenty minutes, the speech was as vague as it was brief. And it was the last the notables heard from the king for some time.

This was to be Calonne's show. It was he who presented a set of six detailed proposals in the king's absence on February 23 and then shepherded these proposals through the assembly. No one thought he would encounter much resistance. Not only had each member been carefully vetted, but the proceedings had been structured to maximize royal control. The notables gathered en masse only for a handful of formal presentations, and they would have no opportunity to raise questions or voice opinions while in the large group. All deliberations would be conducted within the confines of seven "bureaus," each containing about twenty members. Every notable was assigned to a bureau, and every bureau was led by a prince of the blood. It was surely not an accident that Lafayette was placed in the second bureau, where he would work directly under the watchful eye of the Comte d'Artois, one of Calonne's closest and most powerful allies.

The government appeared to be so firmly in control of the Assembly of Notables that Lafayette and his colleagues were widely disparaged as little more than pawns, and all of Paris enjoyed a good laugh at their expense. Within weeks of the assembly's convocation, authors of satirical verses and unflattering prints were outdoing each other with witty

"The Court's Buffet." A 1787 caricature of the Assembly of Notables.

variations on the theme. In one caricature the members of the assembly were portrayed as a bevy of gullible fowl, lined up like hungry diners waiting to be called to their tables at "The Court's Buffet," supervised by chef Calonne. Perched behind a wooden podium, an officious monkey–cum–maître d' informs the misguided flock, "I have gathered you here to learn with which sauce you want to be eaten." On a sideboard seen at the left of the print, a roasted bird served up on a platter foreshadows the birds' collective fate. So widespread was the ridicule that Jefferson opined to Abigail Adams that "the most remarkable effect of this convention as yet is the number of puns and bon mots it has generated. I think were they all collected it would make a more voluminous work than the Encyclopédie." Jefferson's observation was apt, but the conclusion he drew was mistaken; underestimating the staying power of the French, Jefferson predicted "that a good punster would disarm the whole nation were they ever so seriously disposed to revolt."

Neither the jesting nor the cynicism seemed to trouble Lafayette, who had joined the assembly in a spirit of goodwill. He entered its deliberations prepared to listen, learn, and negotiate, and for a few weeks at least, his trust seemed to be well placed. The politically savvy Calonne had placed a popular proposition—the formation of local assemblies—at the top of the notables' agenda. His suggestion was that representative bodies, elected by and constituted of local landholders, be established throughout the nation at municipal, district, and provincial levels. Accorded no real legislative powers, these councils would serve as vehicles for expressing collective concerns and, in limited cases, for managing regional affairs. After less than a week of debate, twenty of the second bureau's twenty-two members supported the idea, as did similar majorities in the other bureaus. Lafayette responded with exuberance, averring that local assemblies would offer "the greatest benefit that could come from the justice and the goodness of the King."

This is not to say that Lafayette stood with the crown on every particular—he would have preferred provincial bodies that were stronger and more broadly representative than those the crown proposed, and he suggested a number of changes with such goals in mind. Joining with the majority of the second bureau, he argued that the provincial bodies needed greater powers if they were to have any chance of withstanding the "baneful authority" of the provinces' government-appointed intendants. On the question of voter qualifications, Lafayette and four other members of his bureau advocated a lower standard than the government suggested: instead of requiring an annual income of 600 livres, Lafayette's group called for a minimum income of 100 livres. Lafayette also objected to the notion that larger incomes should translate into more votes.

Of all the amendments Lafayette supported, the most surprising is also the most revealing: Lafayette believed that the provincial assemblies should grant the clergy and the nobility more authority than commoners. He and his like-minded colleagues would have permitted only members of the First and Second Estates to serve as president of any of the provincial bodies; commoners (the Third Estate) would be barred from the office. Furthermore, Lafayette wanted to see a cap that would limit the proportion of commoners—who constituted some 95 percent of the population—to no more than two-thirds of any provincial assembly. In contrast, the royal ministers planned to open membership and offices in the new provincial assemblies to all eligible voters regardless of their social standing.

To the modern eye, Lafayette's position might seem counterintuitive—America's staunchest French advocate came out in favor of political distinctions based on social class. But while the government seemed to be proposing an egalitarian system, Lafayette and many of his colleagues interpreted things differently. The majority of the second bureau saw the crown attempting to grab power by wresting control from the traditional leaders of each region. To be sure, the notables, who were drawn disproportionately from the ranks of the first two estates, were motivated in part by a desire to preserve their own power. But more than self-interest was at stake. Lafayette and many of his fellow notables believed that France's system of estates served as a bulwark against despotism, ensuring the nation's freedom by limiting the authority of the king.

This was also the logic expounded by the influential political theorist Charles-Louis de Secondat, Baron de Montesquieu, whose 1748 treatise *The Spirit of the Laws* argued that "the most natural intermediate subordinate power is that of the nobility. It is in a sense the essence of monarchy, whose fundamental maxim is: no monarch, no nobility; no nobility, no monarch; but there is a despot." Lafayette owned the complete works of Montesquieu and heard much talk of them from Étienne-Charles de Loménie de Brienne, the archbishop of Toulouse, who served as a kind of mentor among the notables. During the assembly, Brienne summed up the vital position of the so-called landed estates—the nobility and clergy: they served at once as "the people's defense and the monarchy's support." Privileging freedom over equality, Brienne insisted that "the distinctions among citizens are necessary for royal dignity, for the proper order of the state, and even for public liberty."

The matter of provincial assemblies was settled relatively amicably, with the notables assenting to most of the government's desires, but Calonne's second proposal led to a veritable insurrection. The crown planned to tame the deficit by imposing a new land tax but offered none of the traditional exemptions. Such a tax would have fallen disproportionately on the First and Second Estates, who were not willing to give in without a fight.

At the heart of the notables' objections was the fact that no one could calculate the size of the deficit with any certainty. On February 22, in a speech that managed to be simultaneously long, tedious, and unclear, Calonne had pegged the deficit at 80 million livres. Less than two weeks later, he acknowledged that the shortfall was 114 million livres. Confused and mistrusting, the bureaus attempted their own audits, yielding an even wider range of estimates, some of which dwarfed Calonne's worst scenarios. By mid-March, the bureaus' frustrations were starting to boil over. How, asked the notables, could they approve new taxes without knowing whether taxes would help to balance the budget?

The government's dismal financial situation might have raised eyebrows under any circumstances but was especially disturbing at this particular moment because an impressive budget surplus had been reported just six years earlier. In February 1781, when France was expending large sums on the American Revolution, Jacques Necker, the Swiss Protestant banker who was then serving as director-general of finance, had issued a document purporting to offer the first full account of the nation's finances ever presented to the people of France: the *Compte rendu au roi*. Designed to shore up a flagging credit market by boosting public confidence, Necker's account trumpeted the underlying health of the French economy and the government's new commitment to financial transparency. The *Compte rendu* was published in large quantity, translated into several languages, and became an unlikely best seller in France and abroad. Limiting his discussion exclusively to ordinary and ongoing expenses, while making no claims about the extraordinary costs of the war, Necker calculated that France's annual income exceeded its expenses by some 10 million livres. In 1787, however, wartime expenses—including, to Lafayette's embarrassment, unpaid interest still due on loans to the United Sates—were included in the calculations. Although they were comparing apples and oranges, the notables wondered how a surplus could possibly have turned into a deficit in such a short time.

Calonne's reputation for loose ethics added fuel to the fire. In the few years that he held his post, he had been accused more than once of enriching himself at the nation's expense. According to one especially colorful rumor, Calonne was said to have carried on a torrid affair with the fashionable painter Élisabeth Vigée-LeBrun, whose portrait of the comptroller general was exhibited to great fanfare at the Royal Academy's Salon exhibition of 1785. At a time of economic strain, everything about Calonne's appearance in the painting seemed to smack of excess: his sumptuous costume of black silk and white lace, his splendid desk laden with gilt mounts and accessories, and the red brocade drapery that matches the upholstery of his gilt wood armchair. Not only was Calonne said to have raided the nation's coffers to pay an outlandish fee for this flattering portrait, but the tale of his affair with the artist grew increasingly delicious with each telling. The pilfered banknotes, it was whispered, were presented to Vigée-LeBrun in the form of exquisitely expensive wrapping paper, with each bill enveloping an individual piece of candy.

More elaborate and persistent still were the accusations of profligacy and impropriety leveled against the royal family. "Madame Deficit" was one of the kinder nicknames given to the queen, whose infamously extravagant wardrobe, penchant for high-stakes gambling, and purported affairs with men and women alike were constant fodder for rumors spread by myriad political enemies. Her spendthrift ways with other people's money furnished a premise for the notorious "Diamond Necklace Affair"—a scandal that played out in the courts of law and public opinion in 1785 and 1786. A team of con artists duped the ambitious and wealthy Cardinal de Rohan into purchasing the eponymous jewels as a gift for the queen for the staggering sum of 1.5 million livres. Deploying, among other fanciful gambits, a nocturnal assignation with a woman dressed as Marie Antoinette, the swindlers led Rohan to believe that her royal highness coveted the necklace and would provide an influential post at court to anyone who gave her the magnificent gems. When the plot unraveled, the conspirators were dealt with readily—at least those who stayed in France long enough to get caught. But Rohan's culpability was a bone of contention that kept all of Paris rapt. Was it reasonable, went the question before the Parlement de Paris (as the high court of Paris was known), for Rohan to have believed that the queen might act in such a manner? Or was the cardinal guilty of treason simply for having entertained such a low opinion of Marie Antoinette? Rohan's acquittal on May 31, 1786, and the celebrations that greeted the verdict gave the royal family an unwelcome answer.

The widespread talk of spending gone wild put the notables in no mood to accept new taxes landing squarely on their own shoulders. The assembly aimed instead, as one member explained, "to make the king work at economies, as one makes the people work for revenues." The royal household, the notables demanded, must open its books and agree to cut costs in accordance with the assembly's decrees.

The notables also wondered about the limits of their own authority: having been appointed by the crown, rather than elected by the nation, did they, in fact, have the power to levy a permanent tax? On March 1, Jean-François-André Leblanc de Castillon, prosecutor of the *parlement* of Aix assigned to the second bureau, argued that they did not. As the *Mémoires secrets* reported, Castillon had insisted that "neither this Assembly . . . nor the Parlements, nor individual states, nor even the King: the Estates-General alone have this right." Castillon stopped just short of calling for the convocation of the Estates-General, an elected body that had been summoned sporadically since the Middle Ages to help the nation through times of crisis. But the mere mention of the idea quickly became "a sensation."

For his part, Lafayette caused a stir of a different variety: he surprised everyone by demurring on the subject of the new tax. Blindsided by the bitter tenor of the proceedings, he was desperate to do the right thing but had no clear idea of what it might be. As Lafayette confessed to his fellow members of the second bureau on March 3, "The object of the deliberation is so important that my youth requires me to enlighten myself through the discussion of administrators more able than myself." He was, quite simply, unprepared to grapple with such profound matters of political philosophy.

So tepid did Lafayette appear to his compatriots that he managed to disappoint even the low expectations of the *Mémoires secrets,* which lambasted him and other veterans of the American Revolution on March 19. While acknowledging that the group had been "so useful to the nation during the last war," the *Mémoires* lamented that they had "made a very poor showing in the Assembly of the Notables." Accustomed to "the passive obedience of the military and the spirit of despotism that commands troops," the veterans were said to have offered "no vigorous opinions." Mincing no words, the *Mémoires* accused the military men of having demonstrated "the most blind and servile submission" on every matter. To Lafayette, who treasured his reputation as an independent thinker and a staunch defender of liberty, the criticism must have stung.

The preeminent Lafayette scholar Louis Gottschalk cited "a siege of illness" as the root of Lafayette's "uncharacteristic restraint." Certainly, illness might have been a contributing factor. Although Lafayette missed none of the proceedings, he suffered throughout the run of the assembly from a persistent chest cold that might have dissuaded a less eager man. Plagued by coughing, hoarseness, and exhaustion, Lafayette soldiered through with the aid of an assortment of remedies acquired from the Versailles shop of Jean Maury, the apothecary to the stables of the Comte d'Artois. Starting on February 22 and continuing through the month of May, Lafayette went on a veritable spending spree chez Maury. He made purchases nearly every day, running through bottle after bottle of syrup of erysimum, syrup of violet, syrup of mallow, and purified whey in an effort to ameliorate his symptoms and regain his strength. After mounting an all-out campaign to be included among the notables, he was not about to let a bit of congestion keep him from participating.

Finally, in early April, Lafayette began to assert himself. His apothecary bills testify that he was still not completely well, but his health was improving. And having taken time to assess the situation carefully, he began to feel more comfortable issuing bold demands for reform. Most simply, though, Calonne's actions might well have pushed Lafayette past the limits of his tolerance. All of these factors combined to resurrect the fiery spirit that had won the heart of America.

Calonne was growing frustrated with his handpicked notables, who were turning out to be far more independent-minded than anyone had anticipated. At a plenary session held on Monday, March 12, Calonne adopted a new tactic. Rather than grapple with the substance of the assembly's many and varied objections to his plans, he blithely declared the group's oppositions to be immaterial. Taking a moment to thank the notables for their zealous and faithful service, Calonne reported that His Majesty had read the reports of each bureau and had observed "with satisfaction that in general your sentiments are in accord with his principles." He added that "you have shown yourselves to be animated by the desire to contribute to and perfect" the implementation of the government's plans and that "the objections that you have raised, and which relate principally to matters of form, do not contradict the essential points of the goal that His Majesty proposed." This was arrant nonsense.

By Friday—four days later—each of the seven bureaus had submitted its own refutation of Calonne's ludicrous statement. Though phrased in tones ranging from polite rectification to righteous indignation, the seven separate *réclamations* all agreed on one point: the assembly's differences with the crown's proposals were substantive, Calonne's declaration to the contrary notwithstanding. The second bureau's rebuttal was among the mildest; the group asked simply that "an exact record" of their findings be inserted into the record to prevent any misconstruction.

Instead of backing down, Calonne raised the stakes. With the government and the notables at an impasse, the finance minister turned to a third party: the French people. At Calonne's behest, his own speech, the full text of the government's proposals, and an incendiary *avertissement* by an anonymous hand, published both independently and as an introduction to the proposals, were printed and distributed. The *avertissement* caused an instant commotion, not least because it was given out, free of charge, on Saturday, March 31, to parish priests, who were asked to read it from their pulpits the next day. By Monday, April 2, "nothing but the Avertissement" was being spoken of in Paris or Versailles, according to Brienne.

The *avertissement* was an exercise in demagoguery, pure and simple. In an audacious move, the crown was trying to turn the people against the nobility and the clergy. After summarizing the key proposals and extolling their many virtues, the text built to a harangue against the government's critics, reaching a crescendo with a series of rhetorical questions and answers that must have given that week's Mass a lively tone:

What could be the pretexts for concern?
We will pay more! . . . Undoubtedly: but who? Only those who do not pay enough. . . .

Privileges will be sacrificed! . . . Yes: justice desires it, necessity demands it. Would it be better to overcharge those without privilege, the people? There will be loud objections! . . . It's to be expected. Is it possible to advance the common good without damaging some private interests? Can reform be accomplished without complaint?

The fact that the First and Second Estates were under siege was not lost on the notables. Gathered in the Versailles apartments of the Comte d'Artois on Monday, April 2, the members of the second bureau seethed. Brienne denounced the *avertissement*. The Duc de Guines declared that it "misled the people" and served as a "dangerous tocsin." The Duc d'Harcourt maintained that "the government had never addressed the people in this manner." And when Lafayette boldly asserted that "even in Boston this appeal would be regarded as seditious," he was reproving Calonne for rabble-rousing. In Lafayette's view, enraging the public not only risked undermining the nobility and the clergy but jeopardized the very stability of France. Marie Antoinette, too, "highly disapproved" of the *avertissement,* thinking that Calonne was playing a dangerous game. The king, however, predictably failed to understand what the uproar was all about.

His reserves of goodwill depleted, Lafayette went on the offensive. Seizing on rumors that Calonne had manipulated the sale of government lands for personal gain, Lafayette (quite possibly coached by Brienne) rapidly became his bureau's sharpest and most outspoken agitator against the finance minister. Calonne's dabbling in land speculation had already been the subject of a scathing pamphlet that had come to the attention of the second bureau; now Lafayette joined the disparaging chorus by insisting that "we must attack the monster of land speculation, not feed it." On Tuesday, April 3, Lafayette presented the Comte d'Artois with a signed memo to be passed along to the king requesting a "rigorous examination" of recent real estate transactions. "Why," asked his memo, had "finance ministers proposed to the King purchases or exchanges that, having no benefit for the King, served only to benefit certain individuals?" Fighting fire with fire, Lafayette donned the mantle of public interest that Calonne had briefly tried on. The squandered funds, he alleged, had been raised through taxes, and taxes could be justified only in the interest of the nation. The millions of livres that had been "abandoned to depredation and greed," he wrote, "are the fruit of the sweat, the tears and possibly the blood of the people."

Lafayette's memo soon supplanted Calonne's *avertissement* in the public eye. In an entry dated April 30, 1787, the *Mémoires secrets* reported that the denunciation "has been spoken about for a long time and . . . attracted a certain amount of publicity." It had, in fact, generated more than noise. On April 8—five days after Lafayette submitted the memo—Calonne was dismissed. And on May 1, Brienne was appointed to take Calonne's place.

The Assembly of Notables marked an important turning point in Lafayette's life. For the first time, he established himself in his native land as a champion of the downtrodden and a defender of human rights, much as he had already done abroad. Writing to Washington, Lafayette acknowledged that the venture was bound to make him a few enemies. "The King and family and the great men about Court," he noted, "do not forgive me for the liberties I have taken, and the success it had among the other classes of the people."

Triumphing over Calonne seemed to energize Lafayette, who found his footing in the month of May by suggesting a host of reforms. In the name of justice, Lafayette wanted to improve conditions in the nation's prisons, introduce greater leniency in the criminal code, and increase rations for His Majesty's soldiers. Thinking, perhaps, of his American friends, he also sought to restore civil rights to French Protestants. For much of the seventeenth century, the Edict of Nantes, issued by Henri IV—a convert to Catholicism—had guaranteed members of Reformed churches religious freedom and legal equality. But Louis XIV had revoked the edict in 1685, forcing hundreds of thousands of Protestants into exile and exposing those who remained to discrimination and persecution. During the second half of the eighteenth century, pleas for toleration grew steadily louder, as one *philosophe* after another adopted religious freedom as a key principle of Enlightenment thought and coalitions of intellectuals, clergymen, and public leaders sought common ground on the matter.

Lafayette had been involved with the struggle for Protestant rights ever since his return from the American war, but prior to the assembly he had worked only through back channels, collaborating with Calvinist leaders, influential *salonnières,* and sympathetic statesmen in an attempt to persuade the king to soften sanctions. These efforts had come to nothing. But, as Lafayette wrote to Washington in January 1787, he was hopeful that the Assembly of Notables might at last provide some relief on this count. Indeed, Lafayette found a sympathetic audience in the second bureau, where only two members objected. Inspired by Lafayette's words, the group approved a memo to the king on May 24. "A portion of our fellow countrymen," it read, "who do not have the good fortune to profess the Catholic faith, find themselves stricken by a kind of civil death." On behalf of these oppressed individuals, and "in the general interest of the populace, of national industry, and of all moral and political principles," the bureau asked the monarch to demonstrate "a beneficent" tolerance toward the non-Catholics, who, counting among his people, deserved his protection. No immediate action was taken. But by November, with pressure mounting from both domestic and international fronts, the king issued the Edict of Tolerance, restoring to Calvinists a limited range of civil rights.

The proposal of which Lafayette was proudest was one on which he had initially demurred: the calling of the Estates-General. In March, when Leblanc de Castillon had insisted that the Estates-General was the only body that could legitimately impose new taxes on the French people, Lafayette had remained silent. But on May 21, Lafayette predicted that five years hence, the state of the nation's finances would be so altered that a new legislative gathering would be required and asked that the gathering take the form of "a truly national assembly." Artois sought clarification: was Lafayette suggesting a meeting of the Estates-General? Yes, Lafayette confirmed. That was "precisely the object" of his request. Leaving no room for ambiguity, Lafayette asked Artois to "please inscribe his name as putting forth the opinion that the Estates-General of the realm be convened."

On May 25, after three months of deliberation, the Assembly of Notables adjourned. In terms of tangible change, the group accomplished little. Its most important achievement was the establishment of provincial assemblies, and soon Lafayette would be off to participate in the assembly of the Auvergne. The notables had also made headway toward free trade and, by abolishing internal tariffs and modifying the widely despised *gabelle,* or salt tax (which hit the poorest hardest), moved toward a more equitable tax structure. There was some cost cutting as well. Lafayette boasted in a May 5 letter to Washington that they had "got the King to make reductions and improvements to the amount of forty millions of livres a year." Still, by refusing to impose new taxes or authorize new loans, they had all but necessitated that other bodies should undertake additional actions.

The assembly's intangible achievements, however, were of monumental importance. Proving the prognosticators wrong, the notables had not been eaten for dinner. Instead, they'd fired the chef. Lafayette told Washington that the assembly had been a success, writing that "the walls of Versailles had never heard so many good things; and our meeting, particularly in the alarming situation of affairs, when the Kingdom was driving away, like Phaeton's car, will have proved very beneficial." When the Assembly of Notables gathered for its final session in May, the meeting hall looked much as it had at the convocation in February, but looks can deceive: everything had changed.

The months that followed witnessed an epic power struggle between the crown and the highest court of France, with the king repeatedly trying, and repeatedly failing, to persuade the Parlement de Paris to register officially the acts that had emerged from the Assembly of Notables. It was a necessary step; all new laws had to be registered before they could take effect. But as Thomas Jefferson observed, finance minister Brienne, Lafayette's erstwhile mentor, was "slow" to present his edicts to Parlement, "which gave time for the feelings excited by the proceedings of the Notables to cool off, new claims to be advanced, and a pressure to arise for a fixed constitution, not subject to changes at the will of the King." Perhaps, thought the members of Parlement, they should hold out for more.

A game of one-upmanship ensued. Finding Parlement unwilling to act on most of the motions at hand, the king resorted to a tradition as ancient as it was risky: he called a *"lit de justice"*—literally, a "bed of justice," an extraordinary meeting at which the monarch simply declared the controversial legislation to be registered without further ado. On August 6, 1787, the members of Parlement were summoned to Versailles, where they were forced to look on as the king and his ministers announced the registration of the unwelcome edicts. But Louis managed to undermine his authority even as he exerted it. The historian Simon Schama put it perfectly in *Citizens*, his sweeping narrative of the French Revolution, in which he observed that the king evidently "took the presence of the ceremonial 'bed' too literally by falling asleep early in the proceedings." So soundly did the monarch slumber that his snores could be heard throughout the chamber. This performance did nothing to shore up royal power. The very next day, Parlement declared the king's actions null and void on the grounds that new taxes could not be imposed in such a manner. The crown responded by exiling the *parlementaires* to Troyes. And so it went throughout 1787 and into 1788, in a cycle of objections, punishments, and rapprochements that generated much heat but little progress.

Lafayette was appalled. He later related his sentiments to Washington in a 1788 letter: "Government have employed the force of arms against unarmed magistrates, and expelled them. And the people? you will say. The people, my dear General, have been so dull, that it has made me sick, and physicians have been obliged to cool my inflamed blood." Having lost faith in his mentor Brienne, Lafayette wrote to Washington saying that he had decided to cease visiting Brienne's house: "The more I have been connected with him and the Keeper of the Seals [roughly the minister of justice], the greater indignation I have professed against their infernal plan."

Lafayette's outrage was widely shared, most notably by the Duc d'Orléans, the liberally inclined cousin of Louis XVI—the same man who, when he bore the title of the Duc de Chartres, had been Lafayette's rival for the affections of lady-in-waiting Aglaé d'Hunolstein in the 1770s. Orléans let his displeasure be known in dramatic fashion on a day the government hoped would end the conflict between the crown and the Parlement de Paris. On September 20, 1787, after agreeing to a budget compromise to extend existing levies, Parlement was recalled from exile, and on November 19, the magistrates sat in the presence of Louis XVI at a royal session where they were asked to keep the nation afloat by authorizing new loans. After eight hours of discussion, Parlement appeared to be on the verge of approving the borrowing when the king usurped their power and declared the edicts registered. Orléans objected on the spot, announcing to the king and the assembled magistrates that the registration was utterly illegal.

The king banished Orléans from Paris the next day, but his stunning proclamation became the talk of the capital, thanks to a team of writers and printers based at the Palais-Royal—the Paris seat of the Orléans family located across the street from the Louvre. The Duc d'Orléans had inherited the property along with his title in 1785 and had promptly converted its interior courtyard into a bustling commercial emporium whose proceeds helped pay down his extravagant gambling debts. With boutiques, bookstores, and cafés installed throughout the arcade ringing the courtyard (and prostitution flourishing in the garden's shadowy alleys) the Palais-Royal had quickly become a magnet for the wealthy and the dissolute. By 1787, it was also a hotbed of political ferment, a place where agitation against the king and his ministers was continually stoked by Orléans and those in his employ.

The so-called French Prerevolution demonstrated that public opinion could serve as an effective defense against the crown. It would not be long before Lafayette and Orléans—once and future rivals—would use that fickle force as an offensive weapon against each other.

CHAPTER 12

RIGHTS OF MAN

Lafayette found himself in a contemplative mood on January 1, 1788, with his customary optimism tainted by anxiety. He spent the "first moments" of the New Year at home on the Rue de Bourbon, writing an affectionate message to his "beloved General." It was the longest letter he had sent to Washington in months; now that the Assembly of Notables had drawn to a close and the provincial assembly of the Auvergne had completed its work, he had a bit of time to reflect.

As he had since 1777, Lafayette wrote freely to Washington, almost as though he were addressing his better self—a man who knew him intimately and treasured him despite his foibles. On this day, Lafayette's thoughts ranged across a typically broad array of affairs. He shared news of conflicts that threatened to engulf Europe in war and his work on French-American trade as well as an appreciative assessment of Thomas Jefferson, with whom he was "more and more pleased." He wrote with particular pride of the recent meeting of the Auvergne assembly, where he "had the happiness to please the people, and the misfortune to displease the Government to a very high degree." In response to the crown's plea "for an increase of revenue," he explained, "our Province was among the few who gave nothing, and she expressed herself in a manner which has been taken very much amiss." Yet something new had entered into Lafayette's thinking. As a boy, he had yearned to capture the Beast of the Gévaudan without stopping to wonder what, exactly, he would do with the creature if he ever trapped it. Now Lafayette pondered the consequences of his actions. Once tyranny had been vanquished, he wondered, what would take its place?

It was a burning question on both sides of the Atlantic. In 1787, fifty-five men had worked through four steamy Philadelphia months to hammer out provisional answers, and a copy of the resulting document, the Constitution of the United States of America, had since made its way to Lafayette. "It is needless for me to tell you," wrote Lafayette to Washington, "that I have read the new proposed Constitution with an unspeakable eagerness and attention. I have admired it, and find in it a bold, large, and solid frame for the Confederation." Still, Lafayette had concerns. Sensitized by the Assembly of Notables to the dangers of governmental overreaching, he was troubled by the constitutional convention's decision to forgo a bill of rights. Such a document, Lafayette believed, was needed in order to guarantee "that the people will remain in possession of their natural rights and of a perfect equality among the citizens." He was also wary of "the great powers and possible continuance of the President" permitted by the Constitution's vision of the executive branch. Dictatorship, he feared, might be the result. Certain that Washington was the only man capable of leading the nation past these obstacles, Lafayette implored him: "In the name of America, of mankind at large, and your own fame, I beseech you, my dear General, not to deny your acceptance of the office of President. . . . You alone can settle that political machine." Lafayette had unbounded faith in Washington's leadership, which, he felt certain, would set the United States firmly on the right path.

If only France would follow America's lead. "For my part," wrote Lafayette of his homeland, "I am heartily wishing for a Constitution and bill of rights, and wish it may be effected with as much tranquility and mutual satisfaction as it is possible." As Washington knew full well, the constitution that his acolyte envisioned for France bore scant resemblance to the document that was making its way through ratification conventions in every state of the American union. Lafayette and his intimates thought instead of a charter that would reimagine the French monarchy as a version of the English system, with even Jefferson suggesting that they look to England for inspiration. Shortly after the Assembly of Notables convened, Jefferson had sent his best wishes to Lafayette, along with advice that, by "keeping the good model of your neighboring country before your eyes, you may get on, step by step, towards a good constitution." Jefferson acknowledged that a government based on the English "model may not be perfect," but he believed "it would unite more suffrages than any new one which could be proposed."

From a distance of more than two centuries, it may seem unfathomable that a founding father of the United States would encourage France to emulate England, but in 1788, the position espoused by Jefferson was widely shared. Inspired by Montesquieu, many political theorists saw constitutional monarchy as the form of government most likely to ensure liberty in an Old World nation. "Liberty," Montesquieu argued, is not synonymous with unfettered freedom. Rather, in a chapter devoted to the English constitution, Montesquieu wrote that "political liberty . . . is that tranquility of mind that derives from the opinion each person has of his safety." Montesquieu believed that the key to guaranteeing such peace of mind lay in a separation of powers that permitted each branch of government to check the unbridled expansion of the other branches; England, with its legislative Parliament and executive monarchy, had achieved just that. In 1771, the Genevan Jean Louis de Lolme had fleshed out these ideas in his *Constitution of England; or, An Account of the English Government,* a book that found a home in the libraries of Jefferson, Lafayette, and thousands of like-minded thinkers across Europe and the Americas.

On May 25, 1788, Lafayette seized an opportunity to take a public stand against the kind of executive overreach that Montesquieu deemed anathema to liberty. Just as Lafayette was putting the finishing touches on another letter to Washington, a petition drafted by the nobility of Brittany arrived at the Rue de Bourbon. The Breton nobles, to which Lafayette belonged by virtue of his maternal inheritance from the La Rivière family, insisted on preserving their region's historical exemption from certain directives issued by the crown and hoped that Lafayette might add his signature to their declaration. In a postscript to Washington, Lafayette reported, "I very plainly Have Given My Assent."

The twelve noblemen who delivered the document to Versailles on July 12, 1788, promptly found themselves locked up in the Bastille. Lafayette, who was one of some three hundred signatories, suffered a lesser punishment: he was officially "disgraced" by being deprived of a military command he had been scheduled to undertake later that summer. It may well have been the perfect penalty for Lafayette—public enough to burnish his reputation as a defender of freedom but far less onerous than prison. Jefferson acknowledged as much in a letter to James Madison. By way of assuring Madison that Americans need not worry for Lafayette's safety, Jefferson explained that the punishment meted out to Lafayette by the crown was intended "more to save appearances

for their own authority than anything else; for at the very tin
pretended that they had put him into disgrace, they were cor
conferring and communicating with him."

Still, Lafayette was proud to have stood with the nobles of Brittany.
"I associate myself with every opposition to arbitrary acts, present or
future, which threaten or may threaten the rights of the nation," he
wrote to them. But some of Lafayette's allies interpreted the Breton
document rather differently—as a retrograde defense of noble prerogatives intended to halt the nation's progress toward a more democratic
government. The Marquis de Condorcet worried that Lafayette's decision to align with the Breton nobles signaled a weakening of his reformist resolve. Writing to the Italian friend of America, Philip Mazzei,
Condorcet jokingly suggested that Mazzei "try to exorcise the devil of
aristocracy" from Lafayette's home, advising Mazzei to "take along in
your pocket a little vial of Potomac water and a sprinkler made from
the wood of a Continental Army rifle and make your prayers in the
name of Liberty, Equality, and Reason, which are but a single divinity
in three persons."

Condorcet's jest pointed to a dilemma that would hound Lafayette throughout the French Revolution: while partisans on the right
deemed him too radical, partisans on the left found him too conservative. Lafayette loved the United States and believed that—unlike
France—the young nation was a blank slate on which an ideal government could be drawn from scratch. Summing up his view in a letter to
Jefferson, Lafayette wrote that the Americans who collaborated on the
Constitution enjoyed "the advantage to work a new ground, uninflu-
enced by all the circumstances which in Europe necessitate calculations
very different." In France, however, privileges and grievances had deep
roots in centuries of history that could not be easily dismissed. Lafayette believed that any reforms would have to respect this history. The
French abolitionist Jacques-Pierre Brissot discussed Lafayette's stance
with Washington during a 1788 visit to Mount Vernon. According to
Brissot's published account, Washington spoke of Lafayette with paternal concern, describing the marquis's situation with "a joy, mixed with
uneasiness." Washington, Brissot reported, strained to reconcile apparent contradictions in Lafayette's thinking. On one hand, Washington
"recognized the ardor of Frenchmen in going to extremes." But on the
other hand, "their deep veneration for antique governments and monarchs . . . appeared strange to him."

Lafayette saw no conflict. Not only did he deem it possible to create a French constitution that would meld ancient traditions with modern values, but he was one of several men who were determined to help draft an introduction to such a document. On January 12, 1789, Jefferson wrote to Madison from Paris that "everybody here is trying their hand at forming declarations of rights." Knowing that Madison was working on "something of that kind" for the United States, Jefferson was forwarding two examples of French efforts. One was Lafayette's. Acknowledging its hybrid nature, Jefferson explained that, "it contains the essential principles of ours accommodated as much as could be to the actual state of things here." These "accommodations" are evident from the first sentence of an early version of Lafayette's document, preserved in Jefferson's papers, which modifies universal claims to equality with specific exceptions that allow for French realities: "Nature has made men equal, and distinctions among them necessitated by the monarchy are founded upon and must be measured by the general good." The second sentence, too, reveals Lafayette's connections to the values of the sword nobility, naming "honor" one of man's inalienable rights, along with life, liberty, and property. A subsequent passage states that "the command of the army is in the hands of the King alone."

Despite these differences, the fundamental tenets of Lafayette's text had much in common with America's founding documents. After all, they'd emerged from the same traditions and been inspired by the same templates. Condorcet pointed to the Virginia Declaration of Rights, written by George Mason in early 1776, as "the first declaration of rights that truly merits the name," and Mason, in turn, had built on a strain of seventeenth- and eighteenth-century European political theory that identified the citizens of a state as the only legitimate source of sovereignty. The Frenchmen drafting declarations of rights in 1789 were openly borrowing from—and, in their view, improving upon—the Declaration of Independence and Constitution of the United States; not only did they know these documents in translation but they also had the privilege of consulting with Jefferson, Gouverneur Morris (a coauthor of the Constitution who was then in Paris on business), and other Americans. Lafayette, who considered the Federalist Morris too much of an aristocrat, collaborated mostly with Jefferson. As it happened, the men would have less time to focus on the declaration than they might have hoped, for the calendar year of 1789 held many distractions in store.

∙ ∙ ∙

Everyone agreed that France was in crisis, but there was little consensus on how to solve the nation's unrelenting problems. In the months leading up to the convocation of the Estates-General, improvisation reigned supreme as the crown rotated through a series of policies and personnel in the hope of finding the right combination. By the time Brienne stepped down as minister of finance, on August 25, 1788, he had exhausted all of his ideas for salvaging the nation's solvency, leaving France in more or less the same dire straits in which he had found it. In a last-ditch effort to restore the nation's faith in its government, the king replaced Brienne with the one financial figure in whom the people had not lost trust: Jacques Necker, the author of the 1781 *Comte rendu au roi*. But the appointment of the popular Necker only sharpened the battle lines at Versailles, where absolutists and reformers offered competing advice to an indecisive king.

Meanwhile in Paris, Lafayette, Condorcet, and their constitutionally minded colleagues joined together to form a faction of their own. Staunchly opposed to the "party of the Court"—the men and women in the circle of Marie Antoinette and Artois who clung tenaciously to every last shred of absolute power—Lafayette and his circle claimed the name "patriots" and welcomed anyone who shared their views. Many of these figures had come to know each other in the 1780s, when they met at the societies and social assemblies that paved the way for the political clubs that emerged during the revolution: Freemasonic lodges, Mesmer's Society of Harmony, Brissot's Society of the Friends of the Blacks, and gatherings hosted by forward-thinking *salonnières*, including Adrienne's aunt Madame de Tessé. Like the men and women who gathered at such places, the patriots represented every estate and a wide range of viewpoints, from the "aristocratic monarchists" who sought greater powers for the nobility to the "left-wing patriots," like Condorcet, who had already declared himself "republican." Lafayette, the ultimate centrist, occupied a space in the middle.

At the core of this loosely affiliated group stood Adrien Duport, a wealthy member of the robe nobility whose home in the Marais district of Paris became the primary gathering place for a core contingent that became known as the "Society of Thirty" (although its membership ultimately grew to fifty-five). By November 1788, the society was meeting there three times a week for several hours at a time. Lafayette was regularly in attendance, as were the Vicomte de Noailles and other members of his set; having watched their power at court wane since the death of Louis XV, the Noailleses viewed a change in the nation's governing structure as a way to recapture their lost grandeur. When districts throughout France and its colonies began electing representatives to the Estates-General in March 1789, a rudimentary version of a modern-day political campaign got under way, and the Society of Thirty marshaled all of its resources to woo public support of a constitutional monarchy.

As the Estates-General drew nearer, processes were disputed as much as outcomes. Although Louis XVI had named a date in May for the convocation, he had left open the question of how exactly the body should function. On this question, tradition and equity were at odds. In 1614, when the Estates-General had last convened, every district in France had been represented by three men, each of whom had been elected by the members of a single estate: one represented the district's clergy, another its nobility, and a third its commoners. They assembled, debated, and voted by estate, with each estate granted a single vote in the final tally. Such a system made no claims to proportional representation, since the Third Estate could always be outvoted by a coalition of its numerically smaller, but electorally more potent, social superiors. Would the same system be followed in 1789? The king decided not to decide. Each district and each estate would be free to issue its own instructions to its own deputies—some would be told to vote by estate, others by the principle of one man, one vote. Chaos was all but ensured.

Compounding the nation's woes, all the forces of nature conspired to bring France to its knees. In the twelve months preceding the Estates-General, a summer hailstorm followed hard upon a spring drought, devastating the autumn wheat harvest. Jefferson recalled that "the slender stock of bread-stuff had for some time threatened famine," and the cost had risen "to an enormous price." Subsistence quantities were distributed free of charge to the neediest, while those who could pay were relegated to strict rations. So widespread was the impact that Jefferson remembered receiving "cards of invitation to dine in the richest houses" in which "the guest was notified to bring his own bread." He also remembered the winter of 1788–89 as a season "of such severe cold, as was without example in the memory of man, or in the written records of history." If Jefferson's numbers are accurate, the temperature dipped as low as eighteen below zero Fahrenheit. Jefferson described a freeze so bitter that "all out-door labor was suspended, and the poor, without the wages of labor, were of course without either bread or fuel." Bonfires, constructed by the crown, burned at every major intersection in Paris, attracting scores of "people gathered in crowds to avoid perishing with cold." Hunger was continuing to plague the nation when some twelve hundred elected deputies began making their way to Paris and Versailles in the month of April for the convocation of the Estates-General.

With voting procedures still undecided, Jefferson was uneasy. "I am in great pain for the Marquis de Lafayette," Jefferson wrote to Washington. "His principles, you know, are clearly with the people; but having been elected for the Noblesse of Auvergne, they have laid him under express instructions to vote for the decision by orders and not persons. This would ruin him with the Tiers Etat [Third Estate], and it is not possible he could continue long to give satisfaction to the Noblesse." Jefferson shared similar thoughts in a letter to the marquis himself. As a foreign ambassador, Jefferson might have been crossing a line by interfering with the affairs of a host nation, yet he was genuinely concerned, both for France and for Lafayette. On May 6, Jefferson wrote to Lafayette, "As it becomes more and more possible that the Noblesse will go wrong, I become uneasy for you. Your principles are decidedly with the Tiers Etat, and your instructions against them." Jefferson feared that Lafayette's actions

> may give an appearance of trimming between the two parties, which may lose you both. You will, in the end, go over wholly to the Tiers Etat, because it will be impossible for you to live in a constant sacrifice of your own sentiments. . . . But you would be received by the Tiers Etat at any future day, coldly, and without confidence. This appears to me the moment to take at once that honest and manly stand with them which your own principles dictate.

Appealing to Lafayette's desire for popularity, Jefferson advised him that joining the Third Estate now would "win their hearts forever, be approved by the world, which marks and honors the man of the people, and will be an eternal consolation to yourself." The nobility, he added, "will always prefer men who do their dirty work for them. You are not made for that. They will, therefore, soon drop you, and the people, in that case, will perhaps not take you up." Finally, Jefferson put a finer point on the matter when he asked Lafayette to "suppose a scission should take place. The Priests and Nobles will secede, the nation will remain in place, and, with the King, will do its own business. If violence should be attempted where will you be?"

It was no idle question—violence had already been seen on the streets of Paris. Although the popular imagination tends to think of the storming of the Bastille prison on July 14, 1789, as the outbreak of the French Revolution, the first deadly rioting actually began on April 28 at the home of Jean-Baptiste Réveillon—a wallpaper manufacturer. Réveillon lived with his family in an uncommonly grand house near his workshops and warehouses in the heart of the Faubourg Saint-Antoine—the traditional tradesmen's district on the eastern outskirts of Paris, where his business practices made him unpopular among his neighbors. Blithely ignoring time-honored traditions and regulations that assigned different steps of any production process to tradesmen from different guilds, Réveillon produced wallpapers of unparalleled quality by bringing every step of the process in-house. He made a fortune, and his employees—too well trained to be easily replaced—enjoyed a degree of job security that was almost unheard of, even among guild members.

When Réveillon uttered a few ill-chosen words at a meeting of his district's electoral assembly on April 23, 1789, he unwittingly set off a powder keg. Speaking to a select group of men who, like himself, were able to afford the six-livre poll tax required to vote for representatives to the Estates-General, Réveillon complained of the rising costs of doing business, referring to a bygone time when workers were paid only fifteen sous a day. Now it cost nearly that much—fourteen and a half sous—just to buy a loaf of bread. As Réveillon's comments spread throughout the faubourg in the following days, they were garbled into an invidious caricature. Soon, word on the street had it that Réveillon was advocating starvation wages—fifteen sous a day.

One of the most complete accounts of the so-called Réveillon riots comes from the letters of the Marquis de Ferrières, a conservative deputy representing the nobility of Saumur who dutifully wrote home nearly every night of his stay in the capital. As Ferrières reported, "Blood flowed in the Faubourg St-Antoine in Paris." The trouble began when "five or six thousand workers . . . assembled at ten o'clock in the morning, armed with clubs, and descended like furies on the house of a man named Réveillon." Once arrived, "they climbed the walls, broke down the doors, shouting, howling, that they wanted to murder

Réveillon, his wife, his children. They destroyed everything they found, burned the papers, the drawings, and even the bills in the cash register, ravaged the gardens, chopped down the trees." Réveillon and his family escaped over the garden wall, and as Ferrières put it, "The Garde Française fired several rounds, but this only stirred up the mob even more. They climbed up onto houses and threw stones at the troops. The Garde Française advanced with cannons killing many. The rioting lasted until four in the morning and there were as many as seven or eight hundred dead." Ferrières's numbers were exaggerated and his choice of words unsympathetic, but his story is essentially correct. The matter ended badly for a handful of rioters, who were summarily executed on April 29, and for some thirty other participants, who were arrested in the days that followed. The riots were an unmistakable warning of more violence to come.

Lafayette left no record of his response to the unrest in the Faubourg Saint-Antoine, but he was surely troubled by the disorder. In addition to the cost in human lives and personal property, popular uprisings had the potential to derail the nation from the reformed future that Lafayette envisioned. He remained fully committed to a course of action that he termed "moderation," but he had begun to understand the political and pragmatic difficulties that such a path entailed. Having spent most of March in the Auvergne campaigning for election to the Estates-General in the face of well-organized opposition from the party of Artois and Marie Antoinette, Lafayette found himself playing a new and unfamiliar part that required cobbling together fragile coalitions and agreeing to terms that, under other circumstances, he might well have repudiated. Although Lafayette emerged victorious, he was not entirely happy with the deals he cut. He regretted the hodgepodge of instructions he accepted, referring to them, in a letter to his friend and ally the Auvergnat Charles César de Fay de La Tour-Maubourg, as "a composite of great principles and petty details, of popular ideas and feudal ideas." Summing up the intractable problem at the heart of a document that had one foot in the past and one in the future, Lafayette lamented that "there are two hundred years between one provision and another." The position of a moderate was a delicate one, and the slightest disturbance might destroy it completely.

As the opening of the Estates-General approached, political posturing abounded and conspiracy theories flourished. Suspicion, fear, and anger, already widely shared, had been stoked by the recent violence, and in the days before the convocation, Ferrières predicted that the Estates-General would be stormy. "The animosity between the orders is tremendous," he wrote to his wife. On May 15, as the meetings devolved into chaos, he added an ominous postscript: "The orders are neither in accord within themselves, nor in accord with each other." The nobility divided into factions that would form, mutate, and then dissolve as quickly as they arose, and fingers were pointed in all directions, blaming one group or another for each new setback. Lafayette and his allies in the Society of Thirty were at odds with Ferrières and other supporters of an absolute monarchy, and divisions even ran through the princes of the blood. Rumors held that the Réveillon riots had been instigated by the Duc d'Orléans as part of a plot to bring down the king, and Marie Antoinette carried on feuds with everyone from the reform-minded Duchesse d'Orléans to the Mesdames de France, the king's staunchly traditionalist aunts.

Such was the precarious state of affairs on Monday, May 4, 1789, when the deputies to the Estates-General gathered at seven in the morning at the Church of Notre-Dame in Versailles, located just north of the palace, to await the arrival of the king and queen. As the Marquis de Ferrières described the ceremony, three hours passed before the sound of drum, fife, and trumpet announced the approach of the members of the royal family, who were accompanied by the king's ministers, the queen's ladies-in-waiting, and a vast retinue of courtiers. Brilliantly dressed—the women were "covered in diamonds," according to Ferrières—the royal family and courtiers briefly took their seats on banquettes draped with velvet cloth embroidered with fleurs-de-lis while the king gazed upon the spectacle from a throne placed before the choir screen.

Notre-Dame was only a staging ground for the main event: a High Mass was celebrated at the Cathedral of Saint-Louis, located some three-quarters of a mile away, just south of the palace. There, divine blessings would be solicited for the Estates-General. Two by two, the elected deputies made their way from one church to the next in a grand procession through streets hung with rich tapestries, each man carrying a long wax taper to be lit at the cathedral. Royal guards lined the route, and spectators looked on from windows and balconies—or, in the case of Gouverneur Morris, from the street, where he glimpsed what he could "thro a double row of tapestry." Swept up in the pomp and ceremony of the sunny day, Ferrières found his "soul plunged into sweet drunkenness" as his eyes took in the "image of joy, happiness, and satisfaction." Morris saw less but perceived more: observing the progress of the king and queen through the parade, he noted that "the former is repeatedly saluted as he passes along with the Vive le Roi, but the latter meets not a single Acclamation . . . [and] looks . . . with Contempt on the Scene in which she acts a Part." Later in the day Morris learned that Louis, too, was displeased. Not only had the king's "Consort received no Mark of public Satisfaction," but his cousin Orléans had chosen to "walk as Representative and not as Prince of the Blood."

The Duc d'Orléans was a modern man who understood that public opinion would play a dominant role in the nation's reinvention, but Louis XVI believed that affairs of state could move forward simply by following the traditions of the past. When the Estates-General convened on May 5, they met in yet another enormous hall at the Hôtel des Menus Plaisirs. Large enough to accommodate several times the number of participants as the room constructed for the Assembly of Notables, the cavernous space was flanked by side aisles, and loges above the main floor provided additional room for spectators. Delegates were instructed to dress in the costumes specified by the king (although one commoner drew applause when he entered in farmer's garb), and seating arrangements reinforced the hierarchical divisions. The king presided from his golden throne, which had been placed atop a dais surrounded by velvet draperies at the far end of the room, as the queen, ministers, and princes of the blood fanned out around him. Deputies of the clergy and nobility occupied benches arranged in rows

Procession of the Estates-General through the streets of Versailles, May 4, 1789.

CLERGÉ   NOBLESSE   TIERS-ÉTAT

Costume de Cérémonie de Messieurs les Députés des 3 Ordres aux États Généraux

Ceremonial costumes worn by members of the clergy, the nobility, and the Third Estate at the Estates-General.

perpendicular to the throne, while representatives of the Third Estate sat far from the center of power, facing the king from the opposite end of the hall, the two landed estates strategically placed between them and the monarch. The visual messages were neither mistaken nor forgotten. Jules Michelet, the great nineteenth-century historian, wrote that Louis XVI had resurrected "the odious details of a gothic ceremonial, those oppositions of classes, those signs of social distinctions and hatred which it should rather have buried in oblivion. Blazonry, figures, and symbols, after Voltaire, after Figaro! It was [too] late."

The real work of the Estates-General began on May 6, when the deputies reassembled with each estate in its own meeting room. Asked to verify that its membership had been constituted properly, the Third Estate refused, declaring itself unwilling to set a precedent for voting by order and insisting that all decisions be taken up by the Estates-General as a whole. The clergy and nobility, however, proceeded as they were instructed despite some scattered dissension in their ranks. In the weeks that followed, the Third Estate repeatedly tried and failed to persuade the other orders to join them in constituting a unified entity. On June 12, the Third Estate boldly proclaimed itself to be an independent legislative body—operating on a principle of one man, one vote—and adopted the name of the National Assembly. Members of the other orders were welcome. Some clergymen joined the National Assembly, and nobles, too, began to cross over. As early as May 6 one of the noblemen, Mathieu-Jean-Félicité, Comte de Montmorency-Laval, who had attended the Collège du Plessis a few years after Lafayette had departed, argued that the representatives' verification of powers be done jointly, rather than by estate.

As Jefferson had predicted, Lafayette was betwixt and between. On the one hand, his noble constituents had instructed him to vote by estate, and his own inclinations reinforced the idea that an empowered and conscientious nobility was the surest protection against an overreaching monarchy and was, therefore, the nation's best guarantor of liberty. On the other hand, he was keenly aware that his reform-minded colleagues were drifting to the side of the commoners, and he wondered whether this might represent a better and more humane path forward. For a time, Lafayette considered resolving the issue by relinquishing his seat among the nobility and putting himself forward as a candidate representing the Third Estate. But just as he had at the beginning of the Assembly of Notables, he temporized, mired in the conflicting demands of his own belief system.

While the deputies debated in the halls of Versailles, the citizens of Paris were losing patience. The collective voice of the city clamored for a unified National Assembly that might at last begin to address the pressing problems of hunger and inflation. Traveling through France, the English agronomist Arthur Young reported in June that more than a dozen new pamphlets appeared every day in the shops that lined the arcades of the Palais-Royal, with "nineteen twentieths of these productions . . . in favour of liberty, and commonly violent against the clergy and nobility." The people, Young noted, were thronging in such large numbers to the boutiques and coffeehouses on the Orléans property that "one can scarcely squeeze from the door to the counter. . . . They are not only crowded within, but other expectant crowds are at the doors and windows, listening . . . to certain orators, who from chairs and tables harangue each his little audience. The eagerness with which they are heard, and the thunder of applause they receive for every sentiment of more than common hardiness or violence against the present government, cannot be easily imagined."

On the morning of Saturday, June 20, the deputies of the Third Estate arrived at Versailles expecting to welcome the reform-minded clergy into their midst. Instead, all three of the estates found their meeting places locked—the doors barred by armed guards—and signs announcing that a royal session would be held on Monday. Undeterred by the show of force and concerned that the previously unplanned royal session augured ill, the Third Estate and much of the clergy went in search of a new meeting place. Finding an unlocked door leading to an indoor tennis court on the Rue Saint-François, they entered. In an action that would soon be immortalized by the preeminent French painter of the day, Jacques-Louis David, the deputies courageously raised their right arms and pledged not to disband until France had a new constitution. The men who swore the "Oath of the Tennis Court," as it became known, proclaimed the unassailable validity of the National Assembly by insisting that "nothing can prevent it from continuing its deliberations, in whatever locale it may be forced to establish itself; . . . wherever its members are gathered, there is the National Assembly." As the days passed, more clergy joined the commoners, and on June 25, forty-eight nobles declared themselves members of the National Assembly. Lafayette was still not among them. In due course, Louis XVI realized that he had lost the battle. He ordered the clergy and nobility to join the Third Estate in the assembly on June 27.

With the wrangling over process now complete, the National Assembly could turn to the project that Lafayette and many others believed would be the final task of the French Revolution: forging a new constitution. A June letter presumably written to the royalist Madame de Simiane explained Lafayette's goals: "At nineteen, I dedicated myself to the liberty of mankind and the destruction of despotism, as much as a weak individual like myself possibly could. I set out for the New World thwarted by all and helped by no one. . . . I had the pleasure of seeing that revolution completed, and thinking already of revolution in France, I said in a discourse to Congress, printed everywhere except in the [state-sponsored] *Gazette de France:* 'May this revolution serve as a lesson to the oppressors and an example to the oppressed.'" Now he believed that the joyous moment was at hand when he would produce a document that would help France rid itself of oppression in a peaceful and orderly fashion:

> I have tried everything short of civil war, which I could have accomplished except that I feared its horrors. A year ago I developed a plan whose simplest points seemed like extravagances, and which six months from now will be executed in its entirety, yes in its entirety, without changing a single word. I have also created a declaration of

rights which M. Jefferson found so good that he had it sent to General Washington; and this declaration, or something like it, will be the catechism of France.

Unfortunately, circumstances were not conducive to the sort of level-headed deliberation that might right the nation's course. Tens of thousands of royal troops and foreign forces—mostly Swiss and German mercenaries—had been amassing on the outskirts of both Paris and Versailles since May. By early July, some 25,000 soldiers were encamped in a ring around the capital, awaiting orders from their commanding officer, Marshal Victor-François de Broglie, brother of the man at whose table Lafayette had been converted to the American cause. This enormous show of force was widely understood to be the brainchild of the Comte d'Artois and Marie Antoinette. Their absolutist faction still faced opposition from Necker and other moderates in the king's council, but it was steadily gaining strength. Gouverneur Morris's diary entry for June 30 records a conversation with Jefferson, who informed him that "very serious Events are apprehended. That perhaps the King will be prompted to attempt a Resumption of his authority." Widespread rumors held that the National Assembly would be dismantled, the nascent constitution thwarted, and any dissenters slaughtered.

Within the Paris city limits, the authorities were fast losing control. On July 1, Morris wrote to John Jay, a fellow New Yorker who shared his belief in a strong central government, that "the Soldiery in this City . . . declare they will not act against the People . . . and parade about the Streets drunk, huzzaing for the *Tiers*." According to Morris, on June 30 a group of soldiers who had been imprisoned for mutiny were freed by a "Mob"—four thousand strong—with help from military guards. Morris added that when "a Party of Dragoons, ordered on Duty to disperse the Riot, thought it better to drink with the Rioters," jubilation ensued. The prisoners were then "paraded in Triumph to the palais Royal, which is now the Liberty Pole of this City." Versailles, too, saw the streets filled with angry crowds. Summing up the state of affairs in his letter to Jay, Morris concluded that "the Sword has slipped out of the Monarch's Hands without his perceiving a Tittle of the Matter."

The National Assembly could do little more than look on with dismay. On July 8, Honoré Gabriel Riqueti, Comte de Mirabeau—a member of the Society of Thirty who, sharing Lafayette's hope for a constitutional monarchy, had written some of that group's more persuasive pamphlets—proposed that the assembly send a deputation to the king bearing a "very humble address" asking for troops to be withdrawn. Born into the Provençal nobility, Mirabeau had been *"déclassé"*—stripped of the privileges of his order—following a series of scandals. Now a member of the National Assembly, elected by the Third Estate of Aix-en-Provence, he was fast becoming one of the most passionate orators of the French Revolution. The military presence, argued Mirabeau, was causing, not quelling, alarm in the streets of Paris, and jeopardizing "the liberty and honor of the National Assembly." The written appeal that Mirabeau presented for the assembly's consideration the next day elaborated further, declaring for his majesty's edification that "the danger, Sire, threatens the tasks that are our primary duty, and that can have full success, real permanence, only insofar as the people regard them as entirely free." The *Archives parlementaires*—the published record of France's legislative proceedings—reported that Mirabeau's July 9 address "caused the greatest stir in the Assembly, which rose in unison in a sign of support." But the king soon put an end to their enthusiasm, for as Morris wrote in his diary, Louis XVI contemptuously suggested to the deputies that if they felt unsafe at Versailles they could be relocated to a more remote town, such as Soissons or Noyon, in the rural reaches of Picardy.

Lafayette, who seconded Mirabeau's proposal on July 8, grew steadily more wary. Writing to Jefferson, he reported that the king and his council "are very angry with me. If they take me up you must claim me as an American citizen." Rarely did Lafayette invoke the divine, but he closed this letter with the phrase "God bless you," as though these might be his parting words. He had reason to fear trouble from factions other than the king's party as well. Members of the Orléans circle had been making "advances" to Lafayette, seeking an alliance he deemed suspect. In a letter written on July 11, Lafayette explained:

> They tell me that the head of M. le duc d'Orléans and mine have been marked; that sinister plots have been set in motion against me, as the only one capable of commanding an army; that M. le duc d'Orléans and I should coordinate our efforts; that he should be the captain of my guard, and I of his.

Lafayette reported that he had rebuffed these offers in no uncertain terms, responding "coldly" that "M. le duc d'Orléans is, in my view, nothing more than an individual wealthier than myself, whose fate is of no greater interest than that of other members of the minority." Vowing to keep an eye on Orléans, he even dared to imagine a time when he might denounce Artois and Orléans as equally "factious"—inclined to sedition—one prince of the blood being prone to aristocratic scheming, the other employing "more popular means." As far as Lafayette was concerned, neither man had the best wishes of the nation at heart.

On July 9, despite the inauspicious conditions, the thirty-man committee charged with determining a process for writing a new French constitution reported on its work. Lafayette was not a member of the committee, but the report was read into the record by one of his allies, Jean-Joseph Mounier, a lawyer from Grenoble who had devoted many years of study to the English system of government and who, upon reaching Paris in 1789, had been introduced into the salon of Madame de Tessé by Lafayette. Mounier announced that the constitution of France would begin—just as Lafayette hoped—with a preamble articulating the universal rights shared by all of mankind. Mounier's logic was clear: "The goal of all societies being the general good," any valid principle of governance "must be founded on the rights of man." Anxious to act before the window of opportunity slammed shut, Mounier enjoined his listeners to "seize the favorable moment." But before enumerating the committee's proposals, he added a heartfelt plea for a lasting success: "May all the provinces, through the organ of their representatives, finally contract among themselves and with the throne an eternal alliance!"

Lafayette knew he had to act quickly if he wished to be the one to provide France with its declaration of rights. His letter to Jefferson of July 10 included a draft of the document along with a request for Jefferson "to consider it again and make your observations." Lafayette impressed his urgency upon Jefferson: "I beg you to answer as soon as you get up, and wish to hear from you about eight or nine at least."

On July 11, Lafayette presented his "Declaration of the Rights of Man" to the National Assembly. Although he had been eager to solicit Jefferson's advice, Lafayette did not necessarily follow it. Annotations to a copy of the text found among Jefferson's papers suggest that the American was uncomfortable with Lafayette's proposal to include property and honor among man's fundamental rights. In other passages, Lafayette's final copy jettisons ideas inspired by Jefferson found in earlier versions, among them the assertion that "no man may be disturbed . . .

for his religion." Facing a fractious and frightened assembly, Lafayette was in all likelihood more concerned with winning the support of the clergy than with acting immediately on the matter of religious freedom.

It may not have fulfilled all of Jefferson's expectations, but Lafayette's Declaration of the Rights of Man was sufficiently radical to raise red flags among some of the assembly's more outspoken deputies. And it was not only what Lafayette said but what he failed to say that attracted attention. In a striking departure from Mounier's oration, the word "monarchy" was pointedly absent from Lafayette's text. In earlier drafts, Lafayette had made the customary references to the king and his ministers, but in the version he presented on July 11, he asserted that "the principle of all sovereignty resides in the nation" and left the specifics open to debate.

As soon as Lafayette's speech concluded, the Comte de Lally-Tolendal, a supporter of absolute monarchy, took the floor to issue a series of dire warnings couched in words of support. Lally-Tolendal duly noted the speaker's unique history, applauding Lafayette's declaration of "sacred" principles. It was appropriate, he declared, that Lafayette should "be the first to present them to you; he speaks of liberty as he has defended it." Certainly, Lally-Tolendal maintained, this seminal text should be debated in the bureaus. But under no circumstances should such a potentially explosive document—filled as it was with a free-floating array of abstract principles—be circulated to the public at this preliminary stage. "Allow me, Messieurs, to insist more than ever on the danger" that might be produced by "such a declaration isolated from the rest of the constitution," he urged. Publicizing this document would arm the ministry, which would accuse the assembly of wreaking havoc. France, he insisted, was not like America: "There is an enormous difference between a new-born nation announcing itself to the universe, a colonial people breaking ties with a distant government, and an antique, immense nation, one of the greatest in the world." An American solution—he called it "primitive equality"—would not work in France, Lally-Tolendal asserted, where people must be bound "to the monarchical government" and where the rights of "man, citizen, subject, king" must be articulated. The danger of announcing natural rights would be "incalculable." Loud and lengthy applause greeted the termination of Lally-Tolendal's speech. The deputies decided unanimously that Lafayette's declaration would be sent to the bureaus to be refined in tandem with the articles of constitution and would not be shared with a wider audience until the constitution could be published alongside it.

If Lally-Tolendal and his fellow deputies believed they could stop any dissemination of Lafayette's declaration beyond the walls of the Menus Plaisirs, they were mistaken. A new information age was dawning in Paris, as the public's craving for political news was met by an ever-growing cast of publishers, authors, editors, and artists capitalizing on the government's gradual relaxation of censorship laws over the course of the preceding year. The *Journal de Paris,* whose editors traveled in the same circles as the Society of Thirty, was particularly friendly to Lafayette in these days. The paper routinely reprinted Lafayette's speeches and letters alongside a selection of flattering responses. On July 13, the *Journal* reported Lafayette's presentation of his Declaration of the Rights of Man along with a highly partial view of its reception: despite Lally-Tolendal's mixed reaction, the paper published only the absolutist's most generous statement about the declaration: "Its author speaks of liberty as he defended it."

A steady stream of exquisitely varnished reports reached American readers, who avidly devoured news of their favorite Frenchman. Nearly every ship that sailed for the United States carried updates from Paris and Versailles. French and English newspapers, private letters, and diplomatic missives shared cargo space with cases of textiles, wines, and other goods destined for the American market. Word traveled slowly: the crossing to New York or Boston could take more than three months, and another few weeks were generally required for information to reach America's southern and western regions. Sometimes newspapers copied articles word for word from their European or American sources; sometimes they added their own embellishments.

On September 30, Bostonians read the *Journal de Paris* story of July 13 embroidered with local ornament, as the *Massachusetts Centinel* related that "M. Lally was so delighted with the speech that he exclaimed—'The gallant Marquis *speaks* of liberty with the same spirit that he *fought* for it on the plains of America.'" Tellingly, the article's title was also changed in translation. The *Journal de Paris* had reported its news under the headline "National Assembly," but the Boston article was titled simply "Marquis de La Fayette." More than an analysis of France's growing concern for human rights, it was a celebration of Lafayette and a reflection that America wished to claim him as its own. Overstating Lafayette's role in the French Revolution, the *Centinel* went so far as to assert that "to the Marquis de La Fayette may the present emancipation of the citizens of the Commonwealth of France be more justly attributed than to any other of their patriotic characters." But no exaggeration was involved in the paper's description of Lafayette's indebtedness to American precedents: "He has been taught the relative Rights of the Ruler and the Ruled, in the continual correspondence he has kept up with his adopted father, General Washington—the hero and statesman." The author closed the article with a poetic reverie:

Who with th' enlighten'd Patriots met,
On Schuylkill's banks in close Divan,
And wing'd that arrow sure as fate,
Which ascertain'd the Sacred Rights of Man.

It was not simply happenstance that Lafayette's Declaration of the Rights of Man was reported both widely and favorably in France and abroad. Thanks to an aide on a swift horse, Lafayette's words had flown to Paris nearly as quickly as they were spoken. Within hours of Lafayette's July 11 speech, a secretary could be heard reading Lafayette's text aloud in a large chamber of the Hôtel de Ville, an enormous French Renaissance edifice located across from the vast Place de Grève (now Place de l'Hôtel de Ville) on the Right Bank of the Seine, about a mile east of the Palais-Royal. The audience was the city's Assembly of Electors, a group of some 180 men who, having been elected to choose Paris's representatives to the Estates-General, were now serving as the municipality's ad hoc government. That night, printed copies of Lafayette's speech were turned out in quantity, and by the morning of July 12, broadsides proclaiming his enumeration of every French citizen's inalienable rights were available for purchase throughout Paris. But in such tumultuous times, the news of the morning was not always the news of the afternoon, and Lafayette's declaration did not hold the attention of the city for long.

CHAPTER *13*

A STORYBOOK HERO

The Declaration of the Rights of Man had been published less than twenty-four hours earlier, but all anyone was talking about on the afternoon of July 12 was Louis XVI's banishment of Jacques Necker, the director-general of finance, who was the only member of the government whom the people still generally admired. In short order, most of the remaining ministers submitted their resignations or were forced out in a purge orchestrated by the Comte d'Artois and his circle, to be replaced by men loyal to the absolutist cause. Necker had been dining at home on Saturday, July 11, when he'd received a visit from the Comte de la Luzerne, minister of the navy, bearing a letter from the king ordering his immediate exile. Necker calmly finished his meal, and without uttering a word about his plans, he then ushered his wife into a carriage and proceeded to his château at Saint-Ouen, just north of Paris. Less than a day later, the Neckers were safely on the road to Brussels, leaving the king—now stripped of all moderating influences—to attempt a reversal of all the reforms that his coterie of reactionary advisers assured him had already gone too far.

In Paris, word of Necker's dismissal ignited fears that the emboldened forces of absolutism might seek to quell the growing unrest in Paris by attempting an all-out military offensive against the city. From every corner of the capital, angry citizens made their way to the gardens of the Palais-Royal, where orators clambered atop fences, tables, and chairs to declaim the government shake-up and warn of impending danger. *"Aux armes!"* they shouted to the frenzied crowds jostling for space among the trees. According to Gouverneur Morris's diary, roving bands were soon "breaking open the Armorers's Shops" and scouring the streets for weapons and ammunition to be used in defense of the city.

Others set out on missions of a more symbolic variety. The multitudes who gathered at the Palais-Royal had been ruled by a monarchy that was second to none when it came to deploying visual spectacle for political ends; from a fountain erected in the garden of Versailles in the seventeenth century portraying the Roman goddess Latona in the process of transforming disrespectful peasants into frogs, to the costumes prescribed for the Assembly of Notables, the people of France received constant visual reminders of royal authority. Now, as ordinary men and women struggled to wrest control of their destinies from the government, they armed themselves not only with guns and stones but also with symbols. By order of the populace at large, the theaters of Paris would be dark that night. Mourning was to be observed in honor of the exiled Necker, just as it had been in memory of the six-year-old dauphin, who'd died from tuberculosis in June. This time, though, in lieu of a royal proclamation, the news would be delivered by masses of citizens roaming the city, closing places of entertainment as they passed.

Philippe Curtius, an enterprising Swiss anatomist who had adapted his wax-modeling skills for commercial purposes, was at his waxworks gallery on the Boulevard du Temple when hundreds of men and women arrived at the door on the afternoon of July 12. The uncanny likenesses on display in his galleries—one of which was among the many popular attractions at the Palais-Royal—were always up-to-date, as Curtius constantly changed the heads of his figures in accordance with the interests of his public. Curtius, best remembered today as Madame Tussaud's mentor, had both fueled and capitalized on the cults of personality that sustained the political leaders of the day. On this date, the crowd was particularly interested in two of these heads; they demanded that Curtius hand over the busts of Necker and Orléans. Soon, the wax heads were wending their way through the streets in triumph, borne aloft by long poles carried above the crowd. Had anyone wanted to take it, a wax bust of Lafayette was also available at Curtius's shop. But the Palais-Royal crowd, partial to Orléans, was not interested in glorifying the marquis.

Scores of eyewitnesses documented the remarkable events of July 1789, and no account is more revealing than the diary of Gouverneur Morris. Morris—who was a deputy to the Continental Congress, an advocate for Washington's army throughout the American Revolution, a signer of the Articles of Confederation, and an author of the Constitution—had participated in every stage of the American experiment in liberty and was particularly attuned to the implications of each action and reaction of the French situation. On the evening of July 12, he found himself in the midst of the melee as he made his usual Sunday rounds. He had visited the Club Valois in the Palais-Royal, his home away from home, and called on the Comtesse de Flahaut—a mistress whose favors he famously shared with Talleyrand and whose husband supported the faction of Artois and the queen. He had left her apartments and was on his way to see Jefferson when his carriage approached a remarkable scene on the Place Louis XV (known today as the Place de la Concorde). Behind him was "a body of Cavalry with their Sabres drawn"; before him a hundred people were "picking up stones" from the piles of building materials being used to construct the bridge now known as the Pont de la Concorde. Showers of rock rained down upon the mounted soldiers, who responded with pistols. The confrontation between citizens and cavalry continued into the adjacent garden of the Tuileries Palace, where members of the Gardes Françaises, armed with bayonets, joined forces with the people to face off against a detachment of the Royal Allemand—a mounted regiment of the royal army with a name that referenced its German origins. As Morris understood at once, there was no going back. "These poor Fellows," he wrote, "have passed the Rubicon with a witness."

By the next morning, the attention of Paris had shifted to the Hôtel de Ville. Inside that stately edifice, every room, corridor, stairway, and courtyard was filled to overflowing with panicked men and women clamoring for arms; the city was in danger, and the people demanded protection. Thrust into the center of a crisis with few resources at their disposal, the electors were desperate to strengthen their tenuous hold on the city, using whatever means they could. Since late June, they had considered seeking permission from the National Assembly and the king to reestablish a citizens' militia that might ensure the city's safety. The request had never been acted upon. Now, engulfed in chaos around eight in the morning on July 13, the electors tried to calm the crowd by announcing that a citizens' militia had been authorized and urging the assembled multitudes to return to their home districts to report for duty.

With some semblance of calm restored, the flags of the city were carried into the meeting hall and, according to the published proceedings of the electors, mounted "as trophies" on the fireplace, where they flut-

Charles Marville, *Hôtel de Ville*, 1871. In 1789, the electors of Paris and Lafayette established their headquarters in the Paris Hôtel de Ville, seen here in a photograph taken shortly after the building had been burned during the Paris Commune. Most of the city's records from the 1789 revolution were destroyed in the fire, but the façade was left virtually intact.

tered over a marble bust of Lafayette. Carved by Houdon, and received as a gift from the state of Virginia to the city of Paris, the bust had decorated the mantelpiece since 1784, standing as a reminder of France's role in winning American independence. But now, paired with the city flag, the sculpted face seemed to promise liberation closer to home. The minutes of the day's meeting report that the fortuitous pairing of flag and bust gave the electors ideas. "As if by a sudden inspiration," several electors expressed a shared sentiment that command of the militia must be given to Lafayette. Only he, they agreed, could protect Paris from Versailles and save the city from itself. By naming Lafayette to command the militia, the electors had chosen, as Condorcet eloquently put it, "a storybook hero who, thanks to the éclat of his adventures, his youth, his bearing, and his renown, could enchant . . . the imagination and rally all of the popular interests to his side." Any other choice, he added, would have faced "strong opposition" and resulted in "great harm." Only Lafayette—the renowned friend of Washington—had sufficient credibility to reassure the city.

For the time being, the marble bust was the closest the militia would come to seeing Lafayette at its helm. Another man, the Marquis de La Salle, was placed in command while Lafayette was still some five leagues away, at Versailles, where the National Assembly was trying to persuade the king to remove his menacing troops. Angered by the insubordination of the assembly, Louis spurned the deputation sent to him on July 13. "I have already made known to you my intentions regarding the measures that the disorders of Paris have forced me to take," he declared. "It is for me alone to judge their necessity." On July 14, two more groups of deputies again entreated the king. To the second, Louis responded tersely and abruptly ended the discussion by stating, "I have nothing to add."

While Louis XVI held his ground in the palace and debates raged at the Hôtel des Menus Plaisirs, rumors of invasion and massacre swept Paris. At two o'clock in the morning on July 14, several of the Paris electors were holed up in the Hôtel de Ville, trying desperately to cobble together a provisional government that might succeed in controlling the terrified city, when, according to a record of the proceedings, a motley group "wearing on their faces every sign of fright and alarm" burst through the doors "crying that all had been lost, the City taken, and the Rue de Saint-Antoine inundated with 15,000 soldiers who might seize the Hôtel de Ville at any moment." Their story was unfounded. But by six o'clock, the entire populace seemed ready for an imminent siege. Outside city hall, on the Place de Grève, the electors perceived "a countless multitude of people of every age and walk of life" bearing "arms of every variety." Anticipating violence and starvation, crowds rushed to secure provisions from Les Halles, the city's main marketplace, as strong gusts of wind blowing from the west hastened their steps. According to the electors' notes, the roads were packed with "carts of flour, wheat, wine, and other comestibles, cannons, guns, ammunition" being pushed, pulled, or otherwise cajoled in the direction of the Hôtel de Ville.

Around seven o'clock, news of troop movements once again reached the electors. This time, they took action, instructing all citizens of Paris who possessed weapons of any sort to report to the militia's ad hoc leadership, which was dispersed across the city's sixty districts. The electors further ordered all members of the militia to proclaim their allegiance to Paris by wearing the colors of the city in the form of red and blue cockades and to begin constructing defenses by ripping paving stones from the streets, digging trenches, and erecting barricades. Meanwhile, the electors sent formal deputations to two military strongholds: the Hôtel des Invalides—named for its role as a government-sponsored home for aged and disabled veterans—and the Bastille. At these sites, the city's representatives hoped to acquire not only armaments but also solemn pledges that the king's soldiers would not fire upon the citizens. Those sent to the Invalides returned with cannons. Those sent to the Bastille met with less success.

The Bastille has earned a place in history as a site of arbitrary imprisonment, but the massive stone structure was also a fort and a munitions depot. In the preceding weeks, as tensions rose in and around Paris, the army had quietly warehoused thousands of pounds of gunpowder within the seemingly impregnable edifice. Little by little, dozens of cannons, guns, and other weapons had been mounted on its roof, and cannons trained on the Rue Saint-Antoine below. Thus provisioned, the Bastille was both dangerous and desirable. As long as it remained in the hands of the crown, it posed a lethal threat to the citizenry. If it could be taken, it promised the city a nearly endless supply of ammunition.

All of this was known to the three representatives sent to negotiate with Bernard-René de Launay, the royal official in charge of the Bastille. After making their way through the crowd, the municipal delegation presented the city's requests to Launay, who spoke with them in front of an enormous iron gate. Agreeing to continue the conversation inside, Launay ordered the drawbridge lowered and the gate raised and invited the visitors to join him for breakfast. Several hours passed before the electors made their way back to the Hôtel de Ville bearing mixed tidings. They reported that Launay would not surrender, but neither would he permit his men to fire on the people.

The electors were ready to announce the agreement when cries of "perfidy" and "treason" went up from the Place de Grève. Two injured men—one with a wounded arm, the other near death—had been transported there from the Bastille, and fifteen or twenty other casualties were reported. Evidently, the Bastille had again lowered its drawbridge and the people, taking the gesture as an invitation, had begun to cross it when the musketeers guarding the fortress opened fire. A second deputation was immediately dispatched to remind Launay of his promise, but as these men approached the Bastille, they saw that the fortress's soldiers were engaged in a fierce firefight with armed citizens. Observing the crowd, one delegate understood that "a deputation is no longer what they want; it is the siege of the Bastille, the destruction of this horrible prison, it is the death of [Launay] that they demand in great cries."

All of this was accomplished. Before the day was out, the Bastille was captured and its prisoners—seven aged men—were freed, but eighty-three citizens lay dead. In addition, one of the building's defenders was killed in action, and two others were hanged. Launay fought to the end. Taken into custody, he was marched toward the Hôtel de Ville. En route, he lashed out, kicking one of his captors, and was promptly felled by a furious onslaught of blades and guns. Soon, his head was making the rounds of Paris atop a pike, having been unceremoniously hacked off by a cook who had been the recipient of Launay's kick, and who went on to boast of the decapitation. The city leaders lost one of their own: Jacques de Flesselles, the provost of merchants (a member of the municipal council), was shot dead on the steps of the Hôtel de Ville as punishment for the transgression of hedging his bets. He had proclaimed his support of the electors but withheld arms. His became the second head to be paraded through the streets.

News of the Bastille's fall reached Lafayette late that night. Having been elected vice president of the National Assembly, Lafayette was at the Hôtel des Menus Plaisirs, standing in for the president, who had retired for the evening, when two representatives from the Hôtel de Ville arrived to report on the tumultuous day. While Lafayette led a discussion of what steps the assembly should take next, François-Alexandre-Frédéric, Duc de La Rochefoucauld-Liancourt, a deputy from Soissons and a confidant of the king, slipped out of the chamber and made his way to the royal apartments to inform Louis XVI. According to popular legend, Louis asked, "Is it a revolt?" and Liancourt famously replied, "No sire, it's a revolution." In any case, Louis was at last convinced that the troops around Paris were doing more harm than good, and so at approximately eleven in the morning on July 15, he went to the Menus Plaisirs accompanied by his two brothers and announced to the National Assembly—a term he used that day for the first time—that the troops would be removed. Recalling the events years later in his memoirs, Lafayette wrote with satisfaction that "the cause of the people triumphed."

Lafayette's own moment in the spotlight was not far off. Having served as commander of the citizens' militia for less than twenty-four hours, the Marquis de La Salle tendered his resignation on the morning of July 15, clearing the way for Lafayette to take his place. According to the records of the Assembly of Electors, a mere gesture toward Lafayette's bust, which was now accompanied on the meeting hall mantelpiece by the painting *Saint Peter in Chains*—an image of miraculous liberation that had itself been liberated from the Bastille chapel—was all it took to remind the audience that it was time to install Lafayette at the head of the citizens' militia. Médéric-Louis-Élie Moreau de Saint-Méry, the Martinique-born president of the electors, explained succinctly that "the defense of French liberty" belonged in the hands of the "illustrious defender of the liberty of the New World."

Lafayette wrote in his memoirs that he had no knowledge of these events when he set out from Versailles around two in the afternoon. In his capacity as vice president of the National Assembly, he rode in the first of forty carriages that transported more than one hundred deputies to the Hôtel de Ville to celebrate the accomplishments of the city and the nation. It took time to find enough seats for the deputies in the overcrowded meeting hall, but once everyone was in place and the audience's cries of joy were calmed, Lafayette addressed the crowd with a discourse that the electors praised for being "filled with that eloquence which he possesses, so touching, because it is simple and natural." Lafayette's optimism about the future and faith in the king shone through as he "congratulated the Assembly of Electors and all the citizens of Paris on the liberty they had won by their courage" and reminded them that they owed their happiness to "the justice of a beneficent and disabused monarch," whose speech to the National Assembly Lafayette read into the record.

After several more speeches and a great deal more applause, the meeting seemed to be over and the deputies were getting ready to depart when, suddenly, "all the voices joined together to proclaim Monsieur the Marquis de Lafayette Commander-General of the Parisian Militia." Lafayette did not hesitate. "Accepting this honor with every sign of respect and gratitude," he "drew his sword; and swore to sacrifice his life for the preservation of this precious liberty that he was entrusted with defending." Moments later, the chorus of voices resumed, this time to proclaim Lafayette's friend and ally Jean-Sylvain Bailly mayor of Paris.

The offices given to Lafayette and Bailly were municipal, but with the authority of Versailles on the wane, Paris was fast becoming the seat of national power. On July 16, Lafayette asked that his title and his troops be renamed to reflect this new reality—the leader of the Parisian militia would henceforth be known as commander of the National Guard. Yet before the day was out, Lafayette began to wonder if his was an impossible position. He might well have been the most powerful man in the nation, but there was no force on earth that could possibly stop events from spiraling out of control.

CHAPTER 14

"I REIGN IN PARIS"

I reign in Paris," Lafayette wrote on the night of July 16, "and it is over an infuriated people driven by abominable cabals." Casting himself as a calming influence, he explained that he was all but trapped in Paris, held hostage by his own success. "The people, in the delirium of their enthusiasm, can be tempered only by me," he wrote. "Forty thousand souls gather, the fermentation is at its height, I appear, and one word from me disperses them. I have already saved the lives of six people who would have been hanged in various quarters." He insisted, however, that his was not a position to be envied. Although he yearned to go to Versailles, where he hoped that he might persuade Louis XVI to hasten the promised removal of troops, "the well-being of Paris," Lafayette reported, "demands that I not remove myself for a moment. As I write, eighty thousand people surround the Hôtel de Ville and say that they are deceived, that the troops are not withdrawing, that the king must come. Even at this moment, they issue terrible cries. If I were to appear, they would calm themselves; but others will replace them."

Versailles, too, was astir that night. The Comte d'Artois, the Duchesse de Polignac, and a half dozen more of the queen's closest allies were preparing for a timely departure into exile. As the foreign troops dismissed by the king were making their way out of France, Artois and his circle took advantage of the military cover and traveled with the soldiers into more hospitable climes. Marie Antoinette, hoping that the royal family would join the exodus, was making her own preparations. By nightfall, the queen had arranged for all of her matching sets of diamond earrings and necklaces to be packed carefully into a single coffer for safe transport in her personal carriage. Assisted by Madame Campan, a lady-in-waiting, the queen set fire to a stash of papers lest they be seized in her absence; their contents have been lost to history. But Louis, convinced that he could win the people back, was determined to stay. Marie Antoinette was reduced to tears. And the diamonds would have to be unpacked.

As morning arrived on July 17, Louis XVI prepared to humble himself before the crowds of Paris. Accompanied by a handful of his remaining allies, the dispirited king climbed into a waiting carriage, passed through the palace gates, and set out along the Avenue de Paris, where expectant onlookers witnessed a sight unthinkable just a few weeks earlier. The customary royal entourage had dwindled to a skeleton crew; the king's chief escorts consisted of the newly assembled citizens' militia of Versailles, whose ranks were fleshed out by hundreds of the National Assembly's deputies joining the procession on foot. To the eyes of the disapproving Marquis de Ferrières, the troupe looked more like a gang of vagabonds than the retinue of a great monarch. Yet such were the supporting players with whom Louis reached the southwestern edge of Paris, near Sèvres, around three in the afternoon. There, speeches by various officials welcomed the sovereign to his city, with the best-remembered passage coming from the mouth of the mayor, Bailly. "I bring your Majesty the keys to the good city of Paris," he began. "These are the same keys that were presented to Henri IV. He had regained his people; here it is the people who have regained their king." When the pleasantries concluded, the Versailles militia withdrew, and Louis XVI was then in the hands of Lafayette.

For the next ninety minutes, two royal carriages, hundreds of the nation's deputies, and scores of city leaders followed behind Lafayette, who led the way on a white horse, surrounded by his aides-de-camp. Although planned in haste, the convoy was orderly, making its way through streets lined with tens of thousands of Parisian citizen soldiers, who stood six deep, from the city limit to the Hôtel de Ville—a route spanning more than three and a half miles. Unified by their red-and-blue cockades, this ragtag lot of men, women, and children made up in zeal what they lacked in refinement. Those who had gotten to the armaments carried muskets seized from the Bastille and the Invalides, while others equipped themselves with anything that might serve the purpose. Jefferson spotted not only pistols and swords but also "pikes, pruning hooks, scythes, etc." carried by the crowd that day. *"Vive la nation!"* was the cry shouted from doors, windows, balconies, and roof-tops along the route. The king had come to Paris of his own volition, but as Jefferson poignantly observed, "not a single 'Vive le roi' was heard."

At four-thirty, the procession came to a halt at the Hôtel de Ville. A pulsing, cheering crowd surrounded the building, while an honor guard, épées unsheathed, awaited the king at the entrance. Making his way up the steps, Louis was startled to hear the loud clang of metal on metal as a ceremonial arch of swords went up over his head. By the time he took his seat on the throne that had been placed in the electors' meeting hall, he was a badly shaken man.

Bailly approached, carrying in his hand a bouquet of red and blue ribbons. He hoped the monarch would join with the people in wearing the colors of Paris. Silently, Louis accepted the cockade and affixed it to his hat. At last the crowd erupted: *"Vive le roi!"* An address was expected, but the king was unable to stir his voice. Pressed by Bailly, he issued a few halting words audible only to the mayor, who repeated them at greater volume (and perhaps with a measure of embellishment) for the sake of the eager audience. The king, declared Bailly, loved his people and wished only for calm.

Lafayette, too, was silent, but his actions spoke louder than words. For him, the day had been an unmitigated success, and he later said as much to Morris, who watched the spectacle unfold from a well-placed window on the Rue Saint-Honoré—a plum location secured through the good graces of the Comtesse de Flahaut. It seems that Morris had hoped to arrange a government appointment for Lafayette as governor of the Île-de-France—the region that includes Paris—but the marquis had refused, declaring the command of the militia to be "the utmost of his Wishes." No civilian post could possibly have compared. As Morris recalled Lafayette's proud narration of the day's events, "He had his Sovereign during the late Procession to Paris completely within his Power. He had marched him where he pleased, measured out the Degree of Applause he should receive as he pleased, and if he pleased could have detained him Prisoner." Even Morris, who frequently questioned Lafayette's grasp of political nuance, had to concede that "all this is strictly true."

As Lafayette saw it, the king had "turned himself over as my prisoner" on that July day. Writing just a few weeks later, he remembered being moved by what he saw as the monarch's humility. It had, Lafayette wrote, "attached me to his service more fully than if he had promised me half of his kingdom." Still, Lafayette expected more from Louis, and he intended to get it: "If the king refuses the constitution, I will fight him. If he accepts it, I will defend him."

Lafayette was well prepared to fight the king on almost any front— militarily with support from the National Guard, legislatively through his influence in the National Assembly, and rhetorically in the court of public opinion, thanks to allies in the press who became increasingly active in the wake of the Bastille's fall. *Le Patriote français,* one of the new breed of explicitly political newspapers that emerged in 1789, was founded by Lafayette's abolitionist colleague Jacques-Pierre Brissot and was particularly avid in its support of the forward-looking marquis. Brissot had been inspired by the free press he'd encountered during his 1788 visit to the United States, and his paper's prospectus asserted that "without the Gazettes, the American Revolution, in which France played such a glorious role, could never have been achieved." His explicit intent was to make the *Patriote français* into a vehicle for promoting sweeping reform in France. And as soon as Brissot began publishing on a daily basis, praise of Lafayette's plans and speeches became a standard part of his paper's fare.

Lafayette was a formidable rival to the weakened monarch, but his power soon faltered on the streets of Paris. Although the National Guard was charged with keeping the peace, Lafayette could not deploy the militia against the people in time of crisis without losing his credibility—and possibly his life. The predicament weighed on Lafayette. He alluded to it on July 16 when, in a fit of frustration, he wrote, presumably to Madame de Simiane, that "this furious, drunken populace will not always listen to me." On the fateful date of July 22, he came face-to-face with the limits of his authority at a meeting that turned very ugly indeed.

Joseph-François Foulon de Doué understood that his life was in danger. The seventy-four-year-old financier had been named comptroller general of finances after Necker's July 11 exile, only to be dismissed eight days later when the king announced Necker's recall to France. Foulon was no friend of the general population. According to the weekly *Révolutions de Paris*—a paper that published its first issue on July 12—Foulon appeared to have profited at the expense of the nation, amassing "a stunning fortune" through "odious speculation" on the grain market. Worse still, he had reportedly scoffed at the starvation of the people, directing those afflicted by famine to sate themselves on hay. (The oft-repeated but almost certainly apocryphal story that Marie Antoinette, upon learning that the people lacked bread, exclaimed, "Let them eat cake!" may have originated as a variation on the Foulon story.) In a macabre episode that was later adapted by Charles Dickens in *A Tale of Two Cities,* Foulon planted rumors of his own demise, going so far as to fake his own funeral by burying a conveniently deceased servant in his stead. Dead in name only, Foulon quietly stole out of Paris with the probable intention of fleeing the country; he was apprehended by villagers in the town of Viry, having hidden himself at the home of a friend. It was said that one of the widely despised moneyman's own tenants had turned him in.

At five o'clock in the morning on July 22, a motley crowd deposited Foulon at the Paris Hôtel de Ville. Neither Lafayette nor Bailly was present, but the electors on site determined that Foulon, who had not been officially charged with any crime, should be imprisoned in the Abbey of Saint-Germain-des-Prés, located about a mile away, on the Left Bank, where he could later be turned over to the appropriate legal authorities. But with calls for Foulon's death already being voiced, a transfer in broad daylight seemed too dangerous. Foulon would therefore remain in protective custody at the Hôtel de Ville until after dark, when the move could be effected surreptitiously. That, at least, was the plan. As news of Foulon's whereabouts spread throughout the city, throngs of people flocked to the Place de Grève clamoring for instant gratification. "Hang him!" the crowd implored Bailly, as he desperately attempted to assure them that Foulon would be brought to justice after proper procedures had been followed.

Lafayette arrived in the midafternoon. By then, a crush of people had stormed the Hôtel de Ville, forcing their way through the court-yard, past barriers and guards, up the stairs, and into the assembly hall. There, Lafayette found a makeshift tribunal—having lost control of the situation, electors had been ordered by the crowd to judge the prisoner—that was doing its best to forestall a lynching. The room fell silent as Lafayette issued a personal plea. Noting that the people of France knew him well and had named him their general, he declared that his position "obliges me to speak to you with the liberty and frank-ness that form the basis of my character. You want to execute without trial this man before you: it is an injustice that would dishonor you, that would dishonor me, that would dishonor all the efforts I have made on behalf of liberty if I were to be weak enough to permit it; I will not permit it." Lafayette insisted that he did not wish to defend Foulon. He wished "only that the law be respected, the law without which there is no liberty, the law without which I would not have contributed to the revolution of the New World and without which I will not contribute to the Revolution in progress." As the *Journal de Paris* reported, Lafayette's was a speech of rare eloquence. The paper praised "the justice of the ideas, the grace of the expressions, the truth of the movements." Lafayette concluded by ordering that Foulon be conducted to the prison at the Abbey of Saint-Germain. Unfortunately, the words of the "orator hero" could not be heard above the din on the Place de Grève, and thus "served only to prove his talents."

A grand commotion ensued. Bailly wrote that "impatience began to turn into fury, violent clamors arose on the Place; cries announced that the Palais-Royal and the Faubourg Saint-Antoine"—neighborhoods that had become synonymous with revolutionary agitation—"were coming to take the prisoner." A wave of people surged toward the desk, and then toward the chair in which the captive was seated. Foulon was lost. Whisked across the room, down the stairs, and out the door, he was hanged from a lamppost on the Place de Grève—a plaza that had served for centuries as the site of some of France's most gruesome public executions. But Foulon's ordeal was not yet over. According to the *Révolutions de Paris,* no sooner had Foulon been hoisted aloft than the rope broke, sending him crashing to the ground. Instantly "it was reattached, a thousand hands, a thousand arms occupied themselves with his torture: soon, he was no more." Foulon's bloody head was impaled on a pike, a pitchfork full of hay stuffed into the open mouth as a reminder of the hated man's contempt for the starving.

In a gruesome spectacle of a type that was becoming all too familiar, the severed head was carried through the streets. By sheer happenstance, Foulon's son-in-law Louis-Bénigne-François Berthier de Sauvigny, formerly the royal intendant of Paris, had been taken prisoner in Picardy on suspicion of keeping grain from reaching Paris in order to drive up the price of wheat. Berthier was being transported through Paris in an open cabriolet escorted by 500 armed cavalry when it was spotted by celebrants rallying beneath Foulon's hay-filled head near the Hôtel de Ville. "Kiss Papa!" cried the crowd, as the bearer of the gory standard waved his trophy in Berthier's face. So grisly was the scene that a drawing of it was omitted from the series of prints published in multiple

Jean-Louis Prieur's drawing *Foulon's Head Shown to Berthier,* rejected from the *Tableaux de la Révolution française* in favor of a less grisly view of the same episode.

editions between 1791 and 1817 under the title *Tableaux de la Révolution française.* In its place, the *Tableaux* offered a more decorous, bird's-eye view of the Place de Grève with Foulon's unfolding ordeal barely discernible in the far distance. The *Révolutions de Paris* had no such qualms. It included an engraving of the unwelcome family reunion, noting in the caption that Berthier had inevitably suffered the same fate as his father-in-law.

Lafayette was profoundly unsettled. Just over one year earlier he had lamented the lassitude of his countrymen in a letter to Washington. The French, he had written, could not be roused to extremes. "Passive discontent" was the strongest response he had envisioned. Now he was obliged to look on in horror as men were murdered in the streets. The following day, he submitted his resignation, explaining in a letter to Bailly that "the people did not heed my advice; and the day I lack the confidence they promised me I must, as I said in advance, leave a position in which I can no longer be useful." The resignation was refused. Emissaries from the sixty districts of Paris flocked to Lafayette, beseeching him to remain in his post. Once more, his election was affirmed by general acclaim. On July 24, he wrote to a confidant. "What to do? I am in despair . . . I cannot abandon the citizens who place all of their confidence in me, and if I remain, I am in the terrible situation of witnessing evil without remedying it." In the end, he kept his commission, reasoning that if he could not rein in the violence, no one could.

The murders of Foulon and Berthier were still fresh in the collective mind of the deputies to the National Assembly on August 4, 1789, when they voted to alter the French power structure so fundamentally that the date has gone down in history as "the night the Old Regime ended." In a single marathon session that ran from six in the evening until two in the morning, the nation's representatives passed sweeping resolutions abolishing a host of feudal privileges that had endured for centuries. Lafayette was not at the assembly that night, but two men in his circle, the Vicomte de Noailles and the Duc d'Aiguillon, were among the most vocal advocates for reform, which they cast as the surest way to quiet the uprisings that had by then spread beyond Paris and were stirring up the countryside. Reading from prepared texts, they argued that the people had every reason to agitate for changes to a system that was inherently unjust and out of step with Enlightenment values.

Before the night was over, more than a dozen men—nobles, clergymen, and commoners alike—had highlighted injustices in need of redress. The Vicomte de Beauharnais proposed that "all ecclesiastical, civil, and military posts" should be open to "all classes of citizens" and that criminals should expect "equality of punishment" regardless of social status. The bishop of Chartres condemned the exclusive hunting rights enjoyed by the landed estates as "a curse" on rural areas that had been "battered by the elements for more than a year"; with so little nourishment available, "humanity and justice" demanded that peasants be permitted to hunt for food. Throwing itself into a frenzy of reform, the assembly approved all of these motions. It also voted to eliminate serfdom, to strip the nobility of its right to impose local taxes, to end the practice of purchasing military offices, and much else. Even the profoundly conservative Marquis de Ferrières assented to the changes, evidently out of fear. "It would have been useless, even dangerous," he explained to a friend, the Chevalier de Rabreuil, on August 7, "to oppose the general will of the nation. It would have designated you, you and your possessions, as victims of the furor of the multitude."

The significance of August 4 was lost on no one. Before adjourning, the deputies commissioned a commemorative medal immortalizing the date and arranged for a Te Deum to be sung. A deputation was dispatched to the royal chambers to share the news and to hail Louis XVI as the "Restorer of French liberty." At this early moment in the French Revolution, Louis was still widely seen as a benevolent monarch whose sanctioning of reforms had earned him the gratitude of his people. The hopefulness of that day proved to be short-lived, but it was felt deeply and celebrated widely.

In Paris, Lafayette's allies in the press ensured that he, too, would be lauded for his role in bringing about the nation's transformation. Although Lafayette had not been among the deputies who passed the historic legislation, cadre of journalists, artists, and printers reminded the public that his Declaration of the Rights of Man and his leadership after the fall of the Bastille had helped make the change possible. For instance, one triumphant hand-colored print, probably published shortly after August 4, bears the caption "The French nation aided by Lafayette defeats the despotism and feudal abuses that oppressed the people." Seen from a low vantage point, two monumental standing figures tower over their surroundings. Lafayette appears at the right, dressed in the uniform of a militia commander with the sword of authority raised high above his head and the National Guard arrayed behind him, the tricolor flag rising up from a collection of bayonets. Idealizing Lafayette's appearance, the image depicts his tall, slender body positioned in a balletic stance, striking a graceful pose befitting his status. He is not an aggressor but, rather, a well-bred partner who gently holds the outstretched left hand of an allegorical female figure of uncommon strength. Dressed in red and blue, the colors of Paris, this handsome woman sports the helmet and sandals of Athena (the ancient goddess of war and wisdom), clutches in her right hand a sheaf of lightning bolts—the favored weapon of Zeus himself—and wears around her shoulders a blue robe dotted with golden insignia, evoking the traditional regalia of the king of France. The bulging muscles of her exposed calves and the hideous writhing of the winged, humanoid monster trapped beneath her firmly planted right foot attest that her might is not merely a costume. With Lafayette's assistance, the image suggests, the French nation is all powerful—a pleasant interpretation of events but, unfortunately, not an accurate one.

Through the late summer and early fall of 1789, fiscal and political reform ground to a halt in Versailles while hunger and anger reached new heights in Paris. Although the National Assembly approved a final version of the Declaration of the Rights of Man on August 26, Octo-

La Nation Française assistée de M. De la Fayette terrasse le Despotisme et les Abus du Regne Feodal qui terrassaient le Peuple

The French Nation Helped by Mr de la Fayette Stops the Despotism and Abuses of the Feudal King Who Oppresses His People. Engraving. 1791.

ber arrived without the king signing off on it; Louis also neglected to sanction the abolition of feudal privileges approved by the deputies on August 4. As the nation despaired, unscrupulous individuals from every walk of life tried to turn the crisis to their own benefit. With flour scarce and bread prohibitively expensive, the Parisian bakers' guild, angered by the city's imprisonment of one of its members, threatened to go on strike if he was not released. Gouverneur Morris, who was considering going into the business of supplying Paris with flour and other food-stuffs, suspected municipal officials of "casting about for the Ways and Means to make Money out of the present Distress." Worst of all, Morris heard rumors that the Duc d'Orléans was fomenting agitation in the streets, the press, and the assembly, "plunging himself into Debts and Difficulties to support the present factious Temper"—hoping to seize power from Lafayette, Louis, and anyone else who might be toppled in the process. As Lafayette put it in a late August letter, "All hell has conspired against us."

On October 2—a "rainy disagreeable Day" in Paris—Morris felt that it was time to have a heart-to-heart talk with the overmatched marquis. After dinner at the Rue de Bourbon, Morris took Lafayette aside to warn him that he was losing control of the National Guard and, by extension, the city. Believing danger to be imminent, Morris urged that Lafayette "immediately discipline his Troops and make himself obeyed," emphasizing "that this Nation is used to be governed and must be governed, that if he expects to lead them by their Affection he will be the Dupe." Morris evidently agreed with Jefferson that a "canine appetite for popularity" was Lafayette's fatal flaw, but this view was not quite right. Glory, honor, and lasting fame were the treasures Lafayette sought—and his attempts to acquire them sometimes made him deeply unpopular. He expressed affection for the National Guard not because he craved adulation but because he could not imagine, blinded as he was by optimism, that his troops deserved anything less. Regardless of circumstance, Lafayette seldom foresaw the pitfalls ahead.

After months of hunger, the people of Paris became enraged when they learned of a feast held on October 1 in the royal opera house at Versailles. The revolutionary papers described it not merely as a spectacle of gluttony but as an "orgy." Leaders of the King's Bodyguard and officers of a recently arrived Flanders regiment broke bread together, drank toasts to Louis XVI, and sang songs in his honor seated at enormous tables on the opera's stage, while an orchestra provided musical accompaniment to the great delight of spectators who filled the theater's boxes. According to the *Révolutions de Paris,* when Marie Antoinette and the dauphin—both of whom were much beloved by the assembled officers—appeared before the celebrants, cries of "joy and jubilation" echoed through the hall and a lone voice could be heard above the din shouting, "Down with the colored cockades; long live the black cockade!" With that, the revelers began ripping from their hats the ornamental rosettes made of red and blue fabric that signified the revolution, sending a shower of cockades raining to the floor to be gleefully trampled under scores of boots. Soon, the women and children of the court, along with clergymen and other royalists, were merrily distributing black cockades, which may have been intended as a nod to the colors of the queen's native Austria (black and yellow) but in any case were certainly a signal of opposition to the revolution. A group of officers even had the audacity to wear these "insulting signs"—as the *Révolutions de Paris* called them—while reviewing a division of the National Guard.

In the days that followed, the revolution's opponents donned black cockades at their own risk. Rumors about the precise meaning of the black rosettes abounded; one story suggested that they might have been adopted by a coalition of thirty thousand noblemen who intended to sequester the king in the citadel at Metz with the aid of the royal guard before waging "war, in his name, against his people." The *Révolutions de Paris* reported that five black cockades were confiscated in a single afternoon at the Palais-Royal and that one man was struck down by "a hundred canes" after he removed his cockade, only to hold it up in the air and bestow upon it a "respectful kiss." Convinced that these small bundles of fabric signified nothing less than treason, one witness to the attack went so far as to argue that wearing black cockades should be prohibited on pain of death: "The law allows the killing of those who threaten our lives; well, anyone who wears a black cockade endangers the political life of the nation and the natural life of each citizen; the first person who wears an anti-patriotic cockade must therefore hang from the nearest lamppost." It was a twisted bit of logic, but emblematic of the fear and anger raging throughout the capital.

On October 5, 1789, alarm bells sounded through the gray Paris dawn as thousands of marketwomen streamed toward the Hôtel de Ville. The women—known to their critics as *poissardes,* or fishwives—wielded pikes and pitchforks as they hauled heavy cannons across the cobblestones of the Place de Grève. When Lafayette reached the scene later that morning, the National Guard had just managed to roust a crowd of would-be arsonists from the government building. The guardsmen strained to stem the furious tide of people pouring into the quays along the Seine and the adjacent streets. Incensed by the soaring price of flour, which left them unable to feed their families, the women were joined by husbands, brothers, and sons, all of whom shouted for bread. They were certain that an aristocratic plot was at the root of their starvation. "To Versailles!" they clamored, as Lafayette struggled to prevent a march that was rapidly becoming inevitable.

From nine in the morning until four in the afternoon, Lafayette refused to sanction a march to Versailles and forbade the guard, whose loyalties were beginning to waver, to undertake any such action. Back and forth he went, alternating between closed-door meetings with elected representatives of the Paris Commune and high-decibel debates with the crowd on the Place de Grève. Convinced that an attack on Paris was imminent, a young lieutenant in the grenadiers named Mercier cried out, "My general, the king has fooled us all, you and everyone else: he must be deposed." But still, Lafayette refused. Finally, between four and five, he came to understand that any opportunity to prevent a march had passed, as an intrepid contingent dominated by women and men armed with knives, picks, pikes, and pitchforks had started pulling cannons toward Versailles in the late morning. In the meantime, the weather had grown steadily worse—powerful winds had sprung up and a chilling rain was falling—but the crowd's determination showed no signs of flagging. After obtaining a face-saving command from the Paris Commune—who "authorized . . . and even ordered him to transport himself to Versailles"—Lafayette mounted his white horse and took charge of several National Guard regiments. Together, Lafayette and his troops accompanied a crowd of some thirty thousand armed and angry Parisians, arrayed six abreast, on a seven-hour trek along fourteen miles of dark and muddy roads.

According to Marie Antoinette's lady-in-waiting Madame Campan, news that the National Guard had set out from Paris reached Versailles that afternoon while the king was hunting at Meudon, about six miles away, and the queen was alone, lost in "painful thought," in her beloved gardens near the Trianon pavilion, not far from the spot where Lafayette's grandfather Édouard had taken his fatal fall in 1736. The royal household leapt into action: the Marquis de Cubières, equerry to the king, set out on horseback to encourage Louis XVI to abandon that day's hunt and return to the palace; the Comte de Saint-Priest, *secrétaire de l'état de la maison du roi* (the government minister charged with overseeing the king's household), sent a letter to Marie Antoinette urging the royal family to depart immediately for the Château de Rambouillet, some twenty miles southwest of Versailles; and servants began packing bags and loading carriages so that the royal family could be whisked to safety. A few carriages were already on the road when an update arrived—the first Parisian women were drawing near. Versailles had not been designed to withstand a military attack, but now its limited defenses were mobilized: gates that had stood open for a century were pulled shut and locked; the Flanders Regiment assembled on the Place d'Armes, the rounded plaza in front of the château; and the Swiss Guard made ready to stand its ground in the inner courtyards and gardens.

These and other preparations were in progress when Louis XVI and his entourage returned bearing new orders. The king had passed the

Parisian women as he made his way back from the hunt and had been gratified to hear cries of *"Vive le roi!"* from the crowd. Reassured that he would be safe at Versailles, he called off the move to Rambouillet. And, worried that a show of royal force would cause, rather than prevent, an escalation of violence, he ordered the Flanders Regiment to retire to its barracks. The men dutifully obeyed, but as they made their way from the Place d'Armes to their quarters, they found themselves pelted with rocks and gunshot. When Louis heard the news he began to reconsider his decisions but, as Madame Campan put it, "the moment to flee was lost."

Lafayette knew none of this as he rode slowly toward Versailles to meet a fate that was uncertain at best. As Morris described events in his diary, Lafayette "marched by Compulsion, guarded by his own Troops who suspect and threaten him." Yet this was the selfsame Lafayette who had managed to keep his head at Barren Hill as the redcoats bore down on his detachment from three sides, and now, in 1789, he still possessed the composure that had served him so well in 1778. With scores of lives in his hands—not only his own and his companions' but also the lives of the royal family—he did everything in his power to ensure a peaceful resolution. With the sound of drums and the flicker of torches heralding his approach, Lafayette halted the march at around eleven o'clock near the National Assembly's meeting hall in Versailles. There, he administered an oath to remind his troops of their allegiances; the men swore to honor "the nation, the law, and the king" before continuing on. While two officers were sent ahead to the château bearing assurances that Lafayette came to protect the king and not to oust him, a representative of the king appeared to inform Lafayette that Louis "saw his approach with pleasure" and "had just accepted his declaration of rights." Happily, everyone was in agreement on one point: they wanted to see as little bloodshed as possible.

Expectant cries filled the air as Lafayette drew closer to the palace. "Long live the King! Long live the Nation! Long live Lafayette and Liberty!" shouted the contingent of Parisians, who had been driven by fear and desperation to slog through miles of mud on the road to Versailles. Leaving his troops, Lafayette approached the Place d'Armes around midnight, accompanied by two civilians representing the Paris city government. Facing him from the other side of the padlocked grille, the Swiss Guard hesitated; wary though they were of Lafayette's motives, they admitted him to the courtyard and from there into the château, up the stairs, and to the Salon de l'Oeil de Boeuf—the very antechamber where he had awaited the king in 1774, when he was presented at court. But on this occasion, the room was filled with shouts instead of whispers. "There's Cromwell!" went the cry, but Lafayette rejected the comparison to the British general who had helped orchestrate the execution of King Charles I during the English Civil War. "Monsieur," Lafayette snapped, "Cromwell would not have entered alone." Still, the accusation struck a chord. Lafayette knew all too well that, with one false move, "instead of being a guardian, he would have been a usurper." As the Marquise de La Tour du Pin remembered the scene, Lafayette's voice filled with emotion as he explained to Louis the reasoning that compelled him to march: "Sire, I thought it better to come here, to die at the feet of Your Majesty, than to die uselessly on the Place de Grève." Louis XVI was in no position to argue. He gave Lafayette free run of Versailles.

By two in the morning some semblance of order had been established. With the king's guards maintaining calm inside the palace and National Guardsmen patrolling the grounds, Marie Antoinette felt secure enough to go to sleep with four ladies stationed in chairs pushed up against her bedroom door. At four-thirty, hearing shouts and gunshots ringing through the palace, they roused her. Giving the queen no time to dress, they hustled her through a narrow door and down a back passageway toward the king's chambers, tossing a petticoat after her. As though in a French farce gone grievously awry, the ladies reached the king's door only to find it locked. They knocked and were let in, but by then Louis was gone—he had taken the more public route to the queen's bedroom at the first sound of alarm. In the adjacent Salon de l'Oeil de Boeuf, royal guards faced off against armed citizens while the queen, reunited with her children, retreated to the bedroom. At last, a rapprochement involving the exchange of cockades was reached in the Salon de l'Oeil de Boeuf, and calm returned to the château.

Daybreak found Lafayette conferring with the king and queen in their apartments, where the Parisian troops now fraternized with the royal guardsmen. From the marble court below, the clamor grew louder and more menacing. The people were calling in angry tones for Marie Antoinette. At first, they got only Lafayette, who harangued them from the balcony to little effect. He stepped back inside, and speaking again with the uneasy monarchs, he brokered yet another deal. If they came with him to Paris, as the crowd demanded, he would guarantee their safety. They agreed. With that, Lafayette turned to the queen:

"Come with me."

"What? Alone on the balcony?"

"Yes, Madame. Let us go."

Together, Lafayette and Marie Antoinette appeared before the angry crowd. Unable to make himself heard, Lafayette resorted to a gesture that would later be cited by his enemies as a sign of double-dealing: he kissed the hand of the queen. With this gallant pantomime, Lafayette bestowed his blessing on Marie Antoinette and changed the hearts of the people. "Long live the general! Long live the queen!" To the sound of cheers, the pair left the balcony and began preparing for the journey ahead.

At approximately one o'clock in the afternoon on October 6, 1789, the royal family set out from Versailles in a carriage. Inside, Marie Antoinette clutched her coffer of diamonds. Outside, Lafayette rode beside the monarchs on a handsome white horse, keeping pace with the coach. A hundred carriages followed behind, bearing the National Assembly's deputies, while thousands of exhausted citizens and soldiers joined the historic journey on foot. It was six in the evening before Lafayette reached the Hôtel de Ville and quite dark by the time the royal family moved into a rambling suite of hastily evacuated apartments in their new home, the Tuileries Palace, which stretched along the banks of the Seine just west of the Louvre. There, Louis was fated to live by Lafayette's rules and under Lafayette's authority. On the morning of October 7, Lafayette attended what could only have been a very awkward ceremonial levee in the king's new chambers. For better or for worse, it seemed that Louis XVI would always have Lafayette at his side.

That the march to Versailles ended so calmly was nothing short of extraordinary. October 5 had witnessed its share of fatalities—the heads of two royal bodyguards had been transported to Paris on pikes—but large-scale carnage had been avoided, and much of the credit belonged to Lafayette. His uncommon ability to think clearly under pressure and his unparalleled credibility with the crowd had allowed him to wrest control from mayhem. That night, Lafayette proved to the world that he deserved his reputation as Washington's protégé. But the future would bring challenges that might have been too much for any man.

CHAPTER 15

TRIUMPH

Lafayette emerged victorious from a night that could well have been his last, but the time for celebration was not yet at hand. A seasoned general, he quickly surveyed the available options, assessed strategies, and then picked his next battle. He would spend the week from October 7 to October 14 embroiled in a political struggle with his old nemesis the Duc d'Orléans, who, having burnished his populist credentials, now called himself Philippe Égalité.

No one was certain how the tumult of October 5 began—the question remains open to this day—but several theories pinned the blame on Orléans. According to Madame Campan, "Many people averred that they had recognized the duc d'Orléans at four-thirty in the morning . . . at the top of the marble staircase pointing the way to the guardroom that led to the queen's bedchamber." The self-styled prince of equality was said to have been wearing a "redingote" (the word derives from the French attempt to pronounce "riding coat")—a style of jacket imported from Orléans's beloved England—and an unstructured hat with a turned-down brim. The *chapeau rabattu* would have been doubly handy; not only was the style generally worn by commoners, but its drooping edges were useful for shielding one's face from unwanted scrutiny. A pamphlet spelled out what Campan only implied—that Orléans had instigated the march on Versailles as part of a regicide plot that would have rendered him regent, if not king.

Lafayette might or might not have helped spread these rumors, but he was certainly happy to capitalize on them. Meeting with Orléans three times in a span of seven days, Lafayette succeeded in convincing the highborn Anglophile that London might prove a safer haven than Paris, and on Wednesday, October 14, Orléans appeared before the National Assembly to request a passport, claiming that he had been "charged by His Majesty with an important mission." In a letter to his ally Mounier, Lafayette admitted to having no proof that Orléans was conspiring against the king. If he had any, he wrote, "I would have denounced him." Yet Orléans did not call his bluff. Whether acting out of guilt or fear, or perhaps some combination of the two, the duke decamped for England on October 15.

Out of sight was, however, not out of mind. The possibility that Orléans might return to Paris weighed heavily on Lafayette, who enlisted the help of the Chevalier de la Luzerne—then serving as ambassador to London—to keep tabs on the duke's movements. Lafayette also dispatched one of his former aides-de-camp to the British capital to tell Orléans "that it would suit neither you nor [Lafayette] for you to return to Paris before the end of the Revolution." Indeed, if Orléans were to head for home, Lafayette would see him "as his enemy" and would challenge him to a duel on the morning after his arrival.

Even as Lafayette eased Orléans into exile, he choreographed an intricate political dance to stabilize the leadership of the nation and to ensure his own place in the power structure. His town house became a locus of coalition building as a steady stream of carriages made their way to the Rue de Bourbon filled with men seeking places for themselves or their friends in what they hoped might soon be a new government. That Lafayette had no legal authority to establish such a government, much less distribute appointments within it, seems to have been a matter of little concern.

Lafayette's strength rested in part on his military might, which had grown considerably on October 7, when Louis XVI had granted him control over any troops within a forty-five-mile radius of Paris, so that he might guarantee the "provisioning of the capital." Lafayette also wielded another, more symbolic, form of power, deriving from his symbolic role as the French embodiment of American liberty. In the wake of the October Days (as the events of October 5 and 6 became known), journalists friendly to Lafayette repeatedly emphasized the importance of this connection for the benefit of their readers. The *Courrier de Versailles à Paris et Paris à Versailles,* which was edited by Lafayette's former classmate Antoine-Joseph Gorsas, proclaimed on October 8 that the names of "Lafayette and Liberty" were "synonyms . . . made to be reunited." And on October 12, the paper hailed Lafayette as "the champion of liberty in two worlds."

Lafayette played the role to the hilt. The candidates and lobbyists who flocked to his cabinet struck deals in a room lined with English-language books on American politics—William Gordon's *The History of the Rise, Progress, and Establishment of the Independence of the United States of America* (1788), Joel Barlow's *The Vision of Columbus* (1787), and various works by Jefferson, Adams, and other leaders of the American Revolution—and decorated with the golden Declaration of Independence that Lafayette had commissioned in 1784. No one could have emerged from the study unaware of Lafayette's deep connection to the cause of liberty in the New World.

Morris was a frequent visitor to Lafayette's *cabinet* in these days. Reveling in the gamesmanship of French politics, he and Madame de Flahaut had already drawn up their ideal list of government ministers, and on Sunday, October 11, a visit to Lafayette was the first stop on Morris's busy social itinerary. He arrived at nine in the morning but was obliged to wait, as Lafayette was already occupied in conversation despite the early hour. Morris had friends—or, more precisely, friends of friends—whom he wished to see well placed, but first he would have to loosen Lafayette's grip on the reins of power. Morris tried to explain "that [Lafayette] cannot possibly act both as Minister and Soldier, still less as Minister of every Department. That he must have Coadjutors in whom he can confide." Lafayette raised moral objections to some of the names proposed by Morris, but the stubborn New Yorker would not take no for an answer. Continuing his quest to shake Lafayette from the optimism that, remarkably, seems not to have deserted him even during this period of radical social upheaval, Morris insisted that "Men do not go into Administration as the direct Road to Heaven . . . they are prompted by Ambition or Avarice and therefore . . . the only Way to secure the most virtuous is by making it in their Interest to act rightly."

To Morris, it would seem, bedfellows made strange politics. One of the men on whose behalf he was lobbying was his mistress's other lover, Charles Maurice de Talleyrand-Périgord, the bishop of Autun and a representative to the National Assembly—known to history simply as Talleyrand. As the firstborn son of a noble family, Talleyrand should have inherited the family fortune and carried on the name by the rule of primogeniture. But after a childhood accident left him with a club-foot, his image-conscious family settled all of his rights and privileges on a younger brother; they instead steered Talleyrand toward a path traditionally followed by second sons by sending him to the clergy. And yet he was a clergyman more in name than in spirit, as amply evidenced by the Comtesse de Flauhaut's giving birth to his child (a son) in 1784. No cause for embarrassment in the context of Parisian aristocratic mores, the lad was welcomed by the Comte de Flahaut, who was well aware that Talleyrand was the boy's father, and the infant was even portrayed with his mother in a scene of maternal tenderness painted by Adélaïde Labille-Guiard, one of the premier portraitists in Paris, and exhibited at the 1785 Salon. Morris and Talleyrand met frequently at the Hôtel de Flahaut—sometimes one arrived as the other departed, and at other times they sat and chatted amiably with or without the object of their mutual affection.

On Tuesday, November 3, Morris and Talleyrand visited Lafayette together. According to Morris's diary, Talleyrand concluded "that La Fayette has no fixed Plan," and Morris gathered that Lafayette had "a great Deal of the *Intriguant* in his Character" but that "he must be used by others because he has not talents enough to make use of them." Perhaps their jaded ways prevented them from seeing what Lafayette was about. He was in fact quite certain of the end he wished to achieve: a constitutional monarchy that guaranteed the liberty of the French people. But being unsure of the best way to attain his objective, Lafayette adopted the technique he had learned as a nineteen-year-old member of Washington's military family, methodically gathering advisers around himself so that he might listen to their thoughts before doing what generals inevitably must do: command and sally forth.

Many people got Lafayette wrong in those days, almost as though they couldn't believe that his single-minded dedication to the project of a constitutional monarchy might be genuine. Marie Antoinette suspected that Lafayette intended to usurp her husband's throne. As she confided in a conversation with Madame Campan, the queen felt sure "that the whole army was devoted to him and that everything he said about the pressure used against him to make him march on Versailles was merely a feint." In her opinion, Lafayette had orchestrated the October Days to showcase his own power, and rumors that Lafayette was fomenting crises to advance his own interests had been spreading through Paris at least since September. One popular pamphlet asked "Why, Citizens! have Lafayette, Bailly, and the chefs of the Commune

left you wanting for bread? . . . Imbecile residents of Paris and Versailles! . . . These villains [*scélérats*] think that you have too much life in
you." Parisians were fools to believe that their lives were more secure,
insisted the anonymous author, "in the hands of the traitor La Fayette,
this scoundrel, this vampire, than in those of your good king."

In a rare case of agreement across a growing political divide, agita-
tors on the extreme left concurred with traditionalists on the political
right on the issue of Lafayette: it was universally acknowledged that
he posed a grave threat to the liberty of the nation. Jean-Paul Marat, a
writer and the publisher of the radical newspaper *L'ami du peuple,* was
among the first and most outspoken of the republican firebrands who
believed Lafayette to be a military dictator in the making. Marat is perhaps best remembered today for his dramatic demise; he was stabbed to
death in his bathtub by a female assassin in 1793—an episode brilliantly
memorialized by Jacques-Louis David, who was an ardent Jacobin for
a few years and arguably the greatest French painter of the eighteenth
century. But before Marat became a martyr for the revolution, he was a
journalistic force to be reckoned with. Publicizing scandals, fanning the
flames of conspiracy theories, and issuing warnings of imminent doom
were among Marat's weapons of choice. Marat's tasks, in his own eyes,
included "inciting an ignorant, cowardly, and corrupt people to break
its tyrants' yoke." Defending his methods with chilling logic, Marat
insisted that "everything is permitted to shake the populace out of its
deadly lethargy, recall to it the sense of its rights, inspire it with the
courage to defend them." Lafayette's friend Gorsas saw Marat rather
differently, however, roundly denouncing him as "a vile and accursed
man having neither honor to lose nor virtues to risk, but a cowardly
pen to prostitute and black bile with which to infect paper."

The intense animosity that sprang up between Lafayette and Marat
had its roots in a dispute over freedom of the press that began during
the return to order following the October Days. Lafayette's feelings on
the subject were mixed. In 1787, he condemned as "seditious" the *avertissement* in which Calonne attempted to rouse the ire of the people
against the landed classes, and at least one preliminary draft of Lafayette's Declaration of the Rights of Man had allowed for limits on the
press, insisting that "no man may be disturbed either for . . . his opinions, or the communication of his thoughts by speech, writing, or print
unless he has disturbed the peace by slander." The version he presented
in public was far more liberal, though, listing "the communications

of his thoughts by all possible means" among every man's "inalienable and imprescriptible" rights. On October 8, the Châtelet—the criminal court of Paris, which was closely associated with both the city police and Lafayette's National Guard—issued a warrant for Marat's arrest. Officially, Marat was charged with having libeled one of the city's leaders, but behind the accusation lay a series of venomous attacks against the municipal and national governments. In one, Marat had gone so far as to call for the head of Necker, whom Marat had denounced as a traitor. In the wake of the march to Versailles, Lafayette seems to have reconsidered the consequences of unfettered free speech, especially in cases where incitement to violence was concerned.

On January 9, 1790, the National Guard made the first of several unsuccessful attempts to take Marat into custody. He responded in his favorite venue, placing an open letter to Lafayette in *L'ami du peuple*. As Marat described it, forty or fifty armed grenadiers and chasseurs had stormed into his home at eleven-thirty in the evening to arrest him for the high crime of publishing insults and slander. Not only should these "brave warriors" have been embarrassed by such an outsized show of force, wrote Marat, but they "should never forget that, being soldiers of the nation, they must never take up arms to oppress its defenders." He addressed Lafayette directly, insisting that "you, sir, on whom the confidence of the nation rests," should instill sentiments of restraint in the troops. Observing that the soldiers who came "to violate my privacy, and to tear me from my hearth" had been technically sent by the Châtelet, Marat absolved Lafayette of complicity, largely for rhetorical effect: "If this tribunal can make soldiers oppress the people with impunity and without your consent, who will stop them from using the national forces against the public? What will happen to your functions as Commander General? And what will the nation, which regards you as its avenger, think of you?" He concluded with a personal challenge, daring Lafayette "to justify in the eyes of the nation the sincerity of the patriotic sentiments that you profess." Lafayette did not respond to Marat directly, but before the year was out he would profess his patriotism more grandly than ever before.

Since November 29, 1789, cities and towns throughout France had been hosting picturesque "festivals of federation"—elaborately choreographed celebrations organized by local members of the National Guard, in which citizens witnessed their militiamen swearing allegiance to a reborn France and its new constitution. At each event, the local population constructed stage sets, designed costumes, and composed suites of music in an outpouring of creative fervor that swept the nation throughout the spring of 1790. The largest and most spectacular of these festivals was held on July 14, 1790, at the Champ de Mars in Paris—the parade ground for the École Militaire and, today, the home of the Eiffel Tower. The celebration was meant to mark the revolution's culmination, and it was destined to be Lafayette's day of triumph.

Preparations began in June, when Bailly, acting on behalf of the Parisian authorities, presented the city's plan for a Festival of Federation to the National Assembly. "Messieurs," he began, "a new order of things is emerging and will regenerate all the parts of the realm." Divisions among the provinces and their people having been banished, he declared, "There is now only one duty, that of submission to the law and the king; there is now only one sentiment, that of love and fraternity." Recognizing that the nation's future peace and prosperity would rest on this unity, Bailly rallied all "our brothers to come, as deputies of districts and departments, to join with us within our walls, in our presence, and to add to the civic oath already sworn by all the French that of being indivisibly united, to love each other always and to help each other, as the need arises, from one end of the realm to the other." By holding the event on July 14, the city intended to honor the fall of the Bastille, a date, Bailly concluded, that marked the beginning of "the epoch of liberty."

Festival of Federation, celebrated on the Champ de Mars, July 14, 1790.

Louis XVI preparing the ground for the Festival of
Federation at the Champ de Mars.

The assembly approved overwhelmingly. The president envisioned a "union of all the citizens, of all the soldiers of liberty, of all the military," who would join with "the king of a free nation" in swearing "with him to maintain this constitution as long as the sentiment of liberty and the enlightenment of reason exist among men." The curate of Saint-Germain l'Auxerrois was even more effusive. He predicted a veritable paradise on earth, in which "citizens of all ages" would be transported by "the holy joy that will enflame their hearts." As he saw it, July 14, 1790, would be a "beautiful day, which will never be erased from our memory."

The plan approved by the assembly called for the Champ de Mars to undergo massive renovations. An enormous, oval amphitheater would be carved out of the training grounds, stretching the entire length of the field. At the northern end of the arena, near the Seine, a triumphal arch would permit three columns of soldiers to enter in the manner of victorious Romans. And at the center of it all, on a raised, circular platform atop a flight of steps, amid clouds of incense wafting from a ring of braziers, Lafayette would lead the crowd in swearing allegiance to the

Souvenir of the Festival of Federation.

king, the nation, and the constitution, while Talleyrand—who, despite the various worldly roles he played, was a bona fide bishop—would consecrate the occasion with a Roman Catholic Mass. Louis XVI, who by this point had effectively become a bystander in his own realm, was to look on from a viewing platform covered with a canopy of blue and gold fabric to be erected just in front of the École Militaire. In the United States, Lafayette had been feted by every city he'd visited, but nothing in the young American republic could possibly compare with festivities that featured Lafayette upstaging his own monarch.

To bring about this glorious spectacle, the citizens of Paris were unable to tame the heavens, but they were willing to move the earth. After pouring rains delayed construction for weeks, men, women, and children of all ages and classes—including Lafayette, members of the National Assembly, and no less a figure than the king himself—labored for days on end, swinging picks, shoveling dirt, and pushing wheelbarrows for the cause, while their voices joined together to sing "Le carillon national"—*"Ah! Ça ira! Ça ira! Ça ira!"* Louis-Sebastien Mercier waxed rhapsodic about the heartwarming scene of 150,000 citizens peacefully united and recalled witnesses coming away with "their eyes bathed in tears." So picturesque was the sight that an anonymous society of artists took out a classified ad on July 12 offering hand-colored commemorative drawings depicting a "View of the Patriots' Work on the Champ de Mars." Each made-to-order drawing promised "gay scenes, unique tableaux, a striking mélange of varied costumes, an astonishing flurry of cheerful groups brought together by chance." Together, these joyous vignettes would help to "perpetuate the memory of an event that posterity will find hard to believe." Advance orders were welcome; any visitors from the provinces who might wish "to help their countrymen enjoy the view of a spectacle that they were not able to attend" were advised that pictures commissioned before the festival would be ready for pickup four days later.

Such enterprising draftsmen were but a small part of the vast cottage industry that sprang up in Paris in July 1790 as individuals from all walks of life sought to cash in on the opportunities presented by the influx of tens of thousands of men from every corner of the nation. Advertisements for products and services ranging from commemorative souvenirs to ride-shares for the homeward journey vied for the attention of "Messieurs les Députés" in the pages of the daily *Affiches, annonces, et avis divers.* Capitalizing on a fortuitous view of the Champ de Mars, the owner of a "large and comfortable house" situated on the Chaillot hill offered all-inclusive tickets for twenty-four livres apiece, providing "refreshments of all variety," an afternoon concert, "a good dinner" at nine p.m., and a grand ball to cap off the night. Another property owner sold no-frills seats with views of the procession at lower rates varying from three livres to one livre, sixteen sous, depending on proximity and line of sight. Performances and spectacles adopted patriotic themes, as the Comédie Française appended topical verses to its presentation of July 9—for instance, taking liberties with the geography of America's heroes to produce the rhyme "Paris, like Boston / has in Bailly, in Lafayette / its Franklin and its Washington." On July 11, a commercial pleasure ground in the Marais called the Vauxhall d'Été offered illuminations, fireworks, and a spectacular reenactment of "The Taking of the Bastille," described as a "grand pyrotechnic Pantomime ending with The Temple of Liberty." And on July 14, just hours after the national festival concluded, the circus at the Palais-Royal re-created it in a "musical drama," with tickets priced at double the usual cost.

As fate would have it, the festival itself turned out to be a sodden affair, as a cold wind and frequent downpours arrived before dawn on July 14, drenching the crowds camped out on the Champ de Mars. The dreadful weather continued for most of the day, but no item was omitted from the agenda, as the *fédérés,* as members of the National Guard from each of the nation's eighty-three departments were known, started gathering at six in the morning and celebrated through the morning and afternoon, with events culminating in a dinner held in their honor at the nearby Château de la Muette at six in the evening. The opening procession alone lasted hours: representatives from scores of civil and military groups filed through the triumphal arches in fits and starts. The army sent detachments of cavalry, grenadiers, artillerymen, chasseurs, and hussars. Paris was represented by its electors and mayor as well as the presidents of each district, a battalion of veterans, a group of children, and a corps of musicians. The National Assembly was out in full force, joining the Paris National Guard and the *fédérés*. It was not until three-thirty in the afternoon that Talleyrand took his place at the altar to bless the white flags held aloft by the eldest member of every departmental deputation. Following a full Latin Mass, Lafayette's moment finally arrived. Five hundred drums beat as one as he climbed the steps to the altar. Miraculously, the rain abated as Lafayette led the assembled crowd, some 350,000 strong, in swearing allegiance to the nation, the law, and the king.

Helen Maria Williams, an English author who attended the Festival of Federation, surely exaggerated when she called the spectacle "the triumph of human kind," but it was indisputably the triumph of Lafayette. The *Révolutions de Paris,* whose editors had grown wary of Lafayette's overweening success, parodied the day's outsized displays of affection in a tongue-in-cheek report on the *fédérés'* fondness for their hero: "Ten thousand of them dashed towards him, some kissing his face, others his hands, others his uniform: it was only with great difficulty that he managed to remount his horse." Referring to Suetonius's account of the notoriously depraved emperor Caligula, who appointed his horse consul, the authors predicted that "if there had been an election, popular folly might have lavished on M. de la Fayette's horse . . . the honors that a Roman emperor bestowed upon his own in a fit of despotic frenzy."

In contrast to Lafayette's white horse, Louis XVI was barely noticed. Declining to join the grand procession due to the rain, the king entered the royal pavilion through a rear door. He bore no scepter and wore neither crown nor ceremonial robe. Put out by this grandiose display of his own insignificance, the king did not so much as "bother to leave his throne for the altar to give the people who had loaned him twenty-five million [livres] . . . the satisfaction of seeing him take the oath," in the words of the *Révolutions de Paris.*

In the hours and days that followed the oath taking, Lafayette continued to reign triumphant. William Short, Jefferson's private secretary

Lafayette at the altar of the Festival of Federation, July 14, 1790.

who succeeded Jefferson as the American ambassador to France, wrote to Morris, then sojourning in London, to say that Lafayette "seemed to have taken full possession of the *fédérés*—his popular manner pleased them beyond measure." Writing to Jefferson, Short noted that Lafayette had opened the ground floor of his home to the *fédérés*, feeding at first one hundred, then a hundred and fifty, then two or three hundred men every day at tables set up wherever space permitted. According to the Englishwoman Helen Maria Williams, Lafayette, "who is so justly the idol of the French nation," was nearly smothered at the feast at La Muette. Writing to a friend in England, she related that Lafayette had cried out, "But, my friends, you stifle me!" before being whisked away in the interest of his own safety. For the rest of the week, as dances and festivals enlivened the streets of Paris and visiting soldiers filled the arcades of the Palais-Royal with "the air of the general rendez vous of all the votaries of Mars, Bacchus, and Venus," the *Révolutions de Paris* observed that Lafayette "was everywhere, and everywhere he received

the honors of an apotheosis." An illuminated transparency of his likeness and a corresponding image of Bailly were erected on the Pont
Neuf, placed on either side of the equestrian statue of the still-beloved
Bourbon monarch Henri IV, while a vast outpouring of prints, paintings, poems, and songs celebrated Lafayette as the man who brought
liberty to France. According to the *Révolutions de Paris,* as the *fédérés*
began to pack their bags full of souvenirs to share with friends and family at home, "all the editions of the portrait of this hero sold out."

Among the thousands of pieces of revolutionary memorabilia held
in the remarkable collections of the Musée Carnavalet (the museum
of Paris history), one oil painting epitomizes the week's veneration of
Lafayette. The artist, whose identity is unknown, offers a close-up view
of the patriotic altar erected on the Champ de Mars just as Lafayette
begins to read the oath to the expectant crowd. Dressed in his blue-
and-white National Guard uniform, Lafayette stands proudly atop the
circular platform, his upright posture echoed by the columnar altar
in front of him and the triumphal arch in the distance. Talleyrand, in
his bishop's miter, stands a few steps down, in a position so marginal
that his robes seem to flow past the picture's rightmost edge. At the
left, two *fédérés*—perhaps the men who commissioned the painting—
gaze directly at the viewer as their companions tilt their heads upward,
mouths parted in anticipation of the coming pledge. Lafayette's raised
left hand holds a piece of paper, presumably the text of the oath, while
he points with his sword, using his right hand, at the base of a small
crucifix. Although dark clouds occlude much of the sky, three diagonal
beams of light streak down through a clear blue patch at the upper left,
pointing directly at Lafayette, as though the very forces of nature had
conspired to heighten the drama. A gust of wind threatens to topple
the red, white, and blue figure of a patriotic altar boy, who struggles to
remain upright as his tricolor flag, caught in the wind, pulls him back.
Lafayette alone stands effortlessly erect, commanding our admiration.

CHAPTER 16

UNFLATTERING PORTRAITS

illiam Short had been in politics long enough to recognize a missed opportunity when he saw it. Like the vast majority of observers, Short believed that the Festival of Federation had marked "the zenith" of Lafayette's "influence," as he wrote to Gouverneur Morris two weeks after the event. But he was one of the few to express a prescient regret that Lafayette did not capitalize more fully on that triumph. Short lamented that Lafayette had "made no use of it, except to prevent ill." Looking ahead, he worried that "the time will come, perhaps when [Lafayette] will repent having not seized that opportunity of giving such a complexion as every good citizen ought to desire."

In fact, the time was already at hand, as challenges were springing up daily on a national level. Insurrections roiling the army in the far reaches of France were a particularly vexing development, as Lafayette noted in correspondence with his cousin the Marquis de Bouillé, a former governor of Martinique who was stationed in Metz as commander of a portion of the Army of the East. An ardent defender of the monarchy, Bouillé had sworn allegiance to the new constitution only at the king's behest and was now contemplating the various options that lay before him. Uncertain of how much support he should lend, he wrote to sound out Lafayette, who responded, "If I love liberty and the principles of our constitution above all, my second wish, my very ardent wish, is for the return of order, calm and for the establishment of the public force." Lafayette understood as well as anyone that the success of a revolution depended on its army, and he took the opportunity to try to win Bouillé fully to the side of the constitution: "let us serve it, my dear cousin, with all of our power," vanquishing "all that might disturb the happiness and peace of our fellow citizens, from whatever side the attacks might come." Lafayette was being candid; he had no grand plans to hide and no personal agenda beyond ensuring liberty in the best way he knew how.

Three months later, as dissent in the army worsened, Lafayette confessed his deepening troubles to Washington, who was then serving his first term as president. Lafayette was worried not only about the king's émigré brothers, who talked of raising foreign armies to retake France, but also about threats from Orléans and others on the left who had donned the populist mantle. Writing from Paris on August 23, he reported to Washington on "Revolts among the Regiments," explaining that "as I am Constantly Attacked on Both Sides . . . I don't know to which of the two we owe these insurrections." Yet he correctly surmised that the more immediate danger to his own authority came from the left. As he put it, "I Have lately lost Some of My favour with the Mob, and displeased the frantic lovers of licentiousness, as I am Bent on Establishing a legal Subordination."

Lafayette's political rivals had been sharpening their attacks against him prior to the Festival of Federation, and his apotheosis on that day only urged them to bolder actions. Orléans returned to Paris over Lafayette's objections in the first week of July and may well have begun his campaign of defamation as early as May, when a pamphlet bearing many of his hallmarks claimed to recount the *Private, Impartial, Political, Military and Domestic Life of the Marquis de La Fayette, General of the Cornflower.* Featuring more than ninety pages of personal and political calumny, the pamphlet garnered attention from the police and the reading public alike, and in May 1790, a bookseller was arrested and jailed for four days for purveying this scurrilous publication, until a plea from Lafayette led to his release. The arrest did little to dampen interest in the pamphlet, however, and it could still be purchased on the streets of Paris in May 1791. Railing against a topsy-turvy world filled with "pygmies disguised as giants," the anonymous author issued a taunting address to the "honorable followers and zealous partisans of the little Auvergnac Cromwell." Toying with Lafayette's admirers, the pamphlet offered them mock encouragement in a torrent of angry prose:

> Continue to adore your idol, to flatter his pride while beating your drums on the battlefields, as he, all perfumed and dolled up by the

hands of a circle of courtesans, steps out of an elegant carriage, hiding, beneath a coiffure more ridiculous than martial, the horns that he received as a wedding present from his lubricious companion.

Orléans was likely the wealthiest and most influential of Lafayette's rivals in the summer of 1790, but he was not the only man vying for control. Other contenders for power, including the artful Mirabeau and the three deputies to the National Assembly who were known collectively as the Triumvirate—Antoine Barnave, Adrien Duport, and Alexandre de Lameth—were committed to upholding order while embracing reform. Each man attempted to carve a path between the equally undesirable extremes of absolute monarchy and chaos. Together and separately, Lafayette, Mirabeau, and the Triumvirate dominated an unstable political center throughout much of 1790 and 1791 as they established and dissolved alliances, struck side deals with the king, and tacked back and forth between the court and the people.

When Lafayette wrote to Washington on August 23, he expressed hope that he would be able to end the quarrels that prevented the moderates from banding together, although the situation demanded a type of politicking that had never come naturally to Lafayette. Emboldened by the courage of his convictions to the point that he was nearly blinded by certainty, Lafayette adopted a flat-footed negotiating strategy almost guaranteed to alienate would-be allies. Early in August, word reached Morris in England that a growing rift within the Triumvirate had prompted Lameth to reach out to Lafayette in the hope of establishing a new coalition. But Lafayette evidently dismissed the very notion in a phrase that bordered on bombast, responding with "a Declaration that in the present Situation there was no Alternative but Victory or Death."

Others allowed themselves greater latitude. While Lafayette clung fast to his principles, the nimble orator Mirabeau, ever the master of the convenient deal, was busy negotiating with the king and queen in the hopes of supplementing, if not supplanting, the influence he believed Lafayette wielded at court. Whether Mirabeau was using the monarchs or the monarchs were using him is a question that has no clear answer, but Mirabeau was entirely open about his desires. On June 29, 1790, he drafted a letter for Louis XVI to send to Lafayette, ordering "that he agree to consult with Mirabeau on matters concerning the interest, the well-being of the State, my service, and my person." (The king never dispatched the letter, but neither did he discard it. It was found in the notorious *armoire de fer*—a secret iron chest, discovered behind a panel in the Tuileries Palace in 1792 during the search for evidence to be used at the king's trial.) Moderates hoping to quell the infighting made occasional attempts to broker a peace between Lafayette and Mirabeau, but the enmities continued until Mirabeau's death (apparently from natural causes) on April 2, 1791.

Lafayette was as skeptical of Mirabeau as he was of Orléans—he called them both "Cowards" in his August letter to Washington and suggested that "there is something Cloudy in the Present systems of those two men"—yet he remained confident that they would be defeated quickly. In fact, he predicted a rapid conclusion to the entire revolution, writing that "I hope our Business will End with the Year." After that, Lafayette envisioned a retirement much like Washington's. Poking fun at his own reputation, he explained that once the revolution ended, "this So much Blackened Cromwell, this Ambitious dictator, Your friend, Shall most deliciously Enjoy the Happiness to Give up all power, all public Cares, and to Become a private Citizen in a free Monarchy."

Lafayette was jesting, but murmurs that he might be inclined to abuse his military might were growing louder. On August 16, the National Assembly voted "without discussion and unanimously" to place Lafayette's cousin the Marquis de Bouillé at the head of an army charged with quashing open insurrection in three regiments—one Swiss and two French—stationed in the northeastern garrison town of Nancy. Prompted by Lafayette, the assembly authorized Bouillé to use whatever force might be needed. In an August 18 letter apprising Bouillé of the vote, Lafayette made clear that the rebelling troops should be shown no mercy. "The decree concerning Nancy," he wrote, "is good; its execution must be entire and vigorous." As Lafayette saw it, the nation had to be saved before it slid into chaos:

> Now is the moment, my dear cousin, when we can begin the establishment of constitutional order that must replace revolutionary anarchy . . . let us not be discouraged . . . let us hope that by uniting all of our forces for the establishment of the constitution, by steeling ourselves against all domestic and foreign difficulties, we will assure liberty and public order at the same time.

In a "fraternal" rather than "official" capacity, Lafayette also wrote to the commanders of the National Guard of four neighboring regions, asking them to join with Bouillé's forces. Their collective goal, he declared, must be to "strike a mighty blow for the entire army."

The insubordination in Nancy abated briefly only to stir up again on August 25, when a general sent to review the regiments' finances was held captive in his quarters by the Swiss soldiers. As Lafayette promised, members of the National Guard were promptly dispatched, but many of them sided with the Swiss mutineers. When the general escaped to nearby Lunéville on August 28, the soldiers and citizens of Nancy arrested a number of the National Guard's officers and began arming themselves for the anticipated retribution. With Bouillé and an army several thousand strong now advancing toward the city, the soldiers of Nancy sent a deputation to plead their case before the National Assembly. It was their only hope. On August 31, as the assembly debated whether to intervene, the Jacobin Maximilien Robespierre and others on the left called for an inquiry. Lafayette objected. Instead, he argued that "Monsieur Bouillé needs a show of support from the Assembly, and that we must give it to him." Barnave proposed, and the assembly passed, a motion endorsing Bouillé's mission to restore order.

While the assembly weighed the pros and cons, Bouillé marched his troops to the gates of Nancy. At first, it seemed that the soldiers would surrender, and the Swiss were in fact departing when Bouillé's troops came under cannon and gunfire issuing from soldiers and citizens alike. When the shooting was over, hundreds of Bouillé's men lay on the ground, Nancy was obliged to bury ninety-four bodies of its own, and the numbers of casualties mounted as the injured succumbed to their wounds over the course of the next few days. The rebellious Swiss soldiers faced harsh sentences: twenty-three were executed and forty-one were condemned to serve thirty years in the galleys. Another seventy-one soldiers were referred to their regiments for judgment, and several hundred citizens of Nancy were taken into custody. As part of the subsequent crackdown, the Jacobin Club of Nancy, which had supported the uprising, was shuttered, and the wearing of the revolutionary cockade was banned in the city.

When the news reached Paris on September 2, tens of thousands of people took to the streets in protest, and the radical press unleashed a torrent of vitriol. Marat reached the peak of his anger on September 15 with an open letter in *L'ami du peuple* so inflammatory that the municipal authorities ordered the issue confiscated. The letter lambasted "General Motier" (Marat's preferred name for Lafayette) for "pretending to pass for a good citizen, a true patriot, because fifteen thousand automatons" refused to hear otherwise. Writing off the men of the National Guard as "young fools, completely incapable of reflection," Marat blamed Lafayette for preying on their weakness and deployed fiery rhetoric to accuse him of betraying the ideals of George Washington:

> That you, a mature and educated man, you so-called patriot to whom our fellow citizens, seduced by the appearance of virtue that you put on, abandoned themselves in such good faith, that you would be willing to move the earth to turn the Parisian militia into an army of praetorians, is an execration of which few party leaders would be capable; it is reserved for the American hero, the great general, the immortal restorer of liberty.

"Villain!" Marat exclaimed. "Abandon your cowardly machinations if you are not completely dead to honor, or rather, stop deluding yourself, your tricks will get you nowhere."

Marat was hardly the only one raking Lafayette over the coals. Camille Desmoulins, the editor of the left-wing journal *Révolutions de France et de Brabant,* denounced him in a funeral oration for fellow journalist Élysée Loustalot, who'd died of natural causes. Desmoulins avowed that Loustalot had expired with "the name of Lafayette on his lips" after reaching the painful realization that Lafayette was no more than an "an ambitious officer" whose spirit was never great enough "to play the role of Washington." In fact, he insisted, Lafayette had effectively murdered Loustalot: "Yes, it is you, Lafayette, who killed him, not with the dagger of an assassin or the legal blade of the judge, but through the pain of seeing nothing but the most dangerous enemy of liberty in you, in whom we placed all of our confidence, and who should have been liberty's strongest supporter."

Even Brissot was losing faith. In a 1787 letter, he had warned Lafayette that "the art of circumspection, the need always to keep one's options open and to avoid possible traps, the desire to have only friends and to caress one's enemies . . . all these timid maxims will, in the end, extinguish virtue itself." Brissot was now convinced that his fears were finally coming to fruition. On September 1, 1790, his newspaper *Le Patriote français* reported "with regret" that Lafayette had encouraged the assembly to declare its support for Bouillé. "It is difficult for a patriot to believe that he spoke these words," wrote Brissot, who preferred "to suspend judgment until other accounts clarify whether he might not have misheard." As the records show, however, he had heard correctly.

Not only did Lafayette utter those words; he also believed them. He prized liberty, and yet he was certain that it could be achieved only through law and order. And if he'd ever had a moment's doubt, the lynchings he'd seen in 1789 had convinced him of the potential hazards of chaos.

Although Lafayette's principled position left him increasingly isolated, he was still supported by the municipal authorities and the National Guard. The assembly of the city of Paris sent a deputation to express gratitude for his service, and on September 10, members of the National Guard filled the Rue de Bourbon in front of his town house, pledging to "swear a new oath of fidelity" to their general. But this scene only elicited more criticism from the *Révolutions de Paris,* which called it "idolatry" and insisted that Lafayette reject any oaths but those sworn to the nation, the law, and the king. The following week, the paper went further still, placing the blame for the Nancy debacle on Lafayette's shoulders:

> It is M. de Lafayette who plunged the National Assembly into all of the missteps that it made on this subject . . . it is he who named M. de Bouillé, his relative, to march against the patriotic soldiers. . . . It is M. de Lafayette who turned the legislative body against the various corps of the garrison of Nancy. . . . It is your general who, exercising at the same time the functions of legislator and commander of the capital's public forces, mounted the podium at the National Assembly to request advance approval of the conduct of M. de Bouillé.

As the *Révolutions de Paris* saw it, the events at Nancy resulted not from accidents of poor judgment but from a premeditated plot against the nation. The article concluded that Lafayette's maneuvers had been designed "to misdirect the patriotism of the Parisian army [and] have completely succeeded."

On September 22, Lafayette led a procession to the Champ de Mars—the second in little more than two months. This time, the mood was somber. Black draperies interlaced with white crepe hung on the national altar, and doleful music filled the air, as sixty priests presided over a funeral Mass for the soldiers who'd fallen during the siege of Nancy. As the cortège made its way to the ceremonies, people lining the streets looked on in silence. According to the *Révolutions de Paris,* the spectators fixed their eyes on Lafayette, "seeming to accuse him of all the sorrows they had come to mourn on the Field of the Federation."

In the autumn of 1790, one more rancid ingredient fell into the bubbling stew of accusations against Lafayette: he was said to be having an affair with the queen. Although Lafayette and Marie Antoinette had indeed been conferring about the future of the government behind closed doors, all credible sources concur that the queen felt nothing but contempt for the general, who was, in her view, the loathsome man who had led a murderous horde to Versailles during the October Days of 1789. In a letter to her closest confidant, the Austrian diplomat Florimond Claude, Comte de Mercy-Argenteau, Marie Antoinette wrote on July 12, 1790, "Everything goes from bad to worse: the minister [Necker] and M. de la F[ayette] take missteps every day. We go along with all of them, and instead of being satisfied these monsters become more insolent by the moment." But the palpable enmity between them did not prevent Lafayette from becoming a standard character in a steady stream of pornographic prints and pamphlets of a type that, having defamed Marie Antoinette for more than a decade, had surged in popularity with the onset of revolution. The rumors were preposterous, but they made for irresistibly salacious reading.

"What double rapture! What divine pleasure! What a joy to fuck and be fucked at the same time!" Thus Lafayette is purported to exclaim in the first chapter of *The Patriotic Brothel Founded by the Queen of the French for the Pleasures of the Deputies of the New Legislature,* one of the pamphlets that emerged in 1791 from the circle of the Duc d'Orléans, who employed as his primary propagandist Choderlos de Laclos—the author of *Les Liaisons dangereuses*—and who was long presumed to have been behind much of the slander leveled against Marie Antoinette. Now Orléans turned his copious resources against his rivals for the leadership of Paris. In the pamphlet, Lafayette's exclamation comes during a three-way sexual encounter among himself, Marie Antoinette, and Bailly. Lafayette had been accused of playing both sides of the political game, and here he plays both sides in a more carnal sense. But just as the threesome begins to heat up, the queen becomes worried that Lafayette might lose his resolve. "Courage, my friend, don't pull out;

thrust ahead!" she admonishes him. (Perhaps she remembered Lafayette's reputation for dramatic retreats—one might say withdrawals—during the American war.)

Lafayette was just one of many figures taken down a notch in *The Patriotic Brothel,* but still other pamphlets were devoted entirely to imagined goings-on between Lafayette and the queen. Although the details varied, the premise was generally the same: the pair were said to be joined in an unholy alliance to debase the nation and cuckold its king. Such is the immortal theme of *The Amorous Nights of General Motier and the Beautiful Antoinette, by the Austrian Woman's Little Spaniel* (1790)—a tell-all reputedly set to paper by the queen's dog in a fit of jealousy; the spaniel resented having to share his mistress's favors with Lafayette. Similar narratives unfold in *Marie Antoinette in an Awkward Spot; or, Correspondence of La Fayette with the King, the Queen, La Tour du Pin & Saint-Priest* (1790) and *The Confession of Marie Antoinette, Former Queen of France, to the French People, About Her Loves and Her Intrigues with M. de La Fayette, the Principal Members of the National Assembly, and Her Counter-revolutionary Projects* (1792). Even after the queen had been beheaded and Lafayette locked away in an Austrian prison, the sexual libels continued unabated; in 1792 booksellers offered *The Good-byes of La Fayette; or, Capet the Younger, to Antoinette, and His Last Correspondence While Fleeing the Lands of Liberty.*

Visual artists, too, had great fun with such material, using imagined sexual couplings as fodder for prints that depicted Lafayette as he had never before been seen. *My Constitution* is a delicately rendered aquatint engraving filled with astonishingly bawdy humor. The oval composition presents a well-appointed interior where Marie Antoinette reclines against the front edge of a sofa with her skirts lifted, her legs splayed, and the space directly beneath her private parts labeled ironically "res publica"—the state—echoing the quote that appeared on the print of Washington commissioned by Lafayette in 1779. Nothing on the woman's person identifies her as the queen, but royal status is signaled at the right, where a winged putto raises his right hand to his lips in a gesture of silence as he knocks a crown off the top of a royal orb decorated with three fleurs-de-lis. Lafayette kneels before the queen in full uniform, his left hand resting against his chest and his right placed firmly on her pudendum. Lest there be any question as to the precise nature of this liaison, the decoration on the pedestal beneath the orb clarifies the matter: it features a bas-relief of a rigidly vertical penis, evocatively contrasting with the soft folds of the billowing curtains at the left.

This is clearly a dirty picture, but more important, it is a pointed political critique. The title's reference to the "constitution," for instance, is a play on words of a type that abounded in the satirical verse of the era. The term plainly refers to the recent swearing of oaths led by Lafayette at the Festival of Federation, but the first syllable—*con*—is French slang for "idiot" or "jerk" and can also mean "twat" or "cunt." Pornographic pamphlets abounded with the latter usage, as writers of ribald doggerel made hay of the facile pun, often italicizing, capitalizing, or separating "con" from the rest of a word to emphasize the point with an orthographic elbow to the ribs. Just as Lafayette upstaged Louis XVI on that rainy July afternoon, so too does he supposedly usurp the king's prerogative in the graphic imaginings of *My Constitution* by claiming for himself the queen's *con;* and the visual puns don't end there, as Lafayette's gesture subtly mimics the vogue for oath taking that swept the nation. Extending his right arm, he repeats the very motion made by tens of thousands of *fédérés* on the Champ de Mars, who were, in turn, echoing the elected deputies who swore the Oath of the Tennis Court in 1789. But the oath in *My Constitution* differs in one crucial respect from the others: the representatives to the Estates General and the *fédérés* were committing themselves to the public good and affirming their readiness to lay down their lives for the national interest. Lafayette, in contrast, is shown taking an oath of a far more

My Constitution. Pornographic print depicting Lafayette and Marie Antoinette, c. 1790.

private, and far less noble, variety, declaring himself willing to sacrifice the public good in the interest of his own illicit pleasure.

Were this image anomalous, it would be a mere footnote to history. But *My Constitution* is typical of a whole host of prints and pamphlets that cast Lafayette and the queen in comically erotic vignettes. Another of the type, sometimes given the title *L'âge d'or,* depicts a lover's reunion with an astonishing twist. In the center of the image, a mounted officer of the National Guard dressed in full uniform—the conventional visual shorthand for Lafayette—holds a pair of roses in his right outstretched hand. At the right, a standing woman is poised to greet his arrival, raising her left hand as though ready to receive the flowers. Yet these details are mere window dressing to be noticed only after the viewer has recovered from the startling sight of the officer's mount, for this gallant soldier is riding an enormous penis that stands erect on two equine legs, a ring of pubic hair fulfilling the function of a saddle and a feathery white tail protruding from the rear portion of its testicles. An arc of liquid spraying from the top of its head suggests that our hero may be overly excited by the amorous encounter.

Pornographic print depicting Lafayette
greeting Marie Antoinette, c. 1790.

LA POULLE D'AUTRYCHE

or largent avec facilitée|mais la constitution jene

The Austrian/Ostrich Hen. Caricature of Marie
Antoinette, c. 1791.

More than just a crude joke at Lafayette's expense, the bipedal penis
adapts yet another play on words and images to identify the standing woman as Marie Antoinette. With its long neck, feathery tail, and
rounded torso perched on two slender legs, the creature bears a striking
resemblance to an ostrich, known in French as an *autruche,* which in
turn sounds quite a bit like *Autriche*—Austria—the queen's native land,
and the nation with whom she was rumored to be plotting a military
alliance that would restore France to absolute monarchy. The pun is
spelled out in another caricature from the same period that identifies a
female bird with a vaguely human face as both *"la poule d'autruche"* (the
ostrich hen) and *"la poule d'autryche"* (the Austrian hen).

Who commissioned these prints? One can't be certain—most of the
era's pornographic caricatures were produced either anonymously or
under false names—but in the case of *L'âge d'or,* all signs point in the
direction of Orléans. One variant on this print was skillfully executed
in the labor-intensive medium of hand-colored etching, making it
expensive both to produce and to purchase and suggesting an upscale
patron and audience; Orléans and his friends fit the bill. But the most

important Orléans fingerprint, if one can call it that, is the two-legged penis.

Pictures and sculptures of phalluses with legs (as well as phalluses with tails, phalluses with wings, and even phalluses with their own phalluses) were enjoying something of a heyday among the reform-minded French and British elite. Such images had been much repro-duced as part of the ongoing interest in the findings from Herculaneum and Pompeii—the ancient Roman cities near Naples that, having been buried in volcanic ash in A.D. 79, had attracted widespread attention since the middle of the eighteenth century, when excavations began to uncover streets, buildings, and objects that had endured surprisingly intact.

Easily identified by his oversized and always erect penis, Priapus was the god of fertility and, by extension, served as a protector of gardens. In 1791, a herm—or bust on a pillar—of Priapus would play a key role in the frontispiece for the Orléanist satire *The Patriotic Brothel,* in which a pair of women interact with the carved deity in an out-door setting. The woman at the left, identified in the text as Marie Antoinette, rubs the signature stone phallus between her breasts, while the democrat Théroigne de Méricourt (an unlikely companion for the

Tintinnabulum (bell) believed to invoke the Roman god Priapus in order to ward off evil.

Frontispiece to *The Patriotic Brothel,* a pornographic Orléanist pamphlet, 1791.

queen), seen on the right, fondles the statue's testicles from below. The women, the pamphlet reports, are intoning a hymn to Priapus as they "adorn with garlands the vigorous member of this god, heaven and earth's premier fucker of sirens."

Likening Lafayette, the protector of Paris, to Priapus, the protector of gardens, was not just a dirty joke—although it was surely that. It was also a sly critique of Lafayette's provincial origins and clumsy bearing. As anyone schooled in the classics that dominated eighteenth-century French learning would have known, Priapus was renowned for a rough manner attributed, in part, to his rustic beginnings. In one antique epigram, Priapus, lamenting his own coarseness, explains that he was carved neither from fine stone nor by a master sculptor: "Neither Phidias nor Scopas nor Praxiteles produced me, but some bailiff hacked a log and told me 'thou shalt be Priapus.'" In another he seeks the readers' indulgence in excusing his rude behavior (which generally consisted of threatening to rape anyone—man, woman, or child—who attempted to steal from his garden). "Forgive a hick unable to compete with learned types," he implores. From an Orléanist perspective, Lafayette, too, was something of a hick, but unlike Priapus, he was foolhardy enough to try to compete with his social superiors. According to the logic of the old regime, Lafayette had risen to heights that no child of the Auvergne should have been able to attain.

In 1790 and 1791, Priapus was just one of the classical characters pressed into service as stand-ins for Lafayette. The most common of these was probably the mythical beast known as a centaur. Half man, half horse, the centaur took Lafayette's uncommon attachment to his white steed to its logical conclusion by fusing the two into a single monstrous creature. A print entitled *Le sans tort* spells out this conceit through a play on words and images. *Le sans tort* translates literally as "the blameless one"—a reference to Lafayette's tendency to shake off any culpability for acts of violence committed under his watch. But when read aloud, the phrase sounds like *"Le centaur."* Underscoring the double entendre, the picture features the body and legs of a galloping white horse whose neck morphs into Lafayette's torso and head. A shadowy homunculus identified in the caption as "chagrin" rides atop the hybrid steed, its arms wrapped around the neck/torso as if holding on for dear life, while the horse charges full speed ahead, dragging behind it a liberty cap, which has been tied with a neat bow to its trimly cropped tail.

Le sans tort. Caricature likening Lafayette to a centaur, c. 1791.

Signs in the background commemorate episodes that the supporters of Louis XVI saw as Lafayette's greatest failures. Impaled heads preside over the center of the image like a gory totem pole. Beneath the heads, a round medallion reminds viewers of the promise that Lafayette had been unable to keep on the night of October 5, 1789: "Sleep peacefully. I'll take care of everything." At the right, a notice affixed to a wooden post recalls the 1790 execution of the Marquis de Favras—the only man to be put to death for counterrevolutionary activities before 1792. A third road sign, attached to the base of the pikes, simply references the day of February 28, 1791. This was the so-called Day of Daggers, when Lafayette and the National Guard subdued, disarmed, and arrested some four hundred noblemen who had gathered in the Tuileries armed with weapons of all variety—pistols, poignards, sabers, hunting knives—in order, it was believed, to facilitate the king's escape. From the perspective of the aristocrats who opposed the revolution, Lafayette was very much like the ancient centaurs who were said to have battled the ancestors of the Greeks in a primordial struggle between civilization and barbarism. Centaurs were formidable opponents: powerful, lawless, and driven by nature's coarsest instincts. But the forces of order ultimately prevailed. And surely, hoped supporters of absolute monarchy, they would do so again.

Lafayette was well aware that his image had been tarnished. Since the onset of revolution he had kept up avidly with the burgeoning production of pamphlets and prints, purchasing multiple copies of each regardless of whether its treatment of him was good, bad, or indifferent. During this same period, Lafayette appears to have grown steadily more anxious about what the future might hold. He kept a locksmith busy for much of 1791 changing the locks on nearly every door, box, drawer, and cabinet in the Rue de Bourbon town house. Perhaps he sensed that matters were fated to go from bad to worse.

CHAPTER 17

DOWNFALLS

*C*annon fire jolted Paris to attention at nine-thirty on the morning of June 21, 1791. Soon, warning bells were ringing from every church and cries of alarm filled the streets. The king had vanished. Despite the heavy guard that surrounded the Tuileries Palace at all times, Louis XVI, Marie Antoinette, their children, and a handful of others had somehow disappeared overnight. No one knew where or why the royals had gone. It was equally unclear whether they had fled or been abducted. These questions went unanswered throughout the morning and early afternoon as rumors swirled through Paris and fingers were pointed in many directions—especially at Lafayette, the man who was supposed to protect the Tuileries.

In the chamber of the National Assembly, stunned silence gave way to cacophony. Alexandre de Beauharnais was presiding over the assembly and struggling to control the mounting confusion when Jean-Louis Romeuf, one of Lafayette's aides-de-camp, made his way to the bar. Romeuf had not planned to visit the assembly, but he was glad enough to be there. Glad enough to be alive. He was one of several couriers dispatched by Lafayette early that morning to "warn all good citizens that the king has just been carried off by enemies of the public good, and to order them to attempt to block this departure by all available means, and to bring him back if possible," according to the published proceedings of the assembly. But Romeuf had barely made it out of the Hôtel de Ville when a group of workmen forced him from his horse. As they saw it, Lafayette was to blame for allowing, if not abetting, the king's departure; not having Lafayette on hand, they seemed happy to take out their fury on his messenger. While blows and kicks rained down upon Romeuf, a second group of Parisians, in a less bellicose frame of mind, pulled him from the fray and conducted him to the assembly. Plucking Lafayette's orders from Romeuf's hand, Beauharnais read them aloud.

Soon, Lafayette himself was in the chamber, having made his own escape from an angry crowd gathered on the Place de Grève. Speaking from the tribune, he proclaimed that "an attack" on the king had been carried out by "enemies of the public good" who hoped to strike a blow at "French liberty." It was wishful thinking. Had the king been a victim, the nation would have faced a discrete enemy, a malignant force that could be identified and excised without harm to the body politic.

Unfortunately, the arrival of Arnaud II de La Porte, intendant of the King's Civil List, made it clear that Lafayette's optimism was sorely misplaced. De La Porte came to the assembly bearing a document entitled "Declaration of the King, Addressed to All the French, upon his Departure from Paris." Once the king's text was read into the record, there could be no mistake: Louis XVI had not fallen prey to an antirevolutionary conspiracy; he had been chief among the plotters. The king explained that he could no longer stand idly by to "see all my powers unrecognized, prerogatives violated, personal safety endangered everywhere, crimes going unpunished, and complete anarchy established above the law." The new constitution, he complained, left the monarch with nothing more than "the appearance of authority," without sufficient power "to cure a single one of the ills that afflict the realm." And he was just getting started.

The royal declaration was so long that it filled ten columns of print in the *Archives parlementaires,* its criticisms running the gamut from philosophical misgivings about the premises of the new order to grievances stemming from a sense of personal pique. The former are more substantial, but the latter are more telling, as the king's grumblings about creature comforts and interior decoration reveal just how severely he underestimated the gravity of his situation. Recounting the ordeal of the royal family's arrival at the Tuileries on October 6, 1789, Louis wrote, "Nothing had been prepared to receive the King." Moreover, even after he had settled in, "the disposition of the apartments" did not "afford the comforts to which His Majesty had been accustomed in the other royal properties, and which every individual of means is able to enjoy." Vexing, too, was his treatment during the Festival of Federation. At first, the assembly had placed him at the helm of the festivities "by special decree," but they had subsequently "named another"—Lafayette—to the same post. Making matters worse, the seating arrangements were substandard: despite the king's request, the royal family had been directed to a box separate from his own, "a thing hitherto unprecedented." Louis was equally galled by the budgetary limits imposed on his household expenses; these restrictions, he complained, dared to presume "that services rendered to the person of the king are not also rendered to the State." He concluded with a plea to the people: "Come back to your king; he will always be your father, your best friend." The man seemed not to understand that the time for sentiment had passed.

The royal missive heaped such scorn on the various reforms that had accumulated since the Assembly of Notables convened in 1787 that it managed to alienate nearly all but the monarchy's most ardent supporters. The *Révolutions de Paris* termed it "a satire of the Revolution." Even the royalist Marquis de Ferrières had had enough. He summed up the situation in a letter to his wife, writing, "The Declaration written in the hand of the king completes his downfall." By denouncing "all the Assembly's decrees," explained Ferrières, Louis had "declared himself . . . an enemy of the Constitution." One of the several papers that claimed the title *L'ami du roi* ("The Friend of the King") went so far as to remove the reference to the monarch from its masthead: on June 22, the paper was sold as *L'ami des français* ("The Friend of the French").

Given the carelessness of the monarchs' preparations for escape, it seems incredible that the royal scheme was not discovered. According to Madame Campan, plans had been in the works at least since March, when Marie Antoinette began sending Campan on shopping sprees. Buying just a few items from each boutique to elude detection, Campan assembled complete wardrobes for the queen and her children, shipping all purchases to Brussels to await the royal family's arrival. Marie Antoinette had also decided that she could not live in exile without her custom-made *nécessaire de voyage*—an ebony box, some eight inches deep and twenty-two inches long, trimmed with copper and gilt silver, and designed to contain everything that might be desired on a journey, from a complete tea service to a compass to a makeup brush—and so an order was placed with the *ébéniste* Jean-Pierre Charpenat for an exact duplicate to be made and shipped to the Netherlands.

While Madame Campan was working her way through the shops of Paris, General de Bouillé was amassing twelve battalions and twenty-three squadrons, composed primarily of foreign troops, on the French side of the Belgian border. Bouillé, who pointedly did not share his plans with his cousin Lafayette, stationed most of his men in and around the fortress at Montmédy, the king's intended destination, and dispatched others along the route the monarchs were to travel, in order to guarantee safe passage. As the historian Timothy Tackett has observed, if the suspicions of local citizens had not been aroused by the sudden influx of German-speaking soldiers, Bouillé's order for eighteen thousand rations of bread must surely have signaled that something was afoot. Yet Bouillé reported that, "happily," all of his arrangements generated "no suspicion among the people of the surrounding towns and countryside."

When June 20—the planned departure date—finally arrived, events unfolded like a comedy with a tragic dénouement. In the royal apartments at the Tuileries, details of the voyage were still being sorted out as the day went on. Monsieur Léonard, the queen's hairdresser, was added to the passenger list shortly before three in the afternoon and summarily packed into a carriage without being told where he was going, while the royal governess, Madame de Tourzel, was said to have objected to arrangements that had her traveling in a carriage separate from her charges. Meanwhile, horses and carriages of all variety— a hackney cab, a fiacre, a cabriolet, a berlin—were being deposited at locations in and around the city of Paris, where they would be picked up, driven, and exchanged throughout the day. Overseen by Marie Antoinette's rumored paramour, the Swedish count Axel von Fersen, these and other maneuvers were designed to whisk the royal family safely out of the most closely guarded site in Paris and, from there, far beyond the city walls.

Much of the entourage was already on the move by the time the principal players donned the clothing of servants, couriers, and other commoners to camouflage themselves as they began making their way out of the Tuileries. They started to leave around ten o'clock at night, the end of the working day for many of the palace staff. One by one, they stepped into the courtyard at intervals that sometimes stretched to forty-five minutes, doing their best to blend into the flow of men and women walking toward the street. The process was just beginning when Lafayette and Bailly wandered into the scene. By chance, Lafayette had stopped by Bailly's home before turning in for the night. There, he heard news that, both men agreed, should be shared with the king.

So off they went to the Tuileries, where Lafayette's carriage nearly ran directly into Marie Antoinette, and where Madame de Tourzel, waiting in the fiacre with the children, spotted him. The queen was shaken, but Lafayette did not notice her. Inside, Lafayette and Bailly found the king, who, having dismissed his servants for the night, was about to follow behind his wife. The three men conversed for what must have seemed like days to Louis XVI. Finally, sometime after eleven o'clock, the unwelcome visitors took their leave, and the king slipped out the door near midnight. Despite the delays and near misses, the first hurdle of the royal flight had been cleared.

With 160 miles still to cover between Paris and Montmédy, the danger of discovery remained high. The monarchs had chosen a well-traveled route requiring at least nineteen stops to exchange horses along the way, and the choice of yellow as the color of their vehicles did nothing to render them less conspicuous. Nonetheless, with Paris receding farther and farther into the distance, spirits inside the carriages began to lift. As the governess remembered it, Louis XVI passed the time reading aloud the declaration soon to be heard in the National Assembly; "then looking at his watch, which marked eight o'clock, he said, 'La Fayette just now does not know what to do with himself.'" Apparently, the very thought of Lafayette's awkward situation brought the travelers a degree of joy.

Their mirth was to be short-lived. They were more than halfway to their destination when they rode into Sainte-Menehould on June 22. By the time they reached the city gates, local officials were already suspicious, their interest piqued by the curious arrival and departure of first one, then another detachment of mounted soldiers. In both cases, their officers carried orders signed by the despised Bouillé containing a cover story involving "a treasure," due to arrive shortly, that would require an escort to the border. When two carriages, accompanied by couriers in chamois-colored livery, reached the relay post, they aroused the interest of the postmaster, Jean-Baptiste Drouet. As Drouet told the story, the horses were being changed when, out of idle curiosity, he peered into the waiting carriage; there he noticed the queen, whose face he thought he recognized. Looking at the man seated to her left, Drouet "was struck by the resemblance between his physiognomy and the effigy of the king printed on an *assignat* [paper currency introduced in 1790] that I was carrying." This was not an entirely unexpected development. In fact, Louis had been so fearful of recognition that, against

Assignat worth 100 livres featuring the profile of Louis XVI at the upper center.

the advice of Bouillé, he had charted a route circumventing Reims, the site of his coronation, where he believed that his countenance would be too familiar. Evidently, he had not considered that the *assignats* bore his profile, encircled by the words "Louis XVI King of the French," so that any man he passed on the road might have his portrait in his purse. As the story goes, at least one man did, and his tale was repeated by journalists and printmakers seeking to insert a moment of levity into an episode that was, in all other respects, deadly serious.

The King Eating Pigs' Feet at Sainte-Menehould, the Postmaster Comes Across an Assignat *and Recognizes the King.* Engraving. 1791.

Once the carriages had vanished from sight, Drouet and a comrade leapt to their horses and raced to the town of Varennes. There, they hoped to stop the royal caravan. Reaching Varennes at eleven-thirty in the dark of night, the men dispatched a local innkeeper to spread word of the king's arrival before blocking the bridge leading out of the town with an array of vehicles, including a nearby cart filled with old furniture. In less than five minutes, Drouet and a colleague, the mayor and the National Guard commander of Varennes, greeted the approaching carriages—now accompanied by some 150 mounted troops—at the bridge with eight other armed men. Passports were demanded. While the assembled citizens debated the validity of the documents and the identity of their owners, Louis XVI revealed himself, saying, "Here is my wife, here are my children, we beseech you to accord us that regard which the French have always accorded to their king." By this time, one hundred citizens, many of them armed, had gathered in the street. Soon, the National Guard would have two cannons trained on the hussars. The king was lost.

Until word of the arrest reached Paris, Lafayette faced his own set of dangers. On the night of June 21, representatives from the various factions on the left temporarily set aside their differences to meet at the Jacobin headquarters. There, Georges Danton, the editor of *Révolutions de Paris,* denounced Lafayette. As his newspaper reported it, Danton boomed that, since "Monsieur the Commander General swore on his life that the king would not leave, we must have either the person of the king or the head of Monsieur the Commander General." He had long suspected that Lafayette was an enemy of the revolution, and the events of "June 21 removed all doubt." Danton was addressing Lafayette directly when he declared "the most astonishing" fact of the day to be that "people, on first hearing of the escape of Louis XVI, did not set upon your person." Harking back to the murders of July 14, 1789, he added that "Flesselle and Delaunay paid with their heads for treason less criminal than yours." The loyalty of the troops, the loyalty of their officers, and the loyalty of the Paris sections (the city's neighborhood governments) all had to be confirmed, but the loyalty of Lafayette was particularly suspect. "The general of an army of thirty thousand men, who permits the escape of an entire family," declared the paper, "is criminal or imbecile. . . . Soldiers of the nation, he has lost the right to command you."

Fortunately for Lafayette, a messenger arrived from Varennes with news of the king's discovery on June 22, before anyone had acted on Danton's call. In a show of unity, three deputies, representing the political left, center, and right, were dispatched to meet the monarchs, who had already started on the return trip to Paris. So crowded was the road with onlookers that the somber caravan required several days to deliver its passengers to the Tuileries, where Lafayette promptly presented himself. As he recalled, he attempted to assume a deferential stance. "Does Your Majesty have any order to give me?" Lafayette asked. Through bitter laughter, the king replied, "It seems to me that I am subject to your orders more than you are to mine."

Lafayette's position was growing increasingly untenable. While those on the left held him responsible for the king's escape, partisans on the right blamed him for the ignominious spectacle of the royal family's return. The Comte d'Espinchal observed with disgust that Lafayette had "issued orders that no honors should be accorded to the king, and forbade even the doffing of hats. This worthy commander of a troupe of rebels and troublemakers [*factieux*] is, at this moment, the jailer of his sovereign and of the entire royal family." A letter, written by Bouillé from the safety of Luxembourg and read into the record of the National Assembly on June 30, accused Lafayette of standing "at the head" of the party that hoped to replace the monarchy with a republic. Lafayette's "secret ambition," wrote Bouillé, drives "him toward the only goal he has": establishing a government that would be "monstrous for us."

This double accusation—of ambition and republicanism—was more than Lafayette could bear. Two days later, he appeared before the assembly to refute what he termed Bouillé's "calumny." "I am denounced as an enemy of the form of government that you have established," he stormed to vigorous applause. "Messieurs, I will not renew my oath, but I am prepared to shed my blood to uphold it." Lafayette's discomfort with his role in the king's return did not decrease with the passing of years. Writing in his memoirs decades later, Lafayette sought to absolve himself of responsibility by reminding readers that, "happily for him (after the atrocities suffered by these august victims), it was not to his orders, but to the accident of being recognized by a postmaster . . . that their arrest was due."

When the sun rose over a sharply divided Paris at nine minutes past four on Sunday, July 17, discontent had been roiling the city for weeks. The flight to Varennes was just one of the contributing factors. As the historian David Andress has shown, tens of thousands of men had been tossed into the ranks of the unemployed thanks to the closure of a work relief project in mid-June, and these workers, having passed through two years of impromptu schooling in political action, continued to report to work at jobs that were no longer available as they began petitioning the authorities and protesting in the streets. Struggling to maintain order, Bailly and Lafayette deployed the National Guard to break up the workers' gatherings—a move that only compounded the animosity felt by those protesters, who saw the National Guard in general, and Lafayette in particular, as complicit in the king's flight. Mutual distrust continued to mount, with more and more Parisians from nearly every level of society being arrested for insulting, threatening, or assaulting the members of the guard. Andress reports that one man was brought in for opining "in a loud voice" that "it was astonishing that [Lafayette's] head was not on the end of a pike," while another was arrested for averring that Lafayette and Bailly deserved to be hanged.

It was against this turbulent background that the National Assembly stunned a sizable portion of the populace on July 15 by passing legislation clearing Louis XVI of criminal wrongdoing in his attempted escape and leaving the king at the head of the very government he had so recently disdained. Whatever misgivings individual deputies may have felt, their decision was nearly unanimous. The vast majority, apparently, deemed it unwise to disband the monarchy in such unsettled times. As a group, they took cover behind Bouillé's letter, which, aside from castigating Lafayette, indicated that the blame for the king's flight rested entirely on Bouillé's shoulders.

Reactions were swift and loud. Calls for the creation of a French republic went up at the Palais-Royal and at Danton's headquarters, and crowds marched to the Jacobins' meeting room, hoping to unite the left under the republican standard. The Marquis de Ferrières told his wife that "all the firebrands of the capital were unleashed that very evening in the clubs, in the cafés, shouting horrors against Louis XVI and against the Assembly." One group, he reported, tried to close down the Comédie Française and the Opéra but was repelled by the National Guard. The next day, Gouverneur Morris wrote to his fellow American patriot Robert Morris (no relation) that "much Heat" had been generated against the deputies. Observing that "the People are now assembling . . . and the Militia (many of them opposed to the King) are out," he deemed it "far from improbable that I shall have a Battle under my Windows." The National Assembly shared his fear. On July 16, Bailly was summoned before the chamber and instructed, among other things, to produce an address to the people of Paris explaining "the principles that dictated yesterday's decree" and to ensure "public tranquility."

Some of the "heat" Bailly was asked to cool had generated spontaneously, but political factions were busily fanning the flames. Danton's followers were apparently behind the march to the Jacobins, and many believed that the Duc d'Orléans had had a hand in the tumult as well. As Lafayette related the tale in his memoirs, Choderlos de Laclos, acting on behalf of Orléans, had drafted one of several petitions that began to circulate on July 16 demanding that the question of Louis XVI's culpability be sent out to the departments to be decided by the nation at large. The plan was for those supporting the motion to gather at the site of the Bastille at daybreak, then to procede en masse to the Champ de Mars, where they would sign the petition on the altar of the nation— the same altar that had been consecrated one year and three days earlier by Lafayette. Throughout the night and into the morning, members of the National Guard skirmished with would-be signers, who nonetheless made their way to the Champ de Mars early on July 17.

The violence began before noon. Two men, having inexplicably concealed themselves beneath the altar, along with assorted woodworking equipment and a bottle of wine, were spotted and seized by a group of protesters. Convinced that the pair were planting explosives to disrupt the proceedings, the crowd hanged the men from a lamppost, hacked off their heads, and mounted these bloody trophies on pikes. Another man made an attempt on Lafayette's life only to have his pistol misfire at close range. Eventually, the main event got under way. As the afternoon wore on, some six thousand men and women managed to sign their names or, in many cases, leave their marks on the petition. For a few hours, it seemed that order had been restored.

But news of the newfound calm did not reach the National Assembly until the deputies had already renewed their demand that the municipal authorities keep the peace. In the heat of the late-morning debate, Michel-Louis-Étienne Regnaud de Saint-Jean d'Angély went so far as to insist that "were I to be a victim, like those citizens who have just perished, I would demand the proclamation of martial law!" Ignoring murmurs on the extreme left, the assembly supported Regnaud. During the late afternoon, Bailly ordered red flags to be raised, and with that martial law was declared in Paris. Around seven in the evening, Bailly set off from the Hôtel de Ville accompanied by a battalion of grenadiers of the National Guard to rendezvous with Lafayette at the entrance to the Champ de Mars, where Bailly intended to order the crowd to disperse.

According to Lafayette, their arrival was "greeted by a hailstorm of rocks," and soon thereafter, a pistol shot barely missed the mayor as he attempted "to make his proclamation." In the midst of this attack, the National Guard fired into the air. These were warning shots, Lafayette insisted, "meant to avoid injuring anyone." But the assailants were "emboldened by this moderation" and "redoubled their attack against the municipal offers and the National Guard." Two volunteer chasseurs were killed, whereupon "the National Guard fired in earnest [*tout de bon*]." Lafayette's account is vague on the numbers of casualties, maintaining that "the losses on the side of the assailants have been insanely exaggerated; the crowd was dispersed by the cavalry, which injured no one."

Lafayette's was just one of the many accounts of that day, and it was not destined to become the dominant one. In 1910, the French historian Albert Mathiez—a staunch supporter of Robespierre, a committed socialist, and the founder of the influential journal *Annales de la révolution française,* which dominated academic French studies of the revolution for much of the twentieth century—painted quite a different picture by compiling and analyzing the testimonies of scores of participants and eyewitnesses. Mathiez had numerous axes to grind and gleaned much of his evidence from investigations launched by Lafayette's nemeses. Nonetheless, his findings, which have had a tremendous influence on the study of the event, indicate the diversity of reports that circulated during the summer of 1791, with nearly every point of Lafayette's story being contradicted by someone in Mathiez's compendium.

Several people, including Bailly himself, maintained that the mayor never even began to read aloud the proclamation declaring martial law. Moreover, although the legislation required that Bailly enter the stadium ahead of the soldiers, presumably to permit the crowd to disperse of its own free will, Bailly instead trailed the cavalry, which entered the stadium at full charge. Others testified that the National Guard began firing when a shot rang out from the crowd gathered on the embankment—a shot, some said, that was merely a misfire. According to other accounts, rocks were thrown only after the fusillade began. And although one witness claimed that Lafayette ordered the National Guard to hold their fire, neither Lafayette nor his officers were able to control their men. In some versions, the crowd started fleeing after the first round of shots, only to be hunted down by chasseurs who broke ranks, swinging their sabers wildly. Perhaps the most hotly contested part of the story involves the number of casualties: one author, apparently in Lafayette's camp, noted ten deaths and twenty injuries; another man avowed that he had returned to the field after midnight and counted fifty-four bodies strewn about the streets; and Marat wrote that four hundred corpses had been thrown into the river overnight, on Bailly's orders. To this day, we have no solid grasp on the death toll.

If the battle fought with rocks and guns was more or less over by midnight, the war of rhetoric was just getting started. At the July 25 meeting of Danton's Cordeliers club, the membership invoked the specter of a bloody episode in the sixteenth-century wars of religion by terming July 17 the "Patriot's Saint Bartholomew's day." The *Révolutions de Paris* commenced its vivid retelling on the title page of issue 106. It began: "Blood flowed in the field of the federation; the altar of the nation is dyed with it; men, women had their throats slit; citizens are in a state of consternation."

Images, too, reinforced the helplessness of the victims and the brutality of the National Guard. The article in *Révolutions de Paris* was accompanied by a print depicting the Champ de Mars with half a dozen bodies lying on the field. At the right, infantrymen break ranks to fire at close range on a crowd of unarmed people who are trying to run away, while, in the background, a guardsman on horseback chases down a man on foot. Casting the scene as a moment of sacrilege, the caption reads "Men, Women, and Children were massacred on the altar of the nation on the Field of the Federation." Other prints attacked Lafayette explicitly. One image, for instance, shows a microcephalic Lafayette seated atop his enormous white steed with a gang of turkeys leashed to its tail. Referring to the people gathered around the altar in the distance, Lafayette asks his feathered army whether "it will take courage to kill them."

In the two months that followed, Lafayette reached a rapprochement with the only political faction that was still willing to support him: the Feuillants, a group that contained about seventy of the National Assembly's last remaining moderates. In the wake of the Champ de Mars debacle, these men, with the Triumvirate at their center, broke with the Jacobins to form the short-lived club that retained a commitment to constitutional monarchy. Having worked at cross-purposes for

Unfortunate Day of July 17, 1791.

more than a year, Lafayette understood that his only hope of political survival lay in collaborating with Alexandre and Théodore de Lameth, Duport, and Barnave toward remodeling the constitution in light of recent developments. In the end, the revised constitution accepted by Louis XVI on September 13, 1791, carried some of the group's marks, but the constitutional monarchy was already in its death throes; debating its details amounted to little more than selecting a coffin.

Bouillé's memoirs describe a mass exodus in the second half of 1791,

The Day of July 17, 1791.

in which "the roads of France were covered with men, women and children, afraid of being buried under the ruins of the crumbling monarchy." Bouillé had in mind especially the aristocratic émigrés—well-heeled supporters of the monarchy who started trickling out of France in 1789 and began pouring across the borders after the flight to Varennes. Austria, Germany, Belgium, Italy, England, and the United States were popular destinations for these men and women, who counted among their number more than half of all the officers in the French army, some six thousand men, mostly from the nobility. But another group was also taking to the highways that autumn: the newly unencumbered deputies to the National Assembly, who had voted to dissolve their body as of September 30, 1791, giving way to a new crop of representatives that would be known collectively as the Legislative Assembly. Having thus relinquished the reins of power, hundreds of former deputies spent the month of October making their way out of the capital to resume their private lives abroad or in distant provinces.

Lafayette, too, was on the road. On Saturday, October 8, he wrote a formal letter of good-bye to the National Guard, tendered his resignation to the municipality, and began the long journey back to Chavaniac. His appointment as commander of the National Guard had come to an end with the conclusion of the outgoing assembly, and he suggested in his farewell letter that his work had been accomplished. As Lafayette put it, "The constitution has been completed . . . and, after having been sworn to by all the citizens, in every corner of the empire, it has just been legally adopted by the entire people and solemnly recognized by the first legislative assembly of its representatives." Yet he understood that the nation's hard-won freedoms still rested on a precarious base, and he warned the National Guard against believing "that every sort of despotism has been destroyed, and that liberty . . . has been sufficiently established." Echoing a rallying cry he had heard on the other side of the ocean, he implored his men to "live free or die." The men of the National Guard demonstrated their gratitude by voting to present their departing commander with an épée forged from the iron bars of the Bastille.

Although Lafayette was writing to the men who served under him, his letter also addressed generations yet to come. The revolution-weary marquis was painfully aware that his reputation had been damaged: in the minds of a broad swath of the Parisian population, the massacre at the Champ de Mars had destroyed his credibility as the people's protector and the nation's liberator. Seeing no way to redeem his authority in Paris, he was returning to the Auvergne, but hoping to salvage his name for posterity, he summarized his conduct and motives. Lafayette reminded readers that even amid "hostile plots, ambitious intrigues, and licentious unrest," the National Guard had remained firm in its devotion to liberty and love of the nation. And while he lamented that "without doubt, we ourselves made mistakes needing repair," he alluded to his reputation as a hero of two worlds, writing that "liberty and equality, once established in both hemispheres, will never turn back."

Heading south from Paris, Lafayette traveled more than four hundred miles in eleven days. As he neared his ancestral lands, local guardsmen and other citizens expressed their appreciation by serving as escorts as he passed through their towns. At last he reached Chavaniac on October 19—the anniversary, he noted in a letter, of the American day of triumph at Yorktown.

For the first time in his adult life, Lafayette intended to settle in the Auvergne. Declining a post in the departmental administration, he stated that he wished to return to "private life" and to devote himself "to the work of a simple citizen." The American press drew out the connotation that Lafayette surely intended: that in turning to his land, he was emulating Washington. According to the February 1792 issue of the *American Museum; or, Universal Magazine,* published in Philadelphia, Lafayette was "taking the Cincinnatus of America for his model" by retiring to the Auvergne,

> where he means, by his own example, to promote a higher cultivation of the soil, and to teach the people a more comfortable scheme of rural life. . . . Here he proposes to sit under his own vine, in the freedom which he has so largely contributed to establish, and from which he will not depart, unless to defend it from the violence of hostile attack.

As the American author suggested, Lafayette was not interested in farming for its own sake. Instead, like Arthur Young and other English reformers of the era, he saw agricultural improvement as a vehicle for the amelioration of rural poverty and, consequently, a guarantor of civil tranquility. Looking back on the period a decade later, Lafayette mused in a memo, probably written in 1801, that "this manner of serving my neighbors would have been very useful in the interest of peace." To transform Chavaniac into a model farm that might "give the region an example of the best agriculture, and to raise there the most necessary types of animals," he invited an English farmer, John Dyson of Suffolk, to join the household at Chavaniac. Dyson lived with Lafayette's family for about a year, surveying the lands and making recommendations for the selection and care of crops and livestock that would be best suited to the climate and soil. No longer able to advance the cause of humanity through politics, Lafayette hoped that agriculture might give him a second chance.

The architect Antoine-Laurent-Thomas Vaudoyer also joined the family at Chavaniac that season; he left his Paris home for the Auvergne on October 12 and did not return for 380 days. Vaudoyer, a fellow Freemason and a winner of the prestigious Rome Prize, had been in Lafayette's employ for some time, making sketches of Lafayette's many houses scattered about the provinces, assessing their conditions, and reviewing their titles as the marquis attempted to take stock of his assets. Now, seeing few new buildings going up in the tumultuous capital and being increasingly dismayed by the choices made by the revolutionary government, Vaudoyer was content to spend some time in

Jean-Pierre-Louis-Laurent Houël, *The Storming of the Bastille,* 1789, watercolor.
Lafayette owned a version of this painting.

the Auvergne. Vaudoyer served as Lafayette's architect, foreman, book-keeper, and interior designer, responsible for everything from refurbishing doors, floors, and paneling to replacing staircases and creating a new mezzanine in one of the towers. Vaudoyer was also tasked with keeping tabs on the progress of the painted decorations that Lafayette commissioned for the château. As he had in his Paris town house, Lafayette wished to fill his domestic rooms with visual reminders of his political achievements. By July 4, 1792, nine works by the topographic painter Jean-Pierre Houël had arrived, including interior and exterior views of the taking of the Bastille, two scenes of the king's entrance into Paris (one showing the events of July 17, 1789, the other of October 6, 1789), and other significant episodes that Lafayette wished to remember.

Like many a modern-day renovation, the work at Chavaniac generated complaints from the neighbors. Evidently, some villagers were displeased by Lafayette's decision to take down his weather vanes, which they had grown accustomed to consulting as they planned their fieldwork. Perhaps, Vaudoyer suggested, a new weather vane could be erected atop the curate's house or on the church steeple? Or else, to avoid any interference with the cross, maybe a weather vane could be perched on a "liberty tree" planted nearby as a sign of the revolution's regenerating effect on the French nation.

In singling out the cross and the liberty tree, Vaudoyer had—intentionally or not—touched on a problem that vexed Lafayette. At Chavaniac, Lafayette was distressed to encounter a local perception that the revolution was fundamentally anti-Catholic. Writing on December 14, 1791, Lafayette suggested that "all would be well here without the ecclesiastical and aristocratic maneuvers to put the people off the revolution under the pretext that it will send them to hell." Lafayette still saw himself as a proud son of the Auvergne, but his years in the wider world had changed him so fully that he had difficulty understanding why the peasants and villagers might be skeptical about the new order. A particular sticking point was the Civil Constitution of the Clergy—a controversial law approved by the National Assembly on July 12, 1790, and denounced by the pope on March 10, 1791. In essence, the law subordinated the Catholic Church to the state in France. Wary of interference from Rome—a favorite destination for royalist exiles—the assembly required all priests to swear an oath to the national constitution; insisted that priests, curates, and bishops be elected by their flocks rather than appointed by church hierarchy; abolished a host of religious titles and privileges; and set new regulations governing the salaries, duties, and residency requirements of members of the clergy.

Many devout Catholics—especially those in the provinces—saw the Civil Constitution of the Clergy as a usurpation of church authority, but Lafayette thought it best not to address their concerns. Offering advice to a departmental administrator charged with explaining the benefits of the new regime to the peasantry, Lafayette recommended avoiding the matter altogether; "you will never convert a fanatic by tackling him head-on," he explained. The newly established freedom of religion, Lafayette suggested, should be the only religious topic discussed with the local populace. In this way, "the advantages of liberty and equality, the happy consequences resulting from the rights of man in general, and of the French citizen in particular, must stir their hearts, elevate their spirits, and inspire in them horror for the former order of things, and hope for the revolution."

Committed though he was to winning hearts and minds in the Auvergne, Lafayette had not entirely given up on a future in the capital. In November, he stood for election to replace Bailly, who had stepped down as mayor of Paris. But as the Marquis de Ferrières explained to his wife, Lafayette was still viewed with suspicion by both the Left and the Right. "Here," wrote Ferrières on November 1, "all the parties agitate. They say that M. de La Fayette is plotting in the Midi, that he fans the flames of insurrection in Paris, that he wants to make himself necessary, and force the people to call him back." Lafayette made a poor showing against the winner, Jérôme Pétion de Villeneuve, who was installed as mayor on November 13.

Lafayette's retirement would, nonetheless, be a brief one. Thousands of French army officers who had made their way out of the country were regrouping along the nation's borders in the fall of 1791. Led by the brothers of Louis XVI, and supported by neighboring governments, they were determined to restore the absolute monarchy by force. Calls for war sounded throughout France as partisans on various sides seemed to believe that a military conflict would redound to their benefit. Some believed that the war against the royalists in exile would finally unite the nation against a common enemy, while Louis XVI hoped that the émigrés would make quick work of whatever remained of France's armed forces and restore his depleted powers. And yet on December 14, 1791, a beleaguered Louis XVI felt obliged to appear before the Legislative Assembly and announce that he had issued a stern warning to the elector of Trier—a principality under the jurisdiction of the Austrian Leopold II, Marie Antoinette's brother, who had succeeded to the imperial throne of the Holy Roman emperor in 1790. As Louis told the deputies, he had demanded that the elector of Trier put an end to the "amassing of armed French troops" in his territory or face an armed response. The assembly applauded heartily.

Before the day was out, the Comte de Narbonne, the newly appointed minister of war, had established three armies of 50,000 troops each. Narbonne had been named to his post on November 6 after considerable political wrangling; he was not especially favored either by the king or by the assembly, but he was seen as a pawn of neither, which apparently made him acceptable to both. Rumored to be an illegitimate son of Louis XV—Gouverneur Morris had even heard whispers that Narbonne was the product of an incestuous liaison between Louis XV and his devoted daughter Madame Adélaïde—Narbonne was an ally of the Feuillants and a firm believer in constitutional monarchy. Two of the generals he selected to lead the new armies were unsullied heroes: Rochambeau, champion of the Battle of Yorktown, and Nicolas Luckner, who had made his name in the Seven Years' War and to whom the "Song of the Army of the Rhine"—known today as "La Marseillaise," the French national anthem—was dedicated when it was written, in 1792. The third was Lafayette—a choice that pleased almost no one. Lafayette set out to join his troops at Metz on Christmas Day 1791.

By April 20, 1792, when France declared war on the Austrian states, Lafayette had been drilling his men in northeastern France for several months, in a vain attempt to instill discipline in an army that was riddled with conflict and weakened by desertion. But for Lafayette's enemies in Paris, out of sight was not out of mind: even from a distance of two hundred miles, a man with 50,000 troops at his disposal was a force to be reckoned with. That spring, the Jacobin party had been abuzz with false rumors that Lafayette was planning to march his troops into Paris to prevent the city from glorifying the forty surviving soldiers of the Châteauvieux Regiment. These men had been sentenced to a lifetime of hard labor after their mutiny at Nancy had been forcefully put down, with Lafayette's full approval. Having been released from the galleys at Brest after serving just two years, the soldiers became popular heroes, welcomed in the Legislative Assembly's meeting hall and scheduled to be honored by a grand celebration. Jacques-Louis David was charged with choreographing a "Festival of Liberty"—the first of many revolutionary festivals he would organize—to be held on April 15. On that date, the soldiers joined with the people of Paris in a triumphal procession through the streets. The Declaration of the Rights of Man, painted on stone tablets, was borne by marchers at the head of the procession. A train of young girls carried the broken chains that had once bound the soldiers. And a detachment of the National Guard brought up the rear, walking behind a carriage, modeled after ancient Roman precedents, bearing a seated statue of the goddess of liberty.

The Festival of Liberty surely celebrated the Châteauvieux Regiment, but it was also a rebuke to Lafayette—a response in kind to the procession he'd led on September 22, 1790, honoring the soldiers who fell suppressing the mutiny. Lafayette abhorred the event, but he seemed relieved that it was carried out peacefully. In an April 18 letter to Adrienne, who remained at Chavaniac, Lafayette wrote that "the national guard of Paris acquitted itself perfectly in the Châteauvieux affair which, in the end, became nothing more than a disgusting farce" that, in his opinion, reflected badly on the Jacobins. Yet Lafayette's enemies remained convinced that he was plotting against the city. Jacobin newspapers condemned him as a double-dealer, and on April 18 and 19, shouting filled the Hôtel de Ville, as Lafayette's supporters tried to

April 15, 1792: Festival of Liberty honoring the release of forty Châteauvieux soldiers from the galleys of Brest, published in *Révolutions de Paris*, no. 145 (April 14–21, 1792). The depiction of the National Guard, which brought up the rear, as a lone man riding a scrawny donkey suggests the editors' low opinion of Lafayette's supporters.

prevent his detractors from removing the city's busts of Lafayette and Bailly from public view.

Lafayette remained characteristically undaunted. On May 1, he issued a rousing proclamation to the Army of the Center, as his troops were known, urging his men to ignore the partisanship that was roiling national politics. Terming them, variously, soldiers of the nation, soldiers of liberty, and soldiers of the constitution, he implored them to be brave, patient, and indefatigable, to keep their focus on the deadly battles that lay ahead. Let the factions fight among themselves if they would, he counseled. "As to us, armed with weapons blessed by liberty and by the declaration of rights, let us march on the enemy!"

It was sound advice, but Lafayette was unable to heed it himself. Throughout the months of May and June, he struggled to maintain discipline in a poorly equipped and increasingly disorderly army that was engaged in sporadic combat; meanwhile, he fielded frequent updates on the political situation in Paris. He recalled in his memoirs that he was troubled by what he learned: "The clubs usurped all powers, insulted the tribunals and the constitutional authorities, dominated the administration, the legislative body, directed politics and the war." Lafayette was particularly concerned about the "excesses of Jacobinism." So powerful did the Jacobins appear "that no one dared" stand up to them, Lafayette averred. And with so much authority concentrated in the hands of extragovernmental groups, he feared for "the liberty of the nation, its means of defense, the safety and property of its citizens."

On June 16, Lafayette wrote a lengthy letter to the Legislative Assembly denouncing political clubs as antithetical to the constitution and a danger to French freedom. Although he railed against factionalism of all varieties, the Jacobins were his primary target. "Organized like a separate empire . . . blindly controlled by a few ambitious leaders," the Jacobins were, as he put it, a "sect," a "distinct corporation in the middle of the French people, whose powers they usurp by subjugating their representatives." Read into the record two days later and republished in newspapers of every political stripe, the letter generated heated debate. While Lafayette's supporters insisted that he was protecting the constitution as he had always done, his detractors saw something much more dangerous: a thinly veiled threat issued by a general with an army at his disposal. At the Jacobin Club on June 18, Robespierre opened the discussion with a simple directive: "Strike down Lafayette and the nation is saved."

When thousands of armed men stormed the Tuileries Palace on June 20, cornering Louis XVI but leaving peaceably after the monarch donned a red "liberty cap" and raised a glass with the insurgents, Lafayette could not resist the siren call. Informing no one of his departure, he set out for Paris, where he hoped to rescue the king, the nation, and the constitution. Unbidden and unwanted, Lafayette appeared at the bar of the Legislative Assembly on June 28. Against a background of disapproving murmurs, he read a prepared statement declaring that the violence of June 20 had "excited indignation and alarm among all good citizens and especially among the army." Many of his troops, he announced, were "asking themselves whether it is truly the cause of liberty that they are defending." In their name, and in the name of "all the French who love their country, their liberty, their peace," he insisted that "it is time to protect the Constitution from attacks, . . . to assure the liberty of the National Assembly," and to guarantee the protection of the king. He demanded "that the instigators of the violence committed on 20 June at the Tuileries be pursued and punished as traitors [*criminels de lèse-nation*]." Finally, he took direct aim at the Jacobins. Insisting that he was speaking for "all the honest men of the realm," he declared it imperative "to destroy a sect that smothers sovereignty, tyrannizes the citizenry, and whose public debates leave no doubt of the atrocity of its leaders' plots."

It was Lafayette's last stand. His speech enraged the Jacobins, hardening their belief that he was threatening to turn his soldiers against them. In fact, his mere presence gave rise to accusations of dereliction of duty. A general cannot abandon his post at whim, and Lafayette had neither sought nor received permission to leave his army. But so firmly was he convinced of the righteousness of his cause that he seemed not to imagine how his actions might be perceived. If he wished to find out, all he had to do was read a fifteen-page pamphlet published shortly after his proclamation. It bore the title *Crimes of Lafayette in France.* Unable to accept the truth that his dream for a constitutional monarchy had turned into a national nightmare, he had grown blind to the circumstances around him.

Although he never enacted it, Lafayette did harbor one more plan that he believed might at last rescue the country. He would accompany

Louis XVI to the Legislative Assembly, where the king would announce his intention to pass some time at the Château de Compiègne. The Paris Guard would serve as an escort along the route. Once arrived, the king would be protected by the National Guard of Compiègne and by two regiments of chasseurs. Protected in this way, Louis might then "issue a proclamation forbidding his brothers and the other émigrés to advance any farther, while declaring himself prepared to march personally against foreign enemies . . . and pronouncing his support of the constitution in terms that will leave no doubt as to his true sentiments." If only the king had followed his advice, Lafayette mused years later, "it is likely that Louis XVI could have reentered Paris to the acclamations of all the people." However, the king politely declined the offer, with the queen reportedly explaining that "we would be better off locking ourselves away in a tower." As Lafayette archly noted in his memoirs, a tower—the keep of the Temple fortress in Paris's Marais district—became her next and last home.

What was to be done about Lafayette? The question lingered through July and into August as the Legislative Assembly repeatedly circled back to the matter. Among other pieces of evidence, letters between Lafayette and General Luckner, the German-born marshal of France, who was serving as commander of the French Army of the Rhine, were read into the record, their words and phrases parsed and their meanings debated. Were the generals conspiring to enact Lafayette's plan to save the king? Had Lafayette hoped to persuade Luckner to join him in a march on Paris, where, together, their armies might oust the "factions" that, in Lafayette's view, were exerting an extraconstitutional "tyranny over the National Assembly and the king?" Or, in broaching political matters with Luckner, was Lafayette merely expressing personal views to which he, like any citizen, was entitled? After weeks of debate, Marc David Lasource, a Protestant minister who described himself as a former "partisan and admirer" of Lafayette's, proposed on July 21 that the assembly formally accuse Lafayette of conspiracy. Speeches for and against Lafayette were heard throughout the day, with the abolitionist Brissot providing one of the loudest voices against his erstwhile friend, but the session adjourned without a vote. On August 8, the assembly took up the question once more; again debate raged for hours. Finally, just before adjourning at five o'clock that evening, the deputies rejected the accusation against Lafayette by a roll call vote of 406 to 224. According to the *Archives parlementaires,* the news was greeted by "boos from the spectators' galleries, brisk applause from the right and center."

On the morning of August 10, an unstoppable force stormed the Tuileries Palace. Describing the episode, the historian David P. Jordan wrote that "this was not another demonstration, not another spontaneous mass movement. It was a major military operation." Tens of thousands of *fédérés*—National Guardsmen from the provinces—had been gathering in Paris for weeks; many had arrived for the annual celebration of July 14, and more were streaming through the capital with plans to join the army at the northern fronts. With an attack from Austria and its allies expected at any moment, the people of Paris were growing increasingly alarmed, and the Legislative Assembly's quagmire of indecision did nothing to assuage their fears. Over the course of the summer, the city's sectional governments stepped in, filling the leadership void. As the sections produced petition after petition declaring the monarchy overthrown, they also forged closer and closer bonds with the well-armed *fédérés*. The ringing of the tocsin in the early hours of August 10 announced their union: the sections had formed an insurrectionary commune and seized control of Paris while the *fédérés* readied for an offensive against the royal palace. By midmorning, the king and queen had taken refuge in the assembly and a bloody battle was raging at the palace. By midafternoon, some nine hundred bodies littered the Tuileries Palace, its courtyard, and the surrounding streets; two-thirds belonged to the Swiss Guards, whose orders to retreat arrived too late.

By nightfall, everything had changed. Although France was not declared a republic until September, the monarchy had definitively fallen. Declared prisoners of the insurrectionary commune, Louis XVI and Marie Antoinette were transferred to the Temple prison on August 13. Both would be tried and executed for crimes against the nation. Citizen Louis Capet, as the former king was officially known under the new order, climbed the steps of the guillotine on January 21, 1793; his widow followed on October 16. The Legislative Assembly, too, lived only a short time longer; its moderates and monarchists frightened away, the assembly effectively ceded power to the commune and to a hastily assembled Provisional Executive Council, which ruled jointly until a newly elected body—the National Convention—could be seated the following month.

Lafayette's fate was left in the hands of an unforgiving coalition consisting of the Jacobin remnants of the National Assembly, the people of Paris who, Gouverneur Morris believed, would have "torn [Lafayette] to pieces," given the chance, and a newcomer to national politics named Georges Danton, the editor of *Révolutions de Paris* and a long-time foe of Lafayette's. Danton, a lion of a man whose booming rhetoric and renowned lust for life made him a perfect foil to the supremely controlled and calculating Robespierre, was a hero of the Paris sections, and his popularity among the people had led to his appointment as minister of justice. On August 17, the Provisional Executive Council issued an order relieving Lafayette of his command and demanding that he return to Paris to answer for his actions. On August 19, the full assembly passed a decree officially accusing Lafayette of "plotting against liberty and of treason against the nation." On August 21, that accusation ranked thirteenth in the list of fourteen decrees Danton presented to the assembly as those he had certified with the seal of the nation since taking office. By signing off on a denunciation of Lafayette, Danton pleased both the sections and the Jacobins. It had been one of his first orders of business.

Lafayette was at camp in Sedan, in northern France when he learned the news. Emboldened by the knowledge that his motives had always been pure, he was at first inclined to hasten to Paris and confront his accusers. But after a few moments of sober reflection, he understood that entering Paris alone would mean facing certain death. Believing that he still had the support of the army, Lafayette ordered his troops to swear their allegiance to "the nation, the law, and the king." The men remained silent. It was over.

PART FOUR

BETWEEN TWO WORLDS

CHAPTER 18

EXILE

On August 19, 1792, Lafayette rode out of camp at Sedan accompanied by fifteen officers, their servants, and the customary general's escort. Having come to understand, as he put it in his memoirs, that "there was nothing left to do except to seek asylum in a neutral nation in order to save his proscribed head from the executioner, in the hope that he might one day serve liberty and France again," Lafayette set out for his nation's northeastern border. Stopping briefly at Bouillon, about a dozen miles from Sedan, he ordered his army to take up protective positions in case of an Austrian incursion, made temporary arrangements for the chain of command, and dismissed his escorts for their own safety.

Before continuing on the final stage of his journey, Lafayette posted a farewell letter to the municipality of Sedan, explaining his decision to emigrate. Although his letter was addressed to the city's commissioners, it expressed thoughts Lafayette might have wished to share with all of France. "If the last drop of my blood could serve the commune of Sedan," he assured his readers, the commune "would have a right to this sacrifice, and it would be less costly to me than what I am doing." But, he continued, "since my presence among you will serve . . . only to compromise you, I must spare the city of Sedan the troubles of which I would be the cause." The best thing he could do for the city would be to leave it—to "distance from it a head that all the enemies of liberty have proscribed, and that will never bow to any despotism."

Around nine o'clock on that cool and drizzly night, Lafayette and forty-three other Frenchmen approached the gates of the fortified town of Rochefort, in the Austrian Netherlands (present-day Belgium). Like many thousands of men who had passed this way since the outbreak of revolution, they were officers, soldiers, and servants who had abandoned their posts in the French army. Unlike many émigrés, however, they had no intention of joining the coalition forces arrayed against their native land. Lafayette's companions were men who had participated in his struggle to create and protect a constitutional monarchy. Louis Romeuf, the aide-de-camp who had been abused by a Parisian crowd when the king's flight was discovered, was among their number, as was Alexandre de Lameth, a former member of the Triumvirate.

Lafayette and his friends saw themselves as patriots who remained faithful to a constitution that had been travestied and loyal to a monarchy that had been overthrown. As they testified in a signed statement submitted to the authorities at Rochefort, they were honorable citizens who found themselves "unable to withstand any longer the violations of the constitution established by the national will." The Frenchmen were equally adamant that they not "be considered military enemies." Having "renounced" their posts, they presented themselves as noncombatants who deserved to be treated like all other "foreigners who request safe passage" to neutral territory. Had Lafayette not been among their number, they might well have been allowed to pass. As it was, the men were placed under guard and their weapons confiscated. Outraged at being denied the universal right of transit, Lafayette and his companions railed against their detention, but their objections fell on deaf ears. The marquis was a valuable prize.

Austria crowed about the capture, talking up Lafayette's role in the revolution to the point of gross exaggeration. Responding to Lafayette's request for release, the governor of the Austrian Netherlands, Herzog Albert von Sachsen-Teschen, baldly rebuked a man whose name had become inextricably linked with the anti-monarchist cause in the minds of the French king's revanchist foreign allies:

> You were the instigator behind the Revolution that turned France upside down. . . . It is you who placed irons on your king, deprived him of all his rights and his legitimate powers and kept him in captivity. . . . It is you who have been the principal instrument of all the disgraces that befell this unhappy monarch.

In light of these crimes, Sachsen-Teschen continued, Lafayette would remain in captivity "until such a time as your master, after having recovered his liberty and his sovereignty, will be able to decide your fate according to his justice or his clemency."

On August 21, Lafayette put pen to paper in an attempt to explain to Adrienne—and perhaps to himself—how he had arrived at such a predicament. The revolution replayed in his mind as he mulled over the apparent contradictions between his principles and his actions. But the puzzle was so intricate that Lafayette tied himself into a logical knot, musing "that my heart would have been republican if my reason had not given me this nuance of royalism." If Lafayette's heart and mind were divided, his very essence was entirely American, or so he felt. In fact, he envisioned his current location as a stopping point on the way to the United States. He planned to continue on to England as soon as he was released, and he hoped that Adrienne would meet him there so that they could travel together to America. There, he assured her, "we will find the liberty that no longer exists in France, and my tenderness will seek to compensate you for all the joys that you have lost." This was probably not conceived as an empty promise to a disappointed wife. Lafayette—ever as earnest as he was hopeful—fully expected his adopted nation to welcome him with open arms.

To hasten that wished-for embrace, Lafayette was soon drafting a letter to the nearest available American representative, William Short, who was then serving as the U.S. ambassador to the Netherlands in The Hague. Accustomed to seeing his commands carried out, Lafayette expected Short to act promptly. Directing him to the capital of the Austrian Netherlands, Lafayette wrote, "You will greatly oblige me, my dear Sir, by setting out for Brussels as soon as this reaches you, and insist on seeing me. I am an American citizen, an American officer, no more in the French service. That is your right, and I do not doubt of your urgent and immediate arrival." Determined to advance his cause by all possible means, Lafayette also sought Short's assistance in publicizing his plight. He had learned hard lessons about the power of the press, and now he asked Short to arrange the publication of the signed declaration drafted in Rochefort. Lafayette's statement appeared in the *Leyden Gazette,* but Short, a circumspect Virginian, did not hasten to Brussels.

In fact, none of the Americans in Europe leapt to Lafayette's rescue. Rounds of letters circulated among Short, Morris, and Thomas Pinckney, the U.S. ambassador to England, leading the three men to arrive at a unanimous conclusion: neither they nor the nation they represented had the authority to intervene in the matter of Lafayette's detention. Assessing the problem on September 12, Morris wrote to Short that, even "supposing that Monsieur de La Fayette were a natural born Subject of America, and taken under the Circumstances in which he was plac'd, I do not exactly see how the United States could claim him." Would it be possible, asked Morris, for the United States to "interfere in an Affair of this Sort without making themselves Parties in the Quarrel?" Morris expressed himself more bluntly to Pinckney the next day: "The less we meddle in the great Quarrel which agitates Europe the better will it be for us," he wrote. Pinckney concurred. The men also agreed on another point: that Lafayette, for all of his dedication to their nation's cause, was not, in point of fact, an American citizen. As Morris put it, "Monsieur de La Fayette is a Frenchman, and it is as a Frenchman that he is taken and is to be treated." Or, as Pinckey wrote, "A claim of the rights of an American Citizen to a person in the Marquiss's circumstances appears to me to be claiming nothing."

When October arrived with no sign of help from America, Adrienne took matters into her own hands. From that moment on, she would be Lafayette's most ardent champion. On October 8, she wrote directly to George Washington. Where her husband's commands had failed, perhaps her sentimental invocation might succeed. "In this abyss of grief," she wrote, "the idea of owing to the U.S. and to M. Washington—the life and liberty of M. Lafayette re-animates my heart with some hope. I hope every thing from the goodness of a people with whom he has set an example of that liberty of which he is now the victim. . . . Shall I dare speak what I hope?" She dared. Her wish was that an envoy be sent "to reclaim him in the name of the Republic of the U.S." and to carry him to the "bosoms" of the American people. Casting Lafayette as a beloved husband and cherished father, she added that "if his wife & his Children could be comprised in this happy mission, it is easy to judge how sweet it would be to her and to them; but if this would retard or embarrass, in any degree, the process or his success—we will defer the happiness of a reunion yet longer."

Sympathetic though he surely was, there was very little Washington could do about an international affair in which the United States was not a party. He handed the problem over to Vice President Jefferson with only the vaguest of instructions: "Enclosed is a letter from poor Madam La Fayette! How desirable it would be, if something could be done to relieve that family from their unhappy Situation." Three weeks later, he wrote again to Jefferson, asking him to ghostwrite a reply to the distraught Adrienne, sending her "all the consolation I can with propriety give her consistent with my public character and the National policy; circumstanced as things are." Although Washington had issued a gift of personal funds to Adrienne, he deemed it wise to keep the country out of European affairs. At most, he was willing to authorize Morris "to neglect no favorable opportunity of expressing *informally* the sentiments and wishes of this Country respecting M. de la Fayette." Three months would pass before Washington would express his "sincere sympathy" to Adrienne. To this, he added only his "most ardent prayers that you may be again united to M. de Lafayette under circumstances that may be joyful to you both—and that the evening of that life, whose morning has been devoted to the cause of liberty and humanity, may be crowned with the best of heaven's blessings." With that, Washington signed off.

At Chavaniac, Adrienne struggled. She had married one of the wealthiest men in France, but now she was on the verge of penury. As Gouverneur Morris described Lafayette's finances in an August 22 letter to Jefferson, "His circle is completed. He has spent his fortune on a revolution and is now crushed by the wheel which he put in motion." Arch as always, Morris added, "He lasted longer than I expected." Lafayette admitted as much in his letter to Adrienne. Disappointed though he was that he had failed to set France on a safe course, what weighed on him more heavily was that his attempts to do so had depleted the fortunes of his dependents. Still, he insisted that he would "make no excuse, neither to my children, nor to you, for having ruined my family. There is not a person among you who would want to owe your fortune to conduct contrary to my conscience." Lafayette could not even afford to pay for his own upkeep—a grim requirement for prisoners who wished to enjoy a modicum of comfort. On January 23, 1793, Morris instructed agents in Amsterdam to place ten thousand florins at Lafayette's disposal. America could not free its stalwart friend, but it would see to his needs as best it could.

By the time Adrienne received her husband's letter of August 21, it was clear that she and her children would soon be left with nothing. Before the month was out, Lafayette's name had been added to the nation's rapidly expanding list of men and women officially designated as émigrés—a designation with very real consequences. The law required that the belongings of émigrés be inventoried, seized, and, if the nation so desired, sold. By choosing exile, Lafayette had effectively forfeited all of his possessions. On August 30, 1792, four men appointed by local authorities arrived at Chavaniac to begin the inventory. Adrienne and Lafayette's aunt Madame de Chavaniac could only look on as the men opened every door, counted every item, and rifled through every piece of paper in every room of the house. For two days the men worked their way from the kitchen ("42 red copper casseroles . . .") to the chapel ("1 silver-plated Christ . . .") to the barnyard and stables ("2 black cows, one with a calf . . ."), taking note whenever Madame de Chavaniac tried to protect what she could by claiming animals and objects as her own personal property—not that of her émigré nephew.

Madame de Chavaniac had lived in the château far longer than Lafayette, but his imprint was everywhere. When a more expert commission of inspectors arrived in February to assign values to everything they found, they came across mementos of Lafayette's public life scattered about the estate. A stone from the Bastille carved in the shape of the prison and a foot-high statuette of Liberty personified were stashed in an outbuilding near the stables. A framed portrait of George Washington decorated a small room on the second floor of the main house. And the walls of Adrienne's cabinet, where she relaxed by playing the piano or with a game of trictrac, featured five small scenes depicting battles of the American Revolution and a two-foot-wide painting com-

A stone from the Bastille carved in its shape. A similar object was found among
Lafayette's belongings at Chavaniac.

memorating the storming of the Bastille. All of it would be confiscated, and little was ever returned.

Far more tragic were the seizures of Lafayette's possessions in Cayenne, where he had purchased three plantations and the slaves who worked them in order to conduct an experiment in gradual emancipation. Although Lafayette had always intended to free these slaves, he had never actually done so. Now these men, women, and children were the property of an émigré, and they would be impounded, inventoried, and sold like any other assets. On November 28, 1792, Adrienne wrote a pleading letter to the Ministry of the Marine, whose director was also in charge of the colonies, asking for help. Moved by "sentiments of humanity," she hoped to protect "the small number of blacks" who lived on Lafayette's land. Instead of selling the plantations, she suggested, the treasury might instead leave them be while enjoying all the profits they produced. She wrote, too, to the plantations' overseer, Louis de Geneste, explaining that "nothing could have ever impelled me to sell" these people but that she did not have the funds to purchase them from new owners.

When the plantation of Saint Régis was inventoried on April 5, 1794, each family of slaves counted as one item. Sixty-three people, ranging from a newborn girl not yet named to a sixty-six-year-old man named André, appeared under item numbers 31 to 57 and were valued at 73,250 livres. They constituted, by far, the most valuable portion of the plantation's holdings, estimated to be worth 87,068 livres in all. Although the colonial administrators rejected Adrienne's proposal, they made a gesture toward humanitarianism by agreeing to acquire the slaves for the nation. This way, "people accustomed to living together" would not be separated. The sale was completed on June 24, 1795.

After Lafayette's name was stricken from the list of émigrés in 1799, he wrote to the Ministry of the Marine hoping to be reimbursed for "at least 48" of the slaves taken from him. By that time, slavery had been abolished in the French colonies. The people were free, and Lafayette would not be compensated. At an earlier moment in his life, before financial concerns began to impinge on his idealism, Lafayette might not have asked for reimbursement. Condorcet's 1781 *Reflections on Negro Slavery*—which had influenced Lafayette's thinking on the subject—had stated quite clearly that, when slaves are freed, "the Sovereign owes no reparations to the slave master, just as nothing is owed to a thief except a judgment upon depriving him of a stolen object." In this instance, Lafayette seems to have felt that he simply could not afford his principles.

Adrienne's pleas to liberate the slaves came while she was deprived of her own freedom. If several brave men—some friends, some strangers—had not come to her aid, she would not have survived. On August 19, 1792, the day Lafayette crossed the border, a warrant was signed in Paris for the arrest of Adrienne and any of her children found with her. On August 25, Adrienne added an addendum to her last will and testament leaving the management of household affairs to her brother-in-law; it was at least the fourth time in eighteen months she had annotated her will. Adrienne and Anastasie, the elder of her two daughters, were taken into custody at eight o'clock on the morning of September 10. George had been away from home and Virginie hiding in the house when Alphonse Aulagnier, the justice of the peace charged with their capture, arrived at Chavaniac. Aulagnier had traveled through the night from the departmental capital of Le Puy, accompanied by eighty-six soldiers, gendarmes, and members of the National Guard. It was a massive show of force, far out of proportion to any resistance Adrienne might conceivably have offered, but apparently Aulagnier was quietly sympathetic to his captives' plight. Explicitly disobeying orders to escort the women to a prison in Paris, Aulagnier kept them in his municipality. As he explained to Minister of the Interior Jean-Marie Roland, "the events of September 2 and 3" made it clear "what fate would await my illustrious prisoners" in the capital. Aulagnier was referring to the September massacres of 1792, when the streets of Paris ran red with the blood of more than a thousand men, women, and children and triumphant murderers processed through the streets carrying the head (and, according to some accounts, the entrails) of the Princesse de Lamballe, a close ally of Marie Antoinette's. Roland—who might well have fallen victim himself had the bloodshed continued—ultimately relented, allowing Adrienne and Anastasie to return to Chavaniac under house arrest until further notice.

Anxiety filled Adrienne's days. News of her husband arrived only sporadically, and when it did, it generally took the form of rumor or speculation. Even his location was often uncertain, as he was shuttled from city to city and prison to prison, spending time in Nivelles, Luxembourg, and Wesel before arriving at Magdeburg, where he remained for all of 1793. The couple's financial woes also continued unabated.

Despite Grattepain-Morizot's wishful insistence that "after all debts have been settled, there will still be a balance left of nearly two million" livres, the seizure of all of Lafayette's lands and resources meant that there was no balance left at all. Had it not been for a loan of 100,000 livres extended personally by Gouverneur Morris in June 1793, Adrienne would not have been able to pay her most basic bills.

Adrienne's situation was hardly unique: fear and uncertainty gripped French households throughout 1793 as the nation lurched from crisis to crisis and the National Convention clung to power with an increasing sense of desperation. Events transpired at lightning speed. The month of March, which opened with the war abroad going badly, saw the implementation of a massive conscription effort, the outbreak of a full-fledged counterrevolutionary revolt in the Vendée region of western France, and the National Convention's establishment of a Revolutionary Tribunal and a Committee of Surveillance, each vested with extraordinary powers. On April 6, the Jacobin-dominated convention created the Committee of Public Safety—a super-legislative body of nine members (later increased to twelve) authorized to "deliberate in secret," to "oversee and accelerate administrative actions delegated to the Provisional Executive Council," to suspend the council's decrees "when it deems them contrary to the national interest," and "to take, in urgent circumstances, measures for general external and internal defense." With power thus consolidated, a purge of the National Convention's moderates began. And when the "incorruptible" Robespierre—a purist, in his way, who believed that the success of the revolution justified any actions taken on its behalf—joined the Committee of Public Safety on July 27, 1793, the stage was set for the climactic act of the French Revolution's lethal drama: the Reign of Terror.

On September 5, 1793, leaders of Paris's forty-eight sections, joined by the Jacobin Club, appeared before the National Convention to demand drastic measures. Observing that "the nation's dangers are extreme," the deputation insisted that "the remedies must be equally so." Just as the convention had instituted a nationwide draft to repulse foreign attackers, so too must the republic expel "the traitors within, who divide us, who pit us one against the other." The representatives further noted that a "revolutionary army" must be established with powerful tribunals that would make it "a terrible instrument of vengeance," and that they must remain active "until the soil of the Republic is purged of traitors, and until the death of the last of the conspirators." "Terror," their petition demanded, must become "the order of the day." Presiding over the National Convention, and speaking on its behalf, Robespierre averred that "all the French" would bless the Jacobin Club and the city of Paris for seeking such "imperious and definitive measures." He concluded with a promise: "All villains will perish on the scaffold, the Convention solemnly swears it."

On September 17, 1793, the National Convention began to make good on Robespierre's pledge by passing the Law of Suspects. This law, which Adrienne termed the "fatal decree," declared that "all suspects found in the territory of the Republic, and who are still at liberty, will be placed under arrest." The operative definition of "suspects" was both broad and vague. It encompassed not only those who had emigrated, been refused certificates of good citizenship, or been suspended from public functions by the National Convention, but also "those who, whether by their conduct, their relations, their intentions or their writings, have shown themselves to be partisans of tyranny or federalism and enemies of liberty." Likewise targeted for arrest were "those former nobles, including husbands, wives, fathers, mothers, sons or daughters, sisters or brothers, and agents of émigrés, who have not constantly demonstrated their attachment to the Revolution." According to these definitions, Adrienne and her entire family were enemies of the people.

Roundups began almost immediately. Adrienne's mother, the Duchesse d'Ayen, and her sister, the Maréchale de Noailles, were arrested in early October. They were permitted to remain under surveillance in the Hôtel de Noailles until April, at which time they were transferred to the Luxembourg Palace, Lafayette's first home in Paris, which had been requisitioned for use as a prison. Madame de Chavaniac was placed under house arrest in January 1794. Adrienne was imprisoned on November 13 in Brioude—the closest town to Chavaniac—and was subsequently moved to the prison of La Force in Paris. By the time of her arrival in the capital on June 7, some sixty people per day were being sent to the guillotine.

The months leading up to Adrienne's transfer had been bloody indeed, and many of the men who played roles in Lafayette's rise and fall justly or unjustly met their demise. Marat was murdered in his bathtub on July 13, 1793; Jacques-Pierre Brissot went to the guillotine on October 31, 1793; the Duc d'Orléans was guillotined, despite his new republican name of Philippe Égalité, on November 6, 1793; Jean-Sylvain Bailly, former mayor of Paris, followed on November 12; Antoine Barnave, the triumvir who'd developed an affection for Marie Antoinette while escorting her back from Varennes, was guillotined on November 29; the abolitionist philosopher Condorcet died in prison—a likely suicide—on March 28, 1794; Danton was executed on April 5, 1794.

On July 22, 1794, Adrienne's mother, sister, and grandmother joined the roster of victims. Robespierre himself, who had orchestrated the executions of so many real and perceived enemies, was guillotined less than one week later. Had the Noailles women lived just a few days longer, they would have survived the revolution. Adrienne, concluding her privately published narrative of her mother's life, wrote, "I have given up trying to explain anything because what I feel is inexplicable."

Adrienne escaped her family's fate thanks to American intervention. When Gouverneur Morris learned that Adrienne had been transferred to Paris, he understood the dire implications of the move and hastened to her aid. Morris had no official authorization, but he also had no time to spare. Waiting for approval to cross the Atlantic would have taken weeks under the best of circumstances, and recently Morris's letters had been suffering greater delays than usual because, as he wrote to his brother, "the Comité de Surveillance have done me the honor to peruse some of them." So he would have to act first and inform Washington later. As he explained to the president, he had written to France's minister of foreign affairs, Philibert Buchot, on June 29 "as a citizen and not as a commissioner." While taking pains to stress to Buchot that his was an unofficial letter, Morris reminded the minister of Lafayette's place in the hearts of the American public: "The family of Lafayette is beloved in America," he wrote, adding,

that without examining his conduct in this country . . . my fellow-citizens confine themselves to the grateful remembrance of the services he has rendered us, and that therefore the death of his wife might lessen the attachment of some among them to the French Republic; that it would furnish the partisans of England with means of misrepresenting what passes here; that I cannot but think her existence of very little consequence to this government; and that I am sure its enemies will rejoice at the destruction of anything which bears the name of Lafayette.

Morris never received a reply, but Adrienne believed ever after that he had saved her life. Lafayette, whose feelings about Morris were actually quite mixed, preferred to credit Morris's successor—his former comrade-in-arms James Monroe. Whatever the impetus may have been, Adrienne was liberated on February 2, 1795.

She made freeing her husband her first priority. Having developed a strategy as bold as it was selfless, she followed it through, step by step, until she succeeded. After arranging to send her son, George Washington Lafayette, to the United States, where she hoped he would be cared for by his Virginian namesake, Adrienne obtained passports for herself and her daughters, petitioned Emperor Francis II for permission to join her husband in prison, and arrived with Anastasie and Virginie at the door of the fortress of Olmutz on October 15, 1795. If Austrian forces were going to keep Lafayette under lock and key, they would have to suffer the public embarrassment of keeping his wife and daughters as well.

For all of the public and private diplomacy that had gone into obtaining Lafayette's liberty since 1792, nothing did more to further the cause than the outpouring of international sympathy prompted by Adrienne's self-imposed incarceration. The story of the family's imprisonment captured public attention from Paris to Philadelphia, and even those who were unsympathetic to Lafayette were forced to square their views with the poignant drama of the women's self-sacrifice.

Washington, who had hitherto kept a judicious distance from the matter, was finally moved to act. On May 15, 1796, he wrote to the emperor. Washington emphasized that his was a private letter, composed not in his capacity as the leader of a nation but merely as a man. "In common with the people of this Country," Washington wrote, "I retain a strong and cordial sense of the services rendered to them by the Marquis De la Fayette; and my friendship for him has been constant and sincere." He asked the emperor to consider whether Lafayette's "long imprisonment, and the confiscation of his Estate, and the Indigence and dispersion of his family, and the painful anxieties incident to all these circumstances, do not form an assemblage of sufferings, which recommend him to the mediation of *Humanity*?" Private though the letter might have been, Washington was willing to extend the nation on Lafayette's behalf, asking "that he may be permitted to come to this Country on such conditions and under such restrictions, as your Majesty may think it expedient to prescribe."

Around the same time, pressure to release Lafayette began to pour forth in the public sphere, as essays and prints by Lafayette's supporters capitalized on the sentiments inspired by Adrienne's sacrifice to build their case. Philippe Charles d'Agrain, a former adjutant general who had crossed into the Austrian Netherlands with Lafayette in 1792 but had been freed within the year, produced the most ambitious of these works—an eighteen-page poem entitled *Captivity of Lafayette*. Writing in the voice of Lafayette, Agrain tapped into the era's fascination with dark tales of madness and injustice by painting a tragic picture of the erstwhile champion of freedom stooped under the weight of his irons and dying a slow death, forgotten by all of humankind. Driven to delirium, Agrain's Lafayette is tormented by dreams of a reunion with his beloved wife until, as if emerging from a fog, he understands that Adrienne is truly there in his arms, with their daughters in tow. Augmented by forty-two pages of explanatory notes and documents detailing Lafayette's lifelong campaign for righteousness, the poem was reviewed and excerpted in English and American magazines, where it rekindled interest in his imprisonment.

Two poignant engravings underscore the pathos of Agrain's narrative:

Philippe Charles d'Agrain, *Captivité de Lafayette: Héroïde, et des notes historiques, non encore connues du public, sur les illustres prisonniers d'Olmutz, en Moravie* (Paris: Chocheris, 1797), page 16.

one depicts the moment of the women's arrival, and the other shows Lafayette alone in a stone room that is illuminated only by a feeble light shining through a small, barred window near the ceiling. In both, Lafayette's circumstances seem irredeemably bleak, as chains dangle from the wall on the left of the reunion scene, and the words "suffer and die" can be seen inscribed on the masonry above them. Dank and unhealthful though it was, Lafayette's imprisonment at Olmutz was somewhat less grim than Agrain's words and images might suggest. Lafayette's rooms were on the ground floor, not in the basement, and he had not been entirely alone before his family's arrival—a servant lodged with him, as did two of the officers arrested with him at Rochefort, Charles César de Fay de La Tour-Maubourg (whose younger brother would later wed Lafayette's daughter Anastasie) and Jean-Xavier Bureau de Pusy (whose son would marry Lafayette's granddaughter). Agrain may not have been entirely accurate, but his version of events was deeply persuasive.

Anglophones soon took up their pens in support of the cause. In the United States, former attorney general William Bradford contributed "La Fayette: A Song" to the *New-York Weekly Magazine,* while the Philadelphia newspaperman Mathew Carey translated Agrain's engravings into words. Carey was an Irishman who had worked for Benjamin Franklin in France and founded an American newspaper in 1785, with financial backing from Lafayette. In 1797, his paper, the *Daily Advertiser,* published "Lafayette: A Fragment." As the article describes it, Lafayette had been sitting "on a coarse misshapen bench" with "ponderous chains" weighing on his legs when "the door creaked on its rust-eaten hinges," signaling the arrival of Adrienne and her daughters. Recalling with gratitude that Lafayette had entrusted "his fortunes" to America's "tempest-tost bark" and emerged "crowned with laurels at Yorktown," the author urges the United States to remember its hero, who, we read near the end, "casts his longing eyes towards America, that country to which the best, the choicest days of his existence were so zealously and so usefully devoted . . . he trusts she will not cease to reiterate her applications for his relief, till they are crowned with success." Lafayette had helped establish freedom in America, and Americans wanted to return the favor.

Calls to intercede came from England as well. Samuel Taylor Coleridge published "Sonnet to the Marquis de La Fayette" in London's *Freemason's Magazine,* while the fiery Whig politicians Charles James Fox and General Richard FitzPatrick tugged at the heartstrings of their fellow MPs with moving speeches. On May 10, 1796, Fox took the floor of the House of Commons to describe the plight of Adrienne, who, after "enduring a series of most dreadful sufferings under the brutal Robespierre . . . flew on the wings of duty and affection, to Vienna," where she begged for permission to join her husband. When Adrienne arrived at Olmutz, Fox continued, the jailors did their best to shake her determination. They told her that, in the wake of his recent attempt to escape, Lafayette was now subjected to privations that were stricter than usual, and "that if she resolved to go down to the dungeon to her husband, she must submit to share in all the horrors of his captivity." At this, the parliamentary record attests, "a burst of indignation and sorrow broke from every part of the House." Despite every effort to prevent her from taking this fateful step, Fox reported, the virtuous Adrienne refused to be put off.

FitzPatrick reprised the theme on December 16. Asking his listeners to imagine "what a scene must the reunion of this unhappy family have presented in the circumstances under which they met," he related a new slew of horrors that Adrienne had suffered since joining her husband. Seven months in the pestilential prison had taken its toll on Adrienne's health; she was granted permission to seek medical attention in Vienna only on the condition that she not return to Olmutz. Preferring illness to a second separation, Adrienne chose to remain where she was. The most painful injury Adrienne endured, though, was the insult to her piety: a devout Roman Catholic, she was denied the solace of attending Mass or having her confession heard. "It is a torment to her conscience," FitzPatrick explained, to be barred from exercising "that duty which her religion has prescribed." So moving was the speech that, before embarking on a rebuttal, FitzPatrick's archrival William Pitt had little choice but to acknowledge "that a more striking and pathetic appeal was never made to the feelings of the House."

By 1797, France's five-member Directory—the executive branch of the government established after Robespierre's fall—felt pressed by both internal and external forces to act on Lafayette's behalf, but the matter was beyond its control. Not only did Lafayette remain imprisoned by Austria—a foreign power—but the two nations were still at war. Moreover, the directors had little sway in the ongoing peace negotiations, which were being overseen on the French side by a man who was effectively accountable to no one: General Napoleon Bonaparte. The Corsican-born military leader was not yet thirty years old, but as commander of France's victorious Army of Italy, he was one of the most popular men in the nation, and quite possibly the most powerful man in Europe. After months of quiet prodding and unofficial negotiations regarding the Lafayette household's predicament, the president of the Directory wrote to Napoleon on August 1, 1797, asking him to do what he could "to end their captivity as soon as possible." Lafayette's family and their fellow captives were released on September 19.

On October 5, 1797, Samuel Williams, the United States' consul to Hamburg, wrote to Washington that he "had the happiness of embracing our beloved Friend, General La Fayette, accompanied with his Lady & Daughters." Washington was a private citizen now, living under the presidency of John Adams, but his interest in Lafayette had for many years been more personal than political. As Williams reported, the company had been warmly received in every town they passed on their way to Hamburg and all were "in pretty good health, excepting Madame Lafayette, who mends daily." Adrienne had indeed suffered the most severely. When she emerged from prison, a rash covered her body, a gaping sore vexed her leg, and her stomach was constantly unsettled. Williams's assessment that Adrienne's health was improving could best be described as wishful thinking.

The freed captives would not be in Hamburg long. As William Vans Murray, the U.S. consul to The Hague, explained to Washington on August 26, Francis II had "ordered their release provided the necessary steps be taken here to convey them off the territory of the Empire to Holland or America, eight days after their arrival at Hamburgh." Naturally, Lafayette wanted to embark for the United States as soon as possible, but as Williams wrote to Washington, a few obstacles stood in the way. First, Adrienne was not yet well enough to make such a long voyage. Second, France and the United States were perched on the brink of hostilities. Nonetheless, Williams had assured Lafayette that he would find "a most affectionate reception" in America whenever he should choose to sail. Unfortunately, Williams was mistaken.

Lafayette was saddened to learn that relations between his native land and his adopted nation had deteriorated so badly. On October 8, he expressed his dismay to the American Francis Huger, a son of Major Huger, at whose house Lafayette had inadvertently landed when he first set foot in America in 1777. Although he did not yet know what had caused the Franco-American breach, he lamented its consequences, writing that "nothing could be more impolitic for the two countries, and more painful for me." But Lafayette would not give up on his dream, and before putting down his pen he reclaimed the bold optimism that had driven every major decision of his life, for better or for worse, writing, "My most ardent desire is to see these differences resolved quickly." Contemplating a resolution to the international dispute, he prayed, "May it please God that it might be in my power to contribute to it!!"

Lafayette's indefatigable spirit had triumphed over the harsh environs of Olmutz, but even his copious goodwill would not be enough to solve the problems that plagued French-American relations. The once and future allies were on the verge of an international crisis that would go down in history as the Quasi-War. The dispute began with the Jay Treaty—a pact negotiated by John Jay, ratified by Congress, and signed by Washington that settled lingering boundary disputes and reestablished limited commerce between the United States and Great Britain. When the treaty went into effect, on February 29, 1796, France was outraged. From the perspective of a French nation now at war with England—indeed, with most of Europe—the agreement flew in the face of America's proclaimed neutrality in European affairs while abrogating the 1778 Treaties of Amity and Commerce. Soon, French privateers were attacking American merchant ships with abandon, and hundreds of ships were lost in the space of a year.

When Lafayette was released from prison, things were going from bad to worse. Adams, who had never much cared for the French, was losing his patience, and the so-called XYZ Affair of 1798 pushed him to his limit. The ill-fated escapade involved three American envoys who, having been sent to Paris to negotiate a resolution to the ongoing hostilities, were greeted by three shadowy go-betweens—known merely as X, Y, and Z—demanding an apology from Adams and substantial financial payments. Apparently Talleyrand, now serving as French foreign minister, would not meet with the Americans until his own pockets had been sufficiently lined and his nation's coffers replenished by the United States, which, as all of France was well aware, had not yet repaid loans made during the American Revolution. Angry, insulted, and empty-handed, the Americans were told to leave the country.

Meanwhile, in Philadelphia, Adams was pushing for a military buildup in a political climate marked by increasing partisan animosity. On one side stood Adams, Hamilton, and their colleagues affiliated with the Anglophile Federalist Party. On the other side were Jeffer-

son, Madison, and other Francophile members of the Democratic-
Republican Party. Involving, as it did, thorny questions of transatlantic
allegiances, the Quasi-War became hotly contested on the home front
as the country's first two political parties battled for control of national
policy.

So virulent was anti-French sentiment in Federalist circles that even
the beloved name of Lafayette became fair game for political wrangling.
In the spring of 1797, two rival Federalist newspapers—Noah Webster's
American Minerva, published in New York, and *Porcupine's Political
Censor,* published by William Cobbett in Philadelphia—spilled copious amounts of ink in an argument over whether or not it was patriotic
to support Lafayette. Although both papers routinely denounced the
excesses of the French Revolution, Webster believed that Cobbett went
too far in "retailing abuse against Lafayette, whose sufferings (even suppose him to have been in fault, which is doubtful or not admitted) are
far too severe, and call for the sympathy of all mankind." As Webster
saw it, Cobbett's habit of praising France's old regime "denotes a man
callous to the miseries of his species, and extremely disrespectful to the
opinions of the Americans, who entertain friendship and gratitude for
Lafayette." Cobbett, who was never one to back away from a fight,
countered "that a desire to ingratiate yourself with the deceived part of
the public, together with that of injuring me, led [Webster] to bring
forward the stalking horse Lafayette, and not any friendship, gratitude,
or compassion that you entertained for him." Then again, he observed
that Webster had been foolish enough to pin his "political faith on the
sleeve of this unfledged statesman" in the early days of the French Revolution, and that, "like Bailly and Lafayette, you adored the holy right of
insurrection, till it began to operate against yourselves."

Choosing their words carefully, several of Lafayette's American
friends did their best to persuade him to abandon, or at least to post-
pone, his planned emigration. Alexander Hamilton, Lafayette's former
comrade-in-arms who had become a Federalist leader, wrote from New
York on April 28, 1798, bluntly stating the political differences that
now separated them: the execution of Louis XVI and other instances of
violence had, he explained, "cured me of my good will for the French
Revolution." Although he assured Lafayette that "no one feels more
than I do the motives which this country has to love you, to desire and
to promote your happiness," Hamilton concluded that "in the present
state of our affairs with France, I cannot urge you to us."

Even Washington, who just two years earlier had suggested to the emperor that Lafayette be free to immigrate to America, now seconded Hamilton's sentiments. On Christmas Day 1798, Washington wrote to Lafayette that "no one in the United States would receive you with opener arms, or with more ardent affection that I should"—but only "after the difference between this Country and France are adjusted, and harmony between the Nations is again restored." Continuing the letter, which was destined to be his last to Lafayette (Washington died less than a year later), he added:

> It would be uncandid, and incompatible with that friendship I have always professed for you to say, (and on your own account) that I wish it before. For you may be assured, my dear Sir, that the scenes you would meet with, and the part you would be stimulated to act in case of an open rupture, or even if matters should remain in status quo, would be such as to place you in a situation which no address, or human prudence, could free you from embarrassment. In a word, you would lose the confidence of one party or the other, perhaps both—were you here under these circumstances.

Lafayette was still not dissuaded. Replying to Washington on May 9, 1799, he pointed to his half dozen letters as evidence of "how ardently, in spite of difficulties, I long to be in America." Lafayette conceded that Washington had not been alone in warning him away from the United States, but he added, "I am not without some distant hopes, that . . . I may become not quite useless to the purpose of an American negotiation." And although he promised that he would try not to sail before receiving Washington's reply, he left the possibility open by noting that "in the improbable case where I would suddenly pop upon you, be certain, my dear g[ener]al that my motives should be such as to convince you of their urgency, & then I hope individual independence would be left to an harassed old friend by American parties."

Washington and Hamilton, who harbored fond memories of Lafayette, could not have been surprised by his single-minded persistence. But William Vans Murray was just getting to know him and was astounded by Lafayette's unreconstructed optimism. On March 19, 1799, Murray reported to John Quincy Adams, then serving as America's minister to Prussia, about a visit with Lafayette and his family, who were now living in Vianen, near Utrecht. Murray wrote that "Lafayette is young in look and healthy, but what I did least expect he is cheerful." Lafayette was prone to declaring "his attachment 'to Liberty'" without any prompting, Murray observed. "But what exceeded even the pictures of imaginary perseverance, is, that he still . . . wishes to be instrumental in curing political evils—ameliorating mankind!! Lord have mercy upon us!!" Murray could hardly believe it, but Lafayette did not appear to be jesting: the words flowed from Lafayette's mouth most "naturally and unaffectedly."

At the time, Murray felt as though he were in the company of the misguided Doctor Sangrado who, in the picaresque novel *Gil Blas,* admits that "it is indeed true . . . that all my prescriptions have brought people to their graves, and I should change my principles and practice; but I have written a book to support them!" Murray found Lafayette's delusions "lamentable, for he seems to be really governed by a most insatiable thirst after honesty and good intentions, and is certainly generous and amiable." Adams, who had inherited some of his father's wariness of Lafayette's motives, was less generous in his response, writing that, "I am glad you have seen La F[ayette] and not surprised that you found him full of the same fanaticism . . . a great part of which however with him, is what it always was, ungovernable ambition in disguise." Adams admitted that Lafayette "thinks his intentions as good as you allow them to be; but he is a man apt to mistake the operations of his heart as well as those of his head."

Although Lafayette received no encouragement, he continued to plan for an American voyage for most of the year. Writing to Adrienne on July 4, 1799, he declared himself willing to cross the Atlantic in a hot air balloon if need be, and in August he sought Murray's help in obtaining a passport. As before, Murray was flabbergasted. Relating the conversation to Washington, Murray reported that Lafayette had asked "could I not . . . be useful in uniting parties? I told him no!" Yet Lafayette was "much bent on going—Leaving his lady and daughter in France," where they had returned to begin the long process of reclaiming whatever property they could. Intending "to settle for life" on the other side of the Atlantic, Lafayette planned to "land in the Chesapeake" and "pass the winter" as Washington's guest and then "buy a farm near Mount Vernon." So confident was Lafayette of his imminent relocation that by October, correspondents in Europe were addressing his mail to the United States.

To those unfamiliar with Lafayette, this giddy perseverance seemed to cry out for explanation. On June 25, 1799, Major General Charles Cotesworth Pinckney of South Carolina—one of the three American emissaries in the XYZ Affair—forwarded to Washington a letter speculating that Talleyrand was driving Lafayette's plan. Written in cipher by a colleague in The Hague, the document asserted that Lafayette had received "letters from Talleyrand advising him strongly to it, and buoying him up with his canting flattery." The author surmised that "trusting to what popularity, and influence [Lafayette] may still retain in the U[nited] States, especially among the people, Talleyrand expects that on his arrival, [Lafayette] would be courted, flattered and cherished by the Democrats and Anti's." By August, Murray, too, was growing wary that Lafayette might do more harm than good were he to emigrate. Writing to John Quincy Adams, Murray avowed that Lafayette seemed sincere in declaring "explicit federalism, and a support of our government, and abhorrence of the conduct of France towards it and our nation." Yet Murray cautioned, "I think that I know his character—his ambition—too well not to fear that should he go, he will think that he finds reasons to change his tone."

Washington, whose friendship with Lafayette had survived many ups and downs over the course of more than two decades, took all of the speculation in stride. Writing to Secretary of State Timothy Pickering, he initially dismissed allegations that Talleyrand was behind Lafayette's plans. "Surely Lafayette will not come here on such an errand, and under such circumstances," Washington exclaimed. But further reflection led him to amend his views: "And yet—I believe he will, if the thing is proposed to him!" Washington knew all too well that Lafayette "has a blind side, not difficult to assail." In the end, he concurred with Lady Macbeth that "what has been done, cannot be undone. . . . To make the best of it," Washington concluded, "is all that remains to do."

When Washington died, on December 14, 1799, news that Lafayette had abandoned his vision of an American retirement and abruptly returned to France had not yet reached the United States. Had Washington known, he would likely have been relieved. Murray, however, was stunned; Lafayette had left the Netherlands in November without so much as bidding him adieu.

When Napoleon Bonaparte carried out a coup d'état on November 9–10, 1799 (or 18–19 Brumaire year VIII, according to the French revolutionary calendar that dubbed September 22, 1792, the first day of "Year I" to signal the new era created by the foundation of the French republic), Lafayette's aide-de-camp leapt into action. Over the course of two tumultuous days, General Bonaparte, recently returned from Egypt, had overthrown the troubled Directory and installed himself and two colleagues as a three-man Consulate. As Napoleon and his collaborators presented it, they had come to save the republic, not to bury it. The constitution, they argued, had been defiled by the misdeeds of the Directory and could no longer guide the nation. In its place, the consuls would institute a new system designed "to consolidate, guarantee, and inviolably consecrate the sovereignty of the French people, the Republic one and indivisible, the representative system, the division of power, liberty, equality, safety, and property." As Napoleon pledged allegiance to the principles of 1789, and before the dust could settle, the aide hastened to Holland bearing a passport that Adrienne had obtained for Lafayette under an assumed name. Two hours after receiving the forged papers, Lafayette was on the road to France.

Fully understanding that Napoleon might not welcome the sudden appearance of a rival general, Lafayette wrote to Provisional Consul Bonaparte immediately upon reaching Paris. Lafayette acknowledged his "obligations" to Napoleon and minimized the appearance of threat by emphasizing that he was about "to depart for the distant countryside where I will reunite with my family." These were not the first conciliatory words Bonaparte had received from Lafayette. Adrienne had begun laying the groundwork by meeting with Napoleon in October. On her recommendation, Lafayette had written an uncharacteristically succinct letter on October 30 reassuring Napoleon of his gratitude and support.

Nonetheless, Napoleon was incensed when he learned that Lafayette was in Paris. Possessing a keen strategic mind, Napoleon was wary of Lafayette's uncommon "talent for making friends." If allegiances had to be declared, Napoleon wondered, whom could he count on to choose him over of Lafayette?

Lafayette learned of Napoleon's outrage from go-betweens who advised a prompt return to Holland. Lafayette remembered replying that "they surely knew me well enough to understand that this imperious and menacing tone would be enough to set me even more firmly in my course." Moreover, he recalled saying, "It would be quite amusing if I were to be arrested in the evening by the National Guard and locked in the Temple the next day by the restorer of the principles of 89." In other words, Napoleon could not move against Lafayette without undermining his claim to be the true heir of the revolution. Once again, Adrienne brokered a truce. Napoleon would permit Lafayette to remain in France on the condition that he avoid all "éclat" (brilliance or acclaim). In practice, this meant that Lafayette would have to settle outside of Paris and play no role in the public eye.

By far the more practical spouse, Adrienne arranged a retreat perfectly suited to the situation. When she had returned to France, one of her first orders of business had been securing her inheritance of the château and estate of La Grange. Located some forty miles southeast of Paris, La Grange had descended through Adrienne's mother's family and was far enough from the capital to appease Napoleon but near enough to allow Lafayette to keep abreast of current events. Although Lafayette never took his eye off the national and international struggles for liberty, his life would revolve around the house and grounds of La Grange for the next thirty-five years.

CHAPTER 19

HOMAGES

On February 8, 1800, the chapel of the Invalides—which had been deconsecrated during the revolution and renamed the Temple of Mars—hosted a magnificent memorial service celebrating the life and legacy of George Washington. Government officials, army officers, veterans, and other dignitaries gathered beneath the building's soaring dome to gaze upon a sculpted bust of Washington while listening to orations praising the "warrior . . . legislator . . . citizen above reproach!" These panegyrics were dedicated to Washington, but they had been carefully designed to celebrate another soldier-turned-ruler as well: Napoleon Bonaparte, who was the mastermind of the day's events. Handpicked by Napoleon to deliver the official eulogy, the poet Louis de Fontanes lauded Washington in terms that the consul might well have applied to himself. As Fontanes put it, Washington belonged to history's select group of "prodigious men who appear, from time to time, on the world stage," where they are destined by a higher power either "to build a cradle or to repair the ruins of empires." Such men are born for greatness, Fontanes declared. They can only "try in vain . . . to blend into the crowd; the hand of fortune suddenly carries them off and speeds them from obstacle to obstacle, from triumph to triumph, until they reach the summit of power."

If the ceremony's speeches hinted at parallels between Washington and Bonaparte, its decorations made clear which man was more glorious. A vibrant array of ninety-six flags seized by the French army during its Egyptian expedition flew high above the assembly, proclaiming Napoleon's recent triumphs and dwarfing the lifeless bust of Washington, who was effectively upstaged at his own memorial, his honor co-opted and his legacy twisted to legitimate Napoleon's thirst for power. It's probably for the best that neither Lafayette, nor his son, nor any representative of the United States was permitted to attend; true friends of Washington's would have found little to appreciate in the spectacle.

A more suitable homage to Washington was beginning to take shape at La Grange, where Lafayette was transforming Adrienne's ancestral estate into a French version of Mount Vernon. Memories of Washington's retirement on the banks of the Potomac had stayed with Lafayette since his 1784 visit to the United States, and the dream of emulating the American Cincinnatus continued to inspire him. As Lafayette remembered it, his own interest in agriculture had redoubled during the years he spent "within the four walls of a prison," when he read any books he could find on the subject and imagined the pleasures of laboring in the open air. Writing from Vianen in 1799, Lafayette confided to Washington that he dreamed of "retirement on a small farm," and although the details of his plan remained unsettled for quite a while—at times he considered plots of land in Virginia, New England, or New York; at other times he envisioned tending fields in France—he never doubted that he would follow in Washington's footsteps. Whatever its location, the farm would meld ancient virtue with Enlightenment science and civic duty, becoming a site, Lafayette hoped, where new methods would be introduced, tested, and perfected, and the lessons learned shared widely for the betterment of all mankind.

Such were Lafayette's goals when he began afresh at La Grange the agricultural projects that he had abandoned at Chavaniac, and this work would occupy him for the rest of his life. Between 1800 and 1834, Lafayette reconfigured nearly every feature of the 700-acre estate, which, in 1807, included some 416 acres of arable fields, 70 acres of pastureland, and 134 acres of woods and park, crisscrossed by a web of walking, riding, and carriage paths as well as ponds, streams, and irrigation ditches. Lafayette rerouted miles of roads, undertook the large-scale felling of trees, and purchased thousands of plants and seeds, which served a combination of decorative and economic purposes. In one 1806 delivery alone, Lafayette received 203 pear trees and 165 apple trees, which, together with other trees and vines on the property, filled Lafayette's tables with a bountiful selection of preserves and desserts. Not only did Lafayette grow wheat, oats, potatoes, barley, and corn and keep pigs, sheep, cows, turkeys, pigeons, and fish but, determined to make his lands at least as profitable as those of his neighbors, he maintained meticulous records documenting each year's income and expenditures, sought advice from experts near and far, and took copious notes on matters ranging from the best practices in crop rotation to new processes for preparing feed.

Obliged to desist from political activities because of his agreement with Napoleon, Lafayette remained eager to put his energies to good use and became as enthusiastic about his farm as he had once been about the American Revolution; to judge by reports of visitors to La Grange, agriculture ranked with liberty among Lafayette's favorite topics of conversation. Describing an 1802 stay with Lafayette, William Taylor of Norwich wrote, "Before breakfast Lafayette took me over his farm" while speaking of both political and agricultural reform. Taylor was a leading translator of German Romantic literature with no particular expertise in land management, but he was a cousin of John Dyson—the English farmer who had spent a year at Chavaniac back in 1791 and 1792—and the family tie was good enough for Lafayette. Taylor described having been "obliged to answer questions about [Dyson's] farm at Gunton" and quipped that "having by great good-luck fancied that beans would grow on the stiffer and bluer upland . . . I was presented to his farmer as Sir Oracle."

Aesthetic changes were also afoot at La Grange, where, Taylor observed, "the taste of the owner is giving it the appearance of an English park." In late 1800 or early 1801 Lafayette hired Hubert Robert, one of the foremost landscape painters of the day, to design gardens in the "picturesque" manner at La Grange. Sometimes termed "English" because the fashion originated in the United Kingdom, the picturesque style of gardening had become popular in France in the last decades of the eighteenth century as some of the more forward-looking landowners stripped their grounds of symmetrical allées and topiaries pruned *à la française* and replaced them with meandering pathways and plantings that conveyed an air of naturalness. Taylor, who visited while Lafayette's garden was being remodeled, described the changes in progress, noting that the moat around the château "is in part filled up, and is about to assume the form of a passing rivulet. . . . Irregular vistas are breaking into the dark circle of wood . . . [and a few] tall oaks have been singled out on the lawn." The result was a landscape that appeared to be as informal and unaffected as Lafayette himself.

Lafayette's tastes similarly infused the château's interior, which quietly reminded visitors of their host's values and achievements. Taylor wrote to his cousin that he initially found "the bed-chambers . . . furnished with a simplicity which struck me . . . as nakedness." But gradually he "learnt to perceive that not the minutest wish was unforeseen; that the two chairs were enough; that pen, ink, paper, shaving-glass were all at hand." Lafayette's past was displayed proudly in the "round saloon of the south-west tower," where breakfast and tea were served. Taylor described seeing four paintings there: a "portrait of the young Lafayette in his first uniform," as well as a view of the *Victoire*—the "ship which Lafayette at his own expense equipped to carry succour to the army of Washington"— and scenes of "the demolition of the Bastille" and the Festival of Federation. In the library, located in a "round room of the south-east tower," Taylor noted a preponderance of "works on agricultural and political topics, both French and English."

Of the forty-five habitable rooms in the château, the library was the one closest to Lafayette's heart. Nowhere was the link between agriculture and ideas more visible than here, as Sydney, Lady Morgan, the noted Irish author and outspoken advocate of humanitarian causes, observed. In an excerpt from the book *France* (1817), reproduced in American newspapers, Lady Morgan wrote that Lafayette's "elegant and well chosen collection of books, occupies the highest apartments in one of the towers of the château, and like the study of Montaigne, hangs over the farm-yard of the philosophical agriculturalist." As she remembered it, she was standing in the library with Lafayette one day, "looking out of the window at some flocks that were passing beneath," when Lafayette confessed that the lure of the fields often distracted him from his reading: "It frequently happens . . . that my merinos, and my hay carts, dispute my attention with your Hume, or our own Voltaire." An 1826 visitor from the United States drew out the uniquely American implications of the vista, recalling that the library windows "command a view of a rural domain, such as Cincinnatus or Washington would have enjoyed, and such as its own proprietor would not exchange for an empire."

The arrangement was no coincidence; Lafayette had worked closely with Vaudoyer—the same architect he had hired to transform Chavaniac—to design every feature of the library. On May 18, 1802, Lafayette spelled out a decorative scheme, still visible today, featuring nine painted cameos and an array of trophies placed in a ring around the tops of the bookshelves, each commemorating one of his fallen comrades. Of the nine men depicted in paint, two are Americans

(Washington and Franklin) and one is a Dutchman—Albert van Ryssel, who led the Dutch Patriot forces in 1787 and lived the next five years in exile in France as punishment for having adhered to his principles. The other six depict Frenchmen whose deaths resonated deeply with Lafayette. During the French Revolution, all six had shared Lafayette's commitment to a constitutional monarchy, and all were executed on account of it. Among them were Jean-Sylvain Bailly, guillotined on November 12, 1793; Louis-Georges Desrousseaux, the mayor of Sedan, who had been among some two dozen men condemned to death for supporting Lafayette in 1792; and Louis-Alexandre, Duc de La Rochefoucauld, a member of the liberal nobility and a friend of Franklin's; he was assassinated during the September massacres, shortly after Lafayette's flight to Belgium.

The specters of these men accompanied Lafayette for the rest of his life, and they were with him as he sat at a custom-made desk in an alcove of the library—within shouting distance of the farmyard—writing and rewriting his memoirs, one segment of which (a passage of nearly one hundred pages) consists of a letter to the deceased Van Ryssel. This missive to a man who could never read it was completed in 1807—the year Adrienne, who had been plagued by illness since her time in Olmutz, died at the Paris home of her aunt Madame de Tessé. Wrestling with grief while trying to make sense of a tangled life, Lafayette used the letter to Van Ryssel as a forum for examining his vexed relationship to Napoleon. Acknowledging that he had once had faith that Bonaparte might carry on the values of the revolution, Lafayette conceded that he was mistaken. Bonaparte, he had come to understand, was an enemy of freedom. Addressing Van Ryssel directly, Lafayette dedicated the document to "your memory" and posed a poignant question: "Why should I not imagine the text before your eyes when it is the sacred memory of a few friends, more than the opinion of the living universe, to which I wish to report my actions and my thoughts."

Like Washington, Lafayette allowed himself to be lured out of retirement for only one reason: to serve the nation. When Napoleon began to falter in 1814, Lafayette reentered French politics as a staunch opponent of restoring the Bourbon monarchy. Personally and politically, a great deal of bad blood flowed between Lafayette and the returning royals. King Louis XVIII, who took up residence in the Tuileries Palace on May 3, 1814, was no stranger to the aging marquis; formerly Comte de Provence, he was the elder of Louis XVI's brothers and the man

Isidore Laurent Deroy, *La Grange East View,* lithograph, c. 1825, after a painting by Alvan Fisher.

Library at La Grange, designed by Antoine Vaudoyer, c. 1800.

Lafayette had famously snubbed in 1776. Nor was the subsequent king, Charles X, crowned in 1824, a fresh face; he was Louis XVI's younger brother, formerly Comte d'Artois. As Charles X, he kept Lafayette under close scrutiny, lest he conspire to overthrow the monarchy—and it wasn't a case of paranoia; Lafayette was involved with a host of anti-Bourbon conspiracies. None of them came close to succeeding, but all of them kept the government understandably on edge.

Thanks to the Charter of 1814, however, which established a constitutional monarchy in France, Lafayette was able to participate openly in national politics for the first time in more than two decades by putting himself forward for elected office, supporting opposition journalists, and agitating on behalf of liberal causes. Although he did not immediately win a seat in the Chamber of Deputies (as France's lower legislative house was known), he spent the first years of the Bourbon restoration playing the role of civic gadfly. As he put it in an 1816 letter, Lafayette saw Louis XVIII as little more than a pawn of the allied forces that defeated Napoleon, "the protégé, the humble follower, not the leader" of the European monarchies, who wished only to turn back the clock to France's old regime. And Lafayette, who had devoted his life to ending the abuses of absolutism, was determined to do what he could to prevent any such backsliding.

On October 30, 1818, the sixty-one-year-old Lafayette was voted into public office for the first time since the Estates-Gereral. Having failed to win election to the Chamber of Deputies as a representative of the department of the Seine-et-Marne, his home region, he instead went to the legislature as a representative of the department of the Sarthe, located some 150 miles west-southwest of La Grange. In the Sarthe, which imposed no residency requirements on its representatives, Lafayette was fortunate enough to enjoy the support of the liberal journalist Charles Guyot, who, in an 1819 pamphlet, praised his fellow inhabitants of the Sarthe for their choice. "The great, good La Fayette," wrote Guyot, "was not appreciated by his own department; and you supported him for the position that his great virtues deserved—and the only [position] worthy of his immortal name!"

In the weeks leading up to his swearing in on December 10, 1818, Lafayette was once again the talk of Paris. The Chamber of Deputies became the hottest ticket in town, as well-heeled individuals vied for a chance to witness the return of Lafayette—a return that immediately revived the battles over Lafayette's image that had lain dormant during Napoleon's reign. An ally of Lafayette's, the romantic author and leading liberal theorist Benjamin Constant, who would join Lafayette as a representative of the Sarthe in 1819, employed the power of his pen to burnish Lafayette's tarnished credentials as a defender of liberty and to put the best possible spin on the attention Lafayette was generating. Writing in the liberal organ *La Minerve française,* Constant reported that the "curiosity" that animated the audience in the Chamber of Deputies as Lafayette rose to swear his oath could be "easily explained: so many memories of different sorts and all honorable are attached to that name!" In contrast, the ultraroyalist journal *Le conservateur* mocked Lafayette's reappearance by resurrecting the critical conceit that conflated the veneration of Lafayette with that of his horse after the 1790 Festival of Federation and expressing astonishment that "a famous white horse, a horse that shared with its master the idolatrous love of the good people of Paris . . . has not terminated his valorous career: he still lives." Harking back to the wordplay that peppered the political journalism of the old regime, the *Conservateur* concluded by asserting that "the marquis, the master of this horse, is still riding the same hobbyhorse."

Although the newspapers differed wildly in their assessments of Lafayette, they were in complete agreement on one point: the reputation of the general (a title that Lafayette preferred to the aristocratic "marquis") had been formed, for better or for worse, by his actions during the French Revolution. Still, Lafayette continued to take up new causes in the Chamber of Deputies and was often joined in his efforts by his son and fellow deputy, George Washington Lafayette. Singly and together the Lafayettes, *père et fils,* advocated such domestic policies as the establishment of free public education and the lowering of voting requirements, and addressed such contentious international issues as the revolutions and insurgencies in Greece, Italy, and Poland (which they supported) and the slave trade (which they opposed). Almost always, their speeches and letters were laced with references to the years before 1791, when Lafayette's French reputation had seemed unassailable.

Of course, there was still one place where Lafayette's reputation remained uncontested, and Lafayette had not given up on returning to the nation he considered his spiritual homeland. On November 25, 1823, Lafayette wrote to the American president James Monroe expressing his desire to rejoin "the friends with whom I can once more enjoy the sweetest memories, and visit the happy shores of an adopted land which has so filled my first and most presumptuous hopes." He was, he told Monroe, too occupied with his work in the Chamber of Deputies to contemplate an immediate voyage. Yet, he concluded, "I often dream of the day when I will be able, without remorse, to enjoy the happiness of finding myself once again on American ground." Considering the time required for transatlantic mail, Monroe's reply came swiftly. On February 7, 1824, Monroe informed Lafayette that "Congress had passed a resolution . . . to express to you the sincere attachment of the entire nation, and its ardent desire to receive you again." And on July 13, 1824, having lost his seat in the Chamber of Deputies, Lafayette sailed from Le Havre to begin his final tour of the United States, which was to be the grandest celebration the young nation had ever seen.

On August 16, 1824, Lafayette disembarked the packet ship *Cadmus* in lower New York Bay. Unlike Lafayette's first arrival in New York, in 1784, which had gone virtually unnoticed for some time, his second visit was hotly anticipated. Over the course of thirteen months, Lafayette, his son, and his secretary, Auguste Levasseur, stopped in each of the twenty-four states of the union. Municipalities from Vermont to Virginia hailed Lafayette with events ranging from intimate meals in the homes of local dignitaries to balloon ascents witnessed by thousands, and everywhere they went the men were treated to dinners at local taverns, tours of historic battlefields, and reviews of militias and regiments. They marched in parades and attended services at churches of every denomination, often encountering septuagenarian and octogenarian veterans of the War of Independence who wept openly for joy or schoolchildren who serenaded "the nation's guest" with songs written specially for the occasion.

By 1824, many members of America's founding generation had long since passed away—Gouverneur Morris in 1816, Washington in 1799, and Franklin nine years before Washington. Most of the living founders were too frail to revel in the limelight as Lafayette did on this journey; Jefferson and Adams, who were famously fated to die on the same day, July 4, 1826, were eighty-one and eighty-nine years old, respectively. At sixty-seven—roughly the same age as President Monroe, the last president to have participated in the nation's birth—Lafayette was comparatively young and remarkably robust. He was a celebrity. And yet he was more than that. He was a living embodiment of the nation's founding principles, and his enduring vitality augured well for the future of his adopted land.

Every town and county laid out its best for Lafayette, but surely no celebration could have outshone the gala festivities held in New York City on the night of September 14, 1824. Lafayette called it "the most brilliant and magnificent scene ever witnessed in the United States." The event was held at Castle Garden, a decommissioned fort on a man-made island that was linked to lower Manhattan by a bridge and had recently been converted into America's largest commercial pleasure ground. Some six thousand partygoers attended by two hundred servants paid three dollars apiece to join in the revelry. They danced and drank beneath a canopy decorated with the flags of the world and illuminated by a giant chandelier supporting thirteen smaller ones— one for each of the original states. Evoking the grandeur of antiquity, a triumphal arch, nearly ninety feet wide, decorated with sprigs of laurel and surmounted by a bust of George Washington, marked the entrance to the island pavilion. When the guest of honor arrived at ten p.m., he found inside a large transparency, lit from behind, that brought to life the château at La Grange—a structure that, in time, became almost synonymous with Lafayette, as its image was reproduced on objects of all kind, created around the world for sale in the American market, for many years to come. People who attended saved their tickets, their dresses, their gloves—anything that might remind them of the occasion. And those objects have since made their own way throughout the United States, where they have been collected by museums, libraries, and historical societies and exhibited to celebrate patriotic occasions of every variety.

Why did the celebrations in honor of Lafayette loom so large in people's minds? In part, the phenomenon reflected a genuine outpouring of affection and appreciation for a man who had come to our nation's aid at a moment of need and whose dramatic life story had unfolded in the pages of American newspapers, books, magazines, and prints for the better part of fifty years. Words of gratitude and admiration for the French hero of the American Revolution filled the songs and poems written in his honor. One typical set of lyrics was meant to be sung to the tune of "La Marseillaise," the French national anthem. Renamed "Hail! Lafayette!" it implored listeners to "think how then the illustrious stranger, / spurn'd rank and ease. . . . His counsel, sword,

Blue-and-white transfer-
printed plate depicting Lafayette's home at La Grange.
Nineteenth-century American.

and wealth supplying . . . amidst the famish'd—naked—dying!" (Few of those singing the American version would have been aware that the song was originally dedicated to Marshal Nicolas Luckner, the commander of the French Army of the Rhine with whom Lafayette was accused of conspiring against France in 1792 and who was sent to the guillotine in 1794.)

But something more than gratitude was involved, for Lafayette arrived at a time when Americans were beginning to think about their nation's fiftieth anniversary. In many ways, Lafayette's triumphal tour kicked off the jubilation. In celebrating Lafayette, Americans were celebrating their own past and honoring all of the country's early leaders. Nowhere was the collective nature of the tribute more evident than in the entertainments offered on Monday, June 20, 1825, at the Boston Theater in Massachusetts—an imposing, neoclassical edifice located at the intersection of Federal and Franklin Streets in what is now the heart of Boston's Financial District. A broadside advertising that evening's show announced not only that Lafayette would be in attendance, where he would watch *Charles II,* "a comedy in two acts," but also that the auditorium would be ornamented with "appropriate Decorations in honor of the Nation's Guest." These decorations, though, had little if anything to do with Lafayette: the names of every governor of Massachusetts would ring the boxes, while seats in the upper tier would feature the governors of each of the thirteen original states. A new "drop scene" would depict a temple with Corinthian columns described as "a monumental structure to the memory of General Washington," as well as an equestrian statue of Washington and a "correct view of Washington's Tomb at Mount Vernon." Toward the end of the evening, "the Grand Washington Transparency containing a brief sketch of the civil and military life of this illustrious hero" would be displayed.

Fan depicting Lafayette,
Marie Antoinette, and an
allegory of French patriotism,
carried to a ball celebrating
Lafayette at Castle Garden
on September 14, 1824.

Other Lafayette celebrations looked forward to the nation's bright future. One of these was held on September 11, 1824, the forty-seventh anniversary of the Battle of Brandywine, when Lafayette enjoyed a spectacular dinner hosted by the French residents of New York at Washington Hall, located on the northeast corner of Broadway and Chambers Street in lower Manhattan. That night, Washington Hall was reimagined as the crossroads of the globe: four faux-marble piers representing the four corners of the earth were erected at fifty-foot intervals, and a large model of the sun hung from the center of the ceiling, some thirty feet off the ground. All of the decorations were magnificent, but the pièce de résistance was an astonishingly detailed centerpiece representing the Erie Canal that ran the length of a seventy-foot-long table. As described by the *Evening Post* of September 13, "at one end was to be seen Lake Erie—in the centre Lake Ontario, and at the other end Lake Champlain. . . . Passage boats with passengers and baggage" dotted the water, which ran a "winding course" through the mock canals, while "at a distance various kinds of water fowl" sailed gracefully "to and fro." Adding to the "most charming effect" of the scene, the "rich verdure" of the canal's "mossy banks, studded now and then with roses, was here and there interrupted by aqueducts, rocks, and bridges which were thrown over the canal at different places."

To men living in New York as the long-anticipated canal was nearing completion, the visiting marquis and the grand engineering project represented much the same thing: the great potential of the United States to serve as a beacon to all nations and the promise that the New World would, one day, triumph over the Old. By linking the Great Lakes to the Hudson River, which, in turn, flows into New York Harbor—the gateway to the Atlantic Ocean—the canal was destined to become the first waterway to facilitate European commerce with the American interior. More than twenty years earlier, Gouverneur Morris had rhapsodized about the possibilities that such a canal might

WASHINGTON HALL

Washington Hall, New York City.

offer. Writing to his friend John Parish on January 20, 1801, Morris had
described his summer travels in upstate New York and lower Canada,
asking, "Shall I lead your astonishment up to the verge of incredu-
lity?" He answered his own question: "I will." Recounting the rush of
thoughts that came to him on the shores of Lake Erie, Morris predicted
that a relatively small investment of funds dedicated to constructing
an inland navigation system "would enable ships to sail from London,
through Hudson's River, into Lake Erie," providing unfettered access to
the inner reaches of the continent, which, he explained, "excels the part
we inhabit in soil, in climate, in everything." Making a bold but prescient forecast, Morris boasted that "the proudest empire in Europe, is
but a bauble compared to what America *will* be, *must* be, in the course
of two centuries; perhaps of one!" Morris did not live long enough to
witness the creation of the transformative waterway he envisioned, but
the guests assembled in Washington Hall on the night of Lafayette's
fete were about to see Morris's dream fully realized. Soon, America's
promise would be one step closer to fulfillment.

As it happened, Lafayette's triumphal tour also coincided with
America's bitterly fought presidential campaign of 1824. The election
ended infamously: with no candidate winning a majority of electoral
college votes, the decision was thrown into the House of Representa-

tives, which selected John Quincy Adams over Andrew Jackson, who had won the plurality of both the electoral and the popular votes. To this day, the outcome is sometimes referred to as the "corrupt bargain." With praising Lafayette being tantamount to praising America, and with every elected representative setting out to prove himself more patriotic than his neighbor, politicians and their spokesmen throughout the land did everything in their power to associate themselves with the "Nation's Guest." The House and the Senate heard innumerable orations filled with acclaim for Lafayette, and at the urging of Jefferson and Monroe, who were well aware of Lafayette's tight fiscal straits, Congress awarded two lavish gifts to the visiting hero. On December 2, 1824—the final day of electoral college voting—a bill was introduced to the Senate issuing Lafayette $200,000 in stock and 24,000 acres of land, whose location would be determined by the president at a later date. These were certainly gifts of considerable monetary value, but they also had layers of symbolic meaning. In literal terms, they were meant to reimburse Lafayette for the money he had spent during the revolution. To Lafayette, who'd had to borrow heavily to pay for his ocean crossing, the sums received were most welcome. And to Americans, the ability to repay this long-standing debt of gratitude to an old friend signaled their own prosperity and reminded them how far their country had come in just fifty years.

On September 9, 1825, Lafayette's party sailed for France on the frigate *Brandywine,* but Lafayette never quite put the tour behind him. In the course of his thirteen-month stay he had made a host of new American acquaintances and initiated close friendships that lasted until his death. The artist and inventor Samuel F. B. Morse, who painted Lafayette's portrait on commission from the Common Council of the City of New York, described feeling nearly overcome with admiration for his sitter. And the author James Fenimore Cooper, whom Lafayette met in New York, would become a long-term guest at La Grange. In 1828, acting at Lafayette's behest, Cooper published a fictionalized account of Lafayette's tour as *Notions of the Americans: Picked Up by a Travelling Bachelor*. In America, Lafayette had been enriched by a great deal more than money. He had gained a wealth of admiration and, perhaps most significantly, had solidified his place in American memory as states, municipalities, and institutions of all variety immortalized him by naming towns, counties, schools, and streets in his honor.

Lafayette returned to France with an enormous quantity of gifts that he cherished for the remainder of his life, ranging from a canoe, the *American Star,* which had won a race against an English boat on December 9, 1824, and would be kept in a specially built shed at La Grange, to smaller objects, including Native American ornaments, fragments of weapons collected on the Brandywine battlefield, and maps of various states of the union. Much of this material was kept in Lafayette's library, the contents of which, in the words of Jules Cloquet, the doctor who attended Lafayette's final illness, "could constitute a museum." As the years went by, Lafayette's American collections continued to grow, and a tour of these artifacts became part of the standard itinerary for the droves of Americans who flocked to La Grange to pay homage to their aging hero. Indeed, anyone who has the privilege of visiting La Grange today can still see a selection of objects displayed as they were in Lafayette's time.

Although many details of Lafayette's living quarters have been reconstructed according to Cloquet's careful descriptions of daily routines at La Grange, modern-day visitors must use their imaginations to envision the American fauna that once roamed Lafayette's lands. Throughout his years at La Grange, Lafayette maintained an active correspondence with members of America's agricultural community and participated in exchanges of animals, plants, machinery, and ideas. Two cows, a bull, and a sow from Baltimore, a wild turkey and several chickens from Virginia, as well as American deer, tortoises, terrapins, and even a woodpecker were among the creatures that made the transatlantic journey to La Grange, some more successfully than others. American farming equipment was there too: a steaming machine for preparing animal feed, a threshing machine, a Virginia plow, and much else. Seen together as a collection, these varied creatures and objects helped Lafayette propagate the notion that the La Grange was essentially American. He said as much to Mrs. Caleb Cushing of Massachusetts, who visited in 1829. Describing the carriage ride from Paris to Lafayette's estate, Mrs. Cushing recalled that "at length we approached the end of our journey, and as we entered the boundaries of La Grange,—'Now,' cried the General, 'we are upon American ground.'"

One of the last known portraits of Lafayette emphasizes his attachment to those grounds. Seated in dappled shade on a mossy rock, Lafayette, dressed in business attire, has set aside his walking stick and top hat. The rolled-up newspaper jutting from the hat suggests that he has even set aside the outside world, if only for a moment, to enjoy the peace of La Grange. Behind him are an expanse of grass and a curtain of trees that opens just enough to reveal a bit of sky at the upper right, where the pointed top of a cypress tree rises like a church spire in the distance. Lafayette had never been a religious man, but he was known as an apostle of liberty, and La Grange had become a pilgrimage site.

In this portrait, Louise-Adéone Drölling (Madame Joubert) depicted Lafayette seated among the trees at La Grange.

CHAPTER 20

PICPUS

*I*n the late 1820s, as the French economy staggered, the government of Charles X veered sharply to the right. Supported by ultraconservative ministers, the king abolished the Chamber of Deputies and severely curtailed freedom of the press and voting rights. Calls for revolution rang out in July 1830, when government troops faced off against armed citizens at barricades made of paving stones ripped from the streets of Paris. Hoping to avoid the fate of his brother, the executed Louis XVI, Charles fled to England, leaving his nine-year-old grandson to take the throne of France. But the young Bourbon never ascended. Instead, Louis-Philippe, Duc d'Orléans—the son of the man who had been Lafayette's nemesis during the French Revolution—put himself forward as a *juste milieu,* or middle-of-the-road, alternative to his cousins, and Lafayette traveled to Paris from La Grange to lend his support.

On July 29, Lafayette reprised his role as commander of the National Guard. Speaking to a group of former deputies gathered at a private home, Lafayette explained his motives: "an old name of '89," he said, "might be of some use in the grave circumstances in which we find ourselves." Lest anyone deem him too old for the task at hand, he pledged that "my conduct at seventy-three will be what it was when I was thirty-two." Then he left the meeting "to devote myself to the common defense."

Lafayette understood that his was a symbolic role, but it was one that he was happy to play. On July 31, he threw the full weight of history behind Louis-Philippe when he publicly endorsed the pretender. Just as he had with Marie Antoinette some forty years earlier, Lafayette stood on a balcony beside his monarch. But instead of a deferential kiss, he bestowed a tricolor flag on the man who would soon govern France while fully beholden to a constitution.

Lafayette had triumphed, but once again, his triumph was short-lived. Louis-Philippe's "July Monarchy" retained its open-minded bent for only a brief period of time. By 1834, with economic and social crises mounting, freedoms of speech and association were once again curtailed. In a crushing blow to his lifelong faith in constitutional monarchy, Lafayette lived just long enough to see abuses of power running rampant in Paris once more. On April 15, 1834, a workers' demonstration went fatally awry. As military police clashed with protesters on the Rue Transnonain (part of today's Rue Beaubourg), someone began throwing rocks from an apartment. Without taking the time to seek out the actual perpetrators, a band of soldiers retaliated. They entered the building and murdered everyone they found. Twelve people were killed—women, children, elderly men—all gunned down in their homes, as memorialized by Honoré Daumier's famous lithograph of the tragedy.

The following month, Lafayette took to his bed, desperately sick, in the apartment he maintained on the Rue d'Anjou in Paris. His physician, Jules Cloquet, believed that "moral affections" had exerted a "baneful influence" on Lafayette's health. The general had been unwell throughout the year, afflicted first with a urinary infection, then gout, bronchitis, stomach ailments, and more. Finally, in May, he had contracted a fever that could not be brought down despite the quantities of quinine he was imbibing. For weeks, friends and family had been

Honoré Daumier. *Rue Transnonain, April 15, 1834*. Lithograph.

gathering around him, but as the end drew near his doctors forbade visits from all but the closest relatives. At one o'clock in the morning of May 20, 1834, his respiration began to fail, "drowsiness, delirium, and prostration of strength, became more decidedly pronounced." As Cloquet remembered it, "a few moments before he breathed his last, Lafayette opened his eyes, and fixed them with a look of affection on his children, who surrounded his bed, as if to bless them and bid them an eternal adieu." The marquis pressed Cloquet's hand, let out a final sigh, and expired at twenty minutes after four that morning.

Throughout that day, men and women filed in to pay their last respects to Lafayette, whose body was laid out on the bed where he'd died. Mourners did what they could to preserve their last memories: one took a plaster cast of his lifeless features, several were moved to sketch the scene before them, and the romantic painter Ary Scheffer, who had created one of the last portraits of the living Lafayette, put brush to canvas to memorialize the great man as he appeared in his final rest.

A large but muted crowd was in attendance for Lafayette's funeral and burial. From the Rue d'Anjou to the Church of the Assumption, Lafayette's casket was borne aloft by nine men selected to represent the Chamber of Deputies, the National Guard, the army, Poland, the electoral colleges of France, and, of course, the United States. Tricolor flags flew from every corner of the bier, while the sword and epaulets that Lafayette wore as commander of the National Guard were carried behind on a black velvet cushion. Two columns of soldiers in full dress—members of the National Guard and army alike—lined either side of the cortege, which made its way to the Picpus Cemetery, in eastern Paris, for the interment. The site had been chosen years earlier by Adrienne. During the Reign of Terror, Picpus had been a mass grave where victims of the guillotine were buried; Adrienne wished to rejoin her executed mother, sister, and grandmother. After George Washington Lafayette sprinkled the tomb with soil brought back from America, Lafayette would rest alongside his beloved wife. There would be no funeral orations at Lafayette's graveside; the rules of the cemetery forbade it, and the authorities were grateful for the excuse to impose silence on the ceremony. Emotions run high at funerals of controversial figures, and Lafayette was nothing if not controversial.

In fact, on February 1 of that year, Lafayette himself had experienced an unsettling incident at Père-Lachaise Cemetery during the burial of

François-Charles Dulong, a leftist deputy to the National Assembly who had been killed by a political rival in a duel. According to Isaiah Townsend, a visitor from Albany, thousands of agitated mourners were crammed into the cemetery that day—some standing atop monuments, others sitting on trees or fences, and their voices raised in an "uninterrupted thunder . . . like the cataract of Niagara." With the services concluded, Lafayette had climbed into his carriage when, suddenly, "the horses were detached from the vehicle and the General drawn in triumph by a band of young students to the gates. It was evidently their intention to proceed with him in this manner through the streets of Paris." Only a request from Lafayette put an end to the plan.

Louis-Philippe wanted no such dramatics at Lafayette's funeral, but he apparently had little to fear. The people of France remained silent. In a June 6 letter to his mother in Albany, Isaiah Townsend described the mood with chagrin: "A month has scarcely elapsed since the death of the General, yet in Paris his memory would seem almost forgotten. The name of Lafayette is not heard." Despite the indefatigable efforts Lafayette had exerted on behalf of the French people during nearly five decades of public life, his countrymen felt that they had few reasons to mourn his loss.

It was different in America, where news of Lafayette's death reignited the outpouring of affection that had greeted the living man ten years earlier. President Jackson declared a national state of mourning, flags flew at half-mast, government buildings were draped with crepe, and legislatures around the country heard speeches in honor of Lafayette. Speaking to a joint session of Congress, former president John Quincy Adams delivered a funeral oration that lasted more than three hours. In a melancholy recapitulation of Lafayette's triumphal tour, amateur troupes performed plays honoring the deceased hero, and souvenirs were once again sold, now with black ribbons obscuring the beloved face.

AUTHOR'S NOTE

On a brisk Sunday in October 2012, I emerged from the Métro station at the Place de la Nation in eastern Paris and walked into a sea of red. A political demonstration was in full swing. Red hot air balloons emblazoned with the logo of the French Communist Party floated above the crowd; rows of marchers chanted their opposition to proposed austerity measures while carrying white sheets painted with red lettering; and men wearing red scarves passed out leaflets that detailed policy positions in black and red ink. The mood was festive, but the color turned my thoughts grim.

From June 13 to July 28, 1794, the Place de la Nation—known at the time as the Place du Trône Renversé (Place of the Overturned Throne)—had run red with blood as a guillotine erected on the spot claimed 1,306 lives. On July 22, 1794, the mother, sister, and grandmother of Adrienne de Lafayette counted among its victims. I was on my way to their final resting place—Picpus Cemetery.

Some Parisian burial sites attract droves of tourists, but Picpus is not one of them. While mounds of flowers accumulate at Jim Morrison's grave at Père-Lachaise and groups of schoolchildren file past the royal tombs at Saint Denis, only occasional visitors find their way to the low, stucco-covered building with an unmarked wooden door that leads to Picpus. The hours when the cemetery is open vary according to when the groundskeeper is at home. On the day of my visit, a notice on a nearby bulletin board announced that he was out, but I had come too far to give up. Ignoring the barking of a dog, I tried the door. It opened, and I entered.

I found myself standing in a cobblestoned courtyard surrounded by squat beige buildings: the groundskeeper's house, a convent, a chapel, and, in the far left corner next to the chapel, a tall, narrow metal gate supported by two stone pillars. On each pillar was a plaque—one commemorating Lafayette, the other honoring General Pershing, and both indicating proudly that they had been donated by the Benjamin Franklin Chapter of the Paris Daughters of the American Revolution. Beyond the gate lay the cemetery, but the gate was locked.

Not knowing what to do, I climbed the steps to the chapel, opened the door, and took a seat in the front pew. As I sat in the darkness, I began thinking about the convent next door, about the nuns in my family, and about the communities of religious women who had always welcomed me warmly. Quietly, a side door opened and a woman in her seventies with short, white hair and a plain skirt and sweater—with a simple gold cross hanging from a fine chain around her neck—

came in and began tending to the vases of flowers arranged on the floor around the sanctuary.

Mustering my most polite French, I rose and broke the silence: "Excuse me, Madame. Are you a sister?" She was—Sister Marie-Marthe of the Congregation of the Sacred Hearts of Jesus and Mary and of the Perpetual Adoration. "Please forgive me for bothering you," I said, "but I wonder if there might possibly be any way for me to take a photograph of Lafayette's grave? You see, I'm an American writing a book about Lafayette. This is my last day in Paris, and I came here just to take a picture." She looked at me kindly but said that she was very sorry. She couldn't allow me into the cemetery. The groundskeeper would be furious.

I understood, I said, but we continued talking. I told her about my aunt, a sister of Saint Joseph, whose order originated in France but was expelled during the revolution. I explained that I found it moving to be at Picpus, the final resting place of the sixteen nuns who sang as they walked to the guillotine in the summer of 1794, and whose stories were memorialized by Francis Poulenc's opera *Dialogues of the Carmelites.* Sensing that this might be a long conversation, we both sat down, and after a while an idea came to me. Might she possibly be willing to go to the cemetery herself and take photos with my camera? Sister Marie-Marthe's eyes lit up. "Yes! That I could do!" She took my camera, stood up, and walked back out the side door.

Alone again, I began to wander around the sanctuary, examining its walls. Carved into the stone were the names, ages, and occupations of every person guillotined at the Place de la Nation, numbered according to the order of their deaths. Adrienne's grandmother, sister, and mother were numbers 1039, 1040, and 1041 respectively; the Duchesse d'Ayen had watched her mother and daughter beheaded before the blade fell on her own neck. Many of the inscribed names were aristocrats or people who'd traveled in royal circles: Alexandre de Beauharnais, who was the first husband of Napoleon's empress Joséphine; the German Prince Frederick III; Marie Antoinette's architect, Richard Mique. But others were commoners with no particular claim to fame or notoriety: a painter on porcelain, a domestic servant, a police administrator.

Sister Marie-Marthe returned to find me lost in thought. As we sat together on the wooden pew talking about the pictures she had taken, I posed the question that had been on my mind for three years. Would she agree, I asked, that Lafayette is not widely admired in France? Yes, she said. Only Americans visit his grave, and an American flag flies over it. I paused and asked if she had any idea why. She thought for a moment, then gestured to the names on the walls. "The French Revolution was a complicated time," she said, "and Lafayette was a complicated man. People like simple stories; simple stories get remembered. Lafayette's story isn't simple." I nodded. She was right.

As I gathered my belongings and thanked her for her help, I asked if I could make a donation to the sisters as a token of my gratitude. Again, she considered carefully. At length she answered: "No. Thank you, but no. Go back to the United States. Write your book. And tell Lafayette's story."

ACKNOWLEDGMENTS

This book has been more than seven years in the making and has been a collaborative endeavor at every step. It could not have been completed without the generosity and support of innumerable friends, family members, colleagues, mentors, and assistants. I name many of these people below, but I am indebted to many more.

I would never have had the courage to tackle a project as vast as Lafayette's life without the example and encouragement of Simon Schama, University Professor of Art History and History at Columbia University. Schama, who sponsored my dissertation, was the first person I called when I initially contemplated working on Lafayette. My thoughts have returned many times to his enthusiastic words.

My research benefited from the guidance of librarians and archivists on two continents. I spent several fruitful weeks in the Manuscript Reading Room of the Library of Congress in Washington, D.C., where I had the good fortune to work with Laura Kells and Karen Stuart, who, as members of the team that microfilmed Lafayette's papers at the Château de La Grange, provided expert direction. At the Division of Rare and Manuscript Collections of the Carl A. Kroch Library of Cornell University in Ithaca, New York, I was fortunate to be assisted by Laurent Ferri, curator of the library's 2007 exhibition *La Fayette: Citizen of Two Worlds*. Anna Berkes, research librarian, aided me at Thomas Jefferson's Monticello, and Diane Windham Shaw, Special Collections librarian and college archivist at the David Bishop Skillman Library at Lafayette College, in Easton, Pennsylvania, assisted me with the library's extensive Marquis de Lafayette Collections. I am grateful to staff members at the Special Collections Research Center of the University of Chicago Library, who helped me make my way through the Louis Gottschalk Papers housed there. In New York, I relied on the assistance of the staff at Columbia University's Avery Library and Butler Library, the Frick Art Reference Library, New York University's Bobst Library, the New-York Historical Society Library, and the New York Public Library. I am grateful, too, for help received at French archives and libraries, including the Archives Départementales de Seine-et-Marne, the Archives Nationales (CARAN), the Archives Nationales d'Outre-Mer, and the Bibliothèque Nationale de France.

Individuals at museums and historical societies have given generously of their time and resources. I am especially grateful to Susan R. Stein, Richard Gilder Senior Curator and Vice President for Museum Programs at Thomas Jefferson's Monticello, who offered more support, advice, and information than I could have hoped for and introduced me to curator Elizabeth Chew and Director of Gardens and Grounds Peter J. Hatch. At the New-York Historical Society, Kathleen Hulser shared her copious research and, together with Kathleen O'Connor, invited me to contribute to the educational texts and programming associated with the 2007 exhibition *French Founding Father: Lafayette's Return to Washington's America,* and the exhibition's curator, Richard Rabinowitz, met with me at his Brooklyn home.

French institutions have been equally welcoming. I am particularly grateful to Elaine Uzan Leary, executive director of the American Friends of Blérancourt, for facilitating my visit to the Musée Franco-Américain du Château de Blérancourt. Curator Anne Dopffer kindly arranged for my reception there, and Valérie Coindeau and Catherine Dejoye were immensely gracious. At the Musée National des Châteaux de Versailles et de Trianon I was welcomed by curators Frédéric Lacaille, Alexandre Maral, and Juliette Trey, and by Delphine Dubois, *chargée d'études documentaires.* Curator Valérie Bajou provided the introductions. In turn, Frédéric Lacaille introduced me to Anthony Petiteau and Dominique Prévot at the Musée de l'Armée. At the Musée du Quai Branly, Stéphane Martin, Laurence Reculet, and Nanette Snoep conferred with me about the museum's collections of Native American items.

Two foundations were especially helpful. My understanding of Lafayette benefited immeasurably from the kindness of Joseph Baillio and Guy Wildenstein, who provided me with an introduction to Monsieur Renand, president of the Fondation Josée et René de Chambrun, which owns and maintains the Château de La Grange. At the Fondation Chambrun, Isabelle-Sophie Grivet arranged for an unforgettable private tour of La Grange with Madame Houssenbay. Thanks to the hospitality of director Ger Luijten and curatorial assistant Sarah Van Ooteghem of the Fondation Custodia, I was able to spend an afternoon in the Hôtel Turgot, which was built as a mirror image of Lafayette's (now destroyed) Paris town house.

Generous financial support made this research possible. The New School contributed to the project from start to finish through sources including General Research Funds, Student Assistant Funds, and a prepromotion leave. A Fellowship Research Grant from Earhart Foundation in Ann Arbor, Michigan, enabled me to travel to Lafayette's birthplace, the Château de Chavaniac, in the Auvergne region of France, and to many other sites. I cannot express sufficient gratitude to Dennis L. Bark, chairman of the board of trustees, for his unstinting support and true kindness. I must also thank Mr. and Mrs. Bark for their abundant warmth and hospitality, and for introducing me to Monsieur and Madame Aubert-Lafayette, descendants of the marquis, who welcomed me to their home in the Auvergne. Thanks to these financial resources, I have had the pleasure of working with several of the most intelligent, hardworking, and collegial research assistants a person could hope for. In New York, I benefited from the able assistance of Alison Charny and Jenny Florence. In France, I was aided by Rebecca Cavanaugh, Jessica Fripp, Véronica Langberg, and Sara Phenix. I also benefited from the company and driving skills of James Hogan.

Since 2007, I have honed my analysis of Lafayette by delivering papers at conferences and symposia, where I benefited immeasurably from the scholarship and camaraderie of fellow speakers and from the supportive and thought-provoking responses of audiences. I have presented Lafayette material at events organized by: the American Society for Eighteenth-Century Studies; Barnard College; Bard Graduate Center for Decorative Arts, Design, and Material Culture; the College Art Association; the Consortium on the Revolutionary Era; the New-York Historical Society; the Nineteenth-Century French Studies Colloquium; Skidmore College; the Society for French Historical Studies; University of North Carolina, Chapel Hill; University of North Carolina, Charlotte; University of Sydney; and the Western Society for French History. For inviting me to participate in these and other events, I am grateful to colleagues including Giovana Assenso-Termini, Jeffrey Collins, Jim Frakes, Mimi Hellman, Mark Ledbury, Jennifer Milam, Mary Sheriff, and Rebecca Spang. I also thank editors Dan O'Brien and Fritz Allhoff for including my essay "Transplanting Liberty: Lafayette's American Garden" in their volume *Gardening: Philosophy for Everyone—Cultivating Wisdom* (2010).

I have benefited from less formal but no less fruitful exchanges with scholars throughout the United States and France. Lloyd S. Kramer, professor of history at the University of North Carolina, Chapel Hill, helped me understand the field of Lafayette studies. Kramer's UNC colleague Jay M. Smith generously shared his research on the Beast of the Gévaudan before his book on the subject was published. Miranda Spieler, professor of history at the American University of Paris, called my attention to the complications that bedeviled Lafayette's experiment in the gradual emancipation of slaves. I have enjoyed many conversations with Dena Goodman, Lila Miller Collegiate Professor of History and Women's Studies at the University of Michigan, on topics including the intersection of sociability, politics, and Enlightenment in eighteenth-century France. Oren Jacoby, the director of *Lafayette: The Lost Hero* (2010), brought me on as a consultant to his documentary and introduced me to Lafayette descendant Sabine Renault Sablonière, who welcomed me to her Paris home.

Other scholars who have helped advance my thinking include: Samuel Edgerton, professor of art emeritus at Williams College, with whom I had multiple conversations about eighteenth-century stoves; Ulrich Leben, research scholar at the Bard Graduate Center, who shared his vast knowledge about the furniture maker Bernard Molitor; Melissa Hyde, associate professor of art history at the University of Florida, who hosted me at her Paris apartment; Meredith Martin, professor of art history at New York University, who shared unpublished research with me; Ellen G. Miles, curator of painting and sculpture at the National Portrait Gallery, who pointed me in the direction of a portrait presumed to depict Lafayette; Paul S. Spalding, Joel Scarborough Professor of Religion at Illinois College, who spoke with me about Lafayette's imprisonment. In Paris, I learned a great deal from Susan Taylor-Leduc, dean of Parsons Paris, whom I value as a colleague, a friend, and a Paris guide. Carole Blumenfeld, who discussed with me Louise-Adéone Drölling (Madame Joubert); and Laurence Chatel de Brancion, who welcomed me to her home and gave me a copy of her beautiful book on Lafayette.

New York friends and colleagues have provided a steady stream of support by reading drafts, commenting on talks, and more. Jonathan Lopez devoted tremendous amounts of time and effort to the project. I am deeply grateful for his encouragement and for his valuable comments on two complete drafts. At The New School, Elaine Abelson, Oz Frankel, John Vanderlippe, Jeremy Varon, and other members of the Committee on Historical Studies discussed the paper I delivered at a brown bag workshop. David Brody, Alan Gilbert, Sarah E. Lawrence, Michelle Majer, James and Michelle Nevius, and Henry Raine were among those who responded to lectures, commented on drafts of chapters, and directed me to a wide range of material related to Lafayette. Oliver Grubin solved my long-standing problem of locating the pornographic print of Lafayette riding an ostrich.

I am indebted to Caroline Weber, who encouraged me to try my hand at writing for nonacademic audiences and introduced me to our mutual agent, Rob McQuilkin. It was Rob who first suggested that I write on Lafayette, and although the project took longer than he might have hoped, he has been a patient, constant, and charming supporter. My editor at Knopf, Vicky Wilson, has been equally gracious and supportive. Her sound advice and valuable insights have made this a far better book. It has been a pleasure working with her assistant, Audrey Silverman.

NOTES

Note: All translations are my own unless otherwise indicated.

ABBREVIATIONS

ANOM: Archives Nationales d'Outre-Mer, Aix-en-Provence, France.

AP: Archives parlementaires.

Cornell: Arthur H. and Mary Marden Dean Lafayette Collection, #4611. Division of Rare and Manuscript Collections, Cornell University Library, Ithaca, NY.

Encyclopédie: Denis Diderot and Jean Le Rond d'Alembert, eds. *Encyclopédie, ou dictionnaire raisonné des sciences, des arts et des métiers, par une société de gens de lettres.* 28 vols. Paris: Brunet, 1751–72.

Gottschalk: Louis Gottschalk Papers, Special Collections Resource Center, University of Chicago, Chicago, IL.

LAAR: Stanley J. Idzerda, et al., eds., *Lafayette in the Age of the American Revolution: Selected Letters and Papers, 1776–1790.* 5 vols. Ithaca, NY: Cornell University Press, 1977–83.

LOC: Marquis de Lafayette Papers, Manuscript Division, Library of Congress, Washington, DC.

Mémoires: Marie Joseph Paul Yves Roch Gilbert du Motier, Marquis de Lafayette, *Mémoires, correspondance et manuscrits du Général Lafayette, publiés par sa famille.* 6 vols. Paris: H. Fournier l'Aîné, 1837–38.

PGWC: The Papers of George Washington. Confederation Series. 6 vols. W. W. Abbot, et al., ed., Charlottesville: University of Virginia Press, 1987–.

PGWP: The Papers of George Washington. Presidential Series. 17 vols. W. W. Abbot, et al., ed., Charlottesville: University of Virginia Press, 1987–.

PGWR: The Papers of George Washington. Retirement Series. 4 vols. W. W. Abbot, et al., ed., Charlottesville: University of Virginia Press, 1987–.

PGWRW: The Papers of George Washington. Revolutionary War Series. 22 vols. W. W. Abbot, et al., ed., Charlottesville: University of Virginia Press, 1987–.

INTRODUCTION

xvii **Gilbert du Motier:** The name Lafayette has been spelled in various ways, with the most frequent alternative being "La Fayette." My selection of "Lafayette" is in keeping with the preferences of the two most distinguished Lafayette scholars, Louis Gottschalk and Stanley J. Idzerda, and with common American usage. On this spelling, see Louis Gottschalk, *Lafayette Comes to America* (Chicago: University of Chicago Press, 1935), 153–54. Lafayette's first name, too, has variations: although he always referred to himself as Gilbert, he was baptized Marie Joseph Paul Yves Roch Gilbert. Henry Mosnier, *Le château de Chavaniac-Lafayette, description—histoire—souvenirs* (Le Puy: Marchessou Fils, 1883), 15.

xvii **Carved in 1790**: Anne L. Poulet, et al., *Jean-Antoine Houdon: Sculptor of the Enlightenment* (Washington, DC: National Gallery of Art, 2003), 260.

xix **fashionable salons of Paris**: Antoine Lilti, *Le monde des salons: Sociabilité et mondanité à Paris au XVIIIe siècle* (Paris: Fayard, 2005), 382–84.

xix **marten-fur cap**: Stacy Schiff, *A Great Improvisation: Franklin, France, and the Birth of America* (New York: Henry Holt, 2005), 38–39.

xix **"there is more support"**: André Morellet to William Petty, 1st Marquess of Lansdowne, Sunday, May 4, 1777. Schiff, *A Great Improvisation,* 80.

xix **"decidedly inclined"**: Jules Cloquet, *Recollections of the Private Life of General Lafayette* (London: Baldwin and Cradock, 1835), 8.

xx **open and frank expression**: Even the royalist Comte d'Espinchal, who grew to despise Lafayette during the French Revolution, conceded that Lafayette had a "sweet and honest" appearance. Joseph Thomas Anne Espinchal, as quoted in Étienne Charavay, *Le général La Fayette, 1757–1834* (Paris: Société de l'Histoire de la Révolution Française, 1898), 538.

xx **"love of glory"**: *Mémoires,* 1:6.

xx **"a life without glory"**: Lafayette to Adrienne, May 30, 1777, *Mémoires,* 1:85.

xx **"Glory"**: Lafayette to Washington, February 19, 1778, *LAAR,* 1:301.

xx **"reputation"**: *Dictionnaire de l'Académie française* (Paris: Brunet, 1762), 14:61.

xx **hoped for glory**: Christopher Leslie Brown, *Moral Capital: Foundations of British Abolitionism* (Chapel Hill: University of North Carolina Press, 2006), 437–42, argues that a quest for public recognition motivated some of the era's notable abolitionists, including Lafayette. Liliane Willens, "Lafayette's Quest for 'Glory' in the American Revolution," *Studies on Voltaire and the Eighteenth Century* 205 (1982): 167–68, examines the role of reputation in Lafayette's decision to sail for America.

xxi **Washington his adoptive father**: See, for instance, Lafayette to Washington, April 16, 1785, in which Lafayette identifies himself as "your Bosom friend, your adoptive son." *PGWC,* 2:505.

xxi **books on American history**: An analysis of various private libraries confiscated during the French Revolution termed Lafayette's library *"l'illustration extrême"* of collections featuring books on the American War of Independence. Agnès Marcetteau-Paul and Dominique Varry, "Les bibliothèques de quelques acteurs de la Révolution, de Louis XVI à Robespierre," *Mélanges de la Bibliothèque de la Sorbonne* 9 (1989): 201.

xxi **"a favourite Servant"**: Lafayette to Jeremiah Wadsworth, April 16, 1785, *LAAR,* 5:319.

xxi **"he has planted a tree"**: Jared Sparks, *Memoirs of the Life and Travels of John Ledyard, from His Journals and Correspondence* (London: Henry Colburn, 1828), 214.

xxi **"the man has drawn few eulogies"**: Patrice Guennifey, "Lafayette," in *A Critical Dictionary of the French Revolution,* edited by François Furet and Mona Ozouf, translated by Arthur Goldhammer (Cambridge, MA: Harvard University Press, 1989), 224.

xxiii **"true moderation consists"**: *Mémoires,* 6:46. I was directed to this quote by Sylvia Neely, *Lafayette and the Liberal Ideal, 1814–1824: Politics and Conspiracy in an Age of Reaction* (Carbondale: Southern Illinois University Press, 1991), 109. According to his *Mémoires,* Lafayette spoke these words as part of a discourse pronounced in the Chamber of Deputies on June 4, 1819, but Neely places the speech on June 3.

xxiv **"I have been reproached"**: April 19, 1815, *Mémoires,* 5:406. I was directed to this quote by Neely, *Lafayette and the Liberal Ideal,* 23.

CHAPTER 1: FAMILY PRIDE

3 **Château de Chavaniac:** See Hadelin Donnet, *Chavaniac Lafayette: Le Manoir des deux mondes* (Paris: Le Cherche midi, 1990); Mosnier, *Le château de Chavaniac-Lafayette,* 21–22.

4 **"Clermont"**: Arthur Young, *Travels During the Years 1787, 1788 and 1789, Undertaken More Particularly with a View of Ascertaining the Cultivation, Wealth, Resources, and National Prosperity, of the Kingdom of France* (London: 1792), 160–61.

4 **Although the senior branch:** *Mémoires,* 1:6. My understanding of Lafayette's lineage is indebted to Louis Gottschalk, *Lafayette Comes to America,* 6–11. (A note on Lafayette biographies: although myriad authors have told Lafayette's story, I cite only those biographies that provided me with specific interpretations or pieces of information. All of the biographies I consulted do, however, appear in the bibliography.)

4 **descended from the junior branch:** The death of Lafayette's uncle is described by Lafayette in "Autobiographie de La Fayette par lui-même" in Charavay, *La Fayette,* Appendix I, 532.

4 **"left the province"**: "Autobiographie" in Charavay, *La Fayette,* 531–32.

5 **newly titled marquis:** *Mémoires du duc de Luynes sur la cour de Louis XV (1735–1758),* 17 vols. (Paris: 1860–65). I was directed to this source by Gottschalk, *Lafayette Comes to America,* 9, note 15.

5 **"high birth, or so they say"**: *Mémoires du duc de Luynes,* 1:102.

5 **"broke his head"**: *Mémoires du duc de Luynes,* 2:36.

5 **widowed Marquise de Lafayette:** On Lafayette's family, see Gottschalk, *Lafayette Comes to America,* 7–12.

5 **local legend:** "Autobiographie" in Charavay, *La Fayette*, 533.

6 **Roch-Gilbert wed Marie-Julie de La Rivière:** *Mémoires du duc de Luynes,* 13:277.

6 **the convent where:** A convent education was typical for noblewomen and did not signify a religious calling. On women's education in the eighteenth century, see Martine Sonnet, *L'éducation des filles au temps des Lumières* (Paris: Éditions du Cerf, 1987).

6 **1,000 livres a year:** Gottschalk, *Lafayette Comes to America*, 11.

6 **Rivière influence:** Gottschalk, *Lafayette Comes to America*, 11, asserts that Roch-Gilbert owed his rank to his in-laws, noting that no Motier had ever reached that level.

7 **wrote to Louis XV:** Charavay, *La Fayette*, 554–55.

7 **February 28, 1762:** *Table ou abrégé des cent trente-cinq volumes de la Gazette de France, depuis son commencement en 1631 jusqu'à la fin de l'année 1765* (Paris: Imprimerie de la Gazette de France, 1768), vol. 3, supplément 2.

7 **"Although my mother":** "Autobiographie" in Charavay, *La Fayette*, 533.

7 **His grandmother:** Gottschalk, *Lafayette Comes to America*, 5.

7 **Beast of the Gévaudan:** The beast continues to garner popular and scholarly interest, with numerous books, articles, movies, and Internet sites devoted to the subject. The definitive study is Jay M. Smith, *Monsters of the Gévaudan: The Making of a Beast* (Cambridge, MA: Harvard University Press, 2011).

8 **"my heart Beat":** *LAAR*, 1:390.

8 **"the length of a finger":** As translated in Smith, *Monsters of the Gévaudan*, 91.

9 **"caused some damage":** *Mémoires*, 1:8.

9 **"I recall nothing":** Ibid., 1:7.

9 **"separated with the utmost chagrin":** "Autobiographie" in Charavay, *La Fayette*, 534.

10 **"three superb palaces":** Louis, Chevalier de Jaucourt, "Paris," in Denis Diderot and Jean Le Rond d'Alembert, eds., *Encyclopédie*, 11:944.

11 **Paris in the mid-1700s:** Jaucourt, "Paris," *Encyclopédie*, 11:944.

11 **Shop windows:** Paris had become the world's foremost luxury emporium in the late 1600s, as discussed in Joan DeJean, *The Essence of Style: How the French Invented High Fashion, Fine Food, Chic Cafés, Style, Sophistication, and Glamour* (New York: Free Press, 2005).

12 **"virtue alone":** As translated in Jay M. Smith, *Nobility Reimagined: The Patriotic Nation in Eighteenth-Century France* (Ithaca, NY: Cornell University Press, 2005), 50.

12 **France's humiliation:** Jay M. Smith, *The Culture of Merit: Nobility, Royal Service, and the Making of Absolute Monarchy in France, 1600–1789* (Ann Arbor: University of Michigan Press, 1996), 224.

12 ***dérogeance:*** William H. Sewell, Jr., *Work and Revolution in France: The Language of Labor from the Old Regime to 1848* (Cambridge: Cambridge University Press, 1980), 21.

13 **The school dated back:** Jaucourt, "Paris," *Encyclopédie*, 11:953.

13 **"disciples"**: "Autobiographie" in Charavay, *La Fayette,* 535.

13 **"I was not as well-supported"**: Ibid.

13 **"children sporting épées"**: Ibid., 536.

14 **"burning with the desire"**: Ibid., 535.

14 **troops of the Maison du Roi**: Rafe Blaufarb, *The French Army, 1750–1820: Careers, Talent, Merit* (Manchester: Manchester University Press, 2002), 29. Although the nineteenth-century French novelist Alexandre Dumas immortalized the musketeers in his swashbuckling yarns of Athos, Porthos, Aramis, and d'Artagnan, Dumas was harking back to the company's earliest days, in the age of Louis XIII, when they were entrusted with protecting the king of France.

14 **"to ride to Versailles"**: "Autobiographie" in Charavay, *La Fayette,* 535.

14 **won the prize for Latin rhetoric**: Ibid.

15 **all standard reading**: Chantal Grell, *Le dix-huitième siècle et l'antiquité en France, 1660–1789* (Oxford: Voltaire Foundation, 1995); vol. 1, table 1, lists the ancient texts read in the University of Paris colleges.

15 **Books by these authors**: A 1794 inventory of books from Lafayette's Paris town house is maintained in the Archives Nationales, series F/17, box 1194, dossier 23. Documentation concerning books Lafayette purchased for, sold from, or maintained at La Grange in the early 1800s is housed in LOC, reel 9, folders 111b and 111b, bis.

15 **"Rome was the first"**: Louis-Sébastien Mercier, *Tableau de Paris* (1783 ; repr., Paris: Mercure de France, 1994), 1:148–51.

15 **due to grief**: "Autobiographie" in Charavay, *La Fayette,* 534.

15 **wealthy orphan**: The figures concerning Lafayette's income are based on the financial records housed in LOC, reel 8, folders 100–102a.

16 **skilled laborer**: Peter Jones, "Material and Popular Culture: Introduction," in *The Enlightenment World,* ed. Martin Fitzpatrick, et al. (New York: Routledge, 2004), 347.

16 **"the literary celebrities"**: Élisabeth Vigée-LeBrun, *Souvenirs,* ed. Claudine Herrmann, 2 vols. (Paris: Des Femmes, 1984), vol. 1:123.

17 **"Madame l'Étiquette"**: Jeanne-Louise-Henriette Campan, *Mémoires de Madame Campan, Première femme de chambre de Marie Antoinette,* ed. Jean Chalon (Paris: Mercure de France, 1988), 53.

17 **less sanguine**: The dispute between the Duc and Duchesse d'Ayen is narrated in Gottschalk, *Lafayette Comes to America,* 26–30.

17 **"one almost always recognized"**: Louis-Philippe de Ségur, *Mémoires; ou, Souvenirs et anecdotes* (Brussels: 1825), 1:78.

18 **Académie de Versailles**: *Mémoires,* 1:6.

18 **"the same qualities"**: David A. Bell, *The First Total War: Napoleon's Europe and the Birth of Warfare as We Know It* (Boston: Houghton Mifflin, 2007), 34. On the significance of physical grace at court see also Bernard Hours, *Louis XV et sa cour: Le roi, l'étiquette et le courtisan* (Vendôme: Presses Universitaires de France, 2002), 29–30.

CHAPTER 2: THE OUTSIDER

19 **March 26, 1774**: Étienne Taillemite, *La Fayette* (Paris: Fayard, 1989), 18.

19 **denizens of Versailles**: This description of a presentation at court is compiled from several accounts, especially the memoirs of Chateaubriand, one of France's premier Romantic authors, who was presented to King Louis XVI in 1787. François-René de Chateaubriand, *Mémoires d'outre-tombe* (Paris: Penaud, 1849–50), 1:334–37.

19 **powdered wig**: On the significance of wigs for men's fashion in eighteenth-century France, see Michael Kwass, "Big Hair: A Wig History of Consumption in Eighteenth-Century France," *American Historical Review* 111, no. 3 (June 2006): 631–59.

20 **"nobility of old extraction"**: Guy Chaussinand-Nogaret, *The French Nobility in the Eighteenth Century: From Feudalism to Enlightenment,* trans. William Doyle (Cambridge: Cambridge University Press, 1985), 47.

20 **"pale, cold and lifeless"**: Charavay, *La Fayette,* 538.

20 **"a cold and serious bearing"**: Ségur, *Mémoires,* 1:122.

21 **"by the gaucheness"**: All quotations in this paragraph are from *Mémoires,* 1:7.

21 **"concealed the most active spirit"**: All quotations in this paragraph are from Ségur, *Mémoires,* 1:123

21 **"to persuade me to fight"**: Ibid., 1:107.

21 **"to rouse him"**: Ibid.

21 **they amused themselves**: The group's nights out are described in the memoirs of Lafayette and Ségur and summarized in John K. Howat, "'A Young Man Impatient to Distinguish Himself': The Vicomte de Noailles as Portrayed by Gilbert Stuart," *Metropolitan Museum of Art Bulletin* n.s., 29, no. 7 (March 1971): 327–28.

22 ***"bon air"***: Adolphe Fourier de Bacourt, ed., *Correspondance entre le Comte de Mirabeau et le Comte de La Marck,* 2 vols. (Brussels: Meline, Cans, 1851), 1:47. Because Lafayette's role in the French Revolution was so divisive, it is difficult to find a postrevolutionary memoir that offers an objective account of experiences with Lafayette. However, descriptions of Lafayette's social awkwardness in the 1770s abound in memoirs of friends and foes alike, and are even discussed by Lafayette himself. Lafayette's enemies might have particularly enjoyed recounting such tales, but they seem not to have fabricated them.

22 **"to travel the world"**: *Mémoires,* 1:7–8.

23 **the opportunity arose**: Ibid., 1:8.

23 **insult his prospective employer**: Cloquet, *Souvenirs sur la vie privée du Général Lafayette,* 105.

23 **April 7, 1773**: Gottschalk, *Lafayette Comes to America,* 32.

24 **"Secret Ministry"**: Didier Ozanam and Michel Antoine, eds., *Correspondance secrète du Comte de Broglie avec Louis XV (1756–1774),* 2 vols. (Paris: Librairie C. Klincksieck, 1956–61).

24 **Americans' efforts:** See Sudipta Das, *De Broglie's Armada: A Plan for the Invasion of England, 1765–1777* (Lanham, MD: University Press of America, 2009), 14.

24 **eminently replaceable:** On the suggestion that Broglie sought to supplant Washington, see Charles J. Stillé, "Comte de Broglie, the Proposed Stadtholder of America," *Pennyslvania Magazine of History and Biography* 11, no. 4 (1887): 369–405.

24 **"sparkling eyes":** This description of Broglie is based on *Mémoires de l'abbé Georgel,* 1:283, as quoted in Edgard Paul Boutaric, ed., *Correspondance secrète inédite de Louis XV sur la politique étrangère avec le Comte de Broglie, Tercier, etc.,* 2 vols. (Paris: Plon, 1866), 1:65.

24 **Freemasons:** My understanding of French Freemasonry in this period is primarily indebted to Margaret C. Jacob, *Living the Enlightenment: Freemasonry and Politics in Eighteenth-Century Europe* (Oxford: Oxford University Press, 1991), and Margaret C. Jacob, *The Radical Enlightenment: Pantheists, Freemasons and Republicans,* 2nd rev. ed. (Lafayette, LA: Cornerstone Books, 2006).

24 **"stability under a strong":** As the historian Margaret C. Jacob has written, the society "served as a social nexus that promoted . . . stability under a strong, but constitutional monarchy, social mobility under aristocratic patronage, Baconian experimentalism and . . . dedication to the cult of the new science." Jacob, *Radical Enlightenment,* 80.

25 **62 lodges:** Jacob, *Living the Enlightenment,* 205.

25 **many Founding Fathers:** On the crucial role of Freemasonry in the American Revolution, see Steven C. Bullock, *Revolutionary Brotherhood: Freemasonry and the Transformation of the American Social Order, 1730–1840* (Chapel Hill: University of North Carolina Press, 1996), 109–33.

25 **Prince William Henry:** see J. H. Plumb, "The Impact of the American Revolution on Great Britain," in *The Impact of the American Revolution Abroad* (Washington, DC: Library of Congress, 1976), 64–66.

25 **"listened with ardent curiosity":** Sparks as cited in *Mémoires,* 1:9–10, note 1.

25 **"he had conceived of the idea":** *Mémoires,* 1:7–8.

26 **once responded to a schoolmaster's:** Ibid., 1:1.

26 **"pernicious distinction":** Claude Louis, Comte de Saint Germain, *Mémoires de M. le Comte de St. Germain* (Amsterdam, 1779), 45–46.

26 **out of active duty:** Gottschalk, *Lafayette Comes to America,* 157–58.

27 **"father of a wonderfully loving family":** Undated letter from Lafayette to Adrienne as quoted and translated in André Maurois, *Adrienne: The Life of the Marquise de La Fayette,* trans. Gerard Hopkins (London: Jonathan Cape, 1961), 54.

CHAPTER 3: LES INSURGENTS

28 **On a dark December night:** Members of the Committee of Congress for Secret Correspondence met with the French emissary three times in Decem-

ber 1775. This summary is based on: "Rapport de Bonvouloir au Comte de Guines, December 28, 1775"; Henri Doniol, *Histoire de la participation de la France à l'établissement des États-Unis d'Amérique. Correspondance diplomatique et documents* (Paris: Imprimerie Nationale, 1888), 1:287–92.; and *The Life of John Jay: With Selections from his Correspondence and Miscellaneous Papers,* ed. William Jay, 2 vols. (New York: J. & J. Harper, 1833), 1:39–41.

28 **to assess the likelihood**: See Doniol, *Histoire,* 1:153–59.

28 **mutual suspicions**: Although most Frenchmen of the elite classes were only nominally Catholic (Frenchwomen were generally more so), France had a bloody history of religious intolerance, and in the 1770s, Protestants were still barred from practicing their religion openly.

29 **Silas Deane arrived**: "Narrative of Edward Bancroft," August 14, 1777, *The Deane Papers,* 5 vols. (New York: New-York Historical Society, 1886–90), 1:179.

29 **"engaged in the business"**: Secret Committee of Congress to Silas Deane, March 3, 1776, *The Deane Papers,* 1:123.

29 *Le Boston: Dictionnaire de la conversation et de la lecture: inventaire raisonné des notions générales les plus indispensables à tous, par une société de savants et de gens de lettres,* ed. William Duckett, 16 vols. (Paris: Michel Lévy Frères, 1852–60), 3:484.

29 **ditty celebrating Washington**: Louis Petit de Bachaumont, *Mémoires secrets,* March 17, 1777, vol. 10, pp. 68–70.

29 **"continent"**: A slang word for female genitalia, *con* is used in French as an all-purpose term of abuse and disapprobation.

29 **Narragansett horses**: Schiff, *Great Improvisation,* 9.

30 **"some wise contemporaries of Plato"**: Ségur, *Mémoires,* 1:117.

30 **"opinions from every quarter"**: Ibid., 1:165.

30 **"republican maxims"**: Ibid., 1:152–53.

30 **"I have a levee"**: Silas Deane to John Jay, December 2, 1776, quoted in *LAAR,* 1:13–14, note 14.

30 **"Baron" Johann de Kalb**: Johann de Kalb's peasant origins were first discussed by Friedrich Kapp, *The Life of John Kalb, Major-General in the Revolutionary Army* (New York: Henry Holt, 1884), 1, 265–67. On his wife's fortune, see page 37.

30 **"several young gentlemen"**: Silas Deane to the Secret Committee of Congress, August 18, 1776, *The Deane Papers,* 1:213.

30 **"I am well nigh harrassed"**: Silas Deane to the Secret Committee of Congress, November 28, 1776, *The Deane Papers,* 1:375.

31 **"Had I ten ships"**: Silas Deane to John Jay, December 3, 1776, *The Deane Papers,* 1:397.

31 **"we were afraid to visit"**: *LAAR,* 1:390.

31 **"the desire to right the wrongs"**: Ségur, *Mémoires,* 1:117–18.

31 **"circumstances . . ."**: *LAAR,* 1:390.

32 **meeting regularly**: Johann Kalb to Monsieur de Saint Paul, November 7,

1777, "Letter of Major-General Johann Kalb," *American Historical Review* 15, no. 3 (April 1910): 562–67.

32 **"more of my zeal"**: *LAAR,* 1:391.

32 **publicity, a valuable skill**: See Jeremy D. Popkin and Bernadette Fort, eds., *The "Mémoires Secrets" and the Culture of Publicity in Eighteenth-Century France* (Oxford: Voltaire Foundation, 1998), 7–8.

32 **"high Birth, his Alliances"**: Agreement with Silas Deane, December 7, 1776, *LAAR,* 1:17. As translated by Congress upon Lafayette's arrival in Philadelphia.

33 **"hitherto"**: *LAAR,* 1:391.

33 *La Victoire:* On Lafayette's purchase of the ship, see Gottschalk, *Lafayette Comes to America,* 87–88.

33 **"the secrecy"**: *LAAR,* 1:391.

33 **de Kalb insisted**: Kalb, "Letter of Major-General Johann Kalb," 564.

33 **thirteen of the fourteen men**: This figure comes from a letter written by the fourteenth man. The letter was apparently intercepted by Stormont, who reported it to Lord Weymouth. *LAAR,* 1:44.

34 **"too cruelly punished"**: Lafayette to Adrienne, March 16, 1777, *LAAR,* 1:411.

34 **"I have found a unique opportunity"**: Lafayette to d'Ayen, March 9, 1777, *LAAR,* 1:410.

34 **d'Ayen was outraged**: The feints and rumors that marked Lafayette's departure for America are narrated in Gottschalk, *Lafayette Comes to America,* 97–104.

35 **"Relations seem to be much displeased"**: Lord Stormont to Lord Weymouth, April 2, 1777, *LAAR,* 1:42.

CHAPTER 4: FIRST IMPRESSIONS

39 **"had heard so much of the French officers"**: Charles Biddle, *Autobiography of Charles Biddle, Vice-President of the Supreme Executive Council of Pennsylvania, 1745–1831* (Philadelphia: 1883), 148.

39 **"quite ill"**: *LAAR,* 1:417. All quotes in this paragraph are from the same page.

40 **Vicomte de Mauroy**: Charles Louis, Vicomte de Mauroy, "Mémoire du vicomte de Mauroy sur ses services en Amérique et sur la guerre de l'Indépendance," A.N. K1364, as summarized in "Descriptive List of French Manuscripts Copied for New York State Library from National Archives and National Library at Paris 1888," *New York State Library Bulletin* 57, History 5 (1903): 362.

40 **letter of appointment**: *Collections of the New-York Historical Society for the Year 1886* (New York: New-York Historical Society, 1886), 359–60.

40 **"I wanted by my objections"**: Quotes from Mauroy are found in *LAAR,* 1:415–16.

41 **"The manners"**: Lafayette to Adrienne, June 15, [1777], *LAAR,* 1:419.

41 **"the simplicity"**: Lafayette to Adrienne, June 19, [1777], *LAAR,* 1:420.

41 "new products": *LAAR*, 1:393.

42 completely at home: Lafayette to Adrienne, February 28, 1777, *LAAR*, 1:408.

42 "I believe I'll bury": De Kalb to Mme de Kalb, July 23, 1777, as translated from German to French in Doniol, *Histoire*, 3:214.

42 In a lengthy memoir: Memoir by the Chevalier Dubuysson, *LAAR*, 1:427–34.

43 "burning sand": Ibid., 1:427.

43 a great deal like "beggars": Ibid., 1:427–28.

43 "ruined by debt": Ibid., 1:428.

43 "Volunteers and French Officers": "Charles-Town, S.C. June 16," *Independent Chronicle and the Universal Advertiser* [Boston, MA] 9, no. 466 (July 31, 1777), p. 2.

43 The identities are garbled: *LAAR*, 1:405–6, lists the officers who traveled with Lafayette.

43 American audience: This is the first mention I have found of Lafayette's name in an American paper. However, earlier versions of this article might well have appeared in newspapers published between South Carolina and Boston, as was customary in the period.

44 "I started out brilliantly": Lafayette to Adrienne, July 17, 1777, *LAAR*, 1:423.

44 "harder than this voyage": Dubuysson, *LAAR*, 1:429.

45 "speaks French very well": Ibid., 1:429–30.

45 "ended his harangue": Ibid., 1:430.

46 "terms are very high": John Adams to James Warren, June 19, 1777, *Papers of John Adams,* ed. Robert J. Taylor (Cambridge, MA: Harvard University Press, 2006), 5:226.

46 "very bad": Philippe Charles Tronson du Coudray, "Du Coudray's 'Observations on the Forts Intended for the Defense of the Two Passages of the River Delaware,' July, 1777," *The Pennsylvania Magazine of History and Biography* 24, no. 3 (1900): 343.

46 "badly situated": Ibid., 344.

46 "a hundred times more enthusiasm": Duportail to Vergennes, November 12, 1777, as translated in Paul K. Walker, *Engineers of Independence: A Documentary History of the Army Engineers in the American Revolution, 1775–1783* (1981; repr., Honolulu: University Press of the Pacific, 2002), 177.

47 "the rank and commission": Resolution of Congress, July 31, 1777, *LAAR*, 1:88.

47 "zeal, illustrious family": Resolution of Congress, July 31, 1777, *LAAR*, 1:88.

47 "have a Short Campaign": Henry Laurens to John Gervais, August 8, 1777, *LAAR*, 1:88.

48 "that great man": *Mémoires*, 1:19.

48 "the majesty of his figure": Ibid., 1:20.

48 "embarrass me beyond measure": Washington to Major General William Heath, July 27, 1777, *PGWRW,* 10:438.

49 "to learn and not to teach": "Memoir of 1779," *LAAR*, 1:394.

49 **"What the designs of Congress"**: Washington to Benjamin Harrison, August 19, 1777, *LAAR*, 1:104.

49 **"never meant"**: Benjamin Harrison to Washington, August 20, 1777, *LAAR*, 1:106.

49 **Washington welcomed him**: *Mémoires*, 1:20.

50 **"a friendly Affection"**: The American Commissioners to [George Washington], c. August-September 1777, *LAAR*, 1:107.

51 **"rallying the troops"**: *Mémoires*, 1:25.

52 **"surrounded by citizens"**: Ibid., 1:26.

52 **"the Marquis La Fayette was wounded"**: Washington to John Hancock, September 11, 1777, *PGWRW*, 11:201.

52 **seven hundred men**: John W. Jordan, "Bethlehem During the Revolution: Extracts from the Diaries in the Moravian Archives at Bethlehem, Pennsylvania," *Pennsylvania Magazine of History and Biography* 13, no. 1 (1889): 78.

52 **particularly attentive**: Joseph Mortimer Levering, *A History of Bethlehem, Pennsylvania, 1741–1892* (Bethlehem, PA: Times Publishing Company, 1903), 465.

52 **"inaction"**: *Mémoires*, 1:28.

53 **"a very intelligent and pleasant young man"**: Jordan, "Bethlehem During the Revolution," *Pennsylvania Magazine of History and Biography* 12, no. 4 (1888): 406, note 4.

53 **"the gentle religion"**: *Mémoires*, 1:26.

53 **Lafayette proposed his ventures**: This paragraph is based on *Mémoires*, 1:28–29, note 1.436.

53 **"intimate friend"**: Lafayette to Adrienne, October 1, 1777, *LAAR*, 1:437.

54 **"being honour'd with the name of French"**: Lafayette to Laurens, November 18, 1777, *LAAR*, 1:152.

CHAPTER 5: DISENCHANTMENT

55 **"What a date"**: Lafayette to Adrienne, January 6, 1778, *LAAR*, 1:458–59.

55 **some three thousand men**: On January 1, 1778, Lafayette had under his command Brigadier Generals Muhlenberg, Scott, and Woodford with 3,086 men. "Arrangement of the Continental Army," January 1, 1778, *PGWRW*, 13:94–97.

55 **"consider, if you please"**: Lafayette to Laurens, January 2, 1778, *LAAR*, 1:210.

56 **"When I was in Europe"**: Lafayette to Washington, December 30, 1777, *LAAR*, 1:204.

56 **Conway Cabal**: The question of how serious a threat the Conway Cabal actually posed to Washington is still open to debate. See, among many other sources, Gloria E. Brenneman, "The Conway Cabal: Myth or Reality," *Pennsylvania History* 40, no. 2 (April 1973): 168–77, and Thomas Fleming, *Washington's Secret War: The Hidden History of Valley Forge* (New York: HarperCollins, 2005), 166–205.

57 **Lafayette reported hearing:** Lafayette to Washington, January 20, 1778, *LAAR,* 1:238–39. All quotes found on 1:239.

57 **A scheme is, indeed:** My interpretation follows that of Fleming, *Washington's Secret War,* 166–73, 192–96.

57 **"your Ardent Desire":** Horatio Gates to Lafayette, January 24, 1778, *LAAR,* 1:249.

58 **"As I neither know":** Washington to the Board of War, as quoted in *LAAR,* 1:250.

58 **Writing to Laurens:** Lafayette to Laurens, January 26, 1778, *LAAR,* 1:253–56.

58 **a letter of January 31:** Lafayette to [the President of Congress], January 31, 1778, *LAAR,* 1:267–71.

58 **a resolution of Congress:** *LAAR,* 1:273.

58 **"see if some harm can be done":** Lafayette to Adrienne, February 3, 1778, *LAAR,* 1:462–63.

59 **"blunders of madness or treachery":** Lafayette to Washington, February 19, 1778, *LAAR,* 1:299.

59 **"from a precipice":** Lafayette to Laurens, February 19, 1778, *LAAR,* 1:296.

59 **"Why am I so far from you":** Lafayette to Washington, February 19, 1778, *LAAR,* 1:299.

60 **"However sensibly your ardour":** Washington to Lafayette, March 10, 1778, *LAAR,* 1:342–43.

60 **"When a man does all he can":** *George Washington's Rules of Civility and Decent Behaviour in Company and Conversation,* ed. Charles Moore (Boston: Houghton Mifflin, 1926), 11.

CHAPTER 6: ALLIANCES

61 **"with infinite pleasure":** George Washington to Henry Laurens, May 1, 1778, *PGWRW,* 15:5.

61 **"in a transport of joy":** David Ramsay, *The History of the American Revolution* (1789; repr., Trenton: James J. Wilson, 1811), 2:93.

61 **"I am myself fit to receive":** Lafayette to the president of Congress, May 1, 1778, *LAAR,* 2:40.

61 **"that in serving the cause of humanity":** Lafayette to Adrienne, June 16, 1778, *LAAR,* 2:401.

62 **Baron Friedrich Wilhelm von Steuben:** See Paul Lockhart, *The Drillmaster of Valley Forge: The Baron de Steuben and the Making of the American Army* (New York: HarperCollins, 2008), 114–15.

62 **"must have more than the common quantity":** *PGWRW,* 15:41, note 6.

62 **"in order that due honour":** Letter from George Bryan, vice president of the executive council of Pennsylvania, in Lancaster, Pennsylvania, to Washington, May 23, 1778. "As it is apprehended here, that the Marquis-de-la Fayette has been nominated by the Most Christian King Ambassador to the United States of America, and that he may be expected shortly to pass through this borough in his way to Congress, it would highly oblige the

Executive council of this state, if some previous intimation of the time of his Lordships Journey could be given by one of the Gentlemen of your Excellencys family, in order that due honour might be done to so respectable a personage by this state, as far as present circumstances may admit." *PGWRW,* 15:195.

62 **"refused to listen"**: Laurens to Washington, July 31, 1778, *PGWRW,* 16:210.

63 **"if my compatriots make war"**: Lafayette to Lazare-Jean Théveneau de Francy, May 14, 1778, *LAAR,* 2:398.

63 **forty-seven Oneida warriors**: Joseph T. Glatthaar and James Kirby Martin, *Forgotten Allies: The Oneida Indians and the American Revolution* (New York: Hill and Wang, 2006), 205.

63 **"Young warriors often need advice"**: "Address to Oneida Warriors," *Connecticut Journal* 556 (June 10, 1778): 2.

64 **"be all of one mind"**: On Anne-Louis de Tousard (1749–1817), who would go on to lose an arm fighting under General Sullivan at Newport in 1778, see Michael A. Burke, "Tousard, Anne-Louis," in *American National Biography: Supplement 2,* ed. Mark Christopher Carnes (New York: Oxford University Press, 2005), 553–54.

64 **"The detachment under your command"**: Washington to Lafayette, May 18, 1778, *LAAR,* 2:54.

65 **nine dead**: The number of casualties is given by Washington in Washington to Laurens, May 24, 1778, *PGWRW,* 15:210.

65 **"a timely and handsome retreat"**: "York-Town, May 30," *Pennsylvania Packet; or, The General Advertiser* (June 3, 1778): 2.

66 **"The commander of the enemy's party"**: Ibid.

66 **"French mercenaries"**: see, for example, "American News," *Morning Chronicle and London Advertiser* 2864 (July 25, 1778): 2. The British soldier's account appeared in multiple papers, including "Extract of a Letter from Philadelphia, May 23," *General Evening Post* (London), no. 6948 (July 7–9, 1778): 1; *Public Advertiser* (London), no. 13200 (July 8, 1778): 2.

67 **"set up the war whoop"**: "York-Town, May 30," *Pennsylvania Packet; or, The General Advertiser* (June 3, 1778): 2.

67 **in the diary of Joseph Plumb Martin**: James Kirby Martin, ed., *Ordinary Courage: The Revolutionary War Adventures of Joseph Plumb Martin,* 3rd ed. (Malden, MA: Blackwell, 2008), 71–72. I was directed to this source by Glatthaar and Martin, 208–16, which gives a full account of the role of the Oneidas at Barren Hill.

67 **"six Indian scouts"**: Glatthaar and Martin, *Forgotten Allies,* photo opp., 179.

68 **Lee and Washington**: The hostilities between Lee and Washington have received considerable attention. My understanding of the events is particularly indebted to Fleming, *Washington's Secret War,* and Charles Lee, *The Lee Papers,* 4 vols. (New York: New-York Historical Society, 1872–75).

68 **"when my honest quadruped friends"**: *Lee Papers,* 4:322.

68 **"indecision"**: Lee to the president of the Massachusetts Council, *Lee Papers,* 2:303.

69   "the most idle": Lee to James Bowdoin, November 30, 1776, *Lee Papers,* 2:323.

69   "my former letters": Washington to Lee, *Lee Papers,* 2:318.

69   "to move the morning after": "Order of March and Route of the Army from Camp Valley Forge to Newburg on the North River Opposite Fishkill," *Lee Papers,* 2:408.

69   "the most effectual means": Washington to Lafayette, June 25, 1778, *LAAR,* 2:87.

69   "I must repeat": Washington to Lafayette, June 26, 1778, *LAAR,* 2:92.

70   "is undoubtedly the most honorable": Lee to Washington, June 25, 1778, *Lee Papers,* 2:417.

70   "the People here": Lee to Washington, June 27, 1778, *Lee Papers,* 2:426.

70   "exchanging roles": All quotes in this paragraph are from *Mémoires,* 1:52.

70   An outraged Washington: As Washington described it, upon arriving, "to my great surprise and mortification, I met the whole advanced Corps retreating" and the "Rear of the Corps . . . closely pressed by the Enemy." Washington to Henry Laurens, July 1, 1778, *Lee Papers,* 2:444.

71   "what the devil brought us": Lee to Richard Henry Lee, Englishtown, June 28 [29], 1778, *Lee Papers,* 2:430.

71   "that nothing but the misinformation": Lee to Washington, July 1 [June 30], 1778, *Lee Papers,* 2:435.

71   his court-martial began: For the transcript of Lee's court-martial, including Lafayette's testimony, see *Lee Papers,* 3:1–208.

71   "passed the night": *Mémoires,* 1:53.

72   "ill will and insubordination": Mathieu-François Pidansat de Mairobert, *L'espion anglois; ou, Correspondance secrète entre milord All'Eye et milord All'Ear* (London: Adamson, 1786), 9:31.

72   "haughty and presumptuous": *Extrait du journal d'un officier de la marine de l'escadre de M. le comte d'Estaing* (Paris, 1782), 2.

72   "However pleasantly": Lafayette to the Comte d'Estaing, July 14, 1778, *LAAR,* 2:403.

72   "no other ambition": Lafayette to the Comte d'Estaing, July 24, 1778, *LAAR,* 2:405.

72   "no one was better situated": "Rapport du comte d'Estaing au secrétaire d'État de la Marine," November 5, 1778, as published in Doniol, *Histoire,* 3:460.

73   at least six separate letters to d'Estaing: These are included among the twenty-seven letters Lafayette sent to d'Estaing between July and October 1778, all of which are published as "Correspondance inédite de La Fayette: Lettres écrites au comte d'Estaing pendant la campagne du Vice-Amiral de la Delaware à Boston du 14 juillet au 20 octobre 1778," *Revue d'histoire diplomatique* 6 (1892): 395–448.

73   On July 30: D'Estaing to Lafayette, July 30, 1778, *LAAR,* 2:408.

73   serve under Major General John Sullivan: Washington to Lafayette, July 22, 1778, *PGWRW,* 16:127.

73 "Harmony and the best understanding": Washington to Sullivan, July 27, 1778, *PGWRW,* 16:188.

73 **Washington himself remained wary:** Washington to Gouverneur Morris, July 24, 1778, *PGWRW,* 16:157. Aware that his letter touched on a delicate matter, Washington added a postscript explaining that he was writing "with the freedom of a friend" and asking Morris not to "make me enemys [*sic*] by publishing what is intended for your own information & that of particular friends."

74 "militarily inadmissible": D'Estaing to Sullivan, August 7, 1778, as quoted in *LAAR,* 1:135, note 3.

74 "vexing for certain people": Lafayette to d'Estaing, August 5, 1778, *LAAR,* 2:410.

74 "saw among the Fleet": Lafayette to Washington, August 6, 1778, *LAAR,* 2:133.

74 **"This measure gave much umbrage":** John Laurens to Henry Laurens, n.d., John Laurens, *The Army Correspondence of Colonel John Laurens in the Years 1777–8* (New York: Bradford Club, 1867), 220.

74 *"that the Americans do not find"*: Lafayette to d'Estaing, August 10, 1778, *LAAR,* 2:412.

75 "risk our friendship": Lafayette to Washington, August 25, 1778, *LAAR,* 2:149.

75 **"Would you believe":** Lafayette to d'Estaing, August 24, 1778, *LAAR,* 2:416.

75 "Reccomend to the several chief persons": Lafayette to Washington, August 25, 1778, *LAAR,* 2:153.

75 **tended to the young man's wounded honor:** Washington to Lafayette, September 1, 1778, *PGWRW,* 16:461.

75 "palliate and soften matters": Washington to Major General William Heath, August 28, 1778, *PGWRW,* 16:401.

75 "people old in war": Washington to Sullivan, September 1, 1778, *PGWRW,* 16:465.

CHAPTER 7: HOMECOMINGS

77 "I long my dear general": Lafayette to Washington, September 1, 1778, *LAAR,* 2:163.

77 "our Separation has been long enough": Lafayette to Washington, September 21, 1778, *LAAR,* 2:179.

77 **wrote to Silas Talbot:** Lafayette to Silas Talbot, September 8, 1778, *LAAR,* 2:171.

77 "the instrument of her ambition": *LAAR,* 2:182, note 1.

77 "I have nothing very interesting to do here": Lafayette to d'Estaing, September 13, 1778, as cited and translated in *LAAR,* 2:182, note 2.

78 "If you have entertained thoughts": Washington to Lafayette, September 25, 1778, *LAAR,* 2:183.

78 "How dreadful": Lafayette to Adrienne, June 16, 1778, *LAAR,* 2:400.

78 **"Now . . . that France is involv'd"**: Lafayette to the president of Congress, October 13, 1778, *LAAR*, 2:190.

79 **"wisdom and dexterity"**: Gérard to Vergennes, October 20, 1778, John J. Meng, ed., *Despatches and Instructions of Conrad Alexandre Gérard, 1778–1780* (Baltimore: Johns Hopkins Press, 1939), 344.

79 **"personal satisfaction"**: Doniol, *Histoire*, 3:460.

79 **"Zeal, Courage and attachment"**: Congress to Louis XVI, October 21, 1778, *LAAR*, 2:194.

79 **"no one but [Lafayette] has known"**: William Carmichael to Benjamin Franklin, October 30, 1778, *LAAR*, 2:199.

80 **ceremonial sword**: President of Congress to Lafayette, October 24, 1778, *LAAR*, 2:193.

80 **he returned home a hero**: The crossing was not without incident. A plotted mutiny was discovered and thwarted. *Mémoires*, 1:63–64.

80 **"Upon my arrival"**: Ibid., 1:65.

80 **But even this penalty**: *LAAR*, 2:231, note 2.

80 **80,000 livres**: The amount is given in Louis Gottschalk, *Lafayette and the Close of the American Revolution* (Chicago: University of Chicago Press, 1942, rpt. 1974), 7.

81 **"the first battles"**: Ségur, *Mémoires*, 1:128.

81 **John Paul Jones**: Jones had enjoyed great success against the British fleet throughout the war, and he continued to do so. Most famously, the *Bonhomme Richard* captured HMBS *Serapis* on September 23 after a four-hour battle, during which Jones is reputed to have proclaimed defiantly, "I have not yet begun to fight." Evan Thomas, *John Paul Jones: Sailor, Hero, Father of the American Navy* (New York: Simon and Schuster, 2003), 192.

81 **public feud**: Writing to Washington of the rift among the American envoys on June 12, 1779, Lafayette pleaded, "For God's sake prevent theyr loudly disputing together." *LAAR*, 2:277. Discussed by Schiff, *Great Improvisation*.

82 **newborn daughter Virginie**: Technically, the infant had been named for the queen of France—her full name was Marie Antoinette Virginie. But she would always be known by the name that honored the home state of Washington and Jefferson. *Actes de naissances et baptême à St.-Roch en 1782.* LOC, reel 41, folder 435.

82 **"as an offering to My Western Country"**: Lafayette to Franklin, September 17, 1782, *LAAR*, 5:57; Franklin's response, Franklin to Lafayette, September 17, 1782, *LAAR*, 5:57.

82 **"Miss Virginia"**: The anecdote quickly circulated throughout Europe thanks to the *Mémoires secrets*, which published a variation on the story. Louis Petit de Bachaumont, *Mémoires secrets pour server à l'histoire de la république des letters en France depuis 1762 jusqu'à nos jours*, 36 vols. (London: Adamson, 1783), 21:125–26.

82 **"to impress the minds"**: *LAAR*, 2:267, note 2.

82 **"I great deal love our project"**: Lafayette to Franklin, May 19, 1779, *LAAR*, 2:265.

82 **twenty-six possible images**: A partial list of possible prints, in the handwriting of Franklin and Lafayette, is reproduced in *LAAR,* 2:266.

83 **"I never saw a man"**: Lafayette to Washington, September 1, 1778, *LAAR,* 2:164. The Peale painting owned by Hancock is now in the collection of the Brooklyn Museum of Art.

83 **"when you requested me"**: Washington to Lafayette, September 25, 1778, *LAAR,* 2:183.

83 **filled Monticello**: Susan R. Stein, *The Worlds of Thomas Jefferson at Monticello* (New York: Abrams, 1993), 122–37, 166–74, 198–214, 216–33, 434–36.

83 **Lafayette arranged**: Carol Borchert Cadou, *The George Washington Collection: Fine and Decorative Arts at Mount Vernon* (Mount Vernon: Mount Vernon Ladies' Association, 2006), 281, note 95.

84 **"If you are curious"**: Lafayette to Vergennes, July 1, 1779, *LAAR,* 2:455.

84 **Jean-Baptiste Le Paon**: Jean-Baptiste Le Paon, known as Louis, had been rejected from the Royal Academy of Painting and Sculpture and was thus barred from participating in the biennial Salon exhibitions that marked the high point of the Parisian art calendar. Instead, he showed in a notably less prestigious venue organized by Pahin de la Blancherie, discussed on page 108. An established painter of decorative battle and hunting scenes, Le Paon was employed by the Prince de Condé as a battle painter for the Palais Bourbon, just a stone's throw from Lafayette's home, and had several paintings in the École Militaire. Notices of Le Paon's work are scattered throughout *Nouvelles de la république des lettres et des arts* (1779–1782).

85 **"much more advantageous"**: Lafayette to Vergennes, February 2, 1780. *Mémoires,* 1:327–31.

86 **"hasten to join"**: "Instructions from the Comte de Vergennes," March 5, 1780, as translated in *LAAR,* 2:364.

86 **"in the Uniform"**: John Adams to James Lovell, February 29, 1780, as quoted in *LAAR,* 2:352, note 2.

86 **"last week arrived at Boston"**: Abigail Adams to John Adams, May 1, 1780, *Adams Family Correspondence,* L. H. Butterfield, ed. (Cambridge, MA: Belknap Press of Harvard University Press, 1973), 3:334.

86 **"It's to the roar of cannon"**: Lafayette to Adrienne, May 6, 1780, *LAAR,* 3:430.

87 **"particular delight"**: Lafayette to Samuel Adams, May 30, 1780, *LAAR,* 3:41–42.

87 **"If the French troops arrive in time"**: Lafayette to Vergennes, May 20, 1780, *LAAR,* 3:436.

87 **detailed letter to Rochambeau**: Lafayette to Rochambeau and the Chevalier de Ternay, July 9, 1780, *LAAR,* 3:455–60.

87 **Rochambeau had more immediate concerns**: Rochambeau to Lafayette, July 16, 1780, *LAAR,* 3:464–65.

88 **"I am persuaded"**: Washington to Lafayette, July 22, 1780, *LAAR,* 3:106.

88 **"added in my own name"**: Lafayette to Washington, July 31, 1780, *LAAR,* 3:117.

88 "it is very clearly settled": Lafayette to Rochambeau and Ternay, August 9,
     1780, *LAAR,* 3:473.

89 "He proposes Extravagant things": Rochambeau to Luzerne, August 14,
     1780, *LAAR,* 3:477.

89 "inclined to believe": Luzerne to Rochambeau, August 24, 1780, as excerpted
     and translated in *LAAR,* 3:142.

89 "You know me well enough": Rochambeau to Lafayette, August 27, 1780,
     LAAR, 3:484–85.

90 "to act against the corps": Instructions from George Washington, February
     20, 1781, *LAAR,* 3:334–36.

90 "four or five to one": Lafayette to Luzerne, May 22, 1781, *LAAR,* 3:459.

90 "we'll be in a condition": Lafayette to the Vicomte de Noailles, May 22,
     1781, *LAAR,* 3:462.

CHAPTER 8: HONOR

92 **Paris was abuzz:** The festivities in honor of the dauphin are described in
     detail by Ann H. Sievers, Linda Muehlig, and Nancy Rich, *Master Drawings
     from the Smith College Museum of Art,* exhibit catalog (New York: Hud-
     son Hills Press; Northampton, MA: Smith College Museum of Art, 2001),
     105–11, which discusses the elaborate preparatory drawings for prints of the
     events by Jean-Michel Moreau le Jeune.

92 **Marie Antoinette bestowed:** Ségur, *Mémoires,* 242, and Louis-François
     Métra, *Correspondance secrète, politique et littéraire* (London: 1787), 2:607.

93 **Marie Antoinette's grace:** A published dispatch dated January 24, 1782,
     describes the event as "une circonstance qui peint bien l'âme sensible &
     délicate de notre Reine." Métra, *Correspondance secrète,* 2:607.

93 "large and joyous group of fishwives": Ibid.

93 "his conduct throughout the past campaign": November 23, 1781, Worthing-
     ton Chauncey Ford, ed., *Journals of the Continental Congress, 1774–1789,*
     1135, 34 vols. (Washington, DC: U.S. Government Printing Office), 21:135,
     reproduced in *LAAR,* 3:440–41.

94 **no one on either side:** In reading Lafayette's commercial efforts as being
     parallel to, though not prompted by, desires outlined by both French and
     American representatives, I concur with Gottschalk's assessment in *Lafayette
     Between the American and the French Revolution,* 34–52.

94 **"Collecting the Opinions of Every American Merchant":** Lafayette to
     Washington, November 11, 1783, *LAAR,* 5:164.

94 **"Observations on Commerce":** as translated in *LAAR,* 5:168–75. The docu-
     ment was twelve octavo pages per Gottschalk, *Lafayette Between the Ameri-
     can and the French Revolution,* 44.

95 "free ports": Calonne to Lafayette, Versailles, January 9, 1784, as translated
     and entered into the May 3, 1784, *Journals of the Continental Congress, 1774–
     1789,* 26:334–35.

95 **from timber to whale oil**: Gottschalk, *Lafayette Between the American and the French Revolution,* 222–37.

96 **"I Have a Great Value"**: Lafayette to Livingston, February 5, 1783, *LAAR,* 5:89.

96 **"to Have a Resolve"**: Lafayette's request was answered some two months later, when the American legislature resolved, "That Congress . . . have a high sense of the new proofs he has exhibited of his zeal in the cause of the said states, and of his constant attachment to their interests and welfare." April 10, 1783, *Journals of the Continental Congress, 1774–1789,* 24:234.

96 **"Be so kind only as"**: Lafayette to McHenry, Paris, December 26, 1783, *LAAR,* 5:185.

96 **Honor, which had long**: See Chaussinand-Nogaret, *French Nobility,* 34.

96 **"I sometimes contemplate the situation"**: Abigail Adams to Mercy Otis Warren, February 28, 1780, *Adams Family Correspondence,* 3:288.

96 **"the love of fame"**: Alexander Hamilton, Federalist No. 72, in Alexander Hamilton, John Jay, and James Madison, *The Federalist Papers,* Project Gutenberg, December 12, 2011, www.gutenberg.org/files/18/18.txt. On the Founding Fathers' understanding of fame as an important force that compelled men to great deeds, see Peter McNamara, ed., *The Noblest Minds: Fame, Honor, and the American Founding* (Lanham, MD: Rowman and Littlefield, 1999).

97 **"nature strews approbation"**: "Réputation," *Dictionnaire,* 14:161.

97 **"Because that Entrusting Temper"**: *LAAR,* 5:184–85.

97 **"that Your plenipotentiarie's letters"**: Lafayette to McHenry, Paris, December 26, 1783, *LAAR,* 5:185.

97 **"The Marquis's business"**: November 23, 1782, *Diary and Autobiography of John Adams* (Cambridge, MA: Harvard University Press, 1961) 3:71.

98 **"the same Friend to Us here"**: John Adams to James Warren, February 28, 1780, *Papers of John Adams,* 8:376.

98 **Adams was struggling**: My understanding of Adams's vexed relationships with Franklin and Vergennes are indebted to David McCullough, *John Adams,* and Schiff, *A Great Improvisation.*

98 **"so agreeable to my inclinations"**: Adams to Lafayette, February 20, 1782, *Papers of John Adams,* 12:248.

98 **"the Instruction of Congress"**: John Adams to James Warren, April 16, 1783, *LAAR,* 5:122.

98 **"Seeds of Mischief"**: John Adams to James Warren, April 16, 1783, *LAAR,* 5:122.

98 **"ardent to distinguish himself"**: John Adams to James Warren, April 16, 1783, *LAAR,* 5:123.

99 **"during the Treaty at Paris"**: May 9, 1782, Journal of the Peace Negotiations, *The Revolutionary Diplomatic Correspondence of the United States,* ed. Francis Wharton, 6 vols. (Washington, DC: Government Printing Office, 1889), 5:553.

100 **"the expectation of peace is a joke"**: Ibid., 5:576.

100 **"Would Highly flatter"**: Lafayette to Robert R. Livingston, February 5, 1783, *LAAR,* 5:89.

100 **"I Would take it as a Most flattering Circumstance"**: Lafayette to Washington, February 5, 1783, *LAAR,* 5:92.

100 **"the bearer of the Ratification"**: Washington to Robert R. Livingston, March 29, 1783, New-York Historical Society, Robert R. Livingston Papers, MS 388, box 6.

100 **"the honor of the nation"**: Livingston to Washington, April 9, 1783, New-York Historical Society, Robert R. Livingston Papers, MS 388, box 6.

100 **"there is no Man upon Earth"**: Washington to Livingston, April 16, 1783, New-York Historical Society, Robert R. Livingston Papers, MS 388, box 6.

100 **"will not I apprehend"**: Washington to Lafayette, October 12, 1783, *LAAR,* 5:155.

101 **"that it is inconsistent"**: March 16, 1784, *Journals of the Continental Congress, 1774–1789,* 26:144.

101 **Society of the Cincinnati**: On the history of the society, see: Markus Hünemörder, *The Society of the Cincinnati: Conspiracy and Distrust in Early America* (New York: Berghahn Books, 2006), and Minor Myers, *Liberty Without Anarchy: A History of the Society of the Cincinnati* (Charlottesville: University Press of Virginia, 1983).

101 **"to inculcate to the latest age"**: "The Institution of the Society of the Cincinnati as Altered and Amended at Their First General Meeting," in *Proceedings of the General Society of the Cincinnati, 1784–1884* (Philadelphia: Review Printing House, 1887), 13.

101 **Lucius Quinctius Cincinnatus**: Wendy C. Wick, *George Washington: An American Icon,* exhibit catalog (Washington, DC: Smithsonian Institution Traveling Service, 1982), 133–35. The most thorough discussion of Washington's image as a modern-day Cincinnatus is Garry Wills, *Cincinnatus: George Washington and the Enlightenment* (Garden City, NY: Doubleday, 1984).

102 **"a bald eagle of gold"**: *Proceedings of the General Society,* 14.

102 **welcomed fifteen**: Bachaumont, *Mémoires secrets pour servir à l'histoire de la république des lettres en France,* 89.

102 **Duval and Francastel**: Baron Ludovic de Contenson, *La Société des Cincinnati de France et la Guerre d'Amérique, 1778–1783* (1934; repr. Paris: Picard, 2007), 32–33.

102 **Lafayette voluntarily shouldered**: Lafayette to Washington, March 9, 1784, *LAAR,* 5:209.

103 **Adams condemned the group**: Adams to Lafayette, March 28, 1784, *LAAR,* 5:211–12.

103 **"I have been informed"**: Adams to Matthew Ridley, January 25, 1784, *Papers of John Adams,* 15:49. I was directed to the existence of this letter, the original of which is in the Massachusetts Historical Society, by *LAAR,* 5:203, note 1.

103 **"against the confederation"**: Jefferson to Washington, April 16, 1784, *Papers of Thomas Jefferson.*

103 "that the people may look to them": Abigail Adams to Mercy Otis Warren, May 10, 1785, *Adams Family Correspondence,* 6:139.

103 "most of the Americans": Lafayette to Washington, March 9, 1784, *LAAR,* 5:209.

103 "as to your going to America": Adams to Lafayette, March 28, 1784, *LAAR,* 5:212.

104 "A friendly letter I wrote You": Lafayette to Adams, April 9, 1784, *LAAR,* 5:213.

104 "Altho' I have not Been Honoured": Lafayette to Adams, June 2, 1784, *LAAR,* 5:222.

104 "received in Season": Adams to Lafayette, June 11, 1784, *LAAR,* 5:223.

CHAPTER 9: 1784

105 **thousands of escaped slaves:** On African-Americans in the Revolutionary War, see Simon Schama, *Rough Crossings: Britain, the Slaves and the American Revolution* (New York: Vintage, 2009).

105 **the city had hosted a sprawling:** My descriptions of New York in the immediate aftermath of the war are based largely on Edwin G. Burrows and Mike Wallace, *Gotham: A History of New York City to 1898* (Oxford: Oxford University Press, 1999), 277–87, and I. N. Phelps Stokes, *The Iconography of Manhattan Island, 1498–1909,* 6 vols. (New York: Robert H. Dodd, 1915–28), 1:365–473.

105 **equestrian statue of King George III:** Arthur S. Marks, "The Statue of King George III in New York and the Iconology of Regicide," *American Art Journal* 13, no. 3 (Summer 1981): 61–82.

106 **The landing of the ship:** J. Bennett Nolan, *Lafayette in America Day by Day* (Baltimore: Johns Hopkins Press, 1934), 217.

106 **Approaching Philadelphia:** As described by Frederick Eugene Francis, Baron de Beelen-Bertholff, who was in the United States as a trade representative of Emperor Joseph II, in a letter of August 12, 1784. Excerpted in Hubert van Houtte, "Documents: American Commercial Conditions, and Negotiations with Austria, 1783–1786," *American Historical Review* 16, no. 3 (April 1911): 569.

106 **"wherever [Lafayette] passes":** James Madison to Thomas Jefferson, September 7, 1784, *The Writings of James Madison, Comprising His Public Papers and His Private Correspondence, Including His Numerous Letters and Documents Now for the First Time Printed,* ed. Gaillard Hunt, 9 vols. (New York: G. P. Putnam's Sons, 1900), 2:2.

106 **"admitted and received":** *Minutes of the Common Council of the City of New York, 1784–1831,* 19 vols. (New York: City of New York, 1917), 1:73–74, quote on page 74.

106 **For the next five months:** For the itinerary of Lafayette's 1784 visit to the United States, see Nolan, *Lafayette in America,* 217–39.

107 **Republic of Letters:** My understanding of this topic is deeply indebted to

Dena Goodman, *The Republic of Letters: A Cultural History of the French Enlightenment* (Ithaca: Cornell University Press, 1994).

107 **"the search for knowledge"**: Goodman, *Republic of Letters*, 33.

107 **"the cultivation of useful knowledge"**: *Transactions of the American Philosophical Society, Held at Philadelphia, for Promoting Useful Knowledge* (Philadelphia: Robert Aitken, 1786), xi.

107 **"all specimens of natural Productions"**: Ibid., ix.

107 **"the importance or singularity"**: Ibid., iv.

108 **"Geography, Mathematics, Natural Philosophy"**: Ibid., ix–x.

108 **admitted on January 19, 1781**: J. Bennett Nolan, "Lafayette and the American Philosophical Society," *Proceedings of the American Philosophical Society* 73, no. 2 (1934): 120, and Nolan, *Lafayette in America*, 218.

108 **A well-known figure**: On Chastellux's biography, see Marquis de Chastellux, *Travels in North America in the Years 1780, 1781 and 1782*, ed. and trans. Howard C. Rice, Jr., 2 vols. (Chapel Hill: University of North Carolina, 1903), 1:1–41.

108 **"thought to be a mistake"**: Chastellux, *Travels in North America*, 1:178.

108 **"Salon de la Correspondance"**: I discuss the organization in depth in Laura Auricchio, "Pahin de la Blancherie's Commercial Cabinet of Curiosity (1779–1787)," *Eighteenth-Century Studies* 36, no. 1 (2002): 47–61.

108 **"books, paintings, mechanical devices"**: *Nouvelles de la république des lettres et des arts* ([November?] 1777): 4. In La Blancherie's rooms, one would have found, jumbled together in no particular order, paintings, drawings, and sculptures, as well as scientific wonders ranging from "a pair of waterproof leather shoes" (May 1, 1782), to "three blocks of rock crystal" excavated in Switzerland, "each containing views and perspectives of the Alps" (January 22, 1783), to "a living hen" that regularly laid eggs through two different orifices (June 26, 1782).

109 **The American Philosophical Society**: My understanding of the APS in this era is based in large part on: *Early Proceedings of the American Philosophical Society for the Promotion of Useful Knowledge, Compiled by One of the Secretaries, from the Manuscript Minutes of Its Meetings from 1744 to 1838* (Philadelphia: McCalla and Stavely, 1884).

109 **"a serpent in a horse's eye"**: The examples given here are selected from *Early Proceedings*, 116–21.

109 **According to Barthélemy**: Barthélemy Faujas de Saint-Fond, *Description des expériences de la machine aérostatique de MM. de Montgolfier et celles auxquelles cette découverte a donné lieu* (Paris: Cuchet, 1783), 36.

109 **"the grandest, most illustrious"**: Faujas de Saint-Fond, *Description*, 40.

109 **"enclosing an authentic narrative"**: Nolan, "Lafayette and the American Philosophical Society," 120. Although Nolan gives the date of Lafayette's letter as December 10, 1784, the context indicates that it must have been 1783.

110 **"duplicated by one of the secretaries"**: The duplication of Lafayette's materials was reported at the meeting of April 16, 1784; *Early Proceedings*, 125.

110 **attention-seeking ploy**: Robert Darnton, *Mesmerism and the End of the Enlightenment in France* (Cambridge, MA: Harvard University Press, 1968), 23–24. The following paragraphs are indebted to Darnton, although all primary sources have been consulted directly.

112 **"made the greatest discovery"**: Lafayette to Washington, May 14, 1784, Wharton, *Revolutionary Diplomatic Correspondence*, 6:807.

112 **"Sciences and letters are frighted"**: Lafayette to Franklin, May 20, 1784, *LAAR*, 5:222.

112 **newspapers from Massachusetts**: See, for example, "Account of the Report of the Committee, Appointed by Order of the French King, to Inquire into Animal Magnetism," *Massachusetts Spy* (May 19, 1785): 2.

113 **One American author**: "Boston, Nov. 29," *American Herald* (November 29, 1784): 2.

113 **"private citizen"**: Washington to Lafayette, from Mount Vernon, February 1, 1784, *PGWC*, 1:87.

113 **Baltimore stagecoach route**: Oliver W. Holmes, "Stagecoach Days in the District of Columbia," *Records of the Columbia Historical Society* 50 (1948/1950): 1–42.

113 **"the retreat of General Washington"**: Lafayette to Adrienne, August 20, 1784, LOC, reel 31, folder 354. The following discussion of Lafayette's *cabinet* is based on this version of the letter.

114 **"barometer"**: Barometers were quite fashionable among elite men in Paris, and were written about in the newspapers of the day. See, for instance, "Physique," *Journal de Paris* (May 7, 1785), 127:515–55, a front-page article by La Lande announcing the second edition of a sought-after 1772 book by Jean-André De Luc on thermometers and barometers.

114 **An enormous 1859 painting**: On the painting in relation to Rossiter's campaign to salvage Mount Vernon, see Thomas P. Rossiter, *A Description of the Picture of the Home of Washington After the War. Painted by T. P. Rossiter and L. R. Mignot. With Historical Sketches of the Personages Introduced* (New York: Appleton, 1859). Thomas P. Rossiter, "Mount Vernon, Past and Present. What Shall Be Its Destiny?" *Crayon* 5, no. 9 (September 1858): 243–53.

114 **more than two hundred slaves**: My understanding of the role of slaves at Mount Vernon is indebted to sources including: Joseph J. Ellis, *His Excellency: George Washington* (New York: Alfred A. Knopf, 2005), 147–67, and Kenneth Morgan, "George Washington and the Problem of Slavery," *Journal of American Studies* 34, no. 2 (August 2000): 279–301.

115 **"it Has Ever Been My"**: Lafayette to Adams, March 8, 1784, *LAAR*, 5:202. Adams firmly rejected Lafayette's advice, insisting that he saw "no motive of Reason or Prudence, for making a Mystery of our Sentiments upon this Subject in Europe or America, or for reserving them for America. It is a publick Thing about which every Man has a right to think for himself and express his Thoughts."Adams to Lafayette, March 28, 1784, *LAAR*, 5:212.

116 **"a plan . . . Which Might Become"**: Lafayette to Washington, February 5, 1783, *LAAR*, 5:91–92.

116 **"striking evidence of the benevolence of your Heart"**: Washington to Lafayette, April 5, 1783, *LAAR*, 5:121.

116 **"prudent, calm, and intrepid conduct"**: LOC, folder 222.

116 **"proofs of its love for the rights of all of humanity"**: Ibid.

117 **"his or her hand and sealed"**: "Act XXI. An Act to Authorize the Manumission of Slaves," May 1782, ed. William Waller Hening, *The Statutes at Large: Being a Collection of All the Laws of Virginia, from the First Session of the Legislature in the Year 1619*, 13 vols. (Richmond: Samuel Pleasants, 1809–23), 11:39–40. On reactions to the 1782 act, see George William Van Cleve, "Founding a Slaveholders' Union, 1770–1797," in *Contesting Slavery: The Politics of Bondage and Freedom in the New American Nation,* ed. John Craig Hammond and Matthew Mason (Charlottesville: University of Virginia Press, 2011), 123. On the postwar backlash against emancipation in Virginia, see also Michael A. McDonnell, "Class War? Class Struggles During the American Revolution in Virginia," *William and Mary Quarterly* 63, no. 2, 3rd ser. (April 2006): 305–44, esp. 341.

117 **pro-slavery petitions**: See Fredrika Teute Schmidt and Barbara Ripel Wilhelm, "Early Proslavery Petitions in Virginia," *William and Mary Quarterly* 30, no. 1, 3rd ser. (January 1973): 133–46, esp. 138. I was directed to this valuable article by a classic text, originally published in 1973: David Brion Davis, *The Problem of Slavery in the Age of Revolution, 1770–1823* (Oxford: Oxford University Press, 1999), 167–68.

117 **"done Essential Service"**: Recommendation for James, November 21, 1784, *LAAR,* 5:277–78.

118 **His archives include**: See Melvin Dow, ed., *Lafayette and Slavery, from His Letters to Thomas Clarkson and Granville Sharp* (Easton, PA: American Friends of Lafayette, 1950), 29–31; Condorcet to Lafayette, February 24, 1785, *LAAR,* 5:299–300; and Franklin to Lafayette, May 27, 1788, LOC, LaGrange, 221.

118 **In the same year, Lafayette**: Dow, *Lafayette and Slavery,* 6.

118 ***Description of a Slave Ship:*** "Description d'un Navire Négrier," Cornell, box 2, folder 29.

118 **abolitionist contemporaries**: For an excellent overview, see Davis, *The Problem of Slavery.*

118 **"final purposes"**: *The Compleated Autobiography by Benjamin Franklin,* ed. Mark Skousen (Washington, DC: Regnery, 2007), 2:382.

119 **like Jefferson, who wrote**: On Jefferson's proposals, see Christa Dierksheide, " 'The Great Improvement and Civilization of That Race': Jefferson and the 'Amelioration' of Slavery, ca. 1770–1826," *Early American Studies: An Interdisciplinary Journal* 6, no. 1 (Spring 2008): 165–97.

119 **"the double voice of self-interest"**: *LAAR,* 5:172.

120 **acquired two properties in Cayenne**: The sales contracts for the properties and slaves are housed in ANOM COL/C14/81 F° 9 and FR ANOM COL/C14/81 F° 18.

120 **They ranged in age**: Geneste, "Liste des nègres . . . ," Cornell, box 2, folder 18. Dow, *Lafayette and Slavery,* 6, reports that, "according to Thomas

Clarkson . . . Lafayette liberated all of the slaves on his Cayenne plantation toward the end of 1789." However, Clarkson was mistaken. I thank Miranda Spieler for calling my attention to this fact. On slavery in French Guiana, see Miranda Spieler, *Empire and Underworld: Captivity in French Guiana* (Cambridge, MA: Harvard University Press, 2012). As discussed above, evidence that Lafayette never freed his slaves may be found in the archives at Cornell and ANOM. The facts are also presented accurately in John T. Gillard, "Lafayette, Friend of the Negro," *Journal of Negro History* 19, no. 4 (October 1934), 364, and in Liliane Willens, "Lafayette's Emancipation Experiment in French Guiana—1786–1792," *Studies on Voltaire and the Eighteenth Century* 242 (1986): 345–62.

121 **"to free my negroes"**: Lafayette to Washington, February 6, 1786, *PGWC*, 3:546.

121 **"would to God a like spirit would diffuse"**: Washington to Lafayette, May 10, 1786, *PGWC*, 4:44.

121 **Oneidas, whose young men**: Glatthaar and Martin, *Forgotten Allies*, 208–15.

121 **"fell in with the Marquis"**: James Madison to Thomas Jefferson, New York, September 15, 1784, *Papers of Thomas Jefferson*, 7:416.

121 **whose diary offers**: The following description of the journey is based on Barbé-Marbois's "Journal of His Visit to the Territory of the Six Nations," *LAAR*, 5:245–53. Quotes are as translated by the editors.

122 **Shakers**: My understanding of the Shakers is deeply indebted to Stephen J. Stein, *The Shaker Experience in America: A History of the United Society of Believers* (New Haven: Yale University Press, 1994).

123 **"My companions"**: Lafayette to Adrienne, October 4, 1784, *LAAR*, 5:416.

123 **fascinated by Native American**: The classic text on French attitudes toward America in general, and Native Americans in particular, is Durand Echeverria, *Mirage in the West: A History of the French Image of American Society to 1815* (Princeton: Princeton University Press, 1957). More recent treatments include Aurelian Craiutu and Jeffrey C. Isaac, eds., *America Through European Eyes: British and French Reflections on the New World from the Eighteenth Century to the Present* (University Park: Pennsylvania State University Press, 2009), and Philippe Roger, *The American Enemy: The History of French Anti-Americanism*, trans. Sharon Bowman (Chicago: University of Chicago Press, 2005). A wide selection of documents, images, and objects on the theme are published in Betty-Bright P. Low, *France Views America, 1765–1815*, exhibit catalog (Wilmington, DE: Eleutherian Mills Historical Library, 1978).

124 **"noble savage"**: On the concept of the noble savage and its use (and misuse) by anthropologists, see Ter Ellingson, *The Myth of the Noble Savage* (Berkeley: University of California Press, 2001).

124 **"the respect that we have"**: Peter Jimack, ed., *A History of the Two Indies: A Translated Selection of Writings from Raynal's "Histoire philosophique et politique des établissements des Européens dans les Deux Indes"* (Hampshire, UK: Ashgate, 2006), 211.

124 "One calls *sauvages* all the Indian peoples": *Encyclopédie*, 14:729.

124 "five hundred men, women, and children": *Mémoires*, 1:43.

125 "Europeans who are curious": *Our Revolutionary Forefathers: The Letters of François, Marquis de Barbé-Marbois During His Residence in the United States as Secretary of the French Legation, 1779–1789*, trans. and ed. and with an introduction by Eugene Parker Chase (1929; repr., Freeport, NY: Books for Libraries Press, 1969), 189.

126 **address the assembly**: The following description is based on "Relation of What Pass'd at the Opening of the Treaty Between the United States and the Indian Nations at Fort Schuyler, October 3, 1784," *Connecticut Courant* (November 30, 1784): 1. Similar reports appeared in many other papers.

126 "of the immoderate stress": Madison to Jefferson, October 17, 1784, *LAAR,* 5:273.

126 **Lee did not hesitate**: Lafayette wrote to Adrienne that Lee, who "had no desire to be indebted to me," had observed "that the *sauvages* had been too occupied with me to pay attention to the commissioners." Lafayette to Adrienne, October 4, 1784, *LAAR,* 5:416.

126 "was the only conspicuous figure": Madison to Jefferson, October 17, 1784, *LAAR,* 5:273.

126 "I take him to be as amiable": Ibid., 274. Eugene Parker Chase observes that the phrase "as his vanity will admit" was stricken from the letter by a later hand. Chase, *Our Revolutionary Forefathers,* 274. It is omitted from the transcription in *Writings of James Madison,* 2:76, and replaced with "as can be imagined."

127 "personal credit with the *sauvages*": Lafayette to Adrienne, October 4, 1784, *LAAR,* 5:416.

127 "beautiful": Nolan, *Lafayette in America,* 228.

127 **first histories**: For an overview of Ramsay and Warren, see Eve Kornfeld, *Creating an American Culture, 1775–1800: A Brief History with Documents* (New York: Palgrave Macmillan, 2001), 39–48. On Gordon, see George William Pilcher, "William Gordon and the History of the American Revolution," *Historian* 34, no. 3 (May 1972): 447–64.

128 "an eternal Talker": Adams as cited in Pilcher, "William Gordon," 452, note 11.

128 "recollect the train": James McHenry to George Washington, New York, August 1, 1785, *PGWC,* 3:166.

128 "In certain places": William Gordon to Washington, September 26, 1785; Washington to William Gordon, December 6, 1785; William Gordon to Washington, February 16, 1786, *PGWC.* On the role of vegetation in forging the political and intellectual culture of the early American republic, see Andrea Wulf, *Founding Gardeners: The Revolutionary Generation, Nature, and the Shaping of the American Nation* (New York: Alfred A. Knopf, 2011).

128 **Whether because the author mellowed**: Samuel Adams and John Hancock, however, were both dismayed by Gordon's unflattering descriptions of their actions. See Pilcher, "William Gordon," 462–63.

129 **Lafayette's financial problems**: Lafayette's receipts and expenses during the 1780s are thoroughly documented in LOC, reel 8, folders 100–102a. All figures and quotations in my discussion of Lafayette's finances are found in this collection unless otherwise noted.

130 **Hôtel de Noailles**: Adolphe Berty, *Topographie historique du vieux Paris*, 2 vols. (Paris: Imprimerie Nationale, 1885), 1:298; *Plan et façade en six planches, de l'Hôtel, rue St. Honoré à Paris, appartenant au très-honorable Francis Henry Egerton, des Ducs de Bridgewater, prince du S.E.R. &c. &c. &c.* Paris: 1830.

131 **"a house which, if not the most"**: Letter from Lafayette to Prince de Poix, Hartford, October 12, 1784, excerpted in Charles Brabaint, ed., *La Fayette* exhibit catalog (Paris: Archives Nationales, 1957), 166.

131 **Like Turgot's, Lafayette's was**: For a thorough discussion of the area in general, and of Lafayette's home at 119 Rue de Lille, see *La Rue de Lille: Hôtel de Salm* (Paris: Délégation à l'Action Artistique de la Ville de Paris; Musée de la Légion d'Honneur; Société d'Histoire et d'Archéologie du VIIe Arrondissement, 1983).

133 **Adrien Mouton**: For a summary of Mouton's career, see Michel Gallet, *Les architectes parisiens du XVIIIe siècle: Dictionnaire biographique et critique* (Paris: Mengès, 1995), 377–78.

133 **"it is necessary"**: Anatole de Montaiglon and Jules Guiffrey, eds., *Correspondance des directeurs de l'Académie de France à Rome avec les surintendants des bâtiments* (Paris: Noël Charavay, 1902), vol. 12 (1764–1774), 238. See John Goodman, "Jansenism, 'Parlementaire' Politics, and Dissidence in the Art World of Eighteenth-Century Paris: The Case of the Restout Family," *Oxford Art Journal* 18, no. 1 (1995): 74–95, esp. 83–84.

133 **"barbarously murdered"**: February 21, 1785, David Grayson Allen, ed., et al., *Diary of John Quincy Adams* (Cambridge, MA: Belknap Press, 1982), 1:225.

134 **special dispensation releasing**: Lafayette to Elias Boudinot, March 16, 1785, New Jersey Historical Society. Photostat. Gottschalk, box 54, folder 1.

134 **"Bernard Molitor"**: Ulrich Leben, *Molitor: Ebeniste from the Ancien Regime to the Bourbon Restoration* (London: Wilson, 1992), 185.

134 **"mahogany bookcase"**: The inventories and sales of items in Lafayette's home on the Rue de Bourbon are found in "Vente du Mobilier de l'Émigré La Fayette" and other documents housed in the Archives de la Seine, Paris, DQ10, carton 792.

135 **"the true Cincinnatus"**: Lafayette to Adrienne, August 20, 1784, LOC, reel 31, folder 354.

135 **"I have discovered"**: Lafayette to Adrienne, Church's Tavern, October 10, 1784, *LAAR*, 5:417.

135 **quick note to William Temple Franklin**: Lafayette to William Temple Franklin, November 19, 1783. Photostat. Gottschalk, box 53, folder 10.

135 **four large mirrors**: On August 25, 1795, the commune's representatives

itemized every mirror. Eighteen rooms were outfitted with mirrors, valued at 149,010 livres. Archives de la Seine, Paris, DQ10, carton 792.

136 **English was the language:** Abigail Adams Smith and Caroline Amelia Smith de Windt, *Journal and Correspondence of Miss Adams, Daughter of John Adams, Second President of the United States* (New York: Wiley and Putnam, 1841), 1:49.

136 **invitations preprinted in English:** Lafayette to Franklin, March 9, 1784, Gottschalk, box 53, folder 11.

136 **"life of ceremony and parade":** Abigail Adams to Mary Smith Cranch, April 15, 1785, *Adams Family Correspondence,* 6:84.

136 **"dinner was so perfectly to my taste":** Colonel Smith to Abigail Adams Smith, May 5, 1787, *Correspondence of Miss Adams,* 1:132.

136 **"I should always take pleasure":** Abigail Adams to Mary Smith Cranch, April 15, 1785, *Adams Family Correspondence,* 6:84.

136 **"the fondness that Madame":** *Correspondence of Miss Adams,* 1:49.

137 **"I shall lose part":** Abigail Adams to Mary Smith Cranch, May 8, 1785, *Adams Family Correspondence,* 6:120.

137 **"as a favourite Servant":** Lafayette to Jeremiah Wadsworth, April 16, 1785, *LAAR,* 5:319.

137 **"I might well bring back":** Lafayette to Adrienne, *LAAR,* 5:417.

137 **"the difficulty that M. le M[arqu]is":** Barbé-Marbois, *LAAR,* 5:410.

137 **"the whole family who are Oneidas":** Lafayette to Jeremiah Wadsworth, April 16, 1785, *LAAR,* 5:319. A slightly different version of the story is told in Amelia Cornelius with the assistance of Todd Larkin, "The Archiquette Genealogy," in *The Oneida Indian Journey: From New York to Wisconsin, 1784–1860,* ed. Laurence M. Hauptman, L. Gordon McLester, and the Oneida History Conference Committee (Madison: University of Wisconsin Press, 1999), 126–27. This essay mentions "the children of Lafayette's former clerk, a man named Otsiquette, and an Oneida woman named Sarah Hanyost. Otsiquette had long before returned to France, leaving the boys and Sarah behind." It indicates that Lafayette had also hoped to bring Peter's brother, Edward (Neddy), as well, but that Neddy had run away rather than be taken to Europe.

137 **handful of small receipts:** LOC, folder 102a.

138 **"a *sauvage* from America":** Xavier de Schomberg as quoted in Agénor Bardoux, *La jeunesse de La Fayette, 1757–1792* (Paris: Calmann Lévy, 1892), 194.

138 **"rich Indian dresses":** *Ledyard,* 265–66.

138 **"especially colorful description":** Ange Achille Charles, comte de Neuilly, *Dix années d'émigration: souvenirs et correspondance du comte de Neuilly* (Paris, Douniol, 1865), 10–11.

138 **"Four Iroquois Kings":** The London visits of the Four Iroquois Kings in 1710 and Mai in 1776 have received a considerable amount of attention. My understanding of these events is particularly indebted to Kate Fullagar, "'Savages That Are Come Among Us': Mai, Bennelong, and British Imperial Culture, 1774–1795," *The Eighteenth Century* 49, no. 3 (2008): 211–37,

and Joseph R. Roach, *Cities of the Dead: Circum-Atlantic Performance* (New York: Columbia University Press, 1996).

139 **reported in American papers**: "News from New York," *Massachusetts Centinel* (July 30, 1788): 157. The article, which seems to have been published first by the *Centinel,* was reprinted verbatim in papers including *The Cumberland Gazette, The Hampshire Chronicle,* and *The Pennsylvania Gazette.*

139 **"this young aboriginal"**: This article appeared in at least two papers under two different headlines: "Providence," *Norwich Packet* (August 7, 1788): 3; "New-York," *Pennsylvania Mercury* (August 16, 1788): 3.

139 **"a scarlet coat"**: excerpts from the journal of Susan Woodrow Lear as published in *In the Words of Women: The Revolutionary War and the Birth of the Nation, 1765–1799,* eds. Louise V. North, Janet M. Wedge, and Landa M. Freeman (Lanham, MD: Lexington Books, 2011), 239.

139 **died of pleurisy**: *Gazette of the United States* (March 28, 1792): 383.

139 **"highly cultivated"**: Van der Kemp to Mappa, as cited in Gottschalk, *Lafayette Between the American and the French Revolution,* 434. Although Gottschalk concluded that two Native Americans lived with Lafayette on the Rue de Bourbon, there appears to have been only one. A notice from Paris published in the London-based *Gentleman's Magazine* and dated January 30, 1785, announced, "The Marquis de la Fayette is returned from Philadelphia, and brought with him a young *sauvage* of twelve years old." Lafayette intended to provide the young man with "a very good education," according to the *Gentleman's Magazine and Historical Chronicle* 55 (1785): 148. Lafayette did, in fact, return with a young American whom he intended to provide with a good education, but the boy, James Edward Caldwell, was not of Native American descent.

140 **"friendly controversy"**: Louis Gottschalk, *Lady-in-Waiting: The Romance of Lafayette and Aglaé de Hunolstein* (Baltimore: Johns Hopkins Press, 1939), viii.

140 **"I shall spare you also the confession"**: *LAAR,* 1:5–6. Although the editors of *LAAR* refer to this portion of Lafayette's memoirs as "Memoir of 1779," they note that the first four pages were written in the nineteenth century. *LAAR,* 1:12.

141 **telltale letter on March 27, 1783**: A French transcript of the letter is published as Appendix III in Gottschalk, *Lady-in-Waiting,* 128–29, with a photostat of the original inserted between these pages.

141 **The author Stéphanie Félicité**: *Mémoires inédits de Madame la comtesse de Genlis sur le dix-huitième siècle et la Révolution française depuis 1756 jusqu'à nos jours,* 10 vols. (Paris: Ladvocat, 1825), 2:272. I was directed to this source by Gottschalk, *Close of the American Revolution,* 419, note 19.

141 **"pretty" and "amiable"**: Gottschalk, *Lady-in-Waiting,* 97.

141 **"just to see the portrait that I was making"**: Vigée-LeBrun, *Souvenirs,* 2:287.

142 **"Rumor has it that Monsieur the Comte"**: *Mémoires secrets,* 34:286.

CHAPTER *11*: A POLITICAL EDUCATION

145 "the Happiness of 26 millions of People": Lafayette to Washington, January 13, 1787, *PGWC*, 4:515.

146 "French Prerevolution": The term was coined by Jean Egret, *The French Pre-Revolution, 1787–1788,* trans. Wesley D. Camp (Chicago: University of Chicago Press, 1977). My understanding of this crucial period is indebted to Egret and to Vivian R. Gruder, *The Notables and the Nation: The Political Schooling of the French, 1787–1788* (Cambridge, MA: Harvard University Press, 2007).

147 "whose principles are the most": Thomas Jefferson to Edward Carrington, January 16, 1787. The Thomas Jefferson Papers, Series 1, General Correspondence, 1651–1827, Library of Congress. On Jefferson's thoughts on the Assembly of Notables, see William Howard Adams, *The Paris Years of Thomas Jefferson* (New Haven: Yale University Press, 1997), 259–69.

147 "Having a mild and timid character, uneducated": *Mémoires secrets,* 34:184–85.

148 "King's diversions": The following description of the assembly's first session is drawn from *Procès-verbal de l'Assemblée de Notables tenue à Versailles en l'année MDCCLXXXVII* (Paris: Imprimerie Royale, 1787), 32–42.

148 Measuring 120 feet long: *Mémoires secrets,* 34:147. For the details of the renovations conducted in preparation for the assembly, see Armand Brette, *Histoire des édifices où ont siégé les assemblées parlementaires de la Révolution française et de la première République* (Paris: Imprimerie Nationale, 1902), 1:19–34.

149 "any frugal-minded citizen": As translated in Jeremy D. Popkin, ed. and trans., *Panorama of Paris* (University Park: Pennsylvania State University Press, 1999), 190–91.

149 "tossing several millions": *Mémoires secrets,* 34:147.

149 "Gentlemen": The discourse pronounced by Louis XVI is reproduced in *Procès-verbal de l'Assemblée de Notables,* 42.

151 "the most remarkable effect of this convention": Jefferson to Abigail Adams, February 22, 1787, *The Writings of Thomas Jefferson, 1784–1787,* vol. 4, ed. Paul Leicester Ford (New York: Putnam, 1894), 370. On Jefferson's thoughts on the Assembly of Notables, see 259–69.

151 "that a good punster would disarm": Jefferson to Abigail Adams, February 22, 1787, Ford, *The Writings of Thomas Jefferson,* 4:370.

151 He entered its deliberations: Except where noted, my understanding of, and quotations regarding, Lafayette's participation in the second bureau are indebted to Jean Egret, "La Fayette dans la première Assemblée des Notables (février–mai 1787)," *Annales historiques de la Révolution française* 24 (1952): 1–31. Egret's analysis is based on the bureau's unpublished minutes, held at the Bibliothèque de l'Arsenal in Paris.

151 After less than a week: The bureaus completed their work on local assemblies on February 27. *Mémoires secrets,* 34:250, March 4, 1787.

152 **Lafayette also objected**: On this point, though, he was willing to compromise in the interest of moving the proposal along. Whereas eight of his bureau's members categorically rejected the idea, demanding that the provincial assemblies hew firmly to the principle of "one man, one vote," Lafayette requested only that "the rich would never have more than three or four times" as many votes as their less wealthy neighbors. Egret, "La Fayette," 6.

152 **"the most natural intermediate"**: Montesquieu, *De l'esprit des lois* (Geneva: Barrilot, 1758), book 2, chapter 4.

153 **"the people's defense and the monarchy's support"**: Brienne, cited in Egret, "La Fayette," 6.

153 **"the distinctions among citizens are necessary"**: Egret, *French Pre-Revolution*, 7.

153 **size of the deficit**: Gruder, *The Notables*, 41–42.

153 ***Compte rendu***: Jacques Necker, *Compte rendu au roi, par M. Necker, directeur général des finances, au mois de janvier 1781* (Paris: Imprimerie Royale, 1781).

154 **to Lafayette's embarrassment**: "I have been much hurt to hear that the unpaid interest of the American debt was considered as a very uncertain revenue." Lafayette to Washington, May 5, 1787, in Jared Sparks, *Correspondence of the American Revolution; Being Letters of Eminent Men to George Washington, from the Time of His Taking Command of the Army to the End of His Presidency*, 4 vols. (Boston: Little, Brown, 1853), 4:171.

154 **carried on a torrid affair**: Vigée-LeBrun, *Souvenirs*, 1:90–91.

154 **extravagant wardrobe**: On the politics of Marie Antoinette's wardrobe, see Caroline Weber, *Queen of Fashion: What Marie Antoinette Wore to the Revolution* (New York: Henry Holt, 2006).

154 **"Diamond Necklace Affair"**: For a brief but thorough discussion of the scandal, see Sarah Maza, "The Diamond Necklace Affair Revisited (1785–1786): The Case of the Missing Queen," in Dena Goodman, ed., *Marie-Antoinette: Writings on the Body of a Queen* (New York: Routledge, 2003), 73–97.

155 **"to make the king work at economies"**: The archbishop of Aix, as quoted and translated in Gruder, *The Notables*, 42.

155 **"neither this Assembly"**: *Mémoires secrets*, March 5, 1787, 34:253–54. For Castillon's original discourse, see Egret, "La Fayette," 8.

155 **"The object of the deliberation"**: Egret, "La Fayette," 8.

155 **"so useful to the nation"**: Quotes in ths paragraph are from *Mémoires secrets*, 34:301.

156 **"a siege of illness"**: Gottschalk, *Lafayette Between the American and the French Revolution*, 294.

156 **Jean Maury**: Lafayette's apothecary bills from 1787 to 1789 are found in LOC, reel 8, folder 102a.

157 **"with satisfaction that in general"**: *Procès-verbal de l'Assemblée de Notables*, 114.

157 **seven separate *réclamations***: Ibid., 180–86.

157 **"an exact record"**: Ibid., 181.

157 ***avertissement***: reprinted in Charles Alexandre de Calonne, *De l'état de la France présent et à venir* (London: 1790), 436–40.

157 "**nothing but the Avertissement**": Pierre Chevalier, ed., *Journal de l'Assemblée des Notables de 1787 par le comte de Brienne et Étienne Charles de Loménie de Brienne, archevêque de Toulouse* (Paris: Klincksieck, 1960), 43.

157 "**What could be the pretexts**": Calonne, *De l'état de la France*, 439.

158 "**misled the people**": Chevalier, *Journal de l'Assemblée des Notables*, 45.

158 "**highly disapproved**": Ibid., 44.

158 "**rigorous examination**": All quotes from Lafayette's denunciation are from the copy published in *Mémoires secrets*, April 30, 1787, 35:59–62.

159 "**has been spoken about**": *Mémoires secrets*, 35:58.

159 **restore civil rights to French Protestants**: My understanding of the Protestant cause in eighteenth-century France is indebted to Geoffrey Adams, *The Huguenots and French Opinion, 1685–1787: The Enlightenment Debate on Toleration* (Waterloo, ON: Wilfrid Laurier University Press, 1991).

160 **hopeful that the Assembly**: Lafayette to Washington, January 13, 1787, *Mémoires*, 2:191.

160 **memo**: "Arrêté pris le 24 mai et présenté au roi," *Mémoires*, 2:179–80.

160 "**a truly national assembly**": As quoted in Egret, "La Fayette," 26.

160 "**got the King to make**": Lafayette to Washington, May 5, 1787, in Sparks, *Correspondence of the American Revolution*, 4:170.

161 "**slow**": Thomas Jefferson, "Thomas Jefferson: Autobiography, 6 Jan.–29 July 1821," Founders Online, National Archives.

161 "**took the presence of the ceremonial**": Schama, *Citizens*, 263.

162 "**Government have employed**": Lafayette to Washington, May 25, 1788, Sparks, *Correspondence of the American Revolution*, 4:216.

163 **stoked by Orléans**: See George Armstrong Kelly, "The Machine of the Duc D'Orléans and the New Politics," *Journal of Modern History* 51, no. 4 (December 1979): 667–84.

CHAPTER 12: RIGHTS OF MAN

164 "**first moments**": Lafayette to Washington, January 1, 1788, Sparks, *Correspondence of the American Revolution*, 4:198–200.

165 **made its way to Lafayette**: Gottschalk, *Lafayette Between the American and the French Revolution*, 364.

165 "**keeping the good model**": Jefferson to Lafayette, February 28, 1787, Gilbert Chinard, ed., *The Letters of Lafayette and Jefferson* (Baltimore: Johns Hopkins Press, 1929), 109.

166 "**political liberty**": Montesquieu, *L'esprit des lois*, book 9, chapter 6.

166 **twelve noblemen**: Lafayette to Washington, May 25, 1788, *PGWC*, 6:295.

166 "**disgraced**": Jefferson to John Jay, August 3, 1788, *Papers of Thomas Jefferson*, 13:463.

166 "**more to save appearances**": Jefferson to Madison, January 12, 1789, *Papers of Thomas Jefferson*, 14:437.

167 "**I associate myself**": *Mémoires*, 2:183, as translated by Gottschalk, *Lafayette Between the American and the French Revolution*, 388.

167 **"try to exorcise"**: As quoted in ibid., 416.

167 **"the advantage to work a new ground"**: Lafayette to Jefferson [July 12, 1788?], as cited in ibid., 299.

167 **"a joy, mixed with uneasiness"**: Gottschalk, *Lafayette Between the American and the French Revolution*, 427.

168 **"it contains the essential principles"**: Jefferson to Madison, January 12, 1789, *Papers of Thomas Jefferson*, 14:437.

168 **"Nature has made men equal"**: Quotations in this paragraph from Lafayette's early draft of the Declaration of the Rights of Man are as translated in Chinard, *Letters of Lafayette and Jefferson*, 137.

168 **"the first declaration"**: The following discussion of the history of the various declarations of rights drafted in and before 1789 is deeply indebted to Lynn Hunt, *Inventing Human Rights: A History* (New York: Norton, 2007), 113–36.

168 **Frenchmen drafting declarations**: Condorcet offered a critique of various American declarations in his 1789 *Idées sur le despotisme, à l'usage de ceux qui prononcent ce mot sans l'entendre,* ed. Arthur Condorcet O'Connor and F. Arago (Paris: Firmin Didot, 1847), 168–70.

169 **faction of their own**: My understanding of this faction is based on Daniel L. Wick, *A Conspiracy of Well-Intentioned Men: The Society of Thirty and the French Revolution* (New York: Garland, 1987).

170 **modern-day political campaign**: On the pamphlets produced by the Society of Thirty, see Kenneth Margerison, *Pamphlets and Public Opinion: The Campaign for a Union of Orders in the Early French Revolution* (West Lafayette, IN: Purdue University Press, 1998).

170 **"the slender stock of bread-stuff"**: "Autobiography," Ford, *The Writings of Thomas Jefferson*, 1:123.

171 **"I am in great pain"**: Jefferson to Washington, May 10, 1789, *PGWP,* 2:260.

171 **On May 6, Jefferson**: Jefferson to Lafayette, May 6, 1789, Chinard, *Letters,* 125.

172 **Jean-Baptiste Réveillon**: Leonard N. Rosenband, "Jean-Baptiste Réveillon: A Man on the Make in Old Regime France," *French Historical Studies* 20, no. 3 (Summer 1997): 481–501. These events have been treated in many sources with varying inflections. See David Andress, *The French Revolution and the People* (London: Hambledon and London, 2004), 98–101; George Rudé, *The Crowd in the French Revolution* (Oxford: Oxford University Press, 1967); and Simon Schama, *Citizens.*

172 **"Blood flowed in the Faubourg St-Antoine"**: Marquis de Ferrières, *Correspondance inédite (1789, 1790, 1791)* (Paris: Armand Colin, 1932), 37–38.

173 **"moderation"**: Writing from Chavaniac when he was standing for election as a representative to the Estates-General, Lafayette had reported that he had "preached moderation" in preelection discussions with his would-be constituents. Lafayette [to Madame de Simaine?], March 8, 1789, *Mémoires,* 2:240.

173 **"a composite of great principles"**: Louis Gottschalk and Margaret Maddox,

Lafayette in the French Revolution Through the October Days (Chicago: University of Chicago Press, 1969), 37.

174 **Estates-General would be stormy**: Ferrières to Madame de Ferrières, between April 30 and May 4, 1789, Ferrières, *Correspondance*, 40.

174 **"The orders are neither in accord"**: Ferrières to Madame de Ferrières, May 15, 1789, Ferrières, *Correspondance*, 47. On the divisions within each order in April and May 1789, see Timothy Tackett, *Becoming a Revolutionary: The Deputies of the French National Assembly and the Emergence of a Revolutionary Culture (1789–1790)* (University Park: Pennsylvania State University Press, 2006), chapter 4, "The Creation of the National Assembly," 119–48.

174 **As the Marquis de Ferrières described**: The following description is based on Ferrières to Madame de Ferrières, May 6, 1789, Ferrières, *Correspondance*, 41–46.

174 **procession**: This description is based on Ferrières, *Correspondance*, 42–45.

174 **"thro a double row"**: Anne Cary Morris, ed., *The Diary and Letters of Gouverneur Morris*, 2 vols. (New York, 1888), 1:66.

175 **"Consort received"**: Morris, *Diary,* 1:67.

176 **"the odious details"**: Jules Michelet, *Historical View of the French Revolution: From Its Earliest Indications to the Flight of the King in 1791,* trans. C. Cocks (London: Bohn, 1864), 87.

177 **As early as May 6**: Edna Hindie Lemay, *Dictionnaire des constituants, 1789–1791,* 2 vols. (Paris: Universitas, 1991), 2:694.

177 **On the one hand**: Lafayette was hardly the only deputy grappling with this question, as discussed in Robert H. Blackman, "What Does a Deputy to the National Assembly Owe His Constituents? Coming to an Agreement on the Meaning of Electoral Mandates in July 1789," *French Historical Studies* 34, no. 2 (Spring 2011): 205–41.

177 **For a time, Lafayette considered**: *Mémoires,* 2:309–10. Morris, who dined with Lafayette on Tuesday, June 23, wrote that Lafayette "is determined to resign his Seat, which Step I approve of because the Instructions by which he is bound are contrary to his Conscience." Morris, *Diary,* 1:121.

177 **"nineteen twentieths"**: As quoted in William Doyle, *Oxford History of the French Revolution* (Oxford: Oxford University Press, 1989), 104.

178 **"nothing can prevent it"**: July 22, 1789, Ferrières, *Correspondance*, 71.

178 **"At nineteen, I dedicated"**: *Mémoires,* 2:308.

178 **"I have tried everything"**: Ibid., 2:309.

179 **Tens of thousands**: On May 27, Morris wrote in his diary, "Meet Monsr. de Durfort who tells me the Number of Troops in the Neighbourhood of Paris is to prevent Tumult if the States General are dissolved." Morris, *Diary,* 1:93.

179 **"very serious Events"**: Morris, *Diary,* 1:128.

179 **"the Soldiery in this City"**: Morris to John Jay, July 1, 1789, Morris, *Diary,* 1:129. All quotes in this paragraph are from the same letter, Morris, *Diary,* 1: 129–31.

180 **"very humble address"**: July 8, 1789, *AP,* 8:210.

180 "the liberty and honor of the National Assembly": Ibid.

180 "the danger, Sire, threatens the tasks": July 9, 1789, *AP,* 8:213.

180 "caused the greatest stir in the Assembly": Ibid., 8:212.

180 relocated to a more remote town: Morris, *Diary,* 1:142.

180 "are very angry with me": Lafayette to Jefferson, n.d., Chinard, *Letters,* 135.

180 "They tell me that the head": Lafayette to Madame de Simiane [?], July 11, 1789, *Mémoires,* 2:313. In identifying letters as directed to Madame de Simiane, I am following the lead of Louis Gottschalk, who presumes that letters published with no recipient identified were edited by Lafayette's descendants who wished to cleanse the historical record.

181 thirty-man committee charged with determining: Lafayette was not a member of the committee. For the complete membership, see Lemay, *Dictionnaire,* Appendix II. 7 (a), 2:954–55.

181 Jean-Joseph Mounier: Lemay, *Dictionnaire,* 2:703–5, esp. 704.

181 "The goal of all societies": *AP,* 8:216.

181 "seize the favorable moment": Ibid., 8:215.

181 "to consider it again": Chinard, *Letters of Lafayette and Jefferson,* 135.

181 Annotations to a copy of the text: Gottschalk and Maddox, *Lafayette in the French Revolution: Through the October Days,* 89, note 52.

181 Lafayette's final copy jettisons: I am indebted to Gottschalk and Maddox, *Lafayette in the French Revolution: Through the October Days,* 90, for this interpretation.

182 In earlier drafts: See Keith Michael Baker, "The Idea of a Declaration of Rights," in *The French Idea of Freedom: The Old Regime and the Declaration of Rights of 1789,* ed. Dale Van Kley (Stanford: Stanford University Press, 1994), 162–63.

182 "be the first to present them to you": July 11, 1789, *AP,* 8:222.

182 "incalculable": Ibid., 8:223.

183 gradual relaxation of censorship laws: In his classic study of the subject, Jeremy Popkin notes that the gradual liberation of the press began on July 5, 1788, when "Brienne lifted the censorship restrictions and encouraged all authors to publish their ideas about how the Estates-General should proceed," and continued through July 1789. Jeremy D. Popkin, *Revolutionary News: The Press in France, 1789–1799* (Durham: Duke University Press, 1990), 25ff.

183 "Its author speaks of liberty": *Journal de Paris* (July 13, 1789): 875.

183 American market: On French-American commerce in this period, see Peter P. Hill, *French Perceptions of the Early American Republic, 1783–1793,* Memoirs of the American Philosophical Society, vol. 180 (Philadelphia: American Philosophical Society, 1988). On American newspaper response to the events of 1789, see Beatrice F. Hyslop, "The American Press and the French Revolution of 1789," *Proceedings of the American Philosophical Society* 104, no. 1 (February 1960): 54–85.

183 "M. Lally was so delighted with the speech": "Marquis de La Fayette," *Massachusetts Centinel* (September 30, 1789): 17.

184 "**to the Marquis de La Fayette**": "London, August 8," ibid., 18.

184 **Thanks to an aide**: The reading of Lafayette's Declaration of Rights is described in Jean-Sylvain Bailly and Honoré Duveyrier, *Procès-verbal des séances et délibérations de l'Assemblée générale des électeurs de Paris, réunis à l'Hôtel-de-Ville le 14 juillet 1789*, 3 vols. (Paris: Baudoin, 1790), 1:166–67.

CHAPTER 13: A STORYBOOK HERO

185 "**breaking open the Armorers's Shops**": Morris, *Diary*, 1:145.

186 **waxworks gallery**: David McCallam, "Waxing Revolutionary: Reflections on a Raid on a Waxworks at the Outbreak of the French Revolution," *French History* 16, no. 2 (June 2002): 153–73.

187 **his carriage approached**: On the lethal event that Morris happened upon, see Paul G. Spagnoli, "The Revolution Begins: Lambesc's Charge, 12 July 1789," *French Historical Studies* 17, no. 2 (Fall 1991): 466–97.

187 **every room, corridor, stairway**: Bailly and Duveyrier, *Procès-verbal*, 1:184.

187 "**as trophies**": Ibid., 1:186.

188 "**a storybook hero**": Jean-Antoine-Nicolas de Caritat, Marquis de Condorcet, *Mémoires de Condorcet, sur la Révolution française, extraits de sa correspondance et de celles de ses amis,* 2 vols. (Paris: Ponthieu, 1824), 2:53.

189 "**I have already made known**": *AP,* 8:220.

189 "**I have nothing to add**": Ibid., 8:234.

189 **Paris electors were holed up**: The electors' rise to power is summarized in Henry E. Bourne, "Improvising a Government in Paris, July, 1789," *American Historical Review* 10, no. 2 (January 1905): 284–89.

189 "**wearing on their faces**": Bailly and Duveyrier, *Procès-verbal*, 266.

189 **the entire populace seemed ready**: The following description of the events of July 14 are based on Bailly and Duveyrier, *Procès-verbal*, 271–381.

189 "**a countless multitude**": Bailly and Duveyrier, *Procès-verbal*, 271.

189 "**carts of flour, wheat, wine**": Ibid., 272.

190 "**perfidy**": Ibid., 313.

190 "**a deputation is no longer**": Ibid., 334.

191 "**Is it a revolt?**": Lemay, *Dictionnaire*, 2:536.

191 "**the cause of the people**": *Mémoires*, 2:55.

192 "**the defense of French liberty**": Bailly and Duveyrier, *Procès-verbal*, 422.

192 **around two in the afternoon**: Details of the number of carriages and time of departure are given in Gottschalk and Maddox, *Lafayette in the French Revolution: Through the October Days*, 109. The names of all the deputies in the contingent are listed in Bailly and Duveyrier, *Procès-verbal*, 447–49.

192 "**filled with that eloquence**": Bailly and Duveyrier, *Procès-verbal*, 450.

192 "**congratulated the Assembly**": Ibid.

192 "**all the voices joined**": Ibid., 460.

CHAPTER 14: "I REIGN IN PARIS"

193 **"I reign in Paris"**: Lafayette to Madame de Simiane [?], July 16, 1789, *Mémoires*, 2:317.

193 **the queen had arranged**: Madame Campan, *Mémoires*, 272.

194 **gang of vagabonds**: Ferrières, *Correspondance*, 150.

194 **"I bring your Majesty"**: As translated in *European Magazine and London Review* (July 1789): 81. English sources consistently place Bailly in the Hôtel de Ville at the time of the speech, but Bailly indicates that the speech was given at the first meeting place: Jean-Sylvain Bailly, *Mémoires d'un témoin de la Révolution*, 3 vols. (Paris: 1804), 2:58.

194 **two royal carriages**: Bailly, *Mémoires*, 2:63.

194 **streets lined with tens of thousands**: Morris, *Diary*, 1:152–53. Estimated numbers vary: Jefferson reported 60,000 men; Morris, 80,000; Bailly, 200,000; and Ferrières, an astonishing 500,000. Jefferson to John Jay, July 19, 1789, *The Diplomatic Correspondence of the United States of America, from the Signing of the Definitive Treaty of Peace, 10th September, 1783, to the Adoption of the Constitution, March 4, 1789*, 3 vols. (Washington, DC: Blair and Rives, 1837), 2:308; Morris, *Diary*, 1:171; Bailly, *Mémoires*, 61; and Ferrières, *Correspondance*, 1:151.

194 **"pikes, pruning hooks, scythes"**: Jefferson to John Jay, July 19, 1789, *Diplomatic Correspondence*, 2:308.

195 **"the utmost of his Wishes"**: Morris to Washington, July 31, 1789, Morris, *Diary*, 1:171.

195 **"turned himself over"**: July 24 or 25, 1789, *Mémoires*, 2:322.

196 **"If the king refuses"**: Ibid., 2:321–22.

196 **Jacques-Pierre Brissot**: For two different interpretations of Brissot's prerevolutionary career, see Robert Darnton, *The Literary Underground of the Old Regime* (Cambridge, MA: Harvard University Press, 1982), 41–70; Frederick A. de Luna, "The Dean Street Style of Revolution: J.-P. Brissot, *Jeune Philosophe*," *French Historical Studies* 17, no. 1 (Spring 1991): 159–90; and Darnton's reply to de Luna, "The Brissot Dossier," *French Historical Studies* 17, no. 1 (Spring 1991): 191–205.

196 **"without the Gazettes"**: "Prospectus," *Patriote français* (April 1, 1789): 2.

196 **praise of Lafayette's plans**: For example, "Hôtel-de-Ville," *Patriote français* (July 28, 1789): 4; "Suite du plan d'organisation du milice de Paris," *Patriote français* (August 4, 1789): 1.

196 **"a stunning fortune"**: "Détails. Du Mercredi, 23 juillet," *Révolutions de Paris*: 22. The summary execution of Foulon and his son-in-law are recounted with remarkably little variation by Jean-Sylvain Bailly, *Mémoires*, 2:276–305; Ferrières, *Correspondance*, 155–60; *Mémoires*, 2:274–79, and *Révolutions de Paris*.

197 **"obliges me to speak"**: Lafayette's speech as reported by Bailly, *Mémoires*, 2:290–91.

198 **"the justice of the ideas"**: *Journal de Paris* (July 25, 1789): 924.

198 **"turn into fury"**: Bailly, *Mémoires*, 2:293.

198 **"it was reattached"**: *Révolutions de Paris*, 1, no. 11 (July 18–July 25, 1789): 20.

198 **omitted from the series of prints**: Charlotte Hould, ed., *La Révolution par la gravure: Les Tableaux historiques de la Révolution française; une entreprise éditoriale d'information et sa diffusion en Europe (1791–1817)*, exhibit catalog (Vizille: Musée de la Révolution française, 2002).

199 **"Passive discontent"**: Lafayette to Washington, May 25, 1788, *PGWC*, 6:292.

199 **"the people did not heed"**: *Mémoires*, 2:281.

199 **"What to do?"**: *Mémoires*, 2:320.

200 **"the night the Old Regime"**: See Michael P. Fitzsimmons, *The Night the Old Regime Ended: August 4, 1789, and the French Revolution* (University Park: Pennsylvania State University Press, 2002), for a full account of the day's events and significance.

200 **sweeping resolutions**: *AP,* 8:420.

200 **Vicomte de Noailles and the Duc d'Aiguillon**: Ibid., 8:413–14.

200 **Vicomte de Beauharnais**: The representative from Orléans, he was the first husband of Joséphine Tascher de la Pagerie, who, as the wife of Napoleon Bonaparte, reigned as empress of France. On Beauharnais's political career, see Lemay, *Dictionnaire*, 1:69–71.

200 **"all ecclesiastical, civil, and military posts"**: *AP,* 8:346.

200 **"a curse"**: Jean-Baptiste-Joseph de Lubersac, bishop of Chartres, *AP,* 8:346; Lemay, *Dictionnaire*, 2:608–9.

200 **"It would have been useless"**: Ferrierès to Monsieur de Rabreuil, August 7, 1789, Ferrières, *Correspondance*, 116.

201 **"Restorer of French liberty"**: *AP,* 8:350.

202 **the Parisian bakers' guild**: Morris, *Diary,* 1:230.

202 **"casting about for the Ways and Means"**: Ibid., 1:237.

202 **"plunging himself into Debts"**: Ibid., 1:229.

202 **"All hell has conspired"**: Lafayette to [Madame de Simiane?], August [?] 1789, *Mémoires*, 2:322.

202 **"rainy disagreeable Day"**: Morris, *Diary,* 1:240.

203 **"canine appetite for popularity"**: Jefferson to James Madison, January 30, 1787. The Thomas Jefferson Papers, Series 1, General Correspondence, Library of Congress, Washington, DC.

203 **"orgy"**: See, for example, *Révolutions de Paris* 1, no. 13 (October 3–10): 6 and *Patriote français* (October 6, 1789): 2.

203 **broke bread together**: Campan, *Mémoires*, 287.

203 **"joy and jubilation"**: The following discussion of events involving black cockades is given in *Révolutions de Paris* 1, no. 13 (October 3–10): 5–6. All quotations are from these pages.

204 **Lafayette refused to sanction**: This paragraph presents the events as recounted in Gottschalk and Maddox, *Lafayette in the French Revolution: Through the October Days*, 329–51; Sigismond Lacroix, ed., *Actes de la Commune de Paris pendant la Révolution* (New York: AMS, 1973), 2:165–82; and *Mémoires*, 2:329–46. There are nearly as many accounts of the day as there

were people present. Although details vary, the broad outlines given here are consistent with other credible versions.

205 **thirty thousand armed**: Barry M. Shapiro, *Revolutionary Justice in Paris, 1789–1790* (Cambridge: Cambridge University Press, 1993), 86, places the number of protesters between 30,000 and 35,000. The day's weather is described in Morris, *Diary,* 1:244.

205 **Madame Campan**: Except where noted, my description of the events as seen from Versailles is based on Campan, *Mémoires,* 289–98.

205 **royal household leapt into action**: Campan, *Mémoires,* 562, note 144.

205 **the first Parisian women**: The number of women is given in Henriette Lucie Dillon, Marquise de La Tour du Pin Gouvernet, *Mémoires de la marquise de La Tour du Pin: Journal d'une femme de cinquante ans, 1778–1815: Suivis d'extraits inédits* (Paris: Mercure de France, 1989), 136.

206 **"the moment to flee was lost"**: Campan, *Mémoires,* 291.

206 **"marched by Compulsion"**: Morris, *Diary,* 1:243.

206 **drums and the flicker of torches**: Gottschalk and Maddox, *Lafayette in the French Revolution: Through the October Days,* 349.

206 **"the nation, the law, and the king"**: *Mémoires,* 2:339.

206 **"saw his approach with pleasure"**: Ibid., 2:338.

206 **"Long live the King!"**: *Courrier de Versailles* (October 8, 1789): 109.

206 **Place d'Armes around midnight**: La Tour du Pin Gouvernet, *Mémoires,* 139.

207 **"instead of being a guardian"**: *Mémoires,* 2:339.

207 **"Sire, I thought it better"**: La Tour du Pin Gouvernet, *Mémoires,* 140.

207 **Daybreak found Lafayette**: The following description comes from *Mémoires,* 2:341. It is the only source that places Lafayette on the balcony with the queen; Madame Campan, for instance, has Marie Antoinette appearing alone, her "eyes and hands lifted toward the sky" as she steps onto the balcony "like a sacrificial victim" (Campan, *Mémoires,* 295). Gottschalk and Maddox address the discrepancy in Appendix IV, "Did Lafayette Kiss the Queen's Hand?"; they conclude that the balcony scene probably did unfold more or less as Lafayette described it (Gottschalk and Maddox, *Lafayette in the French Revolution: Through the October Days,* 398–99).

CHAPTER 15: TRIUMPH

209 **"Many people averred"**: Campan, *Mémoires,* 294.

209 **A pamphlet spelled out**: On the rumor, see "Nouveaux indices de conjuration. D'un libelle intitulé: Domine salvum fac regem. Avis au peuple," *Révolutions de Paris,* 15:29–30.

210 **"charged by His Majesty"**: "Versailles," *Patriote français* (October 15, 1789): 1.

210 **"I would have denounced"**: Lafayette to Mounier, October 23, 1789, *Mémoires,* 2:416.

210 **Orléans did not call his bluff**: Shapiro, *Revolutionary Justice,* 84–96, esp. 96.

210 **decamped for England**: "Paris," *Patriote français* (October 16, 1789): 2.

210 **weighed heavily on Lafayette**: *Mémoires,* 2:427–29, 431–32, 475–79.

210 "as his enemy": Ibid., 2:430.

210 "provisioning of the capital": Reported in "Paris," *Patriote français* (October 10, 1789): 4. As translated by Louis Gottschalk and Margaret Maddox, *Lafayette in the French Revolution: From the October Days Through the Federation* (Chicago: University of Chicago Press, 1973), 6–7.

210 "Lafayette and Liberty": *Courrier de Versailles* (October 8, 1789): 109.

210 "the champion of liberty": Ibid., October 12, 1789, 158.

211 English-language books: Two commissioners appointed by the municipality to inventory the books in the library of "the émigré Lafayette" on May 2, 1794, found these, among some 230 books and maps. This is in pointed contrast to the books inventoried in Lafayette's office at the Hôtel de Ville, which were almost entirely in French or Latin, with the majority on religious subjects. One study of the libraries seized from twenty-six key figures found books on American topics in several collections but termed Lafayette's library "the extreme illustration." Agnès Marcetteau-Paul and Dominique Varry, "Les bibliothèques de quelques acteurs de la Révolution, de Louis XVI à Robespierre," *Mélanges de la Bibliothèque de la Sorbonne* 9 (1989), 200–201.

211 "Minister and Soldier": Morris, *Diary,* 1:252.

211 "Men do not go into Administration": Ibid., 1:252–53.

212 1785 Salon: On the painting, see Laura Auricchio, *Adélaïde Labille-Guiard: Artist in the Age of Revolution* (Los Angeles: J. Paul Getty Museum, 2009), 39–40. On the Comtesse de Flahaut, see Marie-José Fassiotto, "La Comtesse de Flahaut et son cercle: un exemple de salon politique sous la Révolution," *Studies on Voltaire and the Eighteenth Century* 303 (1992): 344–48.

212 "La Fayette has no fixed Plan": Morris, *Diary,* 1:283.

212 "whole army was devoted to him": Campan, *Mémoires,* 291.

212 "Why, Citizens!": Extract from the pamphlet *Quand aurons-nous du pain?* as quoted in *Courrier de Versailles à Paris et de Paris à Versailles* (October 12, 1789), 95:151–53.

213 "inciting an ignorant, cowardly": Popkin, *Revolutionary News,* 146–51; quotes as translated on 146–47.

213 "a vile and accursed man": *Courrier de Versailles,* 136.

213 "no man may be disturbed": As quoted and translated by Gottschalk and Maddox, *Lafayette in the French Revolution: Through the October Days,* 86.

213 "the communications of his thoughts": *Mémoires,* 2:252–53.

214 Marat had gone so far: On freedom of the press in September and October 1789, see Shapiro, *Revolutionary Justice,* 99–103, and Charles Walton, *Policing Public Opinion in the French Revolution* (New York: Oxford University Press, 2009), 97–99.

214 He responded in his favorite venue: Charles Vellay, ed., *La correspondance de Marat: Recueillie et annotée* (Paris: Eugène Fasquelle, 1908), 118–19.

214 "festivals of federation": The most thorough account of the event is provided by Mona Ozouf, *Festivals and the French Revolution,* trans. Alan Sheridan (Cambridge, MA: Harvard University Press, 1988), 33–60. My understanding of the day is equally indebted to Schama, *Citizens,* 500–513.

215 **"Messieurs"**: *AP,* 16:117.

215 **"our brothers to come, as deputies"**: Ibid., 16:118.

216 **"citizens of all ages"**: Ibid., 16:119.

217 **the citizens of Paris were unable to tame**: The following description is based on Louis-Sébastien Mercier, *Paris pendant la Révolution (1789–1798); ou, Le nouveau Paris,* 2 vols. (Paris: Poulet-Malassis, 1862), 1:66–72; the quotes are on p. 69.

217 **anonymous society of artists**: *Affiches, annonces, et avis divers* (July 12, 1790): 2038.

218 **Advertisements for products**: Ibid., July 17, 1790, 2097–98.

218 **"large and comfortable house"**: Ibid., July 11, 1790, 2025.

218 **no-frills seats**: Ibid., July 12, 1790, 2038.

218 **"Paris, like Boston"**: "Comédie Française," *Révolutions de Paris* (July 10–17, 1790), 53:40.

218 **"musical drama"**: *Affiches, annonces, et avis divers* (July 10, 1790): 2019.

218 **priced at double the usual cost**: "Fédération du 14 juillet," *Révolutions de Paris* (July 10–17 1790), 53:11.

218 **sodden affair**: "Variétés," *Chronique de Paris* (July 16, 1790): 785.

219 **opening procession alone**: The order of ceremonies, including the list of groups participating in the procession, is published as "Proclamation du roi, concernant l'ordre à observer le 14 juillet, jour de la Fédération générale," *Chronique de Paris* (July 13, 1790): 773–74.

219 **"triumph of human kind"**: Helen Maria Williams, *Letters Written in France, in the Summer of 1790, to a Friend in England* (London: T. Cadell, 1791), 14.

219 **"Ten thousand of them"**: "Fêtes publiques," *Révolutions de Paris* 5, no. 54 (July 17–24, 1790): 52.

219 **due to the rain**: "Fédération du 14 juillet," Ibid. 5, no. 53 (July 10–17, 1790): 8–9.

220 **"seemed to have taken full possession"**: William Short to Gouverneur Morris, July 27, 1790, as published in Morris, *Diary,* 1:565–67.

220 **opened the ground floor**: William Short to Thomas Jefferson, July 16, 1790, Thomas Jefferson Papers.

220 **"who is so justly the idol"**: Williams believed that "aristocrats" may have wheedled into the crowd of admirers with the intention of harming Lafayette under cover of the crowd. Williams, *Letters,* 17. *Révolutions de Paris* reports the same event without the sinister overtones.

220 **"the air of the general"**: The description of the Palais-Royal is from Short to Morris, July 27, 1790, Morris, *Diary,* 1:565. The quote about Lafayette is from "Détails du 10 au 17 juillet 1790," *Révolutions de Paris* 5, no. 53 (July 10–17, 1790): 13.

221 **transparency of his likeness**: Williams, *Letters,* 21.

221 **"all the editions"**: "Détails du 10 au 17 juillet 1790," *Révolutions de Paris* 5, no. 53 (July 10–17, 1790): 13.

CHAPTER 16: UNFLATTERING PORTRAITS

222 **"the zenith"**: William Short to Gouverneur Morris, July 27, 1790, as published in Morris, *Diary,* 1:565–67.

222 **Bouillé had sworn allegiance:** See François-Claude-Amour de Bouillé, *Mémoires du Marquis de Bouillé* (Paris: Baudouin Frères, 1821), 122.

222 **"If I love liberty"**: Lafayette to Bouillé, May 20, 1790, *Mémoires,* 2:461.

222 **"let us serve it"**: Ibid.

223 **"Revolts among the Regiments"**: Lafayette to Washington, August 23, 1790, *PGWP.*

223 **pamphlet:** The full French title of the pamphlet, which is available at the Archives Nationales, the New York Public Library, and elsewhere, is *Vie Privée, Impartiale, Politique, Militaire et Domestique, du Marquis de La Fayette, Général des Bleuets, Pour servir de Supplément à la Nécrologie des Hommes célèbres du dix-huitième siècle, et de clef aux Révolutions Françaises et Américaines. Dédiée aux soixante districts de Paris. Ornée de son Portrait.* À Paris, de l'Imprimerie particulière de M. de Bastide, Président du District de Saint-Roch, en 1790.

223 **bookseller was arrested:** "Le Procès encommencé contre le S Le Normand, Imprimeur prévenu d'avoir imprimé en partie l'écrit intitulé *Vie privée et impartiale, politique, militaire et domestique du Marquis de La Fayette,*" Archives Nationales Y/10509. Inventaires des procès pour crimes de lèse-nation instruits au Châtelet 1789–90. "Procédure au sujet du libelle intitulé *Vie privée et impartiale, politique, militaire et domestique du Marquis de La Fayette,*" Archives Nationales, BB/30/160.

223 **"Continue to adore"**: Cloquet, *Souvenirs sur la vie privée,* iv–v.

224 **he expressed hope:** *Mémoires,* 3:137–40.

224 **"a Declaration that"**: Morris, *Diary,* 1:570.

224 **"agree to consult"**: "Lettre du Roi au Général Lafayette," as published in *Mémoires,* 2:496.

225 **"without discussion and unanimously"**: *AP* 18, 93.

225 **garrison town of Nancy:** My understanding of the *affaire de Nancy* is indebted to Samuel F. Scott, "Problems of Law and Order During 1790, the 'Peaceful' Year of the French Revolution," *American Historical Review* 80, no. 4 (October 1975): 865–71. Except where noted, the following discussion is based on Scott's work.

225 **assembly authorized Bouillé:** The *affaire de Nancy* receives little attention in the English-language literature on Lafayette. Gottschalk's final volume ends with the federation, and more recent American texts tend to minimize the event. For a fuller discussion of Lafayette's role in the *affaire de Nancy,* see the French literature, especially Charavay, *La Fayette,* 240–47.

225 **"The decree concerning Nancy"**: Lafayette to Bouillé, August 18, 1790, Bouillé, *Mémoires,* 134.

226 **called for an inquiry:** See Charavay, *La Fayette,* 243–44.

226 **ninety-four bodies:** These figures are based on the report presented to the

National Assembly by a royal commission charged with investigating the matter on October 14, 1790, and published in *AP,* 19:616–35. For Bouillé's version of events, see Bouillé, *Mémoires,* 145–72. Bouillé declines to estimate the number of dead at Nancy but is in rough agreement with the commissioners in his summary of the soldiers' punishment.

226 **Marat reached the peak:** Charavay, *La Fayette,* 245.

226 **"pretending to pass":** "Lettre à Lafayette," *L'ami du peuple* (September 15, 1790): 222, reprinted in Vellay, *Correspondance,* 182.

227 **"That you, a mature and educated man":** Vellay, *Correspondance,* 183.

227 **"the name of Lafayette":** As quoted in Charavay, *La Fayette,* 246. Charavay, in turn, quotes from François-Alphonse Aulard, *La société des Jacobins: Recueil de documents pour l'histoire du club des Jacobins de Paris* (Paris: 1888–97; repr., New York: AMS Press, 1973), 1:295.

227 **"the art of circumspection":** Brissot to Lafayette, April 30, 1787, as quoted and translated by Shapiro, *Revolutionary Justice,* 18–19.

227 **"with regret":** *Patriote français,* September 1, 1790, 2.

228 **"swear a new oath":** *Révolutions de Paris* 5, no. 61 (September 4–11): 419.

228 **"It is M. de Lafayette":** *Révolutions de Paris* 5, no. 62 (September 11–18, 1790): 489.

228 **Lafayette's maneuvers:** *Révolutions de Paris* 5, no. 62 (September 11–18, 1790): 487.

228 **Black draperies:** This description is based on *Patriote français* (September 22, 1790): 4, and *Révolutions de Paris* 5, no. 63 (September 18–25, 1790): 531.

229 **"seeming to accuse":** *Révolutions de Paris* 5, no. 63 (September 18–25, 1790): 532.

229 **"Everything goes from bad to worse":** Marie Antoinette to Comte de Mercy, July 12, 1790, as reproduced in Maxime de la Rocheterie and Marquis de Beaucourt, eds., *Lettres de Marie-Antoinette: recueil des lettres authentiques de la reine,* 2 vols. (Paris: Picard, 1895), 2:177–79, quote on p. 178. First-person accounts of Marie Antoinette are notoriously unreliable, as are compilations of her letters, which are filled with fictions and forgeries. However, the volumes cited here are generally considered authentic.

229 **pornographic prints:** The pornographic texts and images that derided Marie Antoinette have received a considerable amount of attention from scholars since the 1980s. See for example, Dena Goodman, ed., *Marie-Antoinette: Writings on the Body of a Queen* (New York: Routledge, 2003).

229 **"What double rapture!":** *Bordel patriotique institué par la Reine des François pour les plaisirs des Députés à la nouvelle Législation* (Paris: 1791), 35. Through the process of elimination, Dena Goodman concluded that this pamphlet was produced by the Orléanists: nearly every other rival for power in 1791 comes under attack from the pornographer's pen. Lynn Hunt, "Pornography in the French Revolution," in *The Invention of Pornography: Obscenity and the Origins of Modernity, 1500–1800,* Lynn Hunt, ed. (New York: Zone Books, 1993), 316.

230 **"thrust ahead":** *Bordel patriotique,* 35. The verb used is *enfoncer,* which

means both to drive something in (such as a nail) and, in a military context, to vanquish.

233 *"la poule d'autruche"*: Because spelling was not yet standardized, the letters *i* and *y* are frequently used interchangeably, as in *autriche* and *autryche,* both of which mean Austria.

235 **"Neither Phidias nor Scopas nor Praxiteles"**: *The Priapus Poems: Erotic Epigrams from Ancient Rome,* trans. Richard W. Hooper (Champaign: University of Illinois Press, 1999), 54.

236 **Marquis de Favras**: On the "Favras Conspiracy," see Shapiro, *Revolutionary Justice,* 124–47.

237 **He kept a locksmith busy**: LOC, reel 6, folder 42.

CHAPTER 17: DOWNFALLS

238 **Cannon fire**: This description of the morning of June 21 is based on the report given in "Assemblée Nationale," *L'ami du roi* (June 22, 1791): 689. My discussion of the events of June 1791 is deeply indebted to Timothy Tackett, *When the King Took Flight* (Cambridge, MA: Harvard University Press, 2003).

238 **rumors swirled**: Lafayette gives his version of events in *Mémoires,* 3:73–102.

238 **In the chamber**: *AP,* 27:358–97.

238 **Alexandre de Beauharnais**: Ibid., 27:361.

239 **Soon, Lafayette himself was**: *Mémoires,* 3:79.

239 **"an attack"**: *AP,* 27:370.

239 **"Declaration of the King"**: Ibid., 27:378.

240 **"by special decree"**: Ibid., 27:382.

240 **"that services rendered"**: Ibid., 27:379.

240 **"Come back"**: Ibid., 27:383.

240 **"a satire of the Revolution"**: *Révolutions de Paris* 8, no. 102 (June 18–25, 1791): 546.

240 **"The Declaration written in the hand"**: Ferrières, *Correspondance,* 368.

240 ***L'ami du roi***: *L'ami des français, de l'ordre, et sur-tout de la vérité* (June 22, 1791), 173:689. On June 30, the paper reclaimed the title *L'ami du roi.*

240 **at least since March**: Campan, *Mémoires,* 338.

240 ***nécessaire de voyage***: Ibid., 339.

240 **twelve battalions and twenty-three squadrons**: Bouillé, *Mémoires,* 237.

241 **suspicions of local citizens**: Tackett, *When the King Took Flight,* 69.

241 **"happily"**: Bouillé, *Mémoires,* 240.

241 **added to the passenger list**: Tackett, *When the King Took Flight,* 59.

242 **Lafayette's carriage**: *Memoirs of the Duchess de Tourzel, Governess to the Children of France During the Years 1789, 1790, 1791, 1792, 1793 and 1795,* 2 vols. (London: Remington, 1886), 1:323.

242 **"then looking at his watch"**: Ibid., 1:329.

242 **rode into Sainte-Menehould**: "Lettre des officiers municipaux de Sainte-Menehould à l'Assemblée nationale," June 22, 1791, *AP,* 27:424.

242 **As Drouet told**: Jean-Baptiste Drouet, *Récit fait par M. Drouet, maître de*

poste à Ste Menehould, de la manière dont il a reconnu le roi, et a été cause de son arrestation à Varennes: Honneurs rendus à ce citoyen et à deux de ses camarades (Paris: Imprimerie du Journal des Clubs, 1791), 2.

243 **circumventing Reims:** Bouillé, *Mémoires,* 192.

244 **raced to the town:** This account summarizes Drouet, *Récit.*

244 **"Here is my wife":** Drouet, *Récit,* 6.

244 **"Monsieur the Commander General":** *Révolutions de Paris* 8, no. 102 (June 18–25, 1791): 535.

244 **"Flesselle and Delaunay":** Ibid., 102:538.

244 **loyalty of Lafayette:** On June 23, Lafayette would lead a crowd of National Guardsman into the assembly hall to swear an oath reaffirming their commitment to the nation's freedom. *Mémoires,* 3:86–87.

244 **"is criminal or imbecile":** *Révolutions de Paris* 8, no. 102 (June 18–25, 1791): 532.

244 **a messenger arrived:** *AP,* 27:446–47.

245 **"Does Your Majesty":** *Mémoires,* 3:92.

245 **"issued orders that no honors":** Joseph-Thomas d'Espinchal, *Journal d'émigration du Comte d'Espinchal* (Paris, Perrin, 1912), 241.

245 **"at the head":** Bouillé to National Assembly, letter dated June 26, 1791, *AP,* 27:602.

245 **"calumny":** *AP,* 27:671.

245 **"happily for him":** *Mémoires,* 3:79.

245 **When the sun rose:** Sunrise and sunset are given in *Chronique de Paris* (July 17, 1791), 198:799. The following discussion of the social, political, and economic divisions roiling Paris is indebted to David Andress, *Massacre at the Champ de Mars: Popular Dissent and Political Culture in the French Revolution* (Woodbridge, UK: Boydell Press for the Royal Historical Society, 2000), and David Andress, "The Denial of Social Conflict in the French Revolution: Discourses Around the Champ de Mars Massacre, 17 July 1791," *French Historical Studies* 22, no. 2 (Spring 1999): 183–209.

245 **tens of thousands of men:** Andress, "Denial of Social Conflict," 192–93.

246 **clearing Louis XVI:** This discussion is based on Tackett, *When the King Took Flight,* 137–42.

246 **"all the firebrands of the capital":** Ferrières to Madame de Ferrières, July 20, 1791, Ferrières, *Correspondance,* 395.

246 **"much Heat":** Gouverneur Morris to Robert Morris, July 16, 1791, Morris, *Diary,* 2:220.

247 **"the principles that dictated":** *AP,* 28:372.

247 **The violence began before noon:** This description of the uncontested moments of the event is based on Andress, *Massacre,* 4–6; *Mémoires,* 3:103–9; and Tackett, *When the King Took Flight,* 145–50.

247 **renewed their demand:** *AP,* 28:380–81.

247 **"were I to be a victim":** Ibid., 28:380.

248 **"hailstorm of rocks":** *Mémoires,* 3:106.

248 **Albert Mathiez:** The following details are found in Albert Mathiez, *Le club*

des Cordeliers pendant la crise de Varennes et le massacre du Champ de Mars
(Paris: Champion, 1910), 146–52.

249 **"Patriot's Saint Bartholomew's day"**: Mathiez, *Cordeliers,* 152.

249 **"Blood flowed"**: *Révolutions de Paris* 9, no. 106 (July 16–23, 1791): 53.

251 **"the roads of France"**: Bouillé, *Mémoires,* 269.

251 **popular destinations**: Doyle, *Oxford History,* 156.

251 **formal letter of good-bye**: *Mémoires,* 3:120–23.

252 **he reached Chavaniac**: Ibid., 3:189.

252 **"private life"**: Ibid., 3:124.

252 **"where he means, by his own example"**: "The Following account of the
Illustrious Marquis de la Fayette, extracted from a London paper, cannot
fail to be acceptable to every reader who knows how to appreciate real mag-
nanimity and patriotism." *The American Museum; or, Universal Magazine*
(February 1792): 48.

252 **"this manner of serving my neighbors"**: "Note relative à ma fortune person-
elle," n.d. [1801?], Cornell, box 6, folder 16.

253 **"give the region an example"**: Ibid.

253 **Dyson lived with Lafayette's family**: "Extrait du registre d'enregistrement
des créances sur les émigrés du district de Brioude. Chapitre Lafayette, article 18, 9 février 1793," Cornell, box 122, folder 1, D [Miscellaneous accounts,
legal papers, documents, etc.] Chavaniac.

253 **Vaudoyer also joined**: Vaudoyer memo, 20 messidor year 8 (July 9, 1800).
LOC, reel 6, folder 73. On Vaudoyer's career, see Barry Bergdoll, "Vaudoyer,
Antoine-Laurent-Thomas," in *Dictionnaire critique des historiens de l'art
actifs en France de la Révolution à la Première Guerre mondiale,* ed. Philippe
Sénéchal and Claire Barbillon (Paris: INHA, 2009).

254 **Vaudoyer served as Lafayette's architect**: Vaudoyer to Lafayette, July 4,
1792, Archives Nationales, C/358, no. 1900.

254 **"all would be well"**: "Lettre de Lafayette relative à une instruction à adresser
aux paysans de la Haute-Loire pour leur expliquer la constitution de 1791,"
Séances et travaux de l'Académie des sciences morales et politiques, n.s., 62
(1904): 79.

254 **all priests to swear an oath**: See François Furet, "Civil Constitution of the
Clergy," in Furet and Ozouf, eds., *Critical Dictionary,* 449–57.

255 **"you will never convert a fanatic"**: "Lettre de Lafayette," 81.

255 **"the advantages of liberty and equality"**: Ibid., 80.

255 **"Here," wrote Ferrières**: Ferrières to Madame de Ferrières, November 1,
1791, Ferrières, *Correspondance,* 440.

255 **Calls for war**: Gouverneur Morris speculates on the reasons for the widespread desire for war in a letter to Washington of February 4, 1792. Morris,
Diary, 2:355. Some believed that the war against the royalists in exile would
finally unite the nation; Robespierre, in contrast, vehemently opposed the
war, believing with the king that it would ring the death knell of the revolution. For a well-researched and highly readable biography of Robespierre,
see Ruth Scurr, *Fatal Purity: Robespierre and the French Revolution* (New
York: Metropolitan Books, 2007).

256 **"amassing of armed French troops"**: Charavay, *La Fayette,* 291.

256 **three armies of 50,000 troops each**: Ibid.

256 **product of an incestuous liaison**: Morris, *Diary,* 2:354.

256 **Nicolas Luckner**: One of the many tragic ironies of the French Revolution is that Luckner, the man to whom "La Marseillaise" was dedicated, died on the guillotine in 1794.

256 **choice that pleased almost no one**: Charavay, *La Fayette,* 291, reports that Louis XVI initially objected to Narbonne's selection of Lafayette but was quieted by Narbonne's assertion that "if Your Majesty does not name him today . . . the nation will compel you to do it tomorrow."

256 **the Jacobin party had been abuzz**: The rumors are refuted in Charavay, *La Fayette,* 288–90. For an example of the rumor as it circulated in the Jacobin press, see "Derniers efforts de la faction-Lafayette, pour empêcher la fête civique des soldats de Château-Vieux," *Révolutions de Paris* (March 31–April 7, 1792), 143:8–16.

256 **"Festival of Liberty"**: Detailed plans for the festival are spelled out in "Détails & ordre définitivement arrête de la fête des soldats de Château-Vieux," *Révolutions de Paris* 143 (March 31–April 7, 1792): 16–18, and the event is described in "Première fête de la liberté, à l'occasion des soldats de Châteaux-Vieux," *Révolutions de Paris* 145 (April 14–21, 1792): 97–108. For an analysis of the festival, see Mona Ozouf, *Festivals and the French Revolution,* trans. Alan Sheridan (Cambridge, MA: Harvard University Press, 1988), 66–82.

257 **"the national guard of Paris"**: Lafayette to Adrienne, April 18, 1792, *Mémoires,* 3:430. This letter was found on Adrienne's person when she was arrested by revolutionary authorities on September 11, 1792.

257 **Lafayette's supporters**: *Révolutions de Paris* 145 (April 14–21, 1792): 125–28.

258 **rousing proclamation**: *Mémoires,* 3:311–13.

258 **"The clubs usurped"**: *Mémoires,* 3:323–24.

258 **lengthy letter**: The letter was published in *AP,* 45:338–40, and the debate recorded in *AP,* 45:340–43. It is reproduced with annotations in *Mémoires,* 2:325–31.

258 **"Organized like a separate empire"**: *Mémoires,* 3:326–27.

259 **"Strike down Lafayette"**: Charavay, *La Fayette,* 305.

259 **stormed the Tuileries Palace**: For the most recent discussion of the events of June 20, 1792, see Micah Alpaugh, "The Making of the Parisian Political Demonstration: A Case Study of 20 June 1792," *Proceedings of the Western Society for French History* 34 (2006): 115–33.

259 **"excited indignation and alarm"**: *AP,* 45:653.

259 ***Crimes of Lafayette in France***: *Crimes de La Fayette en France, seulement depuis la Révolution et depuis sa nomination au grade de général* (Paris: Imprimerie du Patriote Français, [1792]). An original copy of this rare pamphlet is housed in the Bibliothèque Nationale de France, Tolbiac, LB39-5208. A photocopy is available in Gottschalk, box 56, folder 9.

260 **"issue a proclamation"**: *Mémoires,* 3:345.

260 **"we would be better off"**: Ibid., 3:347.

260 **What was to be done**: Much of *AP* 46 and *AP* 47 is devoted to these questions.

260 **"tyranny over the National Assembly"**: This was the interpretation offered by the Left and voiced by the deputy Jean Debry on August 8, 1792. *AP,* 47:562.

260 **expressing personal views**: This argument was put forth by Vincent-Marie Viénot de Vaublanc, a leader of the Feuillants, in response to Debry. *AP,* 47:565.

260 **"partisan and admirer"**: *AP,* 47:8.

260 **assembly took up the question**: *AP,* 47:578.

261 **"this was not another demonstration"**: David P. Jordan, *The King's Trial: Louis XVI vs. The French Revolution* (Los Angeles: University of California Press, 1979), 35. See also David Andress, *The Terror: The Merciless War for Freedom in Revolutionary France* (New York: Farrar, Straus and Giroux, 2005), 82–90; Doyle, *Oxford History,* 186–90; and Schama, *Citizens,* 611–18.

262 **"torn [Lafayette] to pieces"**: Morris to Jefferson, August 1, 1792, Morris, *Diary,* 2:483.

262 **"plotting against liberty"**: Charavay, *La Fayette,* 327. For the discussion and text of the resolution, see *AP,* 48:387–88.

262 **at camp in Sedan**: *Mémoires,* 3:401.

262 **"the nation, the law, and the king"**: Charavay, *La Fayette,* 326.

CHAPTER 18: EXILE

265 **"there was nothing left to do"**: *Mémoires,* 3:401.

265 **Bouillon**: Bouillon is part of modern Belgium, but Lafayette described it as being "the extreme frontier of France." *Mémoires,* 3:405.

265 **Lafayette and forty-three other Frenchmen**: Charavay, *La Fayette,* 330–31, lists the names of the officers and aides-de-camp who accompanied him. Although Charavay gives the hour of their arrival as eight o'clock and others have placed it closer to midnight, I have accepted the time of nine o'clock, proposed on the basis of archival research published in Paul S. Spalding, *Lafayette: Prisoner of State* (Columbia: University of South Carolina Press, 2010), 1, the definitive account of Lafayette's life from his 1792 arrest to his 1797 release.

266 **"unable to withstand"**: Charavay, *La Fayette,* 331.

266 **"You were the instigator"**: Ibid., 340–41.

267 **Lafayette put pen to paper**: Lafayette to Adrienne, August 21, 1792, Charavay, *La Fayette,* 332.

267 **"You will greatly oblige me"**: Short forwarded Lafayette's letter to Morris. It is included in Morris, *Diary,* 2:551–52.

268 **"supposing that Monsieur"**: Morris to Short, September 12, 1792, Morris, *Diary,* 2:556.

268 **"The less we meddle"**: Morris to Pinckney, September 13, 1792, Morris, *Diary,* 2:557.

268 **wrote directly to George Washington**: Adrienne de Lafayette to George

Washington, October 8, 1792, *PGWP,* 11:204–6. As translated by John Dyson, who forwarded the original and his translation to Washington. Washington received the letter on February 20, 1793, and responded to it on March 16, 1793.

268 **"Enclosed is a letter"**: Washington to Jefferson, February 24, 1793, *PGWP,* 12:207.

269 **"all the consolation"**: Washington to Jefferson, March 13, 1793, *PGWP,* 12:313.

269 **"sincere sympathy"**: Washington to Marquise de Lafayette, June 13, 1793, *PGWP,* 13:70.

269 **"His circle is completed"**: Morris to Jefferson, August 22, 1792, as quoted in Jared Sparks, *The Life of Gouverneur Morris: With Selections from His Correspondence and Miscellaneous Papers; Detailing Events in the American Revolution, the French Revolution, and in the Political History of the United States,* 3 vols. (Boston: Gray and Bowen, 1832), 203.

269 **designated as émigrés**: Massimo Boffa, "Émigrés," in Furet and Ozouf, *Critical Dictionary,* 324–31.

270 **begin the inventory**: Cornell, 4611 bound manuscript 13++ supplement. A portion of this inventory is published by Henry Mosnier, *Le château de Chavaniac-Lafayette, description—histoire—souvenirs* (Le Puy: Marchessou Fils, 1883), Appendix 1, 45–51. However, Mosnier includes only those items inventoried on August 30, 1792. The inventory continued on August 31, 1792, and was conducted again on February 13–15, 1793. The 1793 inventory is more detailed than that compiled in 1792 and includes the estimated values of many of the items listed. I am grateful to Laurent Ferri, curator of the Division of Rare and Manuscript Collections, Carl A. Kroch Library, Cornell University, Ithaca, NY, for signaling the existence of Cornell's complete inventory.

271 **"sentiments of humanity"**: "Mme de La Fayette au ministre, 28 novembre 1792." This letter and several dozen additional documents related to the purchase and sale of Lafayette's properties in Guiyana are housed in "Titres, pièces, correspondance et renseignements concernant l'habitation la Gabrielle, venue à l'État par le marquis de La Fayette suivant contrat passé à Paris, le 13 germinal an X (3 avril 1802) devant Mr Perhet, notaire (1756-1829)," ANOM FM C/14/81.

271 **"nothing could have ever impelled"**: Mme de La Fayette à Geneste, 28 novembre, 1792, ANOM FM C/14/81.

271 **inventoried on April 5, 1794**: "Extrait des Minutes et Registres du Directoire du Département de la Guyane Française," Archives Nationales, AB/XIX/366.

271 **wrote to the Ministry of the Marine**: Au Citoyen Ministre de la Marine, year 8, ANOM FM C/14/81. Lafayette remained in regular contact with the ministry from 1799 to 1802 as he negotiated the restitution of his property and its subsequent sale to the ministry.

271 **slavery had been abolished**: Slavery had, in point of fact, been declared

abolished in 1794. However, actions on this front were evidently not taken immediately.

271 **"the Sovereign owes"**: Jean-Antoine-Nicolas de Caritat, Marquis de Condorcet, *Réflexions sur l'esclavage des Nègres* (Neufchâtel: 1781), 29–30.

272 **last will and testament**: Adrienne's wills are available in LOC, reel 5, folder 67a.

272 **taken into custody**: "Procès-verbal rédigé par Alphonse Aulagnier, juge de paix au Puy, chef-lieu du département de la Haute-Loire, lors de l'arrestation de madame et de mademoiselle Lafayette," reproduced in Virginie de Lasteyrie, *Vie de Madame de Lafayette par Mme de Lasteyrie sa fille précédée d'une notice sur la vie de sa mère Mme la Duchesse d'Ayen* (Paris: Techener, 1868), 461–63. Virginie was in the house as well, but she hid with a servant and was not discovered. Maurois, *Adrienne*, 233.

272 **quietly sympathetic**: Aulagnier comes off poorly in the story as told by Maurois, *Adrienne*, 231–33. However, judging from his willingness to disobey orders at a moment when doing so could well have been fatal, he could not have been the "fanatical Jacobin" that Maurois describes.

272 **Princesse de Lamballe**: The most recent account of the murder of the Princesse de Lamballe and the September massacres is given by David Andress, *The Terror*, 93–115. Andress puts the number killed between twelve hundred and fifteen hundred.

272 **shuttled from city to city**: Spalding, *Lafayette: Prisoner of State*, 14–25.

273 **"after all debts have been settled"**: Grattepain-Morizot to Adrienne, January 5, 1793, as quoted and translated in Maurois, *Adrienne*, 244.

273 **"deliberate in secret"**: *AP,* 61:378.

273 **September 5, 1793**: My understanding of the events of September 5 is indebted to the classic text on the subject, R. R. Palmer, *Twelve Who Ruled: The Year of the Terror in the French Revolution* (1941; repr., Princeton: Princeton University Press, 2005), 44–55, and to Andress, *The Terror,* 205–9.

273 **"the traitors within"**: *AP,* 73:419.

273 **"revolutionary army"**: Ibid., 73:420.

274 **National Convention began to make good**: Ibid., 74:303.

274 **"fatal decree"**: Adrienne uses the term in her account of the life of the Duchesse d'Ayen, as published in Lasteyrie, *Vie de Madame de Lafayette,* 136. The law is published in *AP,* 74:303–4.

274 **arrested in early October**: Lasteyrie, *Vie de Madame de Lafayette,* 305. Adrienne's father had fled to Switzerland where he remained safe.

274 **house arrest**: Ibid., 300.

274 **Adrienne was imprisoned**: Ibid., 294–96, 305.

274 **sixty people per day**: Ibid., 319.

275 **"I have given up trying"**: Ibid., 150.

275 **"the Comité de Surveillance"**: Morris, *Diary,* 2:52.

275 **"as a citizen"**: Morris to Washington, July 25, 1794, Morris, *Diary,* 2:64.

276 **preferred to credit**: *Mémoires,* 4:372. Monroe's papers testify that Adrienne wrote to him repeatedly in the last six months of 1794.

276 **wrote to the emperor:** John C. Fitzpatrick, *Writings of George Washington from the Original Manuscript Sources, 1745–1749,* 39 vols. (Washington, DC: U.S. Government Printing Office, 1931–44), 35:45–46.

277 *Captivity of Lafayette:* Philippe Charles d'Agrain, *Captivité de Lafayette. Héroïde, avec figures et des notes historiques, non encore connues du public, sur les illustres prisonniers d'Olmutz, en Moravie* (Paris: Chocheris, 1797). An English poem, *The Castle of Olmutz: A poem, inscribed to La Fayette* (London, 1797), seems to be a rough translation of d'Agrain. On d'Agrain's arrest and liberation in 1792, see Spalding, *Prisoner of State,* 41.

279 **"enduring a series of most dreadful":** Quotes in this paragraph are from *The Parliamentary History of England from the Earliest Period to the Year 1803,* 36 vols. (London: Hansard, 1818), 32:1109. I was directed to Fox's speech by Spalding, *Lafayette: Prisoner of State,* 151.

279 **"what a scene":** *Parliamentary History,* 32:1353. Upon his release from prison, Lafayette wrote a letter thanking FitzPatrick and Fox for their support. Lafayette to FitzPatrick, October 8, 1797, *Mémoires,* 4:378–80.

279 **"It is a torment to her conscience":** *Parliamentary History,* 32:1355.

279 **"that a more striking and pathetic":** Ibid., 32:1358.

280 **most popular men in the nation:** David A. Bell, *The First Total War: Napoleon's Empire and the Birth of Warfare as We Know It* (Boston: Houghton Mifflin, 2007), 195–207.

280 **"to end their captivity":** *Mémoires,* 4:293.

280 **"had the happiness of embracing":** Samuel Williams to Washington, October 5, 1797, *PGWR.*

280 **"ordered their release":** William Vans Murray to Washington, August 26, 1797, *PGWR.*

280 **expressed his dismay:** *Mémoires,* 4:377. Francis Huger had been one of the conspirators in the failed plot to free Lafayette from prison.

282 **"retailing abuse against Lafayette":** "Mr. Noah Webster's Attack on Porcupine," *Porcupine's Political Censor* (March 1797): 75.

282 **"that a desire to ingratiate yourself":** "Letter II. To Mr. Noah Webster of New-York," *Porcupine's Political Censor* (March 1779): 81.

282 **"cured me of my good will":** Hamilton to Lafayette, April 28, 1798, Harold C. Syrett, ed., *The Papers of Alexander Hamilton,* 26 vols. (New York: Columbia University Press, 1974), 21:451.

283 **"no one in the United States":** Washington to Lafayette, December 25, 1798, *PGWR.* Washington acknowledged having received, but not replied to, six letters from Lafayette written between October 6, 1797, and September 5, 1798. Even in an era of difficult communication, a delay of this length was extremely rare. Washington explained his silence by pointing out that, since the first four of Lafayette's letters had mentioned an imminent departure for America, he had reason to believe that a response would not find Lafayette in Europe.

283 **"how ardently":** Lafayette to Washington, May 9, 1799, *PGWR,* 4:54.

283 **Murray reported:** Worthington Chauncey Ford, ed., "Letters of William Vans Murray to John Quincy Adams, 1797–1803," *Annual Report of the*

American Historical Association for the Year 1912 (Washington, DC: Smithsonian Institution Press, 1914).

284 **"I am glad you have seen"**: Ford, "Letters," 396.

284 **in a hot air balloon**: Lafayette to Adrienne, July 4, 1799, *Mémoires*, 5:61.

284 **"could I not . . . be useful"**: William Vans Murray to George Washington, August 17, 1799, *PGWR*, 4:259.

284 **addressing his mail to the United States**: Secretary of State Timothy Pickering wrote to Washington on October 24, 1799: "I suspect Lafayette is coming to America: I saw lately a letter from an Emigrant in Germany, addressed to him in the United States." *PGWR*, 4:363.

285 **speculating that Talleyrand**: The quotations below are from Charles Cotesworth Pinckney to George Washington, June 25, 1799, *PGWR*, 4:155.

285 **"explicit federalism"**: William Vans Murray to John Quincy Adams, August 19, 1799, Ford, "Letters," 585.

285 **initially dismissed allegations**: Washington to Timothy Pickering, July 14, 1799, *PGWR*, 4:187.

286 **"to consolidate, guarantee"**: F.-A. Aulard, *Registre des délibérations du Consulat provisoire, 20 brumaire–3 nîvose an VIII (11 novembre–24 décembre 1799)* (Paris: Société de l'Histoire de la Révolution Française, 1894), 3–4. On Napoleon's repeated invocation of the original intent of the 1789 revolutionaries as the basis for his consolidation of power, see Isser Woloch, *Napoleon and His Collaborators: The Making of a Dictatorship* (New York: Norton, 2002).

286 **"obligations"**: Lafayette to Bonaparte, n.d., *Mémoires*, 5:154.

286 **laying the groundwork**: Lafayette to Adrienne, October 28, 1799, *Mémoires*, 5:141.

286 **uncharacteristically succinct letter**: Lafayette to Bonaparte, October 30, 1799, *Mémoires*, 5:146–47.

286 **"talent for making friends"**: As quoted in Constance Wright, *Madame de Lafayette* (New York: Henry Holt, 1959), 250.

286 **"they surely knew me well enough"**: Quotes in this paragraph are from *Mémoires*, 5:155. This section of the memoirs was begun at some point before 1805 and completed in July 1807, as discussed in *Mémoires*, 5:148, note 1.

287 **"éclat"**: *Mémoires*, 5:156.

CHAPTER 19: HOMAGES

288 **"warrior . . . legislator"**: Louis de Fontanes, *Éloge funèbre de Washington; Prononcé dans le temple de Mars, le 20 pluviôse, an 8* (Paris: Henri Agasse, 1800), 29.

288 **"to build a cradle"**: Ibid., 19.

289 **permitted to attend**: *Mémoires*, 5:157.

289 **"within the four walls of a prison"**: "Livre de compte sommaire de mon exploitation de La Grange pour l'année 1828," Cornell, box 130, folder 6, xv.

289 **"retirement on a small farm"**: Lafayette to Washington, May 9, 1799, *PGWR*, 4:55.

289 **Virginia, New England, or New York**: Lafayette mentions New England and Virgina to Adrienne in a letter of August 5, 1799, *Mémoires,* 5:71. In an undated letter possibly written around the same time, the Marquis de La Tour du Pin offers Lafayette advice on purchasing and running an American farm and recommends the area near Albany where he had settled during the French Revolution. Marquis de La Tour du Pin to Lafayette, n.d., "Description d'une ferme américaine . . . ," Cornell, box 3, folder 31.

289 **rerouted miles of roads**: Cornell, box 130, folder 11.

289 **203 pear trees and 165 apple trees**: Bill of sale, November 26, 1806; LOC, reel 44, folder 823.

289 **determined to make his lands**: Lafayette explains these goals in the preface to "Livre de compte sommaire de mon exploitation de La Grange pour l'année 1828," Cornell, box 130, folder 6.

290 **"Before breakfast"**: William Taylor to John Dyson, May 15, 1802, reprinted in J. W. Robberds, ed., *A Memoir of the Life and Writings of the Late William Taylor of Norwich* (London: John Murray, 1843), 406–7.

290 **Lafayette hired Hubert Robert**: LOC, reel 44, folder 822. On Robert's work at La Grange, see Jean de Cayeux, *Hubert Robert et les jardins* (Paris: Herscher, 1987), 112–13.

290 **"is in part filled up"**: Robberds, *Taylor,* 404.

291 **"learnt to perceive"**: Ibid., 406.

291 **"portrait of the young Lafayette"**: Ibid., 405.

291 **"works on agricultural and political topics"**: Inventories of Lafayette's books bear out Taylor's observation: a list of works compiled by Lafayette's secretary in 1816 includes some seventy-six books, in both French and English, under the heading "Agriculture," ranging from essays on picturesque gardens, to treatises on cultivation and livestock—such as R. W. Dickson, *Practical Agriculture; Or, A Complete System of Modern Husbandry* (London, 1805)—to a French translation of Virgil's *Georgics,* the writings of Arthur Young, and periodicals published on both sides of the Atlantic, including *Annales d'agriculture, Mémoires d'agriculture,* and the *American Farmer;* LOC, reel 9, folders 1116 and 1116 bis.

291 **forty-five habitable rooms**: "La Grange, Château. [List of rooms and occupants] [before 1834?]," Cornell, box 130, folder 8.

291 **"elegant and well chosen"**: Published in at least two newspapers: "General La Fayette," *Essex Patriot* [Haverhill, MA] (November 29, 1817): 1, and "From Lady Morgan's 'France,'" *American Advocate* [Hallowell, ME] (November 22, 1817): 4.

291 **"command a view"**: This account was published in at least two newspapers: "Lafayette at Home," *American Mercury* [Hartford, CT] (August 22, 1826): 2, and "Travels: Letters from Europe—No. LXXIII," *Torch Light* [Hagerstown, MD] (February 15, 1827): 1.

291 **worked closely with Vaudoyer**: Vaudoyer made his first trip to La Grange on January 28, 1800. This journey and all of the work and expenses for which Vaudoyer charged Lafayette in 1800 and 1801 are itemized in "Relève des

honoraires du Citoyen Vaudoyer, architecte des Travaux Publics . . ." LOC, reel 44, folder 822.

292 **letter to the deceased Van Ryssel:** *Mémoires,* 5:148–240.

292 **"your memory":** Ibid., 5:240.

292 **lured out of retirement:** Lafayette's intellectual and political life in this period have been studied most extensively by Lloyd Kramer, *Lafayette in Two Worlds: Public Cultures and Personal Identities in an Age of Revolutions* (Chapel Hill: University of North Carolina Press, 1996), and Sylvia Neely, *Lafayette and the Liberal Ideal, 1814–1824: Politics and Conspiracy in an Age of Reaction* (Carbondale: Southern Illinois University Press, 1991). My understanding of the topic is indebted to both of them. In many cases, their citations directed me to primary sources quoted in my text.

294 **"the protégé, the humble follower":** Lafayette, *Mémoires,* 6:24. Lafayette's assault on the character of Louis XVIII comes in an 1816 letter to Madame de Simiane in which Lafayette defends his actions in favor of Napoleon, and against the restored Bourbon, during the so-called one hundred days when Napoleon returned to power before being definitively removed in 1815.

294 **voted into public office:** On Lafayette's political affairs in the department of the Sarthe, which also elected his friend and ally Benjamin Constant, see Kramer, *Lafayette in Two Worlds,* 69–73.

294 **"The great, good La Fayette":** Charles Guyot, "On the Elections" (1819), as quoted and translated in Kramer, *Lafayette in Two Worlds,* 70.

295 **"curiosity":** *La Minerve française* (1818), 4:296.

295 **ultraroyalist journal:** *Le conservateur* (1818), 1:389.

295 **"the friends with whom":** Lafayette to Monroe, November 25, 1823, *Mémoires,* 6:160–61.

296 **"Congress had passed a resolution":** Monroe to Lafayette, February 7, 1824, *Mémoires,* 6:162.

296 **each of the twenty-four states of the union:** Auguste Levasseur, *Lafayette in America in 1824 and 1825; or, Journal of a Voyage to the United States,* trans. John D. Goodman (Philadelphia: 1829; rpt. New York: Research Reprints, 1970), 243–306.

297 **"Hail! Lafayette!":** *Hail! Lafayette!* (Philadelphia: 1824), 1.

298 **fiftieth anniversary:** Andrew Burstein, *America's Jubilee: How in 1826 a Generation Remembered Fifty Years of Independence* (New York: Alfred A. Knopf, 2001), 8–33.

299 **spectacular dinner:** Edgar Ewing Brandon, ed., *Lafayette, Guest of the Nation: A Contemporary Account of the Triumphal Tour of General Lafayette Through the United States in 1824–1825, as Reported by the Local Newspapers,* 3 vols. (Oxford, OH: Oxford Historical Press, 1950–57), 1:199–201.

299 **Gouverneur Morris had rhapsodized:** Jared Sparks, *Life of Governeur Morris,* 3:143–44.

302 **"could constitute a museum":** See Jules Cloquet, *Souvenirs sur la vie privée du général Lafayette* (Paris: Galignani, 1836), 195.

302 **La Grange today**: Today, La Grange is owned and operated by the Josée and René de Chambrun Foundation and is open only to scholars and visiting dignitaries.

302 **"at length we approached"**: Mrs. Caleb Cushing, "Visit to La Grange," *The Literary Journal and Weekly Register of Science and the Arts* 1, no. 13 (August 31, 1833): 97. I discuss Lafayette's Americanization of La Grange in Laura Auricchio, "Transplanting Liberty: Lafayette's American Garden," in Dan O'Brien, ed., *Gardening: Philosophy for Everyone—Cultivating Wisdom* (Oxford: Wiley-Blackwell, 2010), 93–105.

CHAPTER 20: PICPUS

304 **"an old name of '89"**: *Mémoires,* 6:388–89.

305 **"moral affections"**: Cloquet, *Recollections,* 262.

307 **"uninterrupted thunder"**: Isaiah Townsend, Jr., to Mary Bennett Townsend, May 30, 1834, Townsend Family Papers, box 15, Manuscripts and Archives Division, New York Public Library.

307 **"A month has scarcely elapsed"**: Isaiah Townsend, Jr., to Mary Bennett Townsend, June 6, 1834, Townsend Family Papers, box 15, Manuscripts and Archives Division, New York Public Library.

AUTHOR'S NOTE

309 **Picpus Cemetery**: See *Les dernières victimes de la Terreur: 26 prairial–9 thermidor an II (14 juin–27 juillet 1794)*, exhibit catalog (Paris: Association du Souvenir de Picpus, 1994).

BIBLIOGRAPHY

MANUSCRIPT SOURCES

UNITED STATES

Dean Lafayette Collection, #4611. Division of Rare and Manuscript Collections, Cornell University Library, Ithaca, NY

George Washington Papers at the Library of Congress, Washington, DC

James Monroe Papers, Manuscript Division, Library of Congress, Washington, DC

John Quincy Adams Papers, Benjamin Thomas Hill Collection, Manuscript Division, Library of Congress, Washington, DC

Louis Gottschalk Papers, Special Collections Resource Center, University of Chicago, Chicago, IL

Marquis de Lafayette Collections, Special Collections and College Archives, Skillman and Kirby Libraries, Lafayette College, Easton, PA

Marquis de Lafayette Papers, Manuscript Division, Library of Congress, Washington, DC

Robert R. Livingston Papers, The New-York Historical Society, New York, NY

Thomas Jefferson Papers, Library of Congress, Washington, DC

Townsend Family Papers, Manuscripts and Archives Division, The New York Public Library, New York, NY

FRANCE

Archives de la Seine, Paris

Archives Nationales de France, Paris

Archives Nationales d'Outre-Mer, Aix-en-Provence

PERIODICALS—UNITED STATES

The American Advocate

The American Herald

The American Mercury

The American Museum; or, Universal Magazine

The Boston Chronicle
The Boston Evening Post
The Boston Gazette
The Connecticut Courant
The Connecticut Journal
The Cumberland Gazette
The Essex Patriot
Evening Post
The Gazette of the United States
The Hampshire Chronicle
The Independent Chronicle and the Universal Advertiser
The Maryland Gazette
The Massachusetts Centinel
The Massachusetts Spy
The Newport Mercury
The New York American
The New York Journal
The New York Times
The Norwich Packet
The Pennsylvania Gazette
The Pennsylvania Mercury
The Pennsylvania Packet; or, The General Advertiser
Porcupine's Political Censor
The Richmond Enquirer
The Torch Light
The Virginia Gazette

PERIODICALS—FRANCE

Affiches, annonces, et avis divers
L'ami du peuple
L'ami du roi
L'année littéraire
Chronique de Paris
Le conservateur
Le constitutionnel
Courrier de Versailles à Paris et de Paris à Versailles
Feuille du jour
Journal de Paris
Journal des débats
Journal général de France
Lettre bougrement patriotique du véritable père Duchêne
Mercure de France
La Minerve française
Le moniteur universel
Nouvelles de la république des lettres et des arts

Le Patriote français
Révolutions de France et de Brabant
Révolutions de Paris

PERIODICALS—UNITED KINGDOM

European Magazine and London Review
Gentleman's Magazine and Historical Chronicle
The Morning Chronicle and London Advertiser
Public Advertiser

PUBLISHED PRIMARY SOURCES

Abbot, W. W., et al., ed. *The Papers of George Washington.* Charlottesville: University Press of Virginia, 1987–.

Adams, John Quincy. *Diary of John Quincy Adams.* David Grayson Allen et al., eds., 2 vols. Cambridge, MA: Belknap Press, 1982.

———. *Oration on the Life and Character of Gilbert Motier de Lafayette.* Washington, DC: Gales and Seaton, 1835.

d'Agrain, Charles. *Captivité de Lafayette. Héroïde, avec figures et des notes historiques, non encore connues du public, sur les illustres prisonniers d'Olmutz, en Moravie.* Paris: Chocheris, 1797.

Allen, Michael, ed. *An English Lady in Paris: The Diary of Frances Anne Crewe.* St. Leonards, UK: Oxford-Stockley, 2006.

Archives parlementaires de 1787 à 1860. Paris: Dupont, 1862–1913.

Arenberg, Auguste Marie Raymond. *Correspondance entre le Comte de Mirabeau et le Comte de La Marck.* Paris: 1851.

Aulard, François-Alphonse. *La société des Jacobins: Recueil de documents pour l'histoire du club des Jacobins de Paris.* 6 vols. Paris: 1889–97. Reprint, New York: AMS Press, 1973.

Bachaumont, Louis Petit de. *Mémoires secrets pour servir à l'histoire de la république des lettres en France depuis 1762 jusqu'à nos jours.* 36 vols. London: Adamson, 1777–90.

Bailly, Jean-Sylvain. *Mémoires d'un témoin de la Révolution.* 3 vols. Paris: Levrault, Schoell et Cie, 1804.

Bailly, Jean-Sylvain, and Honoré Duveyrier. *Procès-verbal des séances et délibérations de l'Assemblée générale des électeurs de Paris, réunis à l'Hôtel-de-Ville le 14 juillet 1789.* 3 vols. Paris: Baudoin, 1790.

Beard, James Franklin, ed. *The Letters and Journals of James Fenimore Cooper.* 6 vols. Cambridge, MA: Harvard University Press, 1960–68.

Beaufort, Raphael Ledos de, ed. and trans. *Personal Recollections of the Late Duc de Broglie, 1785–1820.* 2 vols. London: Ward and Downey, 1887.

Biddle, Charles. *Autobiography of Charles Biddle, Vice-President of the Supreme Executive Council of Pennsylvania, 1745–1821.* Philadelphia: E. Claxton and Co., 1883.

Bordel patriotique institué par la Reine des François pour les plaisirs des Députés à la nouvelle Législature. Paris: 1791.

Bouillé, François-Claude-Amour, Marquis de. *Mémoires du Marquis de Bouillé.* Paris: Baudouin Frères, 1821.

Boutaric, Edgard Paul. *Correspondance secrète inédite de Louis XV sur la politique étrangère avec le Compte de Broglie, Tercier, etc.* 2 vols. Paris: Plon, 1866.

Boyd, Julien P., ed. *The Papers of Thomas Jefferson,* 40 vols. Princeton: Princeton University Press: 1950–.

Brandon, Edgar Ewing, ed. *Lafayette, Guest of the Nation: A Contemporary Account of the Triumphal Tour of General Lafayette Through the United States in 1824–1825, as Reported by the Local Newspapers.* 3 vols. Oxford, OH: Oxford Historical Press, 1950–57.

———. *A Pilgrimage of Liberty: A Contemporary Account of the Triumphal Tour of General Lafayette Through the Southern and Western States in 1825, as Reported by the Local Newspapers.* Athens, OH: Lawhead Press, 1944.

Brenneman, Gloria E. "The Conway Cabal: Myth or Reality." *Pennsylvania History* 40, no. 2 (April 1973): 168–77.

Buffon, Georges-Louis Leclerc, Comte de. *Oeuvres complètes.* 45 vols. Paris: 1824.

Butterfield, L. H., ed. *Adams Family Correspondence.* 11 vols. Cambridge, MA: Belknap Press of Harvard University Press, 1963–2011.

Calonne, Charles Alexandre de. *De l'état de la France présent et à venir.* London: 1790.

Campan, Jeanne-Louise-Henriette. *Mémoires de Madame Campan, Première femme de chambre de Marie-Antoinette,* edited by Jean Chalon. Paris: Mercure de France, 1988.

The Castle of Olmutz; A Poem, Inscribed to La Fayette. London: 1797.

Chase, Eugene Parker, ed. *Our Revolutionary Forefathers: The Letters of François, Marquis de Barbé-Marbois During His Residence in the United States as Secretary of the French Legation, 1779–1789.* Freeport, NY: Books for Libraries Press, 1929. Reprint, 1969.

Chateaubriand, François-René de. *Mémoires d'outre-tombe.* 12 vols. Paris: Penaud Frères, 1849–50.

Chevalier, Pierre, ed. Journal de l'Assemblée des Notables de 1787 par le Comte de Brienne et Etienne Charles de Loménie de Brienne, archevêque de Toulouse. Paris: Klincksieck, 1960.

Chinard, Gilbert, ed. *The Letters of Lafayette and Jefferson.* Baltimore: Johns Hopkins Press, 1929.

Cloquet, Jules. *Souvenirs sur la vie privée du général Lafayette.* Paris: Galignani, 1836.

Collections of the New-York Historical Society for the Year 1886. New York: New-York Historical Society, 1886.

Condorcet, Jean-Antoine-Nicolas de Caritat, Marquis de. *Idées sur le despotisme à, l'usage de ceux qui prononcent ce mot sans l'entendre.* Edited by Arthur Condorcet O'Connor and F. Arago. Paris: Firmin Didot, 1847.

———. *Mémoires de Condorcet, sur la Révolution française, extraits de sa correspondance et de celles de ses amis.* 2 vols. Paris: Ponthieu, 1824.

————. *Réflexions sur l'esclavage des Nègres*. Neufchâtel: 1781.

Constant, Benjamin. *Mélanges de littérature et de politique*. Paris: Pinchon et Didier, 1829.

Cooper, James Fenimore. *The American Democrat and Other Political Writings*. Washington, DC: Regnery Publishing, 2000.

————. *Notions of the Americans: Picked Up by a Travelling Bachelor*. New York: H. Colburn, 1828.

Crimes de La Fayette en France seulement depuis la Révolution et depuis sa nomination au grade de général. Paris: Imprimerie du Patriote Français, s.d.

Davenport, Beatrix Cary, ed. *A Diary of the French Revolution by Gouverneur Morris (1752–1816), Minister to France During the Terror*. 2 vols. Boston: Houghton-Mifflin, 1939.

The Deane Papers. 5 vols. New York: New-York Historical Society, 1887–90.

The Debates and Proceedings in the Congress of the United States. 42 vols. Washington, DC: Gales and Seaton, 1834–56.

De Pauw, Cornelius. *Recherches philosophiques sur les américains, ou mémoires intéressants pour servir à l'histoire de l'espèce humaine*. 2 vols. Paris: J. M. Place, 1774.

Deville, Étienne. *Index du Mercure de France: 1672–1832*. Paris: J. Schemit, 1910.

Dictionnaire de l'Académie française. Paris: Brunet, 1762.

Diderot, Denis, and Jean Le Rond d'Alembert, eds. *Encyclopédie; ou, Dictionnaire raisonné des sciences, des arts et des métiers, par une société des gens de lettres*. 28 vols. Paris: Briasson, David, Le Breton, and Durand, 1751–72.

The Diplomatic Correspondence of the United States of America, from the Signing of the Definitive Treaty of Peace, 10th September, 1783, to the Constitution, March 4, 1789. 3 vols. Washington, DC: Blair and Rives, 1837.

Doniol, Henri. *Histoire de la participation de la France à l'établissement des États-Unis d'Amérique: Correspondance diplomatique et documents*. 5 vols. Paris: Imprimerie Nationale, 1886–92.

————, ed. "Correspondance inédite de La Fayette: Lettres écrites au comte d'Estaing pendant la campagne du Vice-Amiral de la Delaware à Boston du 14 juillet au 20 octobre 1778." *Revue d'histoire diplomatique* 6 (1892): 395–448.

Drouet, Jean-Baptiste. *Récit fait par M. Drouet, maître de poste à Ste Menehould, de la manière dont il a reconnu le roi, et a été cause de son arrestation à Varennes: Honneurs rendus à ce citoyen et à deux de ses camarades*. Paris: Imprimerie du Journal des Clubs, 1791.

Early Proceedings of the American Philosophical Society for the Promotion of Useful Knowledge, Compiled by One of the Secretaries, from the Manuscript Minutes of Its Meetings from 1744 to 1838. Philadelphia: McCalla and Stavely, 1884.

Egret, Jean. "La Fayette dans la première Assemblée des Notables (février-mai 1787)." *Annales historiques de la Révolution française* 24 (1952): 1–31.

Espinchal, Joseph-Thomas, Comte d'. *Journal d'émigration du Comte d'Espinchal*. Paris: Perrin, 1912.

————. "Lafayette jugé par le Comte d'Espinchal." *Revue rétrospective* 20 (1894): 289–320.

Extrait du Journal d'un officier de la marine de l'escadre de M. le comte d'Estaing. Paris[?]: 1782.

Faujas de Saint-Fond, Barthélemy. *Description des expériences de la machine aérostatique de MM. de Montgolfier.* Paris: Cuchet, 1783.

Ferrières, Marquis de. *Correspondance inédite (1789, 1790, 1791).* Paris: Armand Colin, 1932.

Fontanes, Louis. *Éloge funèbre de Washington: Prononcé dans le temple de Mars, le 20 pluviôse, an 8.* Paris: Henri Agasse, 1800.

Ford, Worthington Chauncey, ed. *Journals of the Continental Congress, 1774–1789.* 34 vols. Washington, DC: U.S. Government Printing Office, 1904–37.

———. "Letters of William Vans Murray to John Quincy Adams, 1797–1803." *Annual Report of the American Historical Association for the Year 1912.* Washington, DC: Smithsonian Institution Press, 1914.

Fourier de Bacourt, Adolphe, ed. *Correspondance ertre le comte de Mirabeau et le comte de la Marck.* 2 vols. Brussels: Meline, Cans, 1851.

Genlis, Stéphanie Félicité de. *Dictionnaire critique et raisonné des étiquettes de la cour.* 2 vols. Paris: P. Mongie Ainé, 1818.

———. *Mémoires inédits de Madame la comtesse de Genlis, sur le dix-huitième siècle et la Révolution française, depuis 1756 jusqu' à nos jours.* 10 vols. Paris: Ladvocat, 1825.

Gottschalk, Louis, ed. *The Letters of Lafayette to Washington, 1777–1799.* Philadelphia: American Philosophical Society, 1976.

Hamilton, Alexander, John Jay, and James Madison. *The Federalist Papers.* Project Gutenberg, December 12, 2011. www.gutenberg.org/files/18/18.txt.

Helvétius, Claude Adrien. *De l'esprit.* Paris: Durand, 1758.

Hening, William Waller, ed. *The Statutes at Large: Being a Collection of All the Laws of Virginia, from the First Session of the Legislature in the Year 1619.* 13 vols. Richmond: Samuel Pleasants, 1809–23.

Houtte, Hubert van. "Documents: American Commercial Conditions, and Negotiations with Austria, 1783–1786." *American Historical Review* 16, no. 3 (April 1911): 567–78.

Jay, William, ed. *The Life of John Jay: With Selections from his Correspondence and Miscellaneous Papers.* 2 vols. New York: J. & J. Harper, 1833.

Jimack, Peter, ed. *A History of the Two Indies: A Translated Selection of Writings from Raynal's "Histoire philosophique et politique des établissements des Européens dans les Deux Indes."* Hampshire, UK: Ashgate, 2006.

Jordan, John W. "Bethlehem During the Revolution: Extracts from the Diaries in the Moravian Archives at Bethlehem, Pennsylvania." *Pennsylvania Magazine of History and Biography* 12, no. 4 (1888): 385–406, and 13, no. 1 (1889): 71–89.

Kalb, Johann de. "Letter of Major-General Johann Kalb, 1777." *American Historical Review* 15, no. 3 (April 1910): 562–67.

Lacroix, Sigismond, ed. *Actes de la Commune de Paris pendant la Révolution.* 7 vols. Paris, 1894–1905. Reprint, New York: AMS, 1973.

———. *Le Département de Paris et de la Seine pendant la Révolution.* Paris: Société de l'Histoire de la Révolution Française, 1904.

Lafayette, Gilbert du Motier de. *Mémoires, correspondance et manuscrits du général Lafayette, publiés par sa famille.* 6 vols. Paris: Fournier Ainé, 1837–38.

Lameth, Théodore, Comte de. *Mémoires*. Paris: Fontemoing, 1913.

La Tour du Pin Gouvernet, Henriette Lucie Dillon, Marquise de. *Mémoires de la marquise de La Tour du Pin: Journal d'une femme de cinquante ans, 1778–1815: Suivis d'extraits inédits de sa correspondance, 1815–1846*. Paris: Mercure de France, 1989.

Laurens, John. *The Army Correspondence of Colonel John Laurens in the Years 1777-8*. New York: Bradford Club, 1867.

Lee, Charles. *The Lee Papers*. 4 vols. New York: New-York Historical Society, 1872–75.

"Lettre de Lafayette relative à une instruction à adresser aux paysans de la Haute-Loire pour leur expliquer la constitution de 1791." *Séances et travaux de l'Académie des sciences morales et politiques*, n.s., 62 (1904).

Levasseur, Auguste. *Lafayette in America in 1824 and 1825; or, Journal of a Voyage to the United States*. Translated by John D. Goodman. Philadelphia, 1829. Reprint, New York: Research Reprints, 1970.

Luynes, Charles Philippe d'Albert, Duc de. *Mémoires du duc de Luynes sur la cour de Louis XV (1735–1758)*. 17 vols. Paris: Firmin Didot, 1860–65.

Madison, James. *The Writings of James Madison, Comprising His Public Papers and His Private Correspondence, Including His Numerous Letters and Documents Now for the First Time Printed*, edited by Gaillard Hunt. 9 vols. New York: G. P. Putnam's Sons, 1900.

Memoirs of the Duchess de Tourzel, Governess to the Children of France During the Years 1789, 1790, 1791, 1792, 1793 and 1795. 2 vols. (London: Remington, 1886).

Meng, John J., ed. *Despatches and Instructions of Conrad Alexandre Gérard, 1778–1780*. Baltimore: Johns Hopkins Press, 1939.

Mercier, Louis-Sébastien. *Paris pendant la Révolution (1789–1798); ou, Le nouveau Paris*. 2 vols. Paris: Poulet-Malassis, 1862.

———. *Tableau de Paris*. 2 vols. Paris: 1783. Reprint, Paris: Mercure de France, 1994.

Métra, Louis-François. *Correspondance secrète, politique et littéraire*. 18 vols. London: Adamson, 1787–90.

Minutes of the Common Council of the City of New York 1784–1831. 19 vols. New York: City of New York, 1917.

Montaiglon, Anatole de, et al., eds. *Correspondance des directeurs de l'Académie de France à Rome avec les surintendants des bâtiments*. 17 vols. Paris: Noël Charavay, 1902.

Montesquieu. *De l'esprit des lois*. Geneva: Barillot, 1758.

Moore, Charles, ed. *George Washington's Rules of Civility and Decent Behaviour in Company and Conversation*. Boston: Houghton Mifflin, 1926.

Morris, Anne Cary, ed. *The Diary and Letters of Gouverneur Morris*. 2 vols. New York: Charles Scribner's Sons, 1888.

Necker, Jacques. *Compte rendu au roi, par M. Necker, directeur général des finances, au mois de janvier 1781*. Paris: Imprimerie Royale, 1781.

Neuilly, Ange Achille Charles, Comte de. *Dix années d'émigration: souvenirs et correspondance du comte de Neuilly*. Paris: Douniol, 1865.

Nolan, J. Bennett. "Lafayette and the American Philosophical Society." *Proceedings of the American Philosophical Society* 73, no. 2 (1934).

———. *Lafayette in America Day by Day*. Baltimore: Johns Hopkins Press, 1934.

North, Louise V., Janet M. Wedge, and Landa M. Freeman, eds. *In the Words of Women: The Revolutionary War and the Birth of the Nation, 1765–1799*. Lanham, MD: Lexington Books, 2011.

Ozanam, Didier, and Michel Antoine, eds. *Correspondance secrète du Comte de Broglie avec Louis XV (1756–1774)*. 2 vols. Paris: Librairie C. Klincksieck, 1956–61.

The Parliamentary History of England from the Earliest Period to the Year 1803. 36 vols. London: T. C. Hansard, 1818.

Pidansat de Mairobert, Mathieu-François. *L'espion anglois; ou, Correspondance secrète entre milord All'Eye et milord All'Ear*. 10 vols. London: Adamson, 1782–86.

Plan et façade en six planches, de l'Hôtel, rue St. Honoré à Paris, appartenant au très-honorable Francis Henry Egerton, des Ducs de Bridgewater, prince du S.E.R. &c. &c. &c. Paris: 1830.

Popkin, Jeremy D., ed. and trans. *Panorama of Paris*. University Park: Pennsylvania State University Press, 1999.

Proceedings of the General Society of the Cincinnati, 1784–1884. Philadelphia: Review Printing House, 1887.

Procès-verbal de l'Assemblée de Notables tenue à Versailles en l'année MDCCLXXX VII. Paris: Imprimerie Royale, 1787.

Procès-verbal de l'Assemblée Nationale. Paris: Baudoin, 1789–91.

Rice, Howard C., Jr., ed. *Travels in North America in the Years 1780, 1781 and 1782 by the Marquis de Chastellux*. 2 vols. Chapel Hill: University of North Carolina Press, 1963.

Robberds, J. W., ed. *A Memoir of the Life and Writings of the Late William Taylor of Norwich*. London: John Murray, 1843.

Rocheterie, Maxime de la, and Marquis de Beaucourt, eds. *Lettres de Marie-Antoinette: recueil des lettres authentiques de la reine*. 2 vols. Paris: Picard, 1896.

Rossiter, Thomas P. *A Description of the Picture of the Home of Washington After the War. Painted by T. P. Rossiter and L. R. Mignot. With Historical Sketches of the Personages Introduced*. New York: Appleton, 1859.

———. "Mount Vernon, Past and Present. What Shall Be Its Destiny?" *Crayon* 5, no. 9 (September 1858): 243–53.

Rousseau, Jean-Jacques. *Discours sur l'origine et les fondements de l'inégalité parmi les hommes*. Amsterdam: Marc-Michel Rey, 1755.

———. *Du contrat social; ou, Principes du droit politique*. Amsterdam: Marc-Michel Rey, 1762.

Saint Germain, Claude Louis, Comte de. *Mémoires de M. le Comte de St. Germain*. Amsterdam: Marc-Michel Rey, 1779.

Ségur, Louis-Philippe de. *Mémoires; ou, Souvenirs et anecdotes*. 3 vols. Brussels: Lacrosse, 1825.

Skousen, Mark, ed. *The Compleated Autobiography by Benjamin Franklin*. 2 vols. Washington, DC: Regnery, 2007.

Smith, Abigail Adams, and Caroline Amelia Smith de Windt. *Journal and Correspondence of Miss Adams, Daughter of John Adams, Second President of the United States.* 2 vols. New York: Wiley and Putnam, 1841.

Smith, Paul H., et al., eds. *Letters of Delegates to Congress, 1774–1789.* 25 vols. Washington, DC: Library of Congress, 1976–2000.

Sparks, Jared. *The Life of Gouverneur Morris: With Selections from His Correspondence and Miscellaneous Papers; Detailing Events in the American Revolution, the French Revolution, and in the Political History of the United States.* 3 vols. Boston: Gray and Bowen, 1832.

———. *Memoirs of the Life and Travels of John Ledyard, from His Journals and Correspondence.* London: Henry Colburn, 1828.

———, ed. *Correspondence of the American Revolution; Being Letters of Eminent Men to George Washington, from the Time of His Taking Command of the Army to the End of His Presidency.* 4 vols. Boston: Little, Brown, 1853.

Syrett, Harold C., ed. *The Papers of Alexander Hamilton.* 26 vols. New York: Columbia University Press, 1961–79.

Table ou abrégé des cent trente-cinq volumes de la Gazette de France, depuis son commencement en 1631 jusqu' à la fin de l'année 1765. 3 vols. Paris: Imprimerie de la Gazette de France, 1766–68.

Taylor, Robert J., ed. *Papers of John Adams.* 16 vols. Cambridge, MA: Belknap Press of Harvard University Press, 1977–2012.

Transactions of the American Philosophical Society, Held at Philadelphia, for Promoting Useful Knowledge. Philadelphia: Robert Aitken, 1786.

Tronson du Coudray, Philippe Charles. "Du Coudray's 'Observations on the Forts Intended for the Defense of the Two Passages of the River Delaware,' July, 1777." *The Pennsylvania Magazine of History and Biography* 24, no. 3 (1900): 343–47.

Vellay, Charles, ed. *La correspondance de Marat: Recueillie et annotée.* Paris: Eugène Fasquelle, 1908.

Vie Privée, *Impartiale, Politique, Militaire et Domestique, du Marquis de Lafayette, Général des Bleuets, Pour servir de Supplément à la Nécrologie des Hommes célèbres du dix-huitième siècle, et de clef aux Révolutions Françaises et Americaines. Dédiée aux soixante districts de Paris. Ornée de son Portrait.* Paris: Bastide, 1790.

Vigée-LeBrun, Élisabeth. *Souvenirs.* Claudine Herrmann, ed. 2 vols. Paris: Des Femmes, 1984.

Voltaire. *Essai sur l'histoire générale et sur les moeurs et l'esprit des nations, depuis Charlemagne jusqu'à nos jours.* Geneva: Cramer, 1756.

Wharton, Francis. *The Revolutionary Diplomatic Correspondence of the United States.* 6 vols. Washington, DC: Government Printing Office, 1889.

Williams, Helen Maria. *Letters Written in France, in the Summer of 1790, to a Friend in England.* London: T. Cadell, 1791.

PUBLISHED SECONDARY SOURCES

Adams, Geoffrey. *The Huguenots and French Opinion, 1685–1787: The Enlightenment Debate on Toleration.* Waterloo, ON: Wilfrid Laurier University Press, 1991.

Adams, William Howard. *The Paris Years of Thomas Jefferson*. New Haven: Yale University Press, 1997.

Adelson, Fred B. "Home on La Grange: Alvan Fisher's Lithographs of Lafayette's Residence in France." *Antiques* 134 (July 1988): 152–57.

Alexander, Robert. *Re-Writing the French Revolutionary Tradition: Liberal Opposition and the Fall of the Bourbon Monarchy*. Cambridge: Cambridge University Press, 2003.

Alpaugh, Micah. "The Making of the Parisian Political Demonstration: A Case Study of 20 June 1792." *Proceedings of the Western Society for French History* 34 (2006): 115–33.

Ammon, Harry. *James Monroe: The Quest for National Identity*. New York: McGraw-Hill, 1971.

Andress, David. "The Denial of Social Conflict in the French Revolution: Discourses Around the Champ de Mars Massacre, 17 July 1791." *French Historical Studies* 22, no. 2 (Spring 1999): 183–209.

———. *The French Revolution and the People*. London: Hambledon and London, 2004.

———. *Massacre at the Champ de Mars: Popular Dissent and Political Culture in the French Revolution*. Woodbridge, UK: Boydell Press for the Royal Historical Society, 2000.

———. *The Terror: The Merciless War for Freedom in Revolutionary France*. New York: Farrar, Straus and Giroux, 2005.

Auricchio, Laura. *Adélaïde Labille-Guiard: Artist in the Age of Revolution*. Los Angeles: J. Paul Getty Museum, 2009.

———. "Pahin de la Blancherie's Commercial Cabinet of Curiosity (1779–1787)." *Eighteenth-Century Studies* 36, no. 1 (2002): 47–61.

———. "Transplanting Liberty: Lafayette's American Garden." In *Gardening: Philosophy for Everyone—Cultivating Wisdom*, edited by Dan O'Brien. Oxford: Wiley-Blackwell, 2010, 93–105.

Baker, Keith Michael. *Inventing the French Revolution. Essays on French Political Culture in the Eighteenth Century*. Cambridge: Cambridge University Press, 1990.

Bardoux, Agénor. *La jeunesse de La Fayette, 1757–1792*. Paris: Calmann Lévy, 1892.

Bell, David A. *The First Total War: Napoleon's Europe and the Birth of Warfare as We Know It*. Boston: Houghton Mifflin, 2007.

Bérard, Simon. *Souvenirs historiques sur la révolution de 1830*. Paris: Perrotin, 1834.

Bernier, Olivier. *Lafayette: Hero of Two Worlds*. New York: Dutton, 1983.

———. *La Restauration*. Paris: Flammarion, 1990.

Bertier de Sauvigny, Guillaume de. *La révolution de 1830 en France*. Paris: Colin, 1970.

Berty, Adolphe. *Topographie historique du vieux Paris*. 2 vols. Paris: Imprimerie Nationale, 1885.

Blackman, Robert H. "What Does a Deputy to the National Assembly Owe His Constituents? Coming to an Agreement on the Meaning of Electoral Mandates in July 1789." *French Historical Studies* 34, no. 2 (Spring 2011): 205–41.

Blaufarb, Rafe. *The French Army, 1750–1820: Careers, Talent, Merit.* Manchester: Manchester University Press, 2002.

Bluche, François. *La vie quotidienne de la noblesse française au XVIIIe siècle.* Paris: Hachette, 1973.

Bourne, Henry E. "Improvising a Government in Paris, July, 1789." *American Historical Review* 10, no. 2 (January 1905): 280–308.

Brennan, Thomas. "Beyond the Barriers: Popular Culture and Parisian *Guinguettes.*" *Eighteenth-Century Studies* 18, no. 2 (Winter, 1984–85): 153–69.

Brette, Armand. *Histoire des édifices où ont siégé les assemblées parlementaires de la Révolution française et de la première République.* 2 vols. Paris: Imprimerie Nationale, 1902.

Brown, Christopher Leslie. *Moral Capital: Foundations of British Abolitionism.* Chapel Hill: University of North Carolina Press, 2006.

Bullock, Steven C. *Revolutionary Brotherhood: Freemasonry and the Transformation of the American Social Order, 1730–1840.* Chapel Hill: University of North Carolina Press, 1996.

Burrows, Edwin G., and Mike Wallace. *Gotham: A History of New York City to 1898.* Oxford: Oxford University Press, 1999.

Burstein, Andrew. *America's Jubilee: How in 1826 a Generation Remembered Fifty Years of Independence.* New York: Alfred A. Knopf, 2001.

Cadou, Carol Borchert. *The George Washington Collection: Fine and Decorative Arts at Mount Vernon.* Mount Vernon: Mount Vernon Ladies' Association, 2006.

Cayeux, Jean de. *Hubert Robert et les jardins.* Paris: Herscher, 1987.

Censer, Jack R. "The Political Engravings of the *Révolutions de France et de Brabant,* 1789 to 1791." *Eighteenth-Century Life* 5, no. 4 (Summer 1979): 105–24.

Charavay, Étienne. *Le général La Fayette, 1757–1834.* Paris: Sociéte de l'histoire de la Révolution française, 1898.

Chatel de Brancion, Laurence, and Patrick Villiers. *La Fayette: Rêver la Gloire.* Saint-Rémy-en-l'Eau: Monelle Hayot, 2013.

Clary, David A. *Adopted Son: Washington, Lafayette, and the Friendship That Saved the Revolution.* New York: Bantam Books, 2007.

Clifford, Dale Lothrop. "The National Guard and the Parisian Community, 1789–1790." *French Historical Studies* 16, no. 4 (1990): 849–78.

Cobb, Richard. *The Police and the People: French Popular Protest, 1789–1820.* Oxford: Oxford University Press, 1971.

Collingham, Hugh, and Robert Alexander. *The July Monarchy: A Political History of France, 1830–1848.* New York: Longman, 1988.

Collins, Glenn. "Made for Washington, Given to Lafayette, a Medal Sells for $5.3 Million." *New York Times,* December 12, 2007.

Contenson, Ludovic, Baron de. *La Société de Cincinnati de France et la Guerre d'Amérique, 1778–1783.* 1934. Reprint, Paris: Picard, 2007.

Craiutu, Aurelian, and Jeffrey C. Isaac, eds. *America Through European Eyes: British and French Reflections on the New World from the Eighteenth Century to the Present.* University Park: Pennsylvania State University Press, 2009.

Darnton, Robert. "The Brissot Dossier." *French Historical Studies* 17, no. 1 (Spring 1991): 191–205.

———. *The Literary Underground of the Old Regime.* Cambridge, MA: Harvard University Press, 1982.

———. *Mesmerism and the End of the Enlightenment in France.* Cambridge, MA: Harvard University Press, 1968.

Das, Sudipta. *De Broglie's Armada: A Plan for the Invasion of England, 1765–1777.* Lanham, MD: University Press of America, 2009.

Davis, David Brion. *The Problem of Slavery in the Age of Revolution, 1770–1823.* Oxford: Oxford University Press, 1999.

De Jean, Joan. *The Essence of Style: How the French Invented High Fashion, Fine Food, Chic Cafés, Style, Sophistication, and Glamour.* New York: Free Press, 2005.

De Luna, Frederick A. "The Dean Street Style of Revolution: J.-P. Brissot, Jeune Philosophe." *French Historical Studies* 17, no. 1 (Spring 1991): 159–90.

Les dernières victimes de la Terreur: 26 prairial–9 thermidor an II (14 juin–27 juillet 1794). Exhibit catalog. Paris: Association du Souvenir de Picpus, 1994.

"Descriptive List of French Manuscripts Copied for New York State Library from National Archives and National Library at Paris 1888." *New York State Library Bulletin* 57, History 5 (1903): 319–82.

Dierksheide, Christa. "'The Great Improvement and Civilization of That Race': Jefferson and the 'Amelioration' of Slavery, ca. 1770–1826." *Early American Studies: An Interdisciplinary Journal* 6, no. 1 (Spring 2008): 165–97.

Donnet, Hadelin. *Chavaniac Lafayette: Le Manoir des deux mondes.* Paris: Le Cherche midi, 1990.

Dow, Melvin, ed. *Lafayette and Slavery, from His Letters to Thomas Clarkson and Granville Sharp.* Easton, PA: American Friends of Lafayette, 1950.

Doyle, William. *The Oxford History of the French Revolution.* Oxford: Oxford University Press, 1989.

Duckett, William, ed. *Dictionnaire de la conversation et de la lecture: inventaire raisonné des notions générales les plus indispensables à tous, par une société de savants et de gens de lettres.* 16 vols. Paris: Michel Lévy Frères, 1852–60.

Echeverria, Durand. *Mirage in the West: A History of the French Image of American Society to 1815.* Princeton: Princeton University Press, 1957.

Egret, Jean. *The French Pre-Revolution 1787–1788.* Translated by Wesley D. Camp. Chicago: University of Chicago Press, 1977.

Ellingson, Ter. *The Myth of the Noble Savage.* Berkeley: University of California Press, 2001.

Ellis, Joseph J. *His Excellency: George Washington.* New York: Alfred A. Knopf, 2005.

Fassiotto, Marie-José. "La Comtesse de Flahaut et son cercle: un exemple de salon politique sous la Révolution." *Studies on Voltaire and the Eighteenth Century* 303 (1992): 344–48.

Ferling, John. *The Ascent of George Washington: The Hidden Political Genius of an American Icon.* New York: Bloomsbury, 2009.

Fierro, Alfred. *Dictionnaire du Paris disparu*. Paris: Parigramme, 1998.

Fitzpatrick, John C., ed. *The Writings of George Washington from the Original Manuscript Sources, 1745–1799*. 39 vols. Washington, DC: U.S. Government Printing Office, 1931.

Fitzpatrick, Martin, et al., eds. *The Enlightened World*. New York: Routledge, 2004.

Fitzsimmons, Michael P. *The Night the Old Regime Ended: August 4, 1789, and the French Revolution*. University Park: Pennsylvania State University Press, 2002.

Fleming, Thomas. *Washington's Secret War: The Hidden History of Valley Forge*. New York: HarperCollins, 2005.

French Caricature and the French Revolution, 1789–1799. Los Angeles: Grunwald Center for the Graphic Arts, UCLA, 1988.

Fullagar, Kate. "'Savages That Are Come Among Us': Mai, Bennelong, and British Imperial Culture, 1774–1795." *The Eighteenth Century* 49, no. 3 (2008): 211–37.

Furet, François. *Interpreting the French Revolution*. Cambridge: Cambridge University Press, 1981.

Furet, François, and Mona Ozouf, eds. *A Critical Dictionary of the French Revolution*. Translated by Arthur Goldhammer. Cambridge, MA: Harvard University Press, 1989.

———. *Terminer la Révolution: Mounier et Barnave dans la Révolution française*. Grenoble: Presses Universitaires de Grenoble, 1990.

Gaines, James R. *For Liberty and Glory: Washington, Lafayette, and Their Revolutions*. New York: Norton, 2007.

Gallet, Michel. *Les architects parisiens du XVIIIe siècle: Dictionnaire biographique et critique*. Paris: Mengès, 1995.

Gerbi, Antonello. *The Dispute of the New World: The History of a Polemic, 1750–1900*. Translated by Jeremy Moyle. Pittsburgh: University of Pittsburgh Press, 1973.

Gillard, John T. "Lafayette, Friend of the Negro," *Journal of Negro History* 19, no. 4 (October 1934).

Glatthaar, Joseph T., and James Kirby Martin, *Forgotten Allies: The Oneida Indians and the American Revolution*. New York: Hill and Wang, 2006.

Godechot, Jacques. *La Révolution française: Chronologie commentée, 1787–1799*. Paris: Perrin, 1988.

Goodman, Dena, ed. *Marie-Antoinette: Writings on the Body of a Queen*. New York: Routledge, 2003.

———. *The Republic of Letters: A Cultural History of the French Enlightenment*. Ithaca: Cornell University Press, 1994.

Goodman, John. "Jansenism, 'Parlementaire' Politics, and Dissidence in the Art World of Eighteenth-Century Paris: The Case of the Restout Family." *Oxford Art Journal* 18, no. 1 (1995): 74–95.

Gottschalk, Louis. *Lady-in-Waiting: The Romance of Lafayette and Aglaé de Hunolstein*. Baltimore: Johns Hopkins Press, 1939.

———. *Lafayette and the Close of the American Revolution*. Chicago: University of Chicago Press, 1942, rpt. 1974.

————. *Lafayette Between the American and the French Revolution, 1783–1789.* Chicago: University of Chicago Press, 1965.

————. *Lafayette Comes to America.* Chicago: University of Chicago Press, 1935.

————. *Lafayette Joins the American Army.* Chicago: University of Chicago Press, 1937.

Gottschalk, Louis, and Margaret Maddox. *Lafayette in the French Revolution: From the October Days Through the Federation.* Chicago: University of Chicago Press, 1973.

————. *Lafayette in the French Revolution: Through the October Days.* Chicago: University of Chicago Press, 1969.

Gottschalk, Louis, Phyllis S. Pestieau, and Linda J. Pike, eds. *Lafayette: A Guide to the Letters, Documents and Manuscripts in the United States.* Ithaca: Cornell University Press, 1975.

Grell, Chantal. *Le dix-huitième siècle et l'antiquité en France, 1680–1789.* 2 vols. Oxford: Voltaire Foundation, 1995.

Gruder, Vivian R. *The Notables and the Nation: The Political Schooling of the French, 1787–1788.* Cambridge, MA: Harvard University Press, 2007.

Hammond, John Craig, and Matthew Mason, eds. *Contesting Slavery: The Politics of Bondage and Freedom in the New American Nation.* Charlottesville: University of Virginia Press, 2011.

Hauptman, Laurence M., et al., eds. *The Oneida Indian Journey: From New York to Wisconsin, 1784–1860.* Madison: University of Wisconsin Press, 1999.

Hill, Peter P. *French Perceptions of the Early American Republic, 1783–1793.* Memoirs of the American Philosophical Society, vol. 180. Philadelphia: American Philosophical Society, 1988.

Holmes, Oliver W. "Stagecoach Days in the District of Columbia." *Records of the Columbia Historical Society* 50 (1948/1950): 1–42.

Hooper, Richard W., trans. *The Priapus Poems: Erotic Epigrams from Ancient Rome.* Champaign: University of Illinois Press, 1999.

Hould, Claudette. *Images of the French Revolution.* Québec: Musée du Québec, 1989.

————, ed. *La Révolution par la gravure: Les Tableaux historiques de la Révolution française; une entreprise éditoriale d'information et sa diffusion en Europe (1791–1817).* Exhibit catalog. Vizille: Musée de la Révolution française, 2002.

Hours, Bernard. *Louis XV et sa cour: Le roi, l'étiquette et le courtisan.* Vendôme: Presses Universitaires de France, 2002.

Howat, John K. "'A Young Man Impatient to Distinguish Himself': The Vicomte de Noailles as Portrayed by Gilbert Stuart." *Metropolitan Museum of Art Bulletin* n.s., 29, no. 7 (March 1971): 327–40.

Hünemörder, Markus. *The Society of the Cincinnati: Conspiracy and Distrust in Early America.* New York: Berghahn Books, 2006.

Hunt, Lynn. *Inventing Human Rights: A History.* New York: Norton, 2007.

————, ed. *The Invention of Pornography: Obscenity and the Origins of Modernity, 1500–1800.* New York: Zone Books, 1993.

————. *Politics, Culture, and Class in the French Revolution.* Berkeley: University of California Press, 1984.

Hyslop, Beatrice F. "The American Press and the French Revolution of 1789." *Proceedings of the American Philosophical Society* 104, no. 1 (February 1960): 54–85.

Idzerda, Stanley J., Anne. C. Loveland, and Marc H. Miller. *Lafayette, Hero of Two Worlds: The Art and Pageantry of His Farewell Tour of America, 1824–1825.* Exhibit catalog. New York: Queens Museum, 1989.

Jacob, Margaret C. *Living the Enlightenment: Freemasonry and Politics in Eighteenth-Century Europe.* Oxford: Oxford University Press, 1991.

———. *The Radical Enlightenment: Pantheists, Freemasons and Republicans,* 2nd rev. ed. Lafayette, LA: Cornerstone Books, 2006.

Jordan, David P. *The King's Trial: Louis XVI vs. the French Revolution.* Los Angeles: University of California Press, 1979.

Kale, Steven. *French Salons: High Society and Political Sociability from the Old Regime to the Revolution of 1848.* Baltimore: Johns Hopkins University Press, 2004.

Kaminski, John P., and Jill A. McCaughan, eds. *A Great and Good Man: George Washington in the Eyes of His Contemporaries.* Madison, WI: Madison House, 1989.

Kapp, Friedrich. *The Life of John Kalb, Major-General in the Revolutionary Army.* New York: Henry Holt, 1884.

Kelly, George Armstrong. "The Machine of the Duc D'Orléans and the New Politics." *Journal of Modern History* 51, no. 4 (December 1979): 667–84.

Klamkin, Marian. *The Return of Lafayette, 1824–25.* New York: Scribner, 1975.

Kornfeld, Eve. *Creating an American Culture, 1775–1800: A Brief History with Documents.* New York: Palgrave Macmillan, 2001.

Kramer, Lloyd S. "America's Lafayette and Lafayette's America: A European and the American Revolution." *William and Mary Quarterly,* 3rd series, 38, no. 2 (April 1981): 228–41.

———. *Lafayette in Two Worlds: Public Cultures and Personal Identities in an Age of Revolutions.* Chapel Hill: University of North Carolina Press, 1996.

Kwass, Michael. "Big Hair: A Wig History of Consumption in Eighteenth-Century France." *American Historical Review* 111, no. 3 (June 2006): 631–59.

La Fayette. Exhibit catalog. Paris: Archives Nationales, 1957.

Lane, Jason. *General and Madame de Lafayette: Partners in Liberty's Cause in the American and French Revolutions.* London: Taylor Trade Publishing, 2003.

Lasteyrie du Saillant, Marie Antoinette Virginie de Lafayette, Marquise de. *Vie de Madame de Lafayette.* Paris: Techener, 1868.

Leben, Ulrich. *Molitor: Ebeniste from the Ancien Regime to the Bourbon Restoration.* London: Wilson, 1992.

Leepson, Marc. *Lafayette: Lessons in Leadership from the Idealist General.* New York: Palgrave Macmillan, 2011.

Lemay, Edna Hindie. *Dictionnaire des constituants, 1789–1791.* 2 vols. Paris: Universitas, 1991.

Levering, Joseph Mortimer. *A History of Bethlehem, Pennsylvania, 1741–1892.* Bethlehem, PA: Times Publishing Company, 1903.

Lilti, Antoine. *Le monde des salons: Sociabilité et mondanité à Paris au XVIIIe siècle*. Paris: Fayard, 2005.

Linton, Marisa. *The Politics of Virtue in Enlightenment France*. Hampshire, UK: Palgrave, 2001.

Lockhart, Paul. *The Drillmaster of Valley Forge: The Baron de Steuben and the Making of the American Army*. New York: HarperCollins, 2008.

Loveland, Anne C. *Emblem of Liberty: The Image of Lafayette in the American Mind*. Baton Rouge: Louisiana State University Press, 1971.

Low, Betty-Bright P. *France Views America, 1765–1815*. Exhibit catalog. Wilmington, DE: Eleutherian Mills Historical Library, 1978.

Marcetteau-Paul, Agnès, and Dominique Varry. "Les bibliothèques de quelques acteurs de la Révolution, de Louis XVI à Robespierre." *Mélanges de la Bibliothèque de la Sorbonne* 9 (1989): 189–207.

Margerison, Kenneth. *Pamphlets and Public Opinion: The Campaign for a Union of Orders in the Early French Revolution*. West Lafayette, IN: Purdue University Press, 1998.

Marks, Arthur S. "The Statue of King George III in New York and the Iconology of Regicide." *American Art Journal* 13, no. 3 (Summer 1981): 61–82.

Martin, James Kirby, ed. *Ordinary Courage: The Revolutionary War Adventures of Joseph Plumb Martin*. 3rd edition. Malden, MA: Blackwell, 2008.

Mathiez, Albert. *Le club des Cordeliers pendant la crise de Varennes et le massacre du Champ de Mars*. Paris: Champion, 1910.

Maurois, André. *Adrienne: The Life of the Marquise de La Fayette*. Translated by Gerard Hopkins. London: Jonathan Cape, 1961.

McCallam, David. "Waxing Revolutionary: Reflections on a Raid on a Waxworks at the Outbreak of the French Revolution." *French History* 16, no. 2 (June 2002): 153–73.

McCullough, David. *John Adams*. New York: Simon and Schuster, 2001.

McDonnell, Michael A. "Class War? Class Struggles During the American Revolution." *William and Mary Quarterly* 63, no. 2, 3rd ses. (April 2006): 305–44.

McNamara, Brooks. *Day of Jubilee: The Great Age of Public Celebrations in New York, 1788–1909*. New Brunswick: Rutgers University Press, 1997.

McNamara, Peter, ed. *The Noblest Minds: Fame, Honor, and the American Founding*. Lanham, MD: Rowman and Littlefield, 1999.

Michelet, Jules. *Historical Views of the French Revolution: From Its Earliest Indications to the Flight of the King in 1791*. Translated by C. Cocks. London: Bohn, 1864.

Michon, Georges. *Essai sur l'histoire du parti feuillant Adrien Duport; correspondance inédite de Barnave en 1792*. Paris: Payot, 1924.

Mires, Charlene. *Independence Hall in American Memory*. Philadelphia: University of Pennsylvania Press, 2002.

Mitchell, C. J. "Political Divisions Within the Legislative Assembly of 1791." *French Historical Studies* 13, no. 3 (Spring 1984): 356–89.

Morgan, Kenneth. "George Washington and the Problem of Slavery." *Journal of American Studies* 34, no. 2 (August 2000): 279–301.

Mosnier, Henry. *Le château de Chavaniac-Lafayette, description—histoire—souvenirs.* Le Puy: Marchessou Fils, 1883.

Neely, Sylvia. *Lafayette and the Liberal Ideal, 1814–1824: Politics and Conspiracy in an Age of Reaction.* Carbondale: Southern Illinois University Press, 1991.

———. "The Politics of Liberty in the Old World and the New: Lafayette's Return to America in 1824." *Journal of the Early Republic* 6, no. 2 (Summer 1986): 151–71.

Newton, William Ritchey. *L'espace du roi: La cour de France au Château de Versailles, 1682–1789.* Paris: Fayard, 2000.

Ozouf, Mona. *Festivals and the French Revolution.* Translated by Alan Sheridan. Cambridge, MA: Harvard University Press, 1988.

Palmer, R. R. *Twelve Who Ruled: The Year of the Terror in the French Revolution.* Princeton, 1941. Reprint, Princeton: Princeton University Press, 2005.

Pilcher, George William. "William Gordon and the History of the American Revolution." *Historian* 34, no. 3 (May 1972): 447–64.

Popkin, Jeremy D. *Press, Revolution, and Social Identities in France, 1830–1835.* University Park: Pennsylvania State University Press, 2002.

———. *Revolutionary News: The Press in France, 1789–1799.* Durham: Duke University Press, 1990.

Popkin, Jeremy D., and Bernadette Fort, eds. *The "Mémoires Secrets" and the Culture of Publicity in Eighteenth-Century France.* Oxford: Voltaire Foundation, 1998.

Poulet, Anne L., et al. *Jean-Antoine Houdon: Sculptor of the Enlightenment.* Exhibit catalog. Washington, DC: National Gallery of Art, 2003.

Prévost, M., Roman d'Amat, and H. Tribout de Morembert. *Dictionnaire de biographie française.* Paris: Librairie Letouzey et Ané, 1994.

Purcell, Sarah J. *Sealed with Blood: War, Sacrifice, and Memory in Revolutionary America.* Philadelphia: University of Pennsylvania Press, 2002.

Ramsay, David. *The History of the American Revolution.* 2 vols. Trenton: James J. Wilson, 1811.

Remond, René. *Les États-Unis devant l'opinion française (1815–1852).* 2 vols. Paris: Armand Colin, 1962.

Rétat, Pierre. *Les journaux de 1789, bibliographie critique.* Paris: Éditions du Centre National de la Recherche Scientifique, 1988.

Roach, Joseph R. *Cities of the Dead: Circum-Atlantic Performance.* New York: Columbia University Press, 1996.

Roger, Philippe. *The American Enemy: The History of French Anti-Americanism.* Translated by Sharon Bowman. Chicago: University of Chicago Press, 2005.

Rosenband, Leonard N. "Jean-Baptiste Réveillon: A Man on the Make in Old Regime France." *French Historical Studies* 20, no. 3 (Summer 1997): 481–501.

Rudé, George. *The Crowd in the French Revolution.* Oxford: Oxford University Press, 1967.

La Rue de Lille: Hôtel de Salm. Paris: Délégation à l'Action Artistique de la Ville de Paris; Musée de la Légion d'Honneur; Société d'Histoire et d'Archéologie du VIIe Arrondissement, 1983.

Sarrans, Bernard. *Lafayette et la révolution de 1830.* 2 vols. Paris: Desplaces, 1832.

Schama, Simon. *Citizens: A Chronicle of the French Revolution.* New York: Vintage, 1989.

———. *Rough Crossings: Britain, the Slaves and the American Revolution.* New York: Vintage, 2009.

Schiff, Stacy. *A Great Improvisation: Franklin, France, and the Birth of America.* New York: Henry Holt, 2005.

Schmidt, Fredrika Teute, and Barbara Ripel Wilhelm. "Early Proslavery Petitions in Virginia." *William and Mary Quarterly* 30, no. 1, 3rd ser. (January 1973): 133–46.

Scott, Samuel F. "Problems of Law and Order During 1790, the 'Peaceful' Year of the French Revolution." *American Historical Review* 80, no. 4 (October 1975): 859–881.

Scurr, Ruth. *Fatal Purity: Robespierre and the French Revolution.* New York: Metropolitan Books, 2007.

Sénéchal, Philippe, and Claire Barbillon, eds. *Dictionnaire critique des historiens de l'art actifs en France de la Révolution à la Première Guerre mondiale.* Paris: INHA, 2009.

Sewell, William H., Jr. *Work and Revolution in France: The Language of Labor from the Old Regime to 1848.* Cambridge: Cambridge University Press, 1980.

Sgard, Jean, ed. *Dictionnaire des journalistes (1600–1789).* Grenoble: Presses Universitaires de Grenoble, 1983.

Shapiro, Barry M. *Revolutionary Justice in Paris, 1789–1790.* Cambridge: Cambridge University Press, 1993.

Shovlin, John. *The Political Economy of Virtue: Luxury, Patriotism, and the Origins of the French Revolution.* Ithaca: Cornell University Press, 2006.

Sievers, Ann H., Linda Muehlig, and Nancy Rich. *Master Drawings from the Smith College Museum of Art.* Exhibit catalog. New York: Hudson Hills Press; Northampton, MA: Smith College Museum of Art, 2001.

Smith, Jay M. *The Culture of Merit: Nobility, Royal Service, and the Making of Absolute Monarchy in France, 1600–1789.* Ann Arbor: University of Michigan Press, 1996.

———. *Monsters of the Gévaudan: The Making of a Beast.* Cambridge, MA: Harvard University Press, 2011.

———. *Nobility Reimagined: The Patriotic Nation in Eighteenth-Century France.* Ithaca: Cornell University Press, 2005.

Soboul, Albert. *Dictionnaire historique de la Révolution française.* Paris: Presses Universitaires de France, 1989.

Sonnet, Martine. *L'éducation des filles au temps des Lumières.* Paris: Éditions du Cerf, 1987.

Spagnoli, Paul G. "The Revolution Begins: Lambesc's Charge, 12 July 1789." *French Historical Studies* 17, no. 2 (Fall 1991): 466–97.

Spalding, Paul S. *Lafayette: Prisoner of State.* Columbia: University of South Carolina Press, 2010.

Spieler, Miranda. *Empire and Underworld: Captivity in French Guiana.* Cambridge, MA: Harvard University Press, 2012.

Stein, Stephen J. *The Shaker Experience in America: A History of the United Society of Believers*. New Haven: Yale University Press, 1994.

Stein, Susan R. *The Worlds of Thomas Jefferson at Monticello*. New York: Abrams, 1993.

Stillé, Charles J. "Comte de Broglie, the Proposed Stadtholder of America." *Pennsylvania Magazine of History and Biography* 11, no. 4 (1887): 369–405.

Stokes, I. N. Phelps. *The Iconography of Manhattan Island, 1498–1909*. 6 vols. New York: Robert H. Dodd, 1915–28.

Tackett, Timothy. *Becoming a Revolutionary: The Deputies of the French National Assembly and the Emergence of a Revolutionary Culture (1789–1890)*. University Park: Pennsylvania State University Press, 2006.

———. *When the King Took Flight*. Cambridge, MA: Harvard University Press, 2003.

Taillemite, Étienne. *La Fayette*. Paris: Fayard, 1989.

Thomas, Evan. *John Paul Jones: Sailor, Hero, Father of the American Navy*. New York: Simon and Schuster, 2003.

Tourneux, Maurice. *Bibliographie de l'histoire de Paris pendant la Révolution française*. 2 vols. Paris: Imprimerie Nouvelle, 1894.

Tourtier-Bonazzi, Chantal de, ed. *Lafayette: Documents conservés en France*. Paris: Archives Nationales, 1976.

Tower, Charlemagne, Jr. *The Marquis de La Fayette in the American Revolution*. 2 vols. Philadelphia: J. B. Lippincott, 1901.

Tuckerman, Bayard. *Life of General Lafayette*. 2 vols. New York: Dodd, Mead and Co., 1889.

Unger, Harlow Giles. *Lafayette*. Hoboken, NJ: Wiley, 2002.

Van Kley, Dale, ed. *The French Idea of Freedom: The Old Regime and the Declaration of Rights of 1789*. Stanford: Stanford University Press, 1994.

Walker, Paul K. *Engineers of Independence: A Documentary History of the Army Engineers in the American Revolution, 1775–1783*. 1981. Reprint, Honolulu: University Press of the Pacific, 2002.

Walton, Charles. *Policing Public Opinion in the French Revolution: The Culture of Calumny and the Problem of Free Speech*. New York: Oxford University Press, 2009.

Weber, Caroline. *Queen of Fashion: What Marie Antoinette Wore to the Revolution*. New York: Henry Holt, 2006.

Wick, Daniel L. *A Conspiracy of Well-Intentioned Men: The Society of Thirty and the French Revolution*. New York: Garland, 1987.

Wick, Wendy C. *George Washington: An American Icon*. Exhibit catalog. Washington, DC: Smithsonian Institution Traveling Service, 1982.

Willens, Liliane. "Lafayette's Emancipation Experiment in French Guiana— 1786–1792." *Studies on Voltaire and the Eighteenth Century* 242 (1986): 345–59.

———. "Lafayette's Quest for 'Glory' in the American Revolution." *Studies on Voltaire and the Eighteenth Century* 205 (1982): 167–81.

Wills, Garry. *Cincinnatus: George Washington and the Enlightenment*. Garden City, NY: Doubleday, 1984.

Woloch, Isser. *Napoleon and His Collaborators: The Making of a Dictatorship.* New York: Norton, 2002.

Wright, Constance. *Madame de Lafayette.* New York: Henry Holt, 1959.

Wulf, Andrea. *Founding Gardeners: The Revolutionary Generation, Nature, and the Shaping of the American Nation.* New York: Alfred A. Knopf, 2011.

Zucker, Adolf Eduard. *General de Kalb: Lafayette's Mentor.* Chapel Hill: University of North Carolina Press, 1966.

INDEX

Page numbers in *italics* refer to illustrations.

A Note on the Type

This book was set in Adobe Garamond. Designed for the Adobe Corporation by Robert Slimbach, the fonts are based on types first cut by Claude Garamond (c. 1480–1561). Garamond is believed to have followed the Venetian models, and it is to him that we owe the letter we now know as "old style." He gave to his letters a certain elegance and feeling of movement that won their creator an immediate reputation and the patronage of Francis I of France.

COMPOSED BY NORTH MARKET STREET GRAPHICS,
LANCASTER, PENNSYLVANIA

PRINTED AND BOUND BY BERRYVILLE GRAPHICS,
BERRYVILLE, VIRGINIA

DESIGNED BY IRIS WEINSTEIN